AF304769

Encyclopaedia of the Word

Achille Bonito Oliva

# Encyclopaedia of the Word
## *Artist Conversations. 1968–2008*

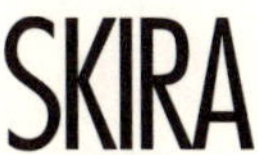
SKIRA

*Back Cover*
Michelangelo Pistoletto
*Portrait of Achille Bonito Oliva*
Courtesy Claudio Abate

*Design*
Marcello Francone

*Editorial Coordination*
Emma Cavazzini

*Copy Editor*
Emanuela di Lallo

*Layout*
Paola Pellegatta

*Translations*
Christopher Evans of behalf
of Language Consulting
Congressi, Milan

First published in Italy
in 2010 by
Skira Editore S.p.A.
Palazzo Casati Stampa
Via Torino 61
20123 Milano
Italy
www.skira.net





*Scientific Coordination*
Martina Cavallarin

*Acknowledgements*
Manuela Pacella
RAM (radioartemobile)
Dora Stiefelmeier
Eleonora Pecorella
Felix Monguilot-Benzal
Incontri Internazionali d'Arte:
Brunella Buscicchio

*We acknowledge the following
for providing some of the
English translations: Claudia
Gian Ferrari, Oredaria Arti
Contemporanee, Magazzino
d'Arte Moderna, Fondazione
Mudima, Galleria Il Ponte
Contemporanea, RAM
radioartemobile, Frittelli Arte
Contemporanea, Galleria
Mazzoli, Galleria Lia Rumma*

# Contents

Foreword in the Form of a
Dialogue on the Labyrinth of Art
*Jorge Luis Borges*

Buenos Aires, 1899 – Geneva, 1986

Buenos Aires
1981

"... We write plays that are not alike... plays that are absolutely different... it's impossible that we have chosen... *Orlando*, for example..."

*It's curious that you always like great writers who are not labyrinthine.*

"Well, Ariosto is a little... Yes, but it's a happy labyrinth, it's like a river with many meanders. It's not a labyrinth in the sense, let's say, of Henry James or Kafka. Piranesi's are labyrinths, it's true, prisons... dimensions. But Ariosto is something else, a happy labyrinth, in the sense of a forest. The whole world is a labyrinth. Once I imagined..."

*What did you imagine?*

"The most impossible thing, impossible to utter in the light of day... I think that the idea is this... on his last journey, Dante went to Venice, didn't he? Let us suppose, if this is supposing, that he intended to write another book after the *Comedy*: what kind of book could have been proposed... it could have been another story... Except that nothing was proposed in the end, because the *Comedy* was everything. A beautiful story... There was a soliloquy, a monologue by Dante: I will write such a book. Well, it is not even necessary for me to write it, because imagining it would be a great deal, would it not? After all, Dante died without writing it. It's an impossible tale, isn't it? Because one imagined, in the golden period of the *Comedy*... But it might have been a fantastic tale, too fantastic... and you interpret it in different ways, all permitted by the text. In general, when you are translating, you choose one interpretation and you emphasize it. But ambiguity, or obscurity, can be a richness, too. It's so mysterious the literature in which you don't know what is clear and what is obscure... It's a very mysterious art... very hard to pull off."

*Is there a contradiction between clarity and the labyrinth?*

"Yes, except that the labyrinth has been conceived with clarity. This means that you don't get to the labyrinth, to chaos, with chaos. You get there with the cosmos. It signifies that the labyrinth has a hidden order. It is laid out for its order and to be understood... perhaps."

*What was the first labyrinth you ever saw?*

"The first one I saw in an engraving; afterwards I went to

Knossos, on Crete; and then to Hampton Court, which is a maze, something different. It's a rather frivolous labyrinth, a bit playful. However, the labyrinth is very often a symbol for happiness… and you, and you have lived for this, because we feel lost in the world, and the obvious symbol is being lost in the labyrinth… and this word 'labyrinth' is so beautiful!"

*What does the word "labyrinth" mean to you?*

"It suggests something terrible. In former times the galleries of mines were referred to as labyrinths… It is curious that in Chaucer, in the fourteenth century, the 'labyrinth' is a labyrinth that moves, made of twigs, circular – very strange. And I've read that Dürer imagined the labyrinth as revolving, but Dürer got lost in the labyrinth that turned. You get in and out of the labyrinth rapidly, a sort of moving circle. *Laborintus* we write, that beautiful word, it invents figures… the Minotaur…"

*Do you think that the circles of hell can be considered a kind of labyrinth?*

"Perhaps they can."

*Until the Renaissance the labyrinth was a structure in which you always got to the centre; after the Renaissance, with Mannerism, on the other hand, the labyrinth became the place of loss. So there is a labyrinth that is closer to our sensibility and that begins with Mannerism and the Baroque.*

"Chesterton said: 'What we all dread most is a maze with no centre.' It was an expression of cosmic fear he used, was it not?"

*Does your labyrinth, that of your writing, Borges, have a centre or not?*

"Yes, it has a centre, a fantastic tale of meanings without explanations; it is apparently a labyrinth, and afterwards you see that it is not, that it is a cosmos, that there is an order, that there is a reasonable explanation. I don't know why I have made so much use of the 'labyrinth'; my attention was caught by the idea of the labyrinth, the idea of the Minotaur, when I was small, and I would not know how to explain it. That obsession was noticed by my readers. I wasn't aware of it. I followed it or was its victim, but I have never tried to explain it to myself. You know, I have never read anything written about me, I have never read a book written on me, either because I wasn't very interested in the subject, or because I found it too interesting. A whole library has been written about me, I haven't read any of it. At home I don't even have my own books. There are other authors, but not my books."

*Borges, your labyrinth, the labyrinth of your stories, of your poems, has a centre...*

"I think I can figure out that they have a centre, but many times they do not, because of my incapacity. I don't seek to be obscure, I try to be classical, but it seems not, it seems that I'm unfortunately modern. A friend of mine, de Chirico, when he meant that something was ugly, used to say: 'It's modern, it's ugly'."

*De Chirico the painter? Giorgio de Chirico?*

"It's ugly, it's modern."

*What do you think of de Chirico's painting?*

"He's a great painter. I can't see his works, because I have lost my sight. My opinion is worth nothing, because I have lost my sight as a reader. In the year 1955 I was able to see a few films, afterwards… I was able to see faces, and now I can't. Now I live in the midst of a mist, a luminous mist, more or less greyish or greenish. I've lost two colors, which are red and black; I see them as *pardo* [a colour that ranges from grey to a greenish hue, and is often used for the skin of mestizos, Editor's note] and as blue shading into green. What I miss now is black. I had the habit of sleeping when it got dark. Now there is no darkness for me, now everything is vaguely luminous and I don't see form, I don't see movement. If I move my hand, I see it moving, but I don't see that it's my hand; and when I move *las tontas* [in the gaucho dialect, 'big legs', 'big feet', 'extremities', Editor's note] I seem to see them, and I get irritated because I don't see them. It's not so terrible though, for it has been such a slow process that there has been no real moment of tragedy. If it had been sudden, then it would have been tragic, and one might have committed suicide. Since I have watched my parents die blind, my grandmother die blind, my English grandfather die blind, and further back still… I don't know."

*It can be said that in your literature...*

"I know very little about my literature. I write it and forget it. You know it better because you've read it. I have read it to correct the proofs, and recently not even that, because I wasn't able to correct the proofs. I try very hard to forget what I have written and to think about what I am going to write next. I think it's unhealthy to look back. Franco Maria Ricci said to me: 'We publish so we don't have to spend our lives correcting manuscripts.' If you publish a book, you free yourself of it. I publish a book and don't know whether it has sold, whether it has been translated, whether it has been a success, whether they have written about it or not. I judge through my friends; if my friends don't talk to me about it it's because they don't like it, and if they do talk to me about they do so in great detail. But very often when I publish a book, they don't say a word. I understand that they didn't like it and change the subject… and look for another subject. I have never wanted to be famous… It's a matter of generations. When I was young people didn't think about success…"

*It could be said that you are the modern Homer owing to the character of universality that your work seems to possess; perhaps for its clarity too…*

"Clarity is a kind of courtesy that you should have for your reader. Apart from his mythical blindness, I don't know what I have in common with the great Homer, with the great poet of the oral tradition."

*Recently you published a book in Italy that is called* Oral, *in which it is possible to discern a sort of Socratic method, a love of oral discourse. And yet the style does not differ from your written one.*

"Blindness has not been able to take from me the sound of words, the pleasure of talking with an audience that I can't see but that I feel silently focused on me. Like what happened in Italy, in Milan, at the exhibition on the labyrinth, when I spoke of my labyrinth before an audience that recited my poems from memory. This perhaps is a comfortable labyrinth…"

# Sol LeWitt
Hartford, Connecticut, 1928 – New York, 2007

New York
1968

*You have said that the material a work is made of is an obstacle for the artist's imagination. It seems to me that your graffiti are made of thought, the idea that presides over your squares.*

"I believe that the choice must be made between content and form, between the spirit and the material through which the artist expresses himself – if this is his choice, the ideas come first. The material is important, but the ideas are more so. The material may be words, sometimes, or even speech itself, and in certain instances even numbers. First of all there's the brain, the lines aren't set down by chance or by whim, but with a sense of direction which, in time, becomes a system that is already preexistent in the brain. Hence, the concept comes first, then the lines that are used to symbolize memory. For instance, music is the final result, but the notes are there just to be read by the musicians. This is what I don't want in my work. I think art has to be read and looked at. I want to say, okay, this can be red, but this can be blue, too. It doesn't matter if the reds and blues are in the right place. In the end, this is how I proceeded in my work, which stems from a single, very simple idea."

*What matters most in these symmetrical compositions of yours, I think, is the thought rather than the activity.*

"The work is done in such a way that the result is predictable. In other words, if one thinks in terms of squares, one can simply say, square, line, or cube; and if I say, cube, this means a three-dimensional form in the pure sense of the word. The word creates the idea, but so does the work, in whatever the artist thinks of doing there is always a final sense: he has to achieve what he sets out to achieve. Once the idea has been defined, the work proceeds; it develops without regard for the rational and the logical. Even if that work and its result are not beautiful, even if the work seems ugly to the artist, he has to follow a sort of magical inner drive that absolutely obliges him to carry it through to the end, step by step, whereas a rational point of view would make him consider what he likes and doesn't like in the work, what he thinks is or is not good. Only in this way can all the creative possibilities, good and bad, beautiful and ugly, mediocre and genial, be included. Logic is always a mechanical process in which the ground rules are set in advance: all the lines going one way are blue, those going the other way are red; and all this is absolute because it can't be changed. Thinking about it, one can tell if the lines pointing a certain way are placed in a manner that's better, more beautiful than another. This way the choice is eliminated because it has already been made at the beginning, and all the rest is mechanical."

*Have you ever used technological means in your work?*

"When I make my drawings I make them by hand. For me it's more interesting to make them this way, because it is the only way it becomes a means of expression; if it is not perfect it becomes more interesting – at least for me – since the ultimate outcome is more complex. But it may also be that I still don't want everything to be absolutely perfect. I don't trust technology. I wouldn't use a computer, because my ideas are very, very plain, as plain as a love letter."

*What importance can colour take on?*

"The use of colour represents a challenge for me, because until recently I had limited myself to black and white, and to greys. Using black and white I found that they cancel each other out, giving a warm, rather beautiful grey. Hence, the use of colour becomes a challenge, it shows me what I can do by placing blues and reds vertically and horizontally. Then, while working, I eliminate everything I can, creating a unity that's all mine. I therefore change as little as possible; sometimes it's necessary to make a decision – two things come into conflict, so a basic programme needs to be established. The basis of this method is to construct a work in which there is a minimum number of decisions to make. My works are always different, because the kinds of ideas that I've used for years have been very similar, whereas the forms I adopt are different. People sometimes get confused, because they look at things formally, as form, and so what they see is always different. They don't realize that the basic idea is always the same, very similar all the time. This is what I want people to think: that I always do the same thing."

*What counts is the repetition of the same concept: not the result, but the mental process. In the final analysis your art is not formalist – it's all-encompassing.*

"Yes, it has this tendency."

# Robert Smithson
Passaic, New Jersey, 1938 – Amarillo, Texas, 1973



*It seems to me that these experiences of yours reproduce the double moment of action and reflection, or the present and memory, in which the mirror and the photograph are the memory of the action.*

"Yes, in a sense it deals with time. I do have an interest in photography as a vehicle for the memory. I think that's a problem that hasn't been really confronted – I mean, the way in which art information is distributed through photography. Thus you get a kind of memory trace: each photograph is an instant of time, and the mirrors are working with what I would call actual colour reflections, joining the ground and the sky. So, the mirror is the medium, and the only area where memory would come in would be the photograph. The mirror is an abstract thing that involves actual colour (the sky is reflected down on the mirror). Then, when you photograph that instant between the sky and the ground, you have a photographic memory trace of it. We have a memory of things forgotten in the distant past, prehistoric time; in other words, there are things we can't remember – but there are traces of them. For instance, I have been working on an idea with making maps of prehistoric continents. We really don't have the memory of these places but we know that they existed one time. I have tried to make maps not out of paper but of rough materials; so I have made maps in the Yucatán out of limestone in the shape of the place."

*Is the tangible feeling of your actions the way you work in nature in the first person, or the traces you create of them?*

"A photograph is an actual thing, but it's only an instant, like a frozen moment. In other words, as I went from site to site I dismantled each piece after I had photographed it. During the travel the experience is very physical; afterwards, the photograph is all that remains, it is the memory, physical evidence in itself. I would call my work in the Yucatán a kind of expeditionary art – not exhibition, but expedition. By studying these different land areas and working – this is very important – I have been dealing with actual light, colours and reflections, not painting. I'm interested in the colour bowling on the mirror, and this is what I would call actual light, and then capturing that actual light in photography, and then having the expedition recorded in both writing and photography… natural colours, colours reflected from different tonalities of sky in brief moments. The existence of nature itself becomes almost ungraspable… the actual places, although being very specific, very physical, are really difficult to see. It isn't simply a matter of vision, there is a kind of breakdown in vision, in an area that isn't defined by white walls and floors. Constructing a work of art not on a wall but on a tree, on the ground instead of the floor. I'm very interested right now only in land for the work to be on; in other words, the work of art needs the actual land. I have planned to cover a whole island with broken glass. I have made a small version of that in the Yucatán, because the Yucatán, in a sense, is a very allusive place, a very ungraspable place to comprehend. That suggested to me the idea, the memory, of Atlantis: so I made a map of Atlantis out of broken glass. And then I've built this map of glass in New Jersey. The Yucatán project stimulated this project. In Canada there are lots of uninhabited islands, so I plan now to cover a whole island with broken glass. And that is the result of the map of glass of Atlantis."

*What gives your experiences their aesthetic value?*

"Photography is information. The whole experience is arrested in the photographic shot, in other words the action is stopped. I'm interested in time, that's to say the process of the work; but my art results in an arresting of that process, so that you get into an area of timelessness. Lévi-Strauss described the primitive mind as constantly involved in a world of timelessness that is made up of all these moments, and then he casually used the reference to the mirror capturing these moments. The camera freezes… I'm interested in that arrested frozen moment. I think that art is about capturing this very moment (it is not vitalistic, it is not kinetic or theatrical, and in any way concerned with movement)."

*Information, then, not communication?*

"That's right. Art is not really about communication."

*What difference is there between your Yucatán experience and the* Asphalt Rundown *you recently made in the former flint quarry near Rome?*

"The work in the Yucatán is unpermanent and timeless, and the work in Rome, the asphalt piece, like the glass island at Vancouver, is permanent and timeless. Nevertheless, they are both concerned with arrested time. But the Yucatán work only exists in terms of an expedition, it's 'unmade'; the work in Rome is 'made' to last. In other words, one is transitory and one is permanent. But mind and matter are always interplaying, and sometimes the work exists only for the mind, some other times it exists only for the matter, so that you have some work that is matter informed by the mind, and other work that is the mind informed by matter. As for the Yucatán work, the mind and perception are crucial important factors, whereas in the asphalt and the glass island the physical matter is what matters. Matter is allusive, fugitive as the mind is; both are in a sense inexplicable, unknowable. You can't be sure of the existence of one or the other, and the work is a sceptical existential assumption. I'm sceptical of both mind and matter, and the role they play in art. There is nothing to communicate automatically."

*When you carry out an action/experience do you develop a predetermined idea or build it up moment by moment? Here in Rome, did you set out with a project?*

"I didn't know what would happen. There is no determined system for what I do, but there is always a sort of double operation between mind and matter – they are always informing each other. But nothing is predetermined. Occasionally, I make notations about what I think I'll do. For instance, here in Rome I had in mind a particular site to look for. I had a general idea of what I wanted – a physical equivalence of my mental image, but then the resolution was in the physical."

*You spoke of Savage Thought. The instant is a suspended moment. Couldn't this discovery lead you to consider the photograph as an instant of magic?*

"I would say that it is a type of totemic logic. In other words, you put yourself in the place, let's say, of an animal or a rock, and you see the world through the eyes of the animal or the rock. It is a kind of totemism. My thinking is more towards that. It is what I would call totemic seeing – not making objects, but an operation of looking."

# Douglas Huebler
Ann Arbor, Michigan, 1924 – Truro, Massachusetts, 1997



*What led you to adopt a variety of media including photography in your work?*

"I started making sculpture and then changed and elaborated maps using locations of points. I made photographs, that's right, but just to put them along the map. It was just about context, and I didn't have a particular care about these first photographs. I used Polaroids – did not have a good camera, anyway. I used photographs sometimes, as a documentation. The real representation was through language, descriptions and maps. The first photographs were almost accidental."

*After you have used photography, in the sense that you have recorded information by taking a series of pictures, are the results subjected to a montage that has a logical character or are they arranged on a formal basis? Can you explain to me the nature of the work presented at the Sperone?*

"Well, there was one of the radio works for instance, done in 1969 in the Californian desert. I buried in the desert some plastic paintings showing still water. It was a play with the mythology of needing water in the desert, and the description of the work tells that the water is buried and there's a map as well that tells where it is buried and what was the meaning of water need: a real mythology, a cultural mythology. In my work I went on trying to find more specific places to work with cultural mythology, cultural forms, to manage phenomena and to use them. I tried to work out a simple cultural idea of mythology without artificial constructions, I was against the photographers wanting to represent phenomena. I thought photography should not represent a specific phenomenon, but general things that are interchangeable in a time system. The first question about my use of photography was that it had to be accidental. A construction regarding time or space means that you think that it is necessary to change the world, and I don't think that I want to change the world, the cultural modes, the technical modes. So I said I go and photograph everything and everybody. To make a documentation like a portrait of mankind by doing that. This is impossible of course, it was just an idea of work. I created a style, I mean, it's my style. Many people use photography now that way, but I was the first one. The point was that I didn't want so much to make photographs, but to create a contraposition between the phenomena of the world and ideas. I did not want to put a pressure on the phenomena, to be mystical, I wanted the phenomenon only as itself. So I didn't change anything. I said nature is there and we may use it the way we like, it's not necessary to change nature. What is important is our relationship with nature and how we think about what we do. So, form to me is not so important, it is only a way of working, a coincidence. We can talk about time, we can talk minutes or centuries, and what we do is to think definitely about ourselves, our universe and how we work with it, how we have a relationship with it. So form and nature go together and, when I make a work, I just put them in juxtaposition without changing anything and allowing concepts to be forms. The world is open, it is free, without history, without the notion 'you must see the world through my eyes'. My work is very open, it doesn't say: you must see the world this way – I just say: it's possible to think about it this way and I wonder what you think that is possible to see. It doesn't matter if I take a photograph every ten seconds or every ten minutes. I get photographs by accident and they are very beautiful because they don't have to be beautiful. I never make a selection, things just happen. This is what I mean by freedom. So when I look at the photographs they are not good photographs. It's not about a good view selected by aesthetic criteria, my photographs are not aesthetic. But for me, when I look at them they are very beautiful, because they are free from having to be beautiful – do you understand? I worked like this two or three years and then I began to use people. I never thought before that I would do it, but then I began to use people in the same way I used natural phenomena. I photographed everybody alive, I used videotapes and movies as well, it didn't matter, I used every media. I'm not interested in media, the media only discovers the world, and everything I discover is absolutely arbitrary."

*Can you explain that?*

"I like to photograph, I may do 36 shots and then look at the contacts and use just one of them, it doesn't matter which one, it's arbitrary. In that photograph you have maybe thirty individuals, and this is already a cultural model. We say in America, for instance, that somebody is 'sweet and lovely'; and in order to represent this topic about people, about everybody alive I show somebody who is really sweet and lovely. But there are of course many topics. We can build a world with the category 'sweet and lovely'. And maybe, at least one person feels represented. You can have a picture of somebody interested in art or part of an art audience. But you immediately think that most people are not interested in art… I mean, there is an idea about how we think about things. But we don't need to say that a photograph means something. Photographs don't mean anything, they become interesting because they do not carry any burden of meaning. It's all fresh again, it's very fresh, new, reborn renaissance. And I like that so much."

*In your work, the medium – photography, videotape, film – is used to establish a set of relationships. But what is the relationship between the real object that you photograph and the object in the photograph?*

"I think photographs are illusions and, well, I said it before, photography allows objects to be free. I don't use photography as art. I don't say the North Pole is art – I say the North Pole is something that comes out as a product of my strategy and the documentation of it. So if I photograph a face or a landscape, for me it is real, in the photograph it represents something that is itself, something that is not modified by my use of it."

*A gap exists between the real object and the object in the photograph. It exists to the extent to which photography is a way of cutting something out of a more complex reality. So it is a work of reduction.*

"And it's arbitrary, when I separate it's arbitrary. You can separate everything and this is again why I use these strategies, but I want to make it very clear that it is arbitrary. I do not say this is better than that, it's by accident that I get this or that. That's what I learned from the first use of these photographs. That it is an accident. Five years ago, when I did those maps with a point here, a point there, a point here, I worked them out in my studio and then I would go out to look and have a surprise. The making of the points on a map is like strategy, a concept that can't be applied everywhere. I enjoyed very much to find out what kind of return my strategy would get. I didn't choose what I get, I didn't know what I get. I always make a strategy, if it's a map or a cultural model – 'sweet and lovely', for instance. The return which I get by my photographs is just a response to my strategy. The strategy which you plan is your model. I work for the general and discover the specific, but of course it's only an example of the specific against the general."

*In this way, then, what counts is not so much the photographed reality but the process of photographing. What I'm asking, in other words, is if in the end what you want to represent through the work is the medium.*

"It is possible, the camera is mechanical, really, it is an instrument and it's only a medium between what I want and the idea, I don't want to make it more interesting, I don't want to get interesting results in terms of media. I don't want people to think 'that's an interesting photograph or an interesting style of camera work or film or videotape'. I use the camera very simply, only simply."

*Is there a connection between this neutral position of yours towards reality and, for example, that branch of philosophy called phenomenology?*

"Well, I think that our relationship with phenomena is language. That's what I mean by cultural constructs. I consider the construct of time or the conceptualism in our map, or the question of beauty. We invent strategies, everybody does – not only artists, everybody. I think that a phenomenon is only itself and that there is no project in it, you see. My intention is to indicate that the projections are vain. You can change things, you can move things, that's less interesting to me as the fact that things are existing with their own energy. We can have a relationship with them by projecting our own energy into the energy of phenomena, and part of that energy can be conceptual. Well, this is energy in energy, but if I think about something, I think about this, it's an energy that is genuinely conceptual and I think that we are dealing with phenomena conceptually and not specifically. As you were saying, the description of what I mean is very simple. For instance, the relationship between men and women, that we can see in terms of love or marriage or sex. It's different from culture to culture, it's different in different times. The phenomenon of sexual relationships is universal and timeless, but it changes according to the institutions that are created – well, you know perfectly well, there are very different cultural ways of dealing with these things, but that's all conceptual. That's what I mean by cultural mythologies."

*So your work can also be regarded as a strategy of mental representation of energy?*

"Yes, the first energy comes from making the idea, that's conceptual energy, a mental energy; my work is a result of that but sometimes there are surprises, things I didn't expect. It's always a matter of fact, I'm not sure what will come out. There is a first energy when I conceptualize what I will do, and what comes after is a surprise – sometimes a very great one. There is a work in the show at Sperone I want to mention. I have been interested for a long time in making work using mannequins, the ones on show in store windows. Once in London I photographed a shopping area: when the model in the window was female, I immediately turned around and photographed the next female being walking down the street. I wanted to make a simple demonstration of a model of reality against true reality. I didn't know exactly what to expect from the work – I just needed to make the idea clear. I didn't want to make decisions about who I would photograph. I have to say that the work is amazing and the coincidences of the mannequins and the persons I photographed next to them are amazing. I expected a very different result. When you see that work, you understand what I mean by 'surprise'. I was not trying to demonstrate anything except a model of reality against reality, and the surprise comes from the way I worked it out, which is definitely unpredictable."

*So, can it also be presented as a form of understanding of the world?*

"Look at my own history. I was a commercial artist, I was a painter, both a realist and an abstract painter, I was a sculptor, I was always concerned with art and the art market. I do believe that what I make now is not concerned with 'art' any longer. I began to see art through my experience of the world. First I was used to adopting models of art, past and present models. Now for me the model for making a work is not any more a specific thing, a formal thing, an aesthetic thing. In a way, it's a kind of effort to undermine art in order to be free again. For my own sake I had to undermine art and to open my mind. I think that what I do is quite simple, the language I use is very simple, everything I use is extremely simple. So it is very accessible, everybody can see it."

*Your art can be defined as an attempt to always create a set of relationships. It is proposed as a set of relationships. In this sense it seems to me that it is linked with that type of Anglo-Saxon culture that is pragmatism. So your work is a set of relationships and in this sense it seems to me that you are rejecting the principle of dialectics.*

"Not that I thought about that very much. Things happen as they happen, in an unpredictable way. Maybe my work is charismatic, I don't know. It's a philosophy. My personal philosophy comes more from some interesting existential notions and from Eastern doctrines as Buddhism. I didn't plan to become an existentialist, I am not necessarily pragmatic, not a linguist, none of that. I believe in the capacity of the simple to be as worthy as the grand."

*Worthy?*

"A snowball is also worthy, it's a tiny little thing that can be worthy as much as a grand thing, that's all. I have a friend who works with the universe, he uses scientific terms and is very intelligent, very bright, and he says I do big art. And I say, if you understand simple things and see that there is an infinite extension, I agree. Everything I do is infinitely extensible."

# Vito Acconci
New York, 1940



*How long have you been working with your body and which value do you give to the gestures you make?*

"This kind of work of mine I have been doing for… I suppose since around the middle of 1968. I don't come out of a painting or sculpture background, I used to be a writer, I used to be a poet. In around 1968 it became clear to me that what I was concerned with, what I was concerned with in poetry wasn't so much the meaning of words, but the act of reading from left to right on a page, from up to down on a page, from one page to another. So what was of interest to me in writing was the activity on a page. And, once that realization became clearer, it just became much more natural to transfer from the page to real space as a stage of action. As for most of the work of the last two or three years, the pieces aren't considered so much as display or exhibition pieces, but rather they set up a situation, a kind of learning session for me, a situation that tests the various ways that I might react to another element, to another person, to my own body. So they are basically learning sessions for me, or tests, experiments. Rather than think of them so much as actions on my own body, I mean, they use the body certainly, but mostly the concern I think is with motivations, decisions, more psychological processes that use the body to be carried out."

*What is theatrical in your actions? What do you mean by theatre? Is there a theatricality in your actions?*

"Theatre in the sense of exhibition or spectacle – probably not. But theatre in the sense of interaction, in the sense of interrelation between one person and another, in the sense of conversation – that I think is really a prime part, a very important one of my work. I have always for some reason kept clear of the term 'theatre', probably because of the connotation it has of a prepared script, a prepared acting. I would not be concerned with theatre, with theatre in that sense, but I would be concerned with theatre in the sense of setting up a kind of stage of action, setting up what I called before a learning task or a learning session. This could probably seem a stage on which I am going to go through a certain activity. Recently I have been much more concerned with the kind of space my work occurs in. More and more I have been concerned with smaller chambers like spaces, cells like spaces, small spaces, in which a very private activity can be performed. So with regards to theatre, the on-lookers are sort of, rather than a theatre audience, in a more traditional sense … the audience in my works usually act almost as a spy, sort of on-lookers to a very private activity. They are not being presented with something for them, but they happen to come in contact with some private activity, so they are almost looking through a key-hole."

*Which is the passage between the daily experience and the aesthetic experience?*

"I guess I would answer by saying that my art activity would be setting up more specialized times, more specialized areas in the middle of my daily activity, in which a more intense concentration can be worked with, than, say, with an ordinary activity. I think the concentration element is probably the most important thing that I look on. So, a certain ordinary activity goes on, followed by a time of withdrawal, a time of exclusion almost, which most of my pieces lately have to do with, going into a kind of withdrawal retreat space in which I am going to go through a specialized and concentrated kind of activity."

*In connection with your concentrated space and your living only by your body, can you tell me about the work where you're blindfolded and about the other clock piece? In these works there's nearly an exile space.*

"The blindfolded catching piece is a film, it's really part of a three-film group. One is a 'hand and mouth' piece in which I push my hand into my mouth as far as I can, until I choke, and keep putting the hand in until I keep choking, until gradually… Now this is one of three, let me tell about the three, in general. The 'hand and mouth' thing goes on until I really can't do it anymore. Then there is this piece that involves standing blindfolded. A rubber ball is repeatedly thrown at me. I attempt to catch the rubber ball, but obviously I can't see it, since I'm blindfolded. So it's an attempt of trying to adapt to the ball being thrown at me, trying to sense through intuit when the ball is going to be thrown at me next. The third film in the group is a 'soap and eyes' piece. It involves staring at the camera for half a minute or so, then throwing soapy water in my eyes, in my face, so that I can't see, my eyes are covered with soap. The film involves trying to blink, not using my hands, trying to blink the soap out of my eyes, until I can look into the camera again, until I can stare at the camera. So the three pieces are mainly three kinds of adaptation. What I was interested in mainly when I was doing the three pieces, was the idea of stress, the idea that when you come into contact with a kind of stress situation, you immediately have a sort of alarm reaction, you immediately react to the stress, then you go through a kind of adaptation stage, you begin to resist and you begin to be able to handle the stress. So there were three basic stages: the alarm-reaction stage, the adaptation stage, the ultimate exhaustion stage.

With regard to the clock piece, it was conceived for a particular occasion. It was an evening of performances in New York and I wanted to do something that was private and public at the same time. So, what I came up with was a clock placed on the wall… I placed the clock, it wasn't already there. The light bulb however was there, there was a light bulb in each of the enclosures. The activity was following the second hand of the clock with my movement around the light bulb. It's a kind of almost going out of my state as a human and becoming a clock, becoming the second hand of a clock. This action seemed very appropriate to me in this particular circumstance, because going in this circular activity as a kind of private activity, I was including myself in my own concentration, including myself in this close, circular world, including myself in my own processes. And all this was very appropriate for that enclosed space, at the same time. The activity took an hour, the other performances were going on in the same hour. So, besides being a private activity, it was also a public activity, in the sense that it timed, it measured the other performances."

*As in Artaud and in the Living Theatre, I find also in your work the attitude to run all through your body. There's the performance where you bit yourself. In this sense you try to give a form to that sort of self-cruelty, you too.*

"Actually, I probably don't think of it in terms of self-cruelty."

*Cruelty in the sense of Artaud, not in the sense of sadism.*

"I guess it can be called self-cruelty, in the sense of me performing an action on myself in order to break through certain boundaries of myself, in order to open myself up, in order to make myself less defensive, maybe, than I ordinarily would have been. So a lot of the work is concerned, I think, with breaking through myself, or breaking through a more public image of myself, or turning in on myself, so that I can be open. With regard to some of the pieces, like the ones I mentioned, with regard to the biting of myself, what I was concerned with then, was mostly defining the limits of my body. I could bite various parts of my body, I could reach various parts of my body, I could turn myself into a kind of close system, including myself in myself by biting my knee, my leg, my arm. But in general I think that the rubbing of my arm or whatever is a matter of breaking through myself, opening myself up. Most of it is just testing various parts of myself, adapting my body to various responses, or adapting my responses to my body."

*Which meaning has the presence of other people, of an audience?*

"What I'm interested in is the idea of me doing a private activity and other people acting as what you said before, as a kind of voyeur, as a kind of spy. I think of my works as sort of possible models or examples. A person walks by, could see what I'm doing, could choose whether to go into the same kind of concentration activity, or could sort of walk out, choose not to. So they are private subjective activities, but presented as a possible inter-subjective kind of thing. Models for possible emulation, possible assimilation by other people. But what I like particularly, as I said before, is the idea of a spectator as a spy, a spectator in a kind of uneasy position: he's seeing something private, so he isn't in the ordinary position of a spectator."

*Why do you photograph, "freeze", your gestures?*

"The fact that a photograph is frozen is completely opposite to the idea of the piece. So I want to try to take, you know, every means possible to almost roughing up the photograph. The photograph gives a much too smooth picture of the piece. And even with regard to film, though a film doesn't freeze it so much, it still presents the work as a kind of finished thing. The ideal situation would be not in an auditorium, where people would be in seats, but rather project the film in a very small room, that only a few people could enter at a time. In other words, the room would exist as almost a kind of meditation chamber, which could be similar to the type of space in which I perform the activity. So the person would have his own meditation chamber, where he could stay as long as he wants, as long as it is necessary for him to get into that same kind of concentration activity. Or he might decide not to, and walk away."

*Is there in the work you make through your body a political or ideological level?*

"In a way, I consider a lot of my work as sort of preparation sessions, which could be appropriate, say, for a kind of guerrilla fighter, or for a kind of revolutionary. In other words, I can set up all sorts of different tasks for myself, different tasks that most people would call arduous tasks, they would call them difficult tasks. This is something that I've never, that I haven't really clearly brought up into the open yet, but more and more lately I have been thinking about it, that my work seems very close to what I was saying before about what can be presented as a model. I believe it is a kind of model for the preparation of your body and mind for various kinds of things, so that we can be kinds of ready guerrilla fighters, revolutionaries. In other words, it's a chain on my body, subjecting my body to various types of stress, so that the body and mind can be strengthened in a sort of warfare against the establishment."

*In which way does Oriental thinking influence you?*

"The attitude in general has influenced me. What specific aspects of it, what specific people, I'm not really sure. But the whole general concentration aim of any Oriental philosophy has definitely been an influence, but I can't really talk about the specifics. There is one thing that I know has really interested me, one kind of anecdote. Apparently in archery, in Zen archery, the master teaches his pupils not so much to hit the target, but he tells them that their aim should be to become the target, and in that way their arrow will hit the target. And it's that kind of thing, I believe, that has been very, very influential."

*To work through your body is for you to move in the real space, not in the metaphoric space. But doesn't it mean also to create a divided body, a body that lives normally and another that, on the contrary, is flowing in the space of art?*

"Yes, I think I agree with that, since my work seems to be so devoted to setting up these concentration chambers, concentration areas, specialized areas. They really are kinds of breakpoints in my ordinary activity, in which this kind of specialization takes place. I think, I was thinking about this, I guess, lately, mostly in these terms, that probably the work I was doing, say, a year and a half ago, two years ago wasn't that much of a break. There would be things like picking up a person in the street, following him as far as I could, until he went into a private place; or there was a piece at the software show in the Jewish Museum that involved standing next to a person or behind him, closer than the ordinary distance, so I would be overtaking the person's space, he would move away. But more and more my work has become, I think, much more involved with specialized, unordinary activities, whereas those two were sorts of almost ordinary activities. One of the reasons, I think, not knowing exactly what to do with these two terms 'art' and 'life'… is the realization that there is a kind of difference, so what I would make of the difference would be taking an ordinary-life activity and in some way concentrating it, specializing it whatever. So it is not so much making a break, but using it to go more deeply into what might be an ordinary life activity."

*Does death exist in your work?*

"Yes, we were talking before about stress situations, and one thing that interests me in a stress situation, is that after the adaptation stage, there follows exhaustion; now, the ultimate exhaustion stage would be death, when the body or whatever can't adapt to anything, and ultimately dies. A lot of people have talked about my work as a kind of desire for death. But I don't think it's that so much, I don't think there is any going towards death, but rather just a kind of allowance of death, or admitting death into my life. In one sense I probably wouldn't agree, in that, what I'm interested in mainly, as I said before, is not so much specific pieces, but a whole system of activity, a whole network of activity. Therefore, death would stop that system of activity – it just couldn't go on. But what I am interested in is not so much reaching death, but always that kind of approach to it."

# Joseph Beuys
Krefeld, Germany, 1921 – Düsseldorf, 1986



*All your works, from the drawings of 1946 up to the current projects, gestures and actions, have contained the same implicit ideology and the same poetics. What are the recurrent themes?*

"During the various phases of my work, I have made environmental spaces and done actions at the same time, and I consider my drawings not as separate things, but in close connection with all the works that follow. Indeed, my drawings foreshadow the actions that I later carried out. There are many themes, but they all revolve around a central issue: man, simply man. In purely scientific terms, I would say the central concern is one of anthropology, illustrated in as many ways as possible. I found out in an elementary manner in my own life that the times we live in are ill suited to man. This problem appears in a purely instinctive way in the early drawings, and gradually becomes more explicit and conscious. Sometimes animals appear, too, for I think there is a relation between animals and man."

*A few of the concerns that appear again and again in your works are recurrent themes of the German Romantic culture. Do you recognize them in what you do?*

"I simply belong to this cultural tradition. But the historical continuity of the German Romantic tradition – the tradition of Novalis, and in part, Goethe – was broken by the positivistic concept of science with which man carried out the industrial revolution. However, the method I've taken up is not the same as Novalis's, because Novalis considered the relation between man and transcendental powers, rather than that between man and matter."

*In Novalis the themes of death and night are means of approaching reality. For you, the themes of cruelty, nature and time are aspects of an art that does not aspire to imagery or form, but to a process of liberation.*

"Yes, I do agree. I can make a sketch here. The concept of science created by the middle class in order to free itself from the feudal system has become very effective, but the revolutionary thought it contains, which was formulated also during the French Revolution – freedom, equality, brotherhood – could not be implemented, because the middle class had protected itself against an even more numerous class (the proletariat) using the discriminating concept of science, calling evolution that which is only the revolution of technical understanding. Thus, it was not possible to attain a global development of human qualities. This method has aided technical progress only, without making history, but acting on man politically in a repressive and authoritarian manner. This is a sociological affirmation, even if sociology is a human science, and thus cannot arise from what is schematically considered science. Science, on the basis of positivistic reasoning, takes a polemical stand towards art: art is worthless, it has no social importance, it's useless, it absolutely is not a vehicle of revolution – only science can be revolutionary. On the contrary, I affirm that only art can be revolutionary, especially when one frees the concept of art from its traditional technical meaning, and passes from the area of art to that of anti-art, from gesture to action, in order to place it at the complete disposal of man. The only vehicle of revolution is an integral concept of art, whence even a new concept of science is born."

*When you say "art-man", you are making an idealistic statement. Which man are you talking about? If it's historical man, man is not free; if it's a-historical man, then it is a man without a model, whom science also hypocritically claims to serve.*

"Here I've written, *art = man = creativity = science.* When the middle class says science is useful to man, it is correct. But you have to look at the content. Let's say this is man – and this is the positivistic concept of science – and this the concept of art: then this concept of art does not negate the concept of science, but includes it. The moment artists, creative people, realize the revolutionary potential of art (creativity) – here I again equate art, creativity and freedom – at that moment they will recognize the true objectives of art and science. Now I'm combining art and science in a larger concept built around creativity. The problem is a broad-ranging one, and embraces a number of concepts. In fact, freedom is linked to the individuality of man. The moment man becomes aware of his individuality, he also wants to be free. By virtue of his antiauthoritarian desire, he longs for self-government and self-determination. The concept of man's self-determination makes sense only as part of the concept of freedom. The individual feels isolated at first. Then he senses the need, as a human being, to communicate, live and talk. This passage is sociology. In my opinion, sociology is nothing more than a scientific concept of love. The reciprocal exchange between man and man is the most important thing. When men have developed awareness, and have learned to live politically in accordance with these powers, then it will be possible to achieve a completely new political configuration."

*Doesn't this vision of art also take up a theory of Schopenhauer's, of art and thought as will and representation of the world?*

"Yes, but I'd also like to mention Kant and Aristotle. The development of philosophical speculation begins, roughly, with Plato. An introductive method comes into use that leads to positivism. What is the sense of this philosophy and of all Western thought? It is a tension towards and an approach to materialistic thought, and hence to technical revolution. There is an analytic force in human thought that was not yet possible in mythic thought before Plato or in even more ancient civilizations. Before, one did not analyse nature, God, or matter. One accepted everything as a coherent whole, and one lacked the strength to make an individual, and hence a free, analysis. This is precisely the awakening of consciousness of Western man from Plato to our own days: the conquest of this power of analysis and criticism. At this point an enormously important figure comes into play: Christ and Christianity. Not the Christianity administered by the churches, but that which has developed along the scientific line, for Christ wanted man to be free. He said, 'I will give you freedom'. That means man must win this freedom through his individual strength. In the churches one practiced old collective mythological rituals. For the power to change human nature, Christianity turned to science. In this way Christ discovered the steam engine and the atomic bomb."

*If the philosophical destiny of art is the liberation of mankind, what significance does the use of various materials like margarine, felt, animals, or even classical texts in your works have?*

"If I want to create a revolutionary concept of man, I have to talk about all the powers that are related to him. If I want to give man a new anthropological position, I also have to attribute a new position to everything than concerns him. To establish his downward ties with animals, plants and nature, as well as his upward links with angels and spirits. I have to talk about these powers once again. To ask myself: what about Christ and God? So, I must again place man in this whole, only then will he be able to acquire his greatness as man and the strength to carry out the revolution. In my actions I have always exemplified the identity, *art = man*. When I did an action with fat and margarine, I set this concept forth. At the beginning of the action the fat appeared merely as chaos, as pure energy. This energy has no direction: that's why it is chaotic. During the action this mass moves, and begins to take on a geometric form, to be part of an architectural whole, a space, a right angle. This is form. At the centre, here, we can put movement. These are the elements that make up human nature. We can even complete it: add volition, feeling, thought. This is the musical score that underlies all of my actions. I've almost always succeeded in making people question, precisely because they felt attacked by my actions. I made something budge. It doesn't matter if I encountered resistance or insults most of the time. I think the man who protests has taken the first step towards becoming a man of action. A revolutionary man."

*Your activity appears, in my opinion, to propose a sort of "Socratic space" in which the works are a pretext for a dialogue with man.*

"This is the most important aspect of my work. The rest – objects, drawings, actions – is secondary. Really, I don't have much to do with art. Art interests me only insofar as it gives me the possibility of a dialogue with man."

*In your work memory is recovered as an anthropological value. What is your position with respect to Freudian psychoanalysis or Jungian deep psychology?*

"I believe they are both important, because they affirm the existence of a collective subconscious. Man must learn how to master the future, and gain an idea of how history evolves. The instant man realizes this, the subconscious will become conscious. Psychoanalysis and psychology aspire only to make peace between man and his subconscious. Man must free himself of his irrational demons, which are the defeats of the past – not only of fascism, but of all history. Only when he has become aware of his historic evolution, and knows his past, man will be ready for revolution, to become a future revolutionary. For this to happen, a new sociology must be created."

*These statements seem to point to a notion of art as information, or better yet, as communication.*

"For me information means everything the world contains: men, animals, history, plants, stones, time, etc. In order to communicate, man uses language, gestures, or writing. He makes a sign on the wall, or takes a typewriter and turns out letters. In short, he uses means. What means can be used for political action? I have chosen art. Making art, then, is a means for man to work in the realm of thought. That this should gradually become an increasingly political task is a matter of my destiny or my ability. In order to communicate, at any rate, there has to be a listener. In technical terms, a transmitter and a receiver. There's no sense in a transmitter if nobody's listening. There's always a consignee and a receiver for every word. But I don't deceive myself in thinking I can talk to everyone: that's why it's important that men learn to talk and discuss things among themselves. Hence, language is indispensable: the concept of language represents the entire content of information to me."

*But capitalism, through the market system, favours your information, and thus interrupts your liberating intention to turn it to account.*

"Yes, but only if the market uses the merchandise inadequately. The potato grown and cared for by the farmer is not damaged, even if the grocer who sells it is dishonest. The ambit of creativity, art, and the freedom of mankind are based on a different principle, the social and democratic principle of an equitable administration of justice. Therefore, art is not degraded by market abuse – it remains absolutely intact."

*The market creates a vicious circle, in that instead of reaching man stripped of his economic power, art reaches only those who can hoard the product.*

"Yes, this too is true, but it doesn't regard art alone. Injustice characterizes all markets, including the art market. It is a consequence of the capitalistic system, which should be abolished. However, we do not yet have a method for doing this. Capitalism has the word, freedom, on the tip of its tongue, affirming that it works for man's freedom, which is exactly why it cannot be trusted. It's the same problem I'm working on at the Academy of Düsseldorf. I say men want to study, they have the right to, because they are free, but the State says they can't. And so, I do all I can to make the majority realize that the system doesn't work. Your judgements stem from pessimistic considerations, but we have no way of knowing how a repressive system would behave with respect to a radical model of freedom. The tools used till now have been based on the concepts of democracy, communism and socialism, which have failed because the notions of freedom, creativity and art, an ideal of absolute freedom, do not exist in their ideology. I don't think the system has any means of power at all against man's desire for freedom. The moment men say, we are free, we want self-determination, capitalism is over."

# Joseph Kosuth
Toledo, Ohio, 1945

New York
1971

*How did you arrive at conceptual art?*

"I don't know exactly… surely if there is a work for me that really began a kind of idea about conceptual art, it was the *Leaning Glass*, which is a five-foot piece of glass that leans against the wall. I realized that the title became very important because it's called 'Any five-foot sheet of glass to lean against any wall'. So, I began to realize that there was that material, that glass that was there and a sort of phenomenology of that, and then again there was the information. I was thinking about the art issues that this obviously brings up, so at a certain point one begins to realize that any glass… it didn't have to do with that particular piece of glass, it exists in an extremely abstract way which was coming out of painting, that was exactly what my interest was, it was an idea about abstraction. Anyway, I put aside my interest in painting and what followed was an interest in making certain kinds of divisions between that phenomenological material state entity that's there and that kind of information. So I did works like a chair and a photograph of a chair and a definition of a chair, which is called *One and Three Chairs*, and other things of that sort. Also, about the same time, I was working with water because water also was interesting to me in the sense that it was clear… it certainly didn't have a colour of a particular sort of emotional type and also did not have a particular form: you know it with the form whatever you put into… which is also the nature of any liquid. I was really ly bypassing a lot of formal concerns, there was a common idea… I had seen them even geometric, or organic, and somehow choosing the form didn't seem to be the issue. The true issue would seem to be to… how does a form function within the context of art, and for me that was really what the issue in art became. Anyway, I was interested in water, again I think a sort of a hold-over from my earlier involvement in classic art, so I did lots of things with water, used steam and ice and set about all sorts of uses of water, like one thing which was several blocks of ice and which only really existed as a kind of documentation of taking these nine pieces of ice and letting them melt, and so the idea that it would remain art regardless of the state it was in. In other words, the ice would become water and should go into the ground and then go back into the whole system, the whole natural system… It would still exist if you are saying that art exists only in a physical sense, or it still exists except you don't know where it is… but then again art exists only as an idea, which one finally realizes it's what exactly art is. Art only exists as an idea. The idea of those water projects belongs to one specific group of works. And the neon ones: I chose neon, it was 1965. Neon was interesting for me only for a real one reason: I needed a material which had a lot of properties. In other words, if I had to write a letter with black, well, then I needed black paint and a board of some sort – two materials. Neon instead had a lot of things. The first neon works I did were the ones that are a whole line of words, let's say… *wide neon electrical*, and so what happens is that you've got a tautology: the work itself describes itself. That was involving an idea about art I had drawn from language and philosophy, the difference between analytic and synthetic sentences, and that emotion about art being analytic and the possibility of making all kinds of comparisons between art and language. It's pretty complicated: I found that certain qualities that art had were analysable and understood, and that one could consider art and understand it if one left art as a model and use language as a model.

For instance, in anthropology they say it's almost impossible for an anthropologist to study his own culture, just because he's inside of it, he is blind, that's his reality so he can't really see it. In the sense that I felt that artists in the twentieth century had always been very much involved in the process of being an artist, and they could never really see what the twentieth century or what modern art was about. And that perhaps my generation, after seventy years of modernism, was the first generation that could say: 'We are no longer part of modern art'. It's really post-modern art. And now we can sit back and look and see what that work was all about. We are the first generation that had the capacity to separate ourselves. I thought I was capable of being an artist, and at the same time of being truly involved in art, but also having an overview and also being able to consider art from another point of view.

I also got involved with glass… actually the glass came before the water because glass was also transparent, didn't have any colour; it still had to be cut into a shape and I had to make a choice about what form the shape would be. Those became aesthetic decisions, and one of the things I've always tried to eliminate from my art is an aesthetic choice. I find art and aesthetics two entirely different issues, and I can talk about that if you want but… it's a thing that… what aesthetics means has to do with your subjective opinion, with your impressions of the world. In other words, whatever information comes in – eyes, nose, mouth, all the senses – you have an opinion and some you like more than others; so, you have a preference based on those opinions and what aesthetics is, is what senses, what arrangements of all those senses you have a preference for. Anything can be dealt with aesthetically, like a sunset can be an aesthetic experience, but it's not art. Art is of course an entirely different matter. And a painting can be dealt with aesthetically, just like a chair could be, or a pile of garbage could be. But the question becomes a question of meaning. Of what it means in terms of your understanding of art. And that's always separate from aesthetics. That's why art has evolved in contemporary art. The notion of a decorative aesthetics is really, in a certain sense, anti-art. Because anything can be decorative, so it has no meaningful connection to the art activity, you see. This is the reason why I always tried to choose a kind of neutral form, so that after a while, for instance after I began doing the photostats with just a dictionary blow-up – and I first did one in 1966 – I only used a definition without any object. That was a photographic blow-up, and there have always been only photostats that were not meant to be considered paintings. But the blow-up could be thrown away. It wasn't considered by me to have any value, it didn't exist as a work of art – it was only what I called the form of presentation. What I want is to separate art from its physical existence in the world, in a certain sense, so that you won't deal with it in an aesthetic sense. But after a while people began to deal with blow-ups like they were paintings. At that point, by 1968, I had worked out probably all I could do with it and I stopped that work. I've used a number of highway bill-boards… whatever the media was for that particular area of the world, it would be in that language and would appear anonymously, so the form of presentation would be clearly something of extemporary and would only exist while the information was existing in that area. That was a deliberate sort of desire to get away from the photostat and the idea that it was a painting. When I did them all, I did those works in French or in Italian or English, my idea was I would want those works to exist in that country, in the language which was spoken there."

*Can we define your work as one about tautology?*

"The works, actually, in terms of the smallest particle, a unit of a proposition, all the way from there to the more ultimate questions, are all tautological. That's the nature of being an artist in the sense of… it's a very tautological one, because it has no specific value of the sort which you can point out and say this is what the value of an artist is: it's clearly tautological, when you think about art you realize there are works of art… when I say works of art I mean only the twentieth century, it's one thing that of course has to be assumed, because for me that's when art began. It's like when you decide where the ape stopped being an ape and became a man. Obviously there is a relation between the ape and the man and so there's obviously a relation between art before the twentieth century and twentieth-century art, but in terms of what the term means… It's so completely different, such as the artists in primitive societies, there is a relation in terms of a kind of cultural energy but otherwise you can't really make any kind of connections that would hold up for long. That's one of the things I found very interesting and fascinating about art and one of the reasons I am an artist is that art in the twentieth century took other dimensions and other implications than it had before that, and this is of course after Romantic periods and after a lot of other attempts to give art an extra meaning. I think art has become something that is equal in terms of its complexity as physics, philosophy or any other field, and this obviously wasn't always so; in a certain sense it has to be taken more seriously because of a lot of implications. Twentieth-century art is tautological. You are saying you can't go outside of art for the verification, right? So in that sense it is analytic: the outside world will give you no information at all about art; it's entirely man-made. It's very much in that sense like logic – which isn't to say it's logical, but its structure is similar to logic. Someone says what an artist is doing is taking something and placing it within a context of art and saying that this is art. You see, this thing is by itself a definition of art, because every artist, when he presents something as his work of art, he's saying that this is his definition of art. One begins to follow how does that set up function and work within a whole system of similar activities, that's where all other ones' engagements with art become complicated because you have to deal with that.

Along with these things, of course once certain very basic, primary questions were raised by Duchamp, with his ready-made, and he understood that – I mean you can give the man credit for understanding the meaning of art very early. In a certain sense, he did that outside of art, in a sort of ironic way. Because there was already a certain kind of almost very internal involvement, which really came from Cubism and its relation to painting, and to a point where you get through Abstract Expressionism, and you come out of that and you could think of Jasper Johns, or Donald Judd: they've arrived to a certain point where they both end up with that sort of realization about art which Duchamp had touched upon earlier."

*However, your conceptual research is still not tied to the object.*

"In a sense, if you have a piece of paper you still have an object and if someone speaks to you the sound waves are physical: so, in a certain sense, they are still objects. The question is not about physical entities, the question is about what do those physical entities mean, how do they function within art. In that sense I do believe that my art, and that of other artists, contemporary artists involved in a similar activity, are completely separate from the earlier attitude about art. What happened is that I think a lot of people who weren't really interested or capable of getting involved in the really complicated issues that we were raising, said 'Well, what this new art is about is that there are no more objects'. And it became very easy, it's a kind of pop idea of conceptual art, to say it simply means no objects. And the fact that there are fewer objects happens to be one of its identifying characteristics. Though, what's important is the question that we raised about the nature of art."

*What criteria do you use to choose your definitions?*

"When I did that work, in 1966–68, I would consider first many things at a different time, because I worked moving from very specific things like the first definition works with water (because I was involved then with water, using also hydrogen and oxygen), and I thought about that and the implications of just presenting the idea of water rather than the actual material. Certain other things, of course, had to do with other kinds of characteristics, colours, for instance, such as the definition of red… they're like the idea of featuring a sort of conceptual presentation of things which really almost had to be sensed. Take the definition of red: red is a very particular thing. When you think about looking at red, there's nothing you can really grasp on to tell why that's red. It's just the experience of it being red. So, to present the definition of red… it exists on various levels. It exists in a very particular, specific sense: you have a personal idea of red instead of an actual red. To other levels, for me it begins to sort of expire, in a certain sense, in a mental sense, it begins to have various stacks of meanings, so that it exists as… I called all those works, for instance, the same, they are all titled the same: *Art as Idea as Idea*, and *Art as Idea as Idea* is a kind of subtitle for all my work since 1966. There's a difference between saying: 'Art as idea' and 'Art as idea as idea'. The point was that once you begin to think of presenting something as an idea instead of presenting it as a form or a physical state of some sort, you then begin to realize that it becomes an idea of art that is built into it. So I said: 'Art as idea as idea', in other words I was calling conceptual art, calling the whole thing. What would be important is to think about the implications of just presenting ideas. And to follow that through – which is what I think I've done. That's what's interesting to me. It isn't only that early work, because that's only really its first level of importance. I could have died after that, and then I would not have been developing enough for some people, if I just did that. For me it's like modern art: it's bound to develop what the implications of these discoveries are. So you go from a very specific thing presenting it as an idea. You're saying: 'I'm presenting the idea instead of the object or the physical sensation'. But when you present the notion of a meaning of something that is not sensible, something you can't physically sense, it means you are presenting the idea of an idea, rather than an idea of something. And this began a whole other sort of issue that came out of it."

*Ad Reinhardt once said: "We need art in order to learn how to see". What is the importance of Reinhardt's work on the conceptual moments experienced today, and on your work as well?*

"For a long time Reinhardt has been perhaps my biggest influence. My first as well. Sometimes I felt he really understood art. I'm talking about the context of the abstract expressionist generation of American artists. He has been the first who understood the nature of art. He did his paintings, the black paintings. And that was really his proposition to art. He was saying that this was art. And at the same time he was writing, he appeared on perhaps more lectures, seminars and discussion groups than the other artists of that generation. His idea about art was very much renowned, and he was open to talk with students and talk with people. You had an art and you had information on it, and you can't separate one from the other. His entire activity is what we consider Reinhardt's art. He didn't just make black paintings and never said a word about them in a sort of mysterious way. He said a lot."

*The main intention in your work is that of the analysis of language. What do you mean by analysis?*

"It's a common usage, it has to do with taking a part, I suppose, and putting together, I mean a very simple definition. To break down and consider, to understand the particular proposition of art, of the entire investigation… since art itself doesn't have any territory of its own, it always uses some other things, materials from other fields or other techniques. When art existed as a kind of very primitive language, one was just interested in the more physical aspects of the language which had to do with the materials. That in the end lost its basic import, but from the artist's point of view it was a very important starting point. Artists realized that anything could function as art, so that our instinct goes to different fields, or different activities or whatever to include into art that becomes material. Because it's man-made. If I man would die, art would still subsist. Trees must still exist, but I wouldn't exist anymore, because I wouldn't have any meaning. Art doesn't have any existence in the natural world, because it is unnatural. It's man-made. So in that case it's going to have to take form in something else. It's like in science-fiction: a Martian comes to Earth and exists only as a mind and must take over other bodies, it's sort of like art. Art takes on different bodies, depending on what artists decide to do. You choose the tool that's best for what you want. So I chose language, as my material, just because it was the most complicated and richest and most versatile for the sort of work I was interested in doing. As far as analysis… To analyse, you take an ideal situation and you break it down to consider it and you think about it. Which others really never want to do. Other people always have done that, historians for instance: but an historian's primary interest is history, not art. Art is only a subject of it. What those persons do, that's a whole separate activity from art. The situation is that there are artists trying to do things of a sort that always other specialists have done who weren't primarily interested in art. I'm talking about the fact that art doesn't have any nature of its own, except a particular kind of skeleton system, but it must only drop on something outside of itself. As a pile. You drop on all other fields that haven't been dealt with in art. I talked with philosophers about art, and they may know a lot about philosophy or philosophic methodology but their idea about art is so naïve and ignorant that it's almost impossible to have a conversation about it. And it's the same for other fields. Their idea of art issues is so kitsch. It's just painting something to hang on walls. Perhaps sometimes they're more sophisticated. They still assume that art is about experience, they have some sort of idea about art that is just useless, you can't even get to know it… For these reasons an artist can get involved in taking all these other areas and fields and linking them to art, in order to make certain things understood about the nature of art. That's all it is about. It's about trying to find out what the nature of art is. And doing it as artists we'll expand the very nature of art. Here's the tautology. In the sense that while you find out about art, you are changing what art is. And that's what being an artist consists of."

# Giulio Paolini
Genoa, 1940



*Your work is made to be looked at, to be seen. Tell me about the process behind your work.*

"The process? 'I look'."

*I suppose "I look" is the poetic impetus that motivates your work.*

"'I look' is in fact the abstract and conceptual scheme of the phenomenon of sight. It's the translation into figures of the phenomenon of seeing. In this activity I traced a number of points on the wall in pencil, which correspond in effect to the quantity of space I had before me, and which the viewer finds before his eyes when he takes my place. For some time now – since 1960, when I began experimenting, but particularly after certain paintings I did in 1963 – I have sought to make an objective image; in other words, during these years I have tried to rescue painting from its role as a vehicle of the image. I begin with a rigid surface that I cover over with another material suitable for receiving visible graphic signs. This second material does not cancel out the support it rests on, for it is deliberately shaped in such a way as to uncover a detail of the latter. So, too, subsequent elements are added, always respecting the presence of those that come before. This way I obtain an effect of the simultaneity of the elements in question. The technique of the painting is its image: which is to say that the design imposed on these materials is nothing other than the presentation of the materials themselves."

*Can we say that, in your work, the object is identified with, and corresponds to, the project?*

"Yes. As a matter of fact, I really try to keep from mystifying the visual image, to make it as objective as possible."

*What do you mean by objective?*

"What seemed to me an objective operation, at the time: absolute respect for process and material. Today, from a distance, I see it as a desire for an absolute image. Roughly speaking, objective and absolute are opposite terms between which my work oscillates."

*What do you mean by absolute?*

"I tend to define as absolute even the works from this period, although at the time I did them I was absolutely convinced I was dealing with a sense of objectivity. Take one of my earliest works, for instance: the geometric squaring of the surface of the canvas. I later tried to destroy the identity of the image, by attributing it in multiple copies to imaginary authors and giving each copy an imaginary title. In this way I was probably trying to rescue this painting and this image from uniqueness, and hence from the objectivity which I had gone to such lengths to give it. I realize it's sort of a play on words. It's probably just a question of changing perspective. It's not a matter of retracting anything, it's just a different idea I have of this work of mine. I once felt the same way about the objectivity of materials; then, I turned my attention to the clarity of formulation."

*It seems to me that your work has always sought its own fulfillment in a context that is strictly linguistic, and hence objective. In your case language and the work are the same thing, as every one of your objects depends on visual language, as an end or as a means of transmission. In this sense I note a leap forward with respect to your strictly linguistic works, characterized by a sort of mirror-play through language: the young man looking at the painting by Lorenzo Lotto, the attribution of two identical works to different artists: almost a sort of turnaround from language to myth, as the language begins to refer to something which is outside of itself.*

"Maybe this great respect I have for language is identified, in the extreme, with a certain distrust. I've never considered language a vehicle for the communication of something else. For me it's always been just a fact in itself, with no collateral meaning, no meanings mediated linguistically. Language is its own meaning. Hence, my basic 'distrust' of language, which invariably appears as absolute respect, probably led me to a disregard for the author, for the matrix of language. I remember certain paintings of mine of 1965, in which I used photography. The first was an image of the wall of my studio, against which I had leaned some paintings, face down. Only one white canvas was turned towards the viewer; on it, the overall image of which it was part was drawn. A detail of a painting by Poussin reproduced on light-sensitive canvas showed a figure who offers the viewer his own reproduction. In this way I rescued the image from the role of service to content."

*This idea of reflection, or of reflective deduction: could this be the ideology of your work?*

"Yes. I don't know if you can speak of ideology, but it's a constant element both when I become the viewer of the painting that my hands make, in close relation to and agreement with its presence; and when I transfer images from past paintings, or become a part of other images that reproduce me as I walk around or work. It is always a matter of non-intervention in a positive sense, of the non-superimposition of a message on the presence of the painting."

*There's almost a voyeur's attitude towards language.*

"As I mentioned earlier, it is an attitude of enormous respect and distrust at the same time. Distrust, in that language should only be a means for imposing your own weakness, sometimes an overly personal hypothesis. It is true that this expectation and non-suggestion become even more personal, but as far as I'm concerned, I've always found myself in this dimension. For Poussin it was a question of emotions caused by certain works of his; whereas in Ingres's case it was above all his attitude, not stiff and reactionary, nor dialectical and invariably inspired. What surprises me is Ingres's 'blindness' – that meticulousness and extreme devotion to detail that drew him away from the problems of painting. He is blind to the integrity of the subject. In speaking of Ingres's 'errors', one must duly consider this attitude of excessive enthusiasm for his *métier* and technique that becomes vocation and 'inhuman' dedication, absolute identity between artist and artwork. Lotto, in contrast, surprised me with the fixity of his painted image, but it was an occasional starting point."

*I always seem to notice a sort of intentional loss of subjectivity in relation to the language used, in these works.*

"When Ingres faithfully – mythically – copies Raphael's *Self-portrait*, this strikes me. I made a work by superimposing the two pictures in such a way that the two things seem the same. I called it *Ingres's Invention* because I wanted to emphasize the absolute quality of invention when it is reduced to identification, and invention can never be so absolute as when it is a reduction of something that is already perfect. The slaver of participation can often be overcome in the acquisition of something that's already there. As far as my distrust in subjectivity is concerned, you will recall my participation in the Bologna Biennale of Painting, where I sent a painting by Picabia. This kind of gesture makes the creation of a work coincide with its perception; the author tries to transmit to the viewer his emotions as viewer. By showing a painting that wasn't mine, I wanted to repropose my relation with that particular painting objectively, by showing this subjective relation between the painting and me, unmediated by language, as a work of my own. I've always left traces of how I arrive at my works in the works themselves. Now I am preparing a new series that embodies an attitude similar to that which I assume before becoming the painter: large canvases in traditional media, which form a kind of scenographic halo, describing in images the paintings I've done up to now. So far, I've confined myself to speculating on what works should be done; here for the first time I intend to propose images, or rather, representations of images that formerly weren't representations for me. The subject is the range of my previous activity, the pictorial description of my past works. It is a mute subject expressing only what I have to communicate, that is, the works I did before this one."

*Your work initially appeared as an application of tautological principles, then there arose a sort of "doubt" about language, followed by an opening towards myth. Now, aren't these new works, whose plan you have described to me, a cyclical return from myth to tautology?*

"It's sort of an anniversary. An important detail in this new group of works is that the canvases will not necessarily be all the same size, although they will all be in the same proportion to my first paintings. The new canvases, scenographic and descriptive of the past, open along the diagonal of that dimension. I've already pointed out that the images of the earlier paintings are the constituent elements of the paintings themselves. Now, the images of these new paintings are no longer the materials that they are made of, but the later flip side of the works done so far – the activity itself. I don't intend to represent past experiences, I want to show that the space of my first canvas of 1960 is still valid, because extending the proposition of that canvas enables me to suggest that all the later works were included in the others – it's like prolonging that initial moment forever. If on the one hand I return to tautology (initially applied to materials, today to images), on the other I maintain a mythical dimension by not cancelling the starting point of my work. No painting of mine is born with the idea of effacing the one before it, it does not arise from a cumulative succession of experiences; it is always an absolute declaration, self-sustaining, suspended in time without developmental relations. Hence, it is logical to suggest that I have never been able to surpass my first painting. Every work is unique; it differs from the others in its emotions, interests, and subsequent misappropriations. But I don't think it can deny or extend what comes before it."

*It seems that this standstill of yours, this running in place before language, also signifies that the work becomes extraneous after it's completed, because, as it is absorbed by culture, it moves away from its maker, and returns to myth. For you then the work of approaching myth, culture and language begins all over again.*

"I felt the need to give the work a sense of growth, the meaning of a conscious series of experiences. Every work has always appeared to be the first, to me; but for just this reason it probably isn't, it is always a different image of the same thought. My return to the dimension of my first painting is intended neither to evoke not to celebrate that work, but merely to point out that there is only one dimension: the ever-changing form of things that follow one another is always essentially the same. The type of image changes by itself not because of a will to surpass or perfect it, but because the succession is part of things."

*Your work consists of drying language out to the point where it is perceptible only from a cultural point of view that is intimately bound up with the act of seeing.*

"We might even say that it is only what one sees, hence it is not at all what one sees – meaning that the absolute quality I always tend to give these images cannot avoid running counter to the act of perception, because it is valid only if considered a certain way. When one attributes absoluteness to the act of perception, and hence to language, the absolute quality paradoxically dissolves, I think. The subjective attribute of this absoluteness is precisely the consciousness of not being able to surpass the limits of language, and hence the application of language's own terms to itself, without forcing it towards inappropriateness and abuse which in my opinion cannot be translated.

Given language's precise but fascinating limits of 'wonder', I'm always careful not to force them, to leave some portion of them unexplored; nor must I compromise them or turn them aside, giving language's latent capacities implications that could not be properly collocated within language itself. This is the paradoxical situation by virtue of which language is everything and nothing. I repeat once again, language is itself."

*It's almost a Borges-like attitude towards language, isn't it?*

"Yes. As a matter of fact, I've always found Borges a very exciting writer. It's not easy, though, to find adjectives for language; there are many ways of interpreting it, but perhaps there's an illusion that language exists *per se*. Clearly, language does not exist, but an intention may exist, a correct devotion to trying to identify it as a fact existing prior to the interpretations made of it. A certain obsession is this fact of being: while recognizing its relativity as a subjective and non-objectifiable fact, one nevertheless attempts to approach its essence. The colour of language is the one everybody gives it; the sense of having it, however, lies in seeking a correct approach to its secrets."

*What would you say is the role of art, of your art, at least?*

"To provide the fascination of its comprehension and contemplation. If a message can come from art, it always does so in spite of art, without an explicit will to affirmation. By comprehension I mean the possibility art gives of watching the spectacle and its author to the same degree, without an opposition of relations, until one reaches an outcome, an involuntary declaration – involuntary for the viewer, who should not expect what he is about to see, and for the artist to the same degree. Just as the viewer is amazed by an artwork (in a contemplative, rather than a violent, sense), so the author is filled with wonder by the unconscious – because unstated – conquest of his idea."

# Lawrence Weiner
New York, 1940



*How do you go over to work simply by concepts, sentences, without actions?*

"Simply by logical deduction."

*What does logical deduction mean for you?*

"It became the only means to make art that was viable in my own time, in my own culture and by the utilization of concepts. One leaves open how the person who is receiving the work envisions things about or sees the work. I began to realize that by placing a unique object in front of a person with the portent of art upon it, you were saying 'this is the way you must see something for it to be art', whereas basically what art is dealing with are general ideas. And if I could keep the work at the point where there are ways one *could* see it, instead of the ways that one *should* see it, I would succeed in making an art viable for my times."

*What's the difference between the words you use today and the materials you used in your previous works?*

"Everyone of the words that I utilize now within the context of the work can be visualized by some person in terms of an absolute material. They are not necessarily to be kept only in their ideal state. I generally prefer just the idea, but if a person chooses to visualize this from a material point of view, there is no difference, it's just visual information. There is nothing that I do that cannot be built physically."

*What do you think to impose today through your aesthetic experience, through your art?*

"I don't think I impose anything. I think I place a cultural alternative within culture itself, I place another way of thinking about art, another way of dealing with art. But I don't impose this, as a way."

*Which alternative?*

"Art is in part a function of the society, and not at all a specific ego-oriented situation, where art itself deals with the culture one is living in. And in dealing with culture, of course, by reentering culture in the form of art, it filters down in its bastardized forms into culture again, becomes very much akin to theoretical physics, where the equation itself, the concept of the physicist, is quite interesting as an idea, and yet it reaches culture again, after it has been bastardized, and reused and put through other terms than the original physics terms, and it reenters from culture again back into physics, and physics' continuity goes on, it is a continuum. And art, I feel is exactly the same situation, you are not making, there is no such a thing as a masterpiece. I don't think that any work of mine is any better than any other work of mine. It's more or less my concept in my dealings with culture and with what it is inclined to call art."

*What's culture?*

"All. All that you are living in, all that constitutes our existences is our culture. One can't define one part of our existence as higher than another part. That's, in a sense, the very fascist concept of art, that art is above men, art is what men should aspire to. And it is impossible for anybody who is just a normal person to make something that another person should 'aspire' to. If one person can make it, almost all other people can comprehend it, so there is no aspiration quality of it. Whatever is part of your life is part of your culture, from your art to your kitchen, to your cigar, to the way people walk in different places. That's culture."

*Which is the difference between culture and experience?*

"It doesn't exist. There is no difference."

*And between culture and politics?*

"There is politics in everything one does. My politics themselves determine, perhaps, the means I utilize to present my art; but politics do not determine art itself. The means that I use, language, I feel, perhaps politically is much more viable for our time to present art, because it makes no imposition of how one thinks of something, it makes a suggestion of what one could think about."

*How do you use words?*

"First I must take exception to the word 'creative'. I don't believe in it. In English the word 'create' has connotations of making something from nothing – but nothing can be made from nothing, or at least I'm not capable of making something from nothing. The work itself is so self-obvious. The work pretends and portends to be nothing but what it is. So I cannot give you a heavy quasi-philosophical idea of what I'm supposed to be doing, what I'm doing is in a sense quite up-front. You can read the words in translation even, there is no right, there is no wrong."

*Which structural value do you give to the word?*

"Whatever structural value is necessary."

*What does this necessity come from?*

"The terms of 'necessity', as you call it, are in relation, I am afraid, only to my concept of culture, only to my concept of the work that I do. The utilization of tenses and of language itself is determined, I think, just again by my take on the situation; there is no overriding religious concept of language involved. Within that point of view follows the work from the very beginning. You will see that there is an awareness of new things about language that I have discovered. Many of these discoveries have not been made by me, but have been made by my contemporaries, have been made by people in other disciplines, and I use everything that I can find out about to make my art, it's that simple, for the manufacture of my art."

*Your work organizes language, gives a different structure to language.*

"My work is the presentation of my ideas about art and my feelings about art and the part of our culture that has been designated as 'art'. They have in no way manner or form or any reason to structure the language or to structure words. If, in turn, my ideas about art, and my utilization of language in art change the structure of the language, and change the structure of the culture – then what I do is profiling its function as art."

*What's art for you?*

"What the culture around me designates as art, and also my product. A definition of my art? The definition of my art is very simply my art."

*Is your art a tautology?*

"In one sense everything that we affirm in relation to any discipline is a tautology, but art itself is not based on tautological thought. It is based, rather, on the thought of one logical approach to the production of art. Why not? We might tell each other what isn't art – and yet, we really can't even tell each other that. Art is the part of our culture that is designated as art. It's art because it deals with problems that have previously been presented within the context of art. Outside of the context of art many of the ideas of art are useful, but at the same time it's not a quality judgement, of whether it is useful outside of its own context. My art is useful within the context of art, which is determined basically by the fact that we are sitting here making an interview in relationship to it; so it has entered the culture successfully within the context of art. There is no doubt that it is art – there is a doubt if it is correct or not correct."

*What's the ideology of your art?*

"The making of a product that has a definite function within culture."

*Can your art intervene on life?*

"Once it becomes part of the culture, I have no control over it any more. And its intervention is completely determined by culture itself, by the necessity of culture: if culture finds something within the construct of my art, that's useful, it will take it. If it finds nothing that is useful, it will not take it, and it will not become art history, and there is no problem, it won't be being discussed in three years."

*Your work starts from a conceptual purpose, but ends always in an object as a result.*

"There is no intention on my part on how the work is to be received. I can make no judgement on whether receiving it just as an idea, or receiving it as a physical object, or receiving it as an action, itself, is better or worse. So there is no intention on my part, other than to present my conclusions. There is no intention to present them in any specific way. I may personally have a liking or a disliking for a means of representation, but I don't have an aesthetic judgement about this liking or disliking."

*Is your work creative or reflexive?*

"I don't even like the word 'reflection'. The work, my work is just, again, a presentation of my conclusions, concerning art. It is the end product of a logical series of thoughts."

*Life is also cruelty, violence, negative themes. How do you choose some words and leave out other words?*

"Necessity for what I'm attempting to present. Both questions of life and death enter into a relationship with metaphysics that I don't particularly like, because in the end I will have to answer back: 'I'. And my work has no relationship to the 'I', the work is presented out of context with me. You need not know me nor speak to me, to either dislike, appreciate or not understand what I do. But to understand anything about my concepts about life and death you must know who I am and what I am, and my life and my death. So I am not very interested in art where its object is 'I'. I really do not mind art where the subject of the art is 'I'."

*What is part of your art?*

"The only thing that one can usually speak of, when one discusses art, is art itself. If you discuss an automobile or you discuss a shoe, you don't discuss what the man who made the automobile or made the shoe had for breakfast."

*Your work is an analytical presentation of language, a presentation of concepts through language, isn't it?*

"No, it is a dialectic utilization of the language."

*Dialectic with what?*

"Dialectic with culture. In the future artists will be thought of as semiologists, rather than as anything else. By my own way of thinking, at this point, I believe that the acceptance of art as culture dialectics would be a very 'healthy' thing politically, for it would place the artist in a context of a functioning use within the society, as opposed to profit, or somebody coming off from a mountain to tell the society something. He's just somebody who is there working along with the society in the same sense that everybody else is working within the society. And to place the artist in that context is perhaps the most important thing I can think of right now."

*But ideas are always production of objects.*

"That's fine. I've never said that I was anti-object. I chose to utilize language as my major means of expressing ideas, but if someone can present logical and lucid ideas employing objects, no problem. I find much object production by my contemporaries highly enlightening and highly interesting and very exciting. My art is not taking a position against or for objects, or against or for the utilization of just the core idea. This position is unimportant in relationship to art. What is important in art is what the position itself is, what conclusions I have reached in relationship to art. I think that my conclusions have already shown that any kind of specific object purporting to be more important than any other object of its like, any other similar object, is asinine."

# Ian Wilson
Great Britain, 1940



*Do you use language as a way of conveying information or as a way of communicating?*

"It appears I do both. If we assume I am communicating, it follows I am communicating certain information."

*Can you please describe your last exhibition, here at the Weber Gallery?*

"In the last exhibition I was present at the opening and those people who were not familiar with what I do asked me questions about it, I responded by explaining that I was concerned with pursuing a discussion of art."

*Why do you use speech instead of other media?*

"I am, as I have said, interested in discussing art."

*What is the difference between speaking with an artist and other persons?*

"I speak to people who are interested in art and I seldom speak to people who are not interested in art, when I am speaking about art.

And when I speak to someone who is not interested in talking about art we talk of other things."

*Do you use speech because it does not leave a trace? Is there an ideological reason for using speech?*

"There is, but it is difficult for me to talk about it."

*Could you say something about this, because it is the most important thing about your work...*

"But perhaps the most important thing cannot be said..."

*There is a distance between men. Do you think language can lessen this distance? I believe language at this time has lost its power. Why have you chosen language?*

"Well, I don't understand why you think language has lost its power."

*Why do you use this Socratic proceeding? Instead of answering, you ask a question.*

"Why do I use a Socratic proceeding? This is not particularly a Socratic proceeding. I am asking questions because we are translating from Italian to English and I just want to be sure I understand you."

*What do you think is the function of art in our society?*

"This is a difficult question. It is difficult because there are many functions of art in our society."

*Do you think you can say what the function of your art is?*

"The function of my work is to continue a discussion of art."

*So it is more important to reflect on art instead of creating other works of art. Do you think that when you speak you are making a work of art? Do you think your discussions are a creation or a reflection?*

"They may be both."

*So why do you not write?*

"The reason I discuss art, the reason I speak about art is that I have not found a position that I want to write."

*What is art for you?*

"The question is too general."

*Do you use speech because you don't want to make objects and commodities?*

"It doesn't matter whether someone wants to or whether someone can buy what I do. This is secondary. I don't think I speak particularly to avoid making objects."

*This is not a problem?*

"No, it is not a problem."

*So you prefer a warm communication, to speak directly, instead of a cold communication…*

"No, it doesn't matter. I read other artists writings on art and I find them interesting."

*When you are alone you like to read the writings of other artists, but when you make art you always use speech and not other media.*

"Yes."

*Why?*

"Because it is not necessary."

*But if you are interested in other people's writings why do you always speak?*

"The reason I speak is that I want to discuss art and understand how other artists think of their work. I want to ask them questions and discuss art with them."

*I don't understand.*

"My position is that it is appropriate that there be a discussion of art in order that we may find out whether it is appropriate that there be a discussion of art."

*Do you question people or do people question you?*

"Both."

*How long have you worked in this way?*

"I have been working in this way for four years."

*And before?*

"Before I was a painter and sculptor."

*When you use language do you think that everything exists in the language and nothing out of the language? Do you understand?*

"Yes, that's a very good question. To say everything exists in language is interesting because it presumes the British philosopher Berkeley's position, according to which this table exists because I think of it and does not exist aside from my thoughts about it. But this is not necessarily true. If the table exists also when I am not thinking about it, then not everything exists in language. But there are many issues in this. It raises the question of whether language determines the world or the world determines language. And perhaps both are the cases."

*Why did you leave sculpture for pure reflection? I mean thoughts, language and speech.*

"The last sculpture I made was a white chalk circle drawn on the floor. It was more interesting to talk about it than draw it."

*Why?*

"Because what was interesting about it was that it was a circle and you can speak about a circle as well."

*Does your art regard Wittgenstein in some way?*

"I am very interested in his writings."

*What of Wittgenstein has influenced your work?*

"Which works? Which ideas? In the *Tractatus* Wittgenstein says that substance is both form and content. I am led to believe from this that there is no art in which the form or the presentation is irrelevant."

*So, does your art regard the logical problem of the language, or does it regard also other realities?*

"I am concerned with the use of language to describe reality. It is as we said before. It is not clear whether language determines the world or whether it is the world that determines language."

*But do you think art is a way of organizing our thoughts?*

"Art is a way we try to organize thoughts. Whether or not we do that, is another question. It appears that when we discuss art we assume we can make art clearer, and it may be that when we say we cannot we fall under our own criticism. By that I mean that it can be made clear that art cannot be made clear. But this doesn't mean that art can be made clearer."

# Carl Andre
## Quincy, Massachusetts, 1935



*Can you tell me something about your first works made in wood in 1958? Which sense did they have for you?*

"Carvings in wood, mostly, were much inspired by Constantin Brancusi, whom I was a great admirer of at the time, and whom of course I remain a great admirer of… In 1958–59, when I was working in New York and was absolutely penniless, the only materials I had to work with were the things I could steal in the streets, and one of the few materials you could find to work with in the streets was wood, timber. I've never had the kind of studio training in sculpture where people work with clay, or plaster, or even stone, marble, such things. I know I always hated clay, even as a child, I hated plaster because plaster was not a material that was real, you always had to turn plaster into something else. So I've always been drawn to materials that were strong and durable, and would be final themselves. Of course, this is the doctrine of direct cutting that came along at the end of the nineteenth century or beginning of the twentieth, when sculptors were turning away from the idea of making models and having them transformed into bronze, or then cut in the stone. They wanted to cut directly into whatever material they were using.

*Can we tell that you've chosen wood because it's a hot material?*

"I've never cut in stone, I don't know how to cut in stone. I've never really cut in metals either, I've used sections of metal. Yes, wood was the material I actually formed myself with, carved and cut into it. And one big day in the early 1960s I was using concrete, I was mixing concrete and using it, not like plaster, as a model, but using it actually as a material to make pieces… There is a distinction I've made in my own work between the 'plastic' sense, that is beginning to mould a continuous form, and the 'clastic' sense, which is to break up (a form is not a form, it's made by combining elements, which are parts and combining parts)…

*Which is your idea of space in these works?*

"Well, to bring up the word conceptual, my work has been

associated with the so-called conceptual artists and it has nothing to do with it whatsoever. I don't really work with ideas at all. As you see I work with material things, quite directly, and it is not an idea that precedes my work. My work has always really begun with matter and the direct manipulation… I don't feel I deal with ideas, in any degree. I feel that I deal with desires. Like: there's the world of matter and I wish to act in the world of matter, and to combine elements in the world of matter, but not in order to realize an ideal, or an idea. And you know the story of the hedgehog and the fox. There are foxes who can leap in many directions – a person like Bob Morris, who's, you know, a dazzling artist because he is going in so many different directions, and very strongly. But for me, I must really keep very close to one kind of line, because that is my strength. So, this extent of 'minimal' I would accept, because of that idea of rigour. But aside from that, I really don't know, I'm not very close to the intellectual currents that go into it."

*Can we state that space grows with the work?*

"Exactly. The work is not existent until it's done, and… well, the space is around all the time. It's a matter of deforming and reforming and manipulating the space, because every object, in a sense, is a kind of space, and when you combine, you deform and you rearrange the space itself, but it doesn't exist beforehand. And this is the confusion… There is the desire to change the space, and there is the idea of changing the space, and for me the desire exists, the idea does not exist. After the work is done the idea can be raised, because then one can comprehend; but for me the action is what generates the idea, not the idea that generates the action."

*Can you tell me something about* Pyramid?

"I met Frank Stella at this time, and he was starting to work at his stripe paintings. And the way he treated a painting as a work to be accomplished by a consistent, rigorous application entirely across the surface of the canvas… It's also very obvious in the pyramid, this is taking an operation and just rigorously carrying in through a form. And it was this kind of rigour and the kind of breaking down of a form into elements, and then combining them, that was very much influence of Frank Stella… He insisted that

I, in a sense, worked at the strongest potential that I could, he would not tolerate himself working at less than highest, most extreme potential, and he wouldn't tolerate my doing it either. It is this kind of rigour of application by the artist that is always for me the most, you know, inspiring, or the greatest influence; it's almost that kind of ethical example, rather than just what the final work looks like.

*Which is the margin and the value of casualness in finding and elaborating materials?*

"Not really accident, because as you see, the material I choose in the world is that which has generally gone through industrial process. I don't pick up stones from the seashore, because each one is unique, in a sense; what I pick are materials that are usually parts that have been discarded from some industrial process, some machine process, and these are the parts that are not wanted, that clip off, they are too long, or too short, whatever. The degree of accident is very low, because the whole idea of an industrial process is to reduce accidents; so, what is left over from an industrial process is even less accidental, in a sense, than the final product, because it's the shape of the final product's sort of leftover. But I tend to want the forms that are, in a sense, the simplest, and have the least accident to them. Squares and rectangles and cubical forms. I have great difficulty with curved forms, because they don't come together very well. So, the materials I use have, you know, rectilinear surfaces, because they just fit together."

*So you try to avoid any accident, any casualness…*

"I don't want the detail of a structure to be interesting, you know, beautiful effects and so forth. This doesn't interest me at all. I want the material in its clearest form."

*Why do you recover mass-produced materials?*

"I don't go out in the world really with an idea of what I'm seeking, rather I come upon the elements. Of course I do have preferences, but these are hardly preferences on the level of a conception, rather on the level of what I can use, you know, what I need, what combines. But there is a difference here between me and, let's say, the pop and neo-realist artists. They took cultural products too – I mean these materials I use that of course are cultural products – but the cultural products of the pop, neo-realist and neo-dada guys are completed objects: I mean, Andy Warhol takes a box, which has already been printed, it's final, and then puts it in art. This is very Duchampian, that's the idea of a completed cultural artefact. What I use is the material in a sense like the brick, which becomes a wall. I don't use the wall, really, I use the brick; in other words, it's the raw material of the society, not its final product."

*Up to 1960 you made vertical pieces, afterwards you gave yourself up to horizontal works. I'd like to know the reason of this shift.*

"I would say that, for instance, there was the work of Morris which was very low, horizontal, and the work of Judd that is on the wall, which is very horizontal too. It has been sometimes said that the major issue of sculpture, let's say, in the 1960s was a problem of getting rid of the base. This was not true, the problem in sculpture was exactly to get away from this vertical anthropomorphic sense, from that sculpture always in the column, or in the sense of human figure. And there hadn't been too much sculpture that was extended in the horizontal way, and my own work was still, I think, influenced very much by this verticality. I suppose it was a contribution of Judd and Morris that freed me from this necessity of verticality. I can't really say it explicitly, all I know is that it's true. Even later, I wasn't really doing, extending the horizontal pieces until late 1964. I've always worked on the floor, but the vision certainly became horizontal around that time. Well, it's certainly a very practical reason, which I would tell is even stronger, because when you build high you become unstable, when you build low, you remain firm all the way through. And this probably is the deepest reason, because I wasn't ever really interested in structures, I never built a box, you know, which is the primary minimal form…"

*At the level of language doesn't the passage to horizontal works mean the possibility of a greater participation too?*

"I know I did not invent the floor, I'm certain of this. I don't think artists really make innovations at all. What is beautiful in art, is not that someone is original, but that someone can find a way of creating in the world the instance of his temperament. This is a problem of every age, because the cultural dominance of the age is always the strongest thing, stronger than the individual. And what is very difficult to the artist is to find a way through the culture that will indeed reflect him. And this is not a business of originality, this is much more difficult than to be original. To be original in a way is easy, but to be true is difficult."

*Couldn't the meaning of these horizontal works be the turning upside down of the vertical lines of the city?*

"Of course I've never lived very much in the vertical parts of New York, I live in the horizontal parts, and I think the subways of New York have been much more an influence on my work than the tall buildings. I've never been at the top of the Empire State Building, you can see it from here, but they are not really 'skyscrapers' as you can see from here. And I've not lived, really, in that part… But I think it may also be that living in New York with something like the Empire State Building, one realizes that, in order to be really impressive in a vertical thing, one has to be very, very high, and that in a sense it's so much more efficient to be extensive across the land. And also there aren't too many great vistas in New York, it is true… and I suppose that might have had something to do with it."

*Which sense has in your work the passage from wood to more opaque materials, like aluminium, and to other heavier materials? Did that choice determine the minimal turning point in your work?*

"In terms of temperament pieces like the *Pyramid* are essentially minimal. I mean, even, that carving as well is minimal in the sense that Brancusi is minimal, that kind of rigour and clearness and simplicity of his forms. Anyway, minimalism was already there, that's not the point. But when the division comes to elements and particles, my first problem was that if you use blocks of wood, they are very light, and if you make a row of blocks they do not have a mass that keeps them stable and they would tend to drift around, somehow. But something like a brick, or a piece of metal, or something that has a great mass… If you take a very small element and it's made of wood, it's too light, it lacks mass: somehow this is a very fundamental sense of sculpture. That's why I've never done hollow works. I like the sense of heaving of it, this is very much how I came to sculpture. The great characteristic of wood is that it's amazingly light for its strength. It's stronger, for its weight, than metal is. But it lacks this kind of heavy mass, which in a sense I wanted. Once I began to get simple groups and sets, I felt that the mass of the individual group had to be greater because it had to keep the stability – and that's something which is just, again, a deep part of one's temperament. And so, going from woods to metals is a matter of passing from structure to placement. When one reaches the horizontal state, then comes the great issue of the durability of the sculpture. In other words, if one puts something low on a floor, people will walk on it. Now, at first I thought that this was a problem, but then I realized that with metals, it makes no difference whether you will walk on it or not. People can enter into the metal floor pieces and stay in the middle of them. Certainly one characteristic of these metal pieces is that they are sculptures that one can enter non-architecturally into; in other sculptures one enters into a structure, rather than into a place. In that way my work is more like gardens than like figures. And this I like very much. I've always liked very much the Japanese gardens, things of this sort, where you don't actually enter but usually pass through. This is a possibility of being within the sculpture, but not as in a house or it being around; you would look at it, and of course one must have a durable material for this, and if one made a wooden piece on a floor it just simply wouldn't have such a long life. I have made pieces that had a very short life, but somehow… why shouldn't they last… And it's the nature of metals that they should stand this."

*Your works from 1958 onwards and the wooden pieces are works to be seen; others, like these in aluminium, are spaces to live in. What do you think about?*

"Yes, the metal pieces are very much to be traversed, so there is this distinction, because before there was a sort of frontality, whereas now the piece is horizontal. The tendency has been always towards the elimination of this kind of frontality, and this is a quality of the horizontal as opposed to the vertical. I like works which sort of ambush you, that is, in a sense take you by surprise because you can be in a place for some time and not even know that they are there. Then suddenly you see them and realize them and let you, in a sense, come and go with the work, even if it's there, but you can forget about it. I don't like art that dominates you, that is coming at you, and is assailing you, and is making attack. I like a work that is just there until it needs you and you need it, and then you don't have to worry about it. That's again inverse of the vertical: the vertical is always there, you arrive and that's confronting you all the time."

*Can we call your art a "city art" because your work rectifies this space?*

"Oh, I don't know, I have no such grand starts about the work, my work is very much subjective, I cannot say that it is any such great ambition."

*Do these works have a political meaning?*

"Well, all work has a political meaning, because every work is an expression of its time. Unfortunately I sometimes feel that my work has aggressive principles, that the work itself may be reactionary in a sense, the same way that abstract art has been using the Cold War as to say that the NATO countries, you know, on this side of the Iron Curtain, they are free, they can make this silly-looking art, but in the Soviet Union they are not free, they must make 'tractor art'. But of course the Great Commissaries of the West like the same kind of art as the Great Commissaries of the East. They all like nice paintings of their models and their tractors and automobiles and things they understand. I'm not saying that intrinsically abstract art is reactionary, but it has been used by reactionaries in the social struggle – and in this sense I am used by reactionaries in the social struggle. Well, I think art is sort of agricultural, that it is involved with maintaining life, and feeding life and offering people peace and happiness, and these very simple things.

And I don't look at art in a business sense, think of it much more as of a life furnishing power. But the thing is that one can make one's art in all the truth that one can summon from oneself, and then it goes into the world, and how the world uses it is something one cannot control. As I have said before: art is what we do and culture is what is done to us. And it's difficult, I try my best to track down how my work is being used, I won't let, for instance, you know, my work be the representative of the US government as long as the war in Vietnam is going on."

*In which sense can your work be called minimal?*

"Only with a small m not a capital M, because the capital M is the name of a movement that was created by critics, and does not exist, it's just a name. But with a small m it would just mean an attempt to create, in a sense, the greatest sufficiency in a work of art, that is to free the work from detail and from distraction, and to give an opportunity that everything in the work shall allow the work, the attention to the work, to be drawn inward, rather than the idea that this work will suggest everything out in the world. The work will suggest only itself. I suppose it's a sense of an unmoving centre, a still point in a way, to bring the attention to itself… just the opposite to making a work which reminds you of all different other things in the world. This is a typical Western view of art, I think it's that which reminds you of all the things that are happening in the universe. My skill tends towards the intensive rather than the extensive. So to that extent it can certainly be minimal."

*Do you work with objects?*

"I suppose, it's just work. They are, but I've never been in trouble. This is a problem artists have today: worrying about the art object. I've never worried about this because since our life is a process, and this is going on, an art object, I don't worry that it's a thing, it doesn't bother me at all, I like things, I like matter, so I would never wish to go beyond matter, to pure idea. I'm not even a mystical. It's not a mystical vision I want, but it's a calm, it's a peace that I want, which is quite a stability. Not a stability in the face of the horrors of the world, not that, but some moments of calm in the world. And I find that the contemplation, perhaps, of certain objects and certain art works, you know, can bring this. But I don't wish to think of art as a narcotic either, this would be very wrong. There is a false way of using art or religion or mysticism or drugs, to paralyze one's self and to make one's self indifferent to the things of the world. I don't believe in being indifferent to the world."

*Which is the relation between the works in heavy materials or aluminium, and concrete poetry made with very light materials: words?*

"I think of heavy and light in terms of matter, again, of mass. As for words, there are some heavy words and some light words, but it's entirely different. Though, it's the same temperament, I bring the same temperament – or I have brought the same temperament – both to the poems and to the material, and in a sense my efforts in poetry have been to try to use words as bricks, you might say, as separate and not in the structure of grammatical form, but without grammar and in a more absolute sense. That sense of isolation that is like sculpture. I don't consciously select them this way. But obviously words have different properties… If all words had the same properties, there might not be poetry, because I treat the words as particles. They retain their meaning, but they do so as atoms, as particles. Usually in a discourse the element of meaning is not the word at all, but the whole sentence, the phrase. Now, I wanted to go back to the word itself and make each individual word the sense of the poem, or at least one element of the poem. And to use the individual word as the bearer of the meaning."

*How do you consider the space of the page and the space of the gallery that you occupy with your works?*

"A gallery space is in a sense like a book, not like a page. A gallery is a place to present work, and a book is a way of presenting poems. Certainly my poems don't have to be in a book to be seen, they can be, they can exist on separate pages, just as my works don't have to be in a gallery in order to be seen. But this is the social mechanism by which art is brought forth."

*Which meaning has the outside work for you?*

"I have done this very little. I've worked outside very little. I've done it so little that I hardly feel so strong about. I'm not a person of the countryside, I'm a person of the town. So I generally think of art as being inside this kind of limitations of houses and dwellings or galleries or studios. I'm just not a person who, you know, climbs mountains and I don't go hiking in the woods. It's just not really very close to my temperament."

*Which is the function of art?*

"I never set out to be an artist, I found myself being an artist. I think if you take small children, before they begin their education, and you put them out in the fields to be together, there are two things that they will always do: they will make love and they will make art. And these are, I believe, the two things in life that

I find myself doing. It's just a memory of my own childhood. I think that the play of children usually is involved in two areas: either they are touching and looking at each other, holding each other, or being together physically in a really kind of erotic and love-making way; or they are changing the world in ways that give them pleasure, picking flowers or making holes, you know, building shelter or whatever. But, I mean, that's really very much what I feel about subjectively."

*Does art have an ideological function?*

"All activities we share with all other forms of life don't need an excuse. We need excuses to go to war, we need ideologies for war, we need ideologies for profiteer exploitations, you know, injustices. It depends on the leverage of art within culture. For instance, I'm sure that in the cinema Jean-Luc Godard is the strongest artist of the second half of the twentieth century so far, and his work is tremendously, consciously political."

# Robert Morris
Kansas City, Missouri, 1931

New York
1972

*In your experiences you used many materials. What's the meaning of that?*

"Well, I don't think that it should be hard for an Italian critic, familiar with the Futurists, to understand… The Futurists were people who involved themselves with a number of different materials… I think artists are, since the 1960s I suppose, investigating many different kinds of materials. Then, I've not only changed lots of materials, I worked in a lot of different formats, film and theatre, dance; so it's a way of just keeping loose, I guess, of keeping more things open on my horizon."

*Are you interested in Duchamp's work?*

"I think so, because I've thought much about Duchamp. Maybe his most important message to me was that he seemed to be a man who was very much concerned with being free, both in terms of his life and in terms of his art, and freedom was achieved by a certain kind of very complicated strategy that involved certain things that he wanted to avoid and certain things that he wanted to achieve. The strategy even involved a very subtle, and I think far-reaching, attack on language itself, in terms of how people formulate problems, and even that he refused: he said 'there are no solutions because there are no problems, problems are an invention of man'. So he was constantly concerned to transcend, to define his freedom, not even in terms of problem solving."

*I think that your work has a double polarity: gesture and the measure of gesture, a sort of reflexive attitude.*

"I wouldn't use the term polarity, which seems to denote a kind of opposition. I wouldn't use the term polarity, but I think there is often in my work a kind of attempt, there has always been an attempt, to do something other than just have an object sitting there. I was always interested in recovering other aspects of it, like my behaviour that went into it, or the time that went into it. One thing or another I was always involved, I think, in pushing it off of that axis – here's a plastic art object that can be taken as a formal arrangement of things. And in so far as I have done things to push it off that axis, I've engaged a number of ways of doing that. It's not my only concern, but I've seen that in the past as I look back to the number of things I've done, I've included this other aspect of things, frequently a temporal aspect. I see that as very natural for me, because I consider that to do anything is a continuum, existing in time as well as in space, and you can choose as much hazard as you want, or as little as you want. And I have certainly done that sort of thing."

*Can you tell me something about that exhibition of yours where each day a work, an object was taken from the space?*

"There have been a couple of exhibitions that involved change throughout the exhibition itself. There was one early work (it was 1967 maybe) with a number of a very minimal type of sculptures, but it had parts that permuted, you know, could be changed, either taken away or rearranged within that given complement of parts. That was, maybe, the first time I did something that was evolving throughout a space of time, as not having a definite configuration, only a limiting set of possibilities. So, that was done some time ago. A couple of years ago I did a piece where I more or less used a gallery situation as a studio, where I just worked every day with a certain number of materials, ending up with the piece finally just being taken away, and some photographs left. That was a development, I suppose, of the original idea that things have a number of possible existences, rather than any definitive, ended kind of existence."

*What did the transition from the gallery to the outside mean for you?*

"I don't think it's a transition between moving out or having an object, a specific object to do a situation… it really extends beyond that. There are other aspects too, I mean social aspects, too, because it functions differently when you work outside, and your work becomes available to, say, a community, rather than to the very particular kind of person who comes to a gallery. In most of the work that has been done outside, certainly the kind of formal concerns has not changed – it's very much process in minimal art – but the function is changed, and in that, I think, is its more interesting aspect. To see whether or not art can have an alternative function, because it's very institutionally bound, at this point, in a gallery, museum, media kind of syndrome. I think that the most interesting aspect is the possibility for it to actually change the function of art, rather than any kind of formal interest."

*What's the relation between outside works and the works of the minimal period?*

"Well, I think I had ideas for… things, you know, 1966, 1965. I'll show you something, it's easier. This is a full-strong hand-made work, that involved what you might call an attempt to extend my ideas of minimal things to the outside. There is a steep beam, placed in a mound of earth. It was never built but, you see, the idea of extending scale and sightlines and so on came naturally out of working with the forms I had been using, and so it just went outside in a very natural kind of way. This is another model for an earth piece, I think that's about 1966. It's a very simple form, but to be done on a very, very large scale. So it's an easy transition, or it seems like a natural transition."

*Has the transition from inside to outside also a political meaning according to you?*

"I think that when you change the function of art from having it inside, either with the collector or with even a museum, and you put it outside, in a community, that whole idea has political implications. I am not about to say that my work has a political ideology behind it, but I believe that everything people do is political, has political implications…"

*What's the function of art?*

"I think art always does have a number of functions and I think that, take earthworks themselves, the way in which that function has changed is, somehow, that it allows the works to be used in a different way, at almost every level… It subverts a whole way, a whole critical way of dealing with art. And that is a very subtle way of changing the function of art, as well as having it accessible to people in a different way… That is not very clear at this point because some people make earthworks out in the desert where they are inaccessible. And I don't want my things to be inaccessible. I think that it's a very complicated subject to talk about, the function of art: it functions in a number of ways, and I think that what's happening with some of the things which have been made outside is that there is a possibility for a kind of alternative way of dealing with art, I mean, it almost forces that."

*Can art modify reality?*

"I guess, I guess so. I mean, I suppose it shares that with science in some ways, or shares that with probably a number of kinds of endeavours certainly. I think it shares that with art history, as anything that's concerned to redefine our notions is modifying reality..."

*Is art useful for you?*

"It's such a broad question that it requires a broad answer. It is my life, it's the way I live my life, because it gives my life meaning to make art. I don't think my life would have very much meaning without it. So art is in itself the means by which I generate meaning for myself."

*Are you interested in Oriental cultures?*

"In general, I would say that prehistoric art always meant more to me than any Western art, any sort of Renaissance, anything like that. Now, also city design, Oriental city design, layouts of cities, planning, not only China, but India, the architecture of India and China – all this has always been very important to me. I mean I've always responded to it a lot, their concerns were so... the response to the land... Like the city of Fadabrasycra I always found fascinating: they built a city that had all these terraces, and had different zones to live in, for the different parts of the year – of course they didn't have any water there, so the city was abandoned right after they built it."

*In what does Western art influence you?*

"Undoubtedly I am influenced. There is no doubt about it, I think everybody is. It's just that there is something about Oriental and prehistoric art that has a kind of fascination for me... Maybe it's that special comprehensive response that their art has to so many things – nature, the cycles of nature, the positioning, the time; a building that has always something to do with an orientation towards a star, or the sun, it can be a temple, also be a tower, also be a court. The complexity of functions of certain Neolithic buildings fascinates me, you know."

*What's the meaning of the use of the body?*

"It's a convenient subject, you know, it's a convenient material, the artist's body has the age of the subject, self-portrait to the artist, and I have used things, from impressions of my own brain waves to a number of other things. It was a concern I had for a while… Finding processes that would initiate and that would complete the work. Initiating the work, finding processes that would complete it, that I didn't have to necessarily make any effort for. For example, once I wanted to make a self-portrait of myself, a drawing, so rather than make the drawing physically, I connected myself to an electroencephalogram machine that records the brain waves, and I thought about myself, for the amount of time that it took the needle to travel the length of my height, so my thinking made the drawing for me, and it happened to be connected with my own body."

*What did theatre mean in your work?*

"Well, I suppose it was a situation where I could explore time in a more direct way than with objects. I also had some training as a dancer, so I was naturally inclined to do that. There were certain kinds of issues that interested me in the dance, as I saw it. Certain images I could use more conveniently in a theatre than in objects. Certain kinds of equivalencies I could manage for myself in real time, that I couldn't manage for myself in recaptured or indicated time."

*Your interest in architecture means also an interest in theatre as a relation between works and people?*

"I have made one theatre piece that did involve directly the audience, only one. This piece I describe, in Holland, obviously involved people. If you are going to experience it, you go into it. Well, you can experience it from the outside too, but it's not really complete unless you enter it, like a building. It simply requires your presence inside it to experience it; in order to be in it, you change it in some way, and you have also changed it for other people. I don't know if that is theatrical, because the first thing you learn about theatre is that there is a great separation between the audience and the performers, although that's breaking down now. But that kind of frontality between performers and audience is something I was always bothered with in theatre, I didn't like it, and I set about doing things where, say, the chairs were all randomed and the performance would emerge out of the audience."

*Can you tell me something about your works that have a greater relation with Dadaism?*

"Those works were done together, in that series of things I made that had to do with the body; foot-prints, or brains, or electro-brainwaves – there are a number of pieces. I made that sort of catalogue of the body, information about the body, what the body could do, what was inside it – this was all about what was inside the body."

*Which is the relation between this part of your work and the minimal experience?*

"The experience of these things had very much to do with your own body, you know. How high your eyes are, what sense of weight you get from the thing, how much you can move around it; so, the mobility and the perception available to the body are part of the term in describing something like this. In other words, it's a phenomenological analysis that has to be made, it seems to me, in terms of minimal art, and that includes the body."

*In the minimal experiences there's this phenomenological position; in your first objects there's a relation with Dadaism, on the level of language too.*

"I believe Dadaism is in everybody's blood at this point. It's in each one of those little bottles [bottles of what is inside the body]. Probably Dadaism has been transformed, tamed, but as an attitude about making, it's sort of filtered into the art tradition."

*What does the transition to the anti-form experience consist in?*

"I don't think that anti-form is possible, it's not my term. But we know what we mean. I think it started by analysing why it is that one makes something, or analysing not only that, but the making itself. I knew that if I would make something like so or have it made, I could preconceive in my mind what it would be, not finally in detail, or how I would feel about it, but I knew it would look this way, it would measure so and so and so. Then I began to search for a way of working that was not so a priori. So I began, I found felt. I found that I was interested in felt because I could prick and take a piece of felt, so, and I could, say, cut it here. Now, that's the information. But the second step is what you do with that, if you drop it on the floor like that, it can exist that way, being hanged on a wall it can do this, come down, like so… It extended the kind of existential qualities of something, right; in other words, it existed in a broader way. I was interested in a whole range of information I could a priori put into something, and see it either come out this way, or this way. In some cases I would take, say, six or eight pieces, I would make a geometric progression, cut it here once, cut it here that many times, keep doubling the cuts. Then you have strips. This information is completely cancelled out, because no one can understand that you made it this way. So there is a range of information and action, behaviour, that is either going to be retained or lost. And I was interested in that spectrum, that's what led me away from rigid things to using things that I could preconceive in terms of what I was going to do with them, but not in terms necessarily of how they would exist."

*Is art a close or an open anthropological activity?*

"What do you mean by anthropological? I mean, obviously I'm not involved in ethnology, I don't study other people, but in so far as… I think of making in a kind of anthropological way, yes, yes. I mean, different ways of structuring, making, premises for making, and so far as you can… I would not call it anthropology, but… I'm not quite sure how you're using that word, I mean, it's a very foreign word to apply to art, in some way. Unless you have a special meaning for it. I would say that there exists a kind of lethal language of artists today, deriving from the analyses of Lévi-Strauss, certainly, that gives investigations about art a kind of horror of anthropology. I know that a lot of artists are very much involved with the kinds of analyses that Lévi-Strauss carried out. I think he is quite useful to understand art up to a certain point, but I do not believe he is any more useful than the analyses of Piaget about the emergence of language, for example. So… no, I don't think it is… I would say that, because I doubt that artists are proceeding in a very anthropological way. They are dealing with certain kinds of analyses, to speak critically, that have been used in anthropology."

*What does art mean in our society?*

"When these issues come up, I'm always reminded of the Russians, because the Russians took all the options possible for artists vis-à-vis the society at large. Now, Malevich opted to have pure art, he said 'I want to be a pure artist because it's necessary to do these researches, because this filters down in society'. Tatlin said 'I want to improve the quality of life, and I'm going to design clothes and stoves and things like that, for people'. In other words art should be applied, so it will have a function for the people at large. And then there are other people like Ejzenstejn and so on, who really just wanted to make propaganda, it didn't mean that any of these people didn't make also good art from one point of view or another, but the fact is: all art is political and the talking of it, and the making of it, is… You cannot avoid the fact that it's a class, it's involved in a class situation, and most of modern art itself is a very bourgeois undertaking. We may have very strong feelings, very strong critical feelings about how this whole enterprise proceeds along; nevertheless, we seem to have a great deal of allegiance to the kinds of structures and intentions and investigations and changes that have happened within this class structure. There are a lot of oppressive factors built into the way the art world moves along, irrespective of the sensibility or the invention going on. In some of the things we talked about we may not have made a clear enough distinction between certain forms, certain social forms, the way the art world is constituted, for example, the fact that certain kinds of things, obviously objects, are encouraged to be made, whereas other things like vast changing of landscape are very difficult to be realized. Now that's an economic, you have to look at economics as soon as you see these kinds of things. And the fact that women don't get as many shows as men, and the whole question about black people…"

# Vettor Pisani
Ischia, Naples, 1934



*The idea of a "tailed" theatre has entered your work. What does it mean?*

"R. C. Theatrum, a Theatre of Artists and Animals: we can quite rightly define it a tailed theatre or a theatre with a tail because here everything and everyone has a tail. It is a democratic theatre, a school of art open to everyone. Of course the rabbit's got a tail in the Small Theatre. The dancer called Gio (her stage name is Rose Baby Casta) has got one, and wears a bunny costume, performing a whirling strip-tease in the Large Theatre. The musician who resembles Oedipus by Khnopff and accompanies the dancer with music by Satie has got one. To tell the truth, he exaggerates; he's got two tails, he wears a tail-coat. The musical instrument played by the musician has got one: a grand piano, black in colour. All the theatre's got one. In point of fact we can view the river the theatre is built on like the tail of its architecture in the form of a Cross. Finally I wouldn't like to forget the tail of the theatre writer. Personally, I think of my fantasy (which is never-ending) as the tail of my own imagination, of my ego."

*What does R. C. Theatrum mean?*

"R. C. Theatrum: Rose Casta Theatre, the theatre of Rose Casta, the baby with her unfledged sex.

R. C. Theatrum: Rotating Cross Theatre, the theatre of the rotating Cross, a propeller that makes the world go round.

R. C. Theatrum: Rose Cross Theatre, the theatre of Rose the stripper plus Cross, the architecture.

R. C. Theatrum: Rose Carnal Theatre, the flesh-pink theatre, the shaved sex and pink face-powder of the noble Jocasta, the mother of Oedipus, the hero.

R. C. Theatrum: Renato Celant Theatre, the theatre of Mr Renato Celant, the commonplace man. (Ah, all those many errors and the jesting philology of Germano Celant, the tailed critic! The island of my childhood is called Ischia, and not Ponza as appears in one of his catalogues full of mistakes).

R. C. Theatrum is a labyrinth: it means an infinite number of things, everything that begins with R. C. But it's above all the theatre of a naïve rabbit in love, who dies of love for his mistress: Rose Baby Casta, the bunny."

*Is art awareness?*

"Error is the brother of sin,
the two wicked brothers
beloved sons
of their mother, ignorance."

*Is art opposed to error?*

"To Oedipus,
famous for his intelligence
and maker of errors… (God, what a cruel destiny!)
sweet and in love, who moistens his mother's lips.
And to Jocasta, the beautiful virgin of the moist lips:
the R. C. artists have decided to build on the river
a dam to insanity, a theatre to beauty
that brings luck and certain victory."

*Is art wandering?*

"To Oedipus the hawk, suspended in infinity,
who in flight awaits the solitary sparrow
who to the country singing goes till the sun dies
and harmony wanders over this valley… alas, of tears: hapless sparrow!

Oh little one, what an error! You could have, singing, gone to the sea
instead of the country! how sorry I am!
And to Jocasta of the beautiful nest
and love-trap for Oedipus and the hawk."

*Is art joy?*

"To Oedipus the sparrow,
the lonely child bound to his mother
who to bed comes and plays… on and on with Jocasta in her beautiful nest.

Yes… sparrow, play, play with Jocasta and with rhyming couplets!

Meanwhile time passes and life fades."

*Is art an Oedipal figuration?*

"Oedipus, what a wretch you are!
To kill your father
where three roads meet;
and what a disgrace!
to have with your mother
not one, but four children.
Chorus: There, I knew it! Four invariably follows three: the
ternary playing with the quaternary! What a lack of seriousness,
one always plays in this theatre! And then what a paranoid, dull
and repetitive artist: he always says the same things! I bet the red
and the green will be here shortly.
Oh Oedipus teaser,
You are up to all sorts of mischief, of every nuance:
red and green and ultramarine blue.
Your errors, God are countless!
and some are even innocent.
You marked the passage
from the state of nature
to the state of culture
and eliminated, oh villain!
the matriarchate.
You invented history,
civilization and civilizations,
the West all male-oriented and phallocratic.
Run, run Oedipus,
oh unlucky one
if the women catch you!
You will end up as a solitary sparrow
featherless
who to the country crying goes
until the sun dies
and harmony wanders…
over this valley."
*Is art an incestuous figuration?*
"To Oedipus tightly bound
who sheds his ties and moistens his mother's lips.
Oh love come! You great and small sail of all my desires:
I desire you

You are beautiful, please, please, be obscene!
blind with love I want to see you."
*Is art amoral?*
It is a great error to speak badly of Evil.
For the triumph of Good
Evil is… (so to speak)
an outside hand.
Chorus: What gnostic, dialectic, and wicked artists are these R .C.!
Alas, the redemption and excessive tolerance of Evil!
We the chorus, moralists, old and moderate affirm that: the evil must not be saved but shoved, and once and for all, to the bottom of the abyss from which they came!"
*Is the artist a prophet?*
Oedipus – the prophet of intelligence. (Be smart).
Christ – the prophet of Goodness. (Be good).
Chorus: … and good God, please. If you can't be smart, at least try to be good."

# Michelangelo Pistoletto
Biella, Italy, 1933

Turin
1972

*I have the impression that, ever since the beginning, your work has betrayed a sort of double vision. Your objects have never been tautological, but specular, as they tend to represent the mechanism with which they have been made. To start with, I wonder if you could describe the mental and cultural process by means of which you came to do mirrors, for instance.*

"I believe the problem of the double is one of the human mind's oldest concerns, the focal point around which the artist always moves. Without going back to the very beginning, to the time, let's say, when man discovered his double reflected, for instance, in a pool of water, or in his fellow man, that other person who moved as he did, we can start at a point when the art of painting had already attained extraordinary refinement and complication as in the fifteenth or sixteenth centuries. At that time, painters in Florence and Rome succeeded in reproducing reality in a way that was genuinely exciting, in creating the illusion that someone really was doubled (a person, landscape, or place), or even in reproducing through painting the actions and movements of the masses. Through these images they set forth ideas, they communicated. These men had progressed in the science of doubling things to communicate a thought, an idea, a necessity; and moreover – indeed, primarily – they told how far the science of the brain had come. Then, little by little, human science progressed at various levels and with various results, to discoveries such as photography, which, had it not existed, would not have allowed Picasso to do the paintings he did, for he would have continued in this profoundly fascinating science of reproducing nature. Instead, Picasso found himself supplanted, as a man, by a phenomenon that took the appeal out of his possible courses of action. So, he reacted with all the virulence of his will to survive, and did things that distorted the reproduction. He carried out a revolution with respect to a constant trend that crowded him and crowded that wonderful capacity man has of rediscovering his own wonder. From Picasso on, the situation has always been hastened along in this direction. Many things have taken place on the artistic level, ranging from his rebellion against abstraction to the understanding that it is actually possible to create matter, to reproduce a psychological reality of pure feeling, rather than a visual reality.

Abstract art, however, immediately became imagery again; it became self-contemplative, instead of stimulating the progress of understanding. I must say that, in a certain sense, whoever is strongly attracted by the surface of things, by the more or less beautiful, the more or less abstract, carries on in this direction of abstract art, and I think that's alright. The problem concerns those artists who have continued to call themselves 'figurativists'. They have always demanded a reason for things. They have never been satisfied with spending a good day making a good painting, but have sought to understand the continuous movement of the world that conditions the work of the artist. In this direction, one makes progress.

For instance, when I began working, I became deeply involved in the work of two artists, Jackson Pollock and Francis Bacon, who only on the surface of things appear to be opposites. Pollock led his uneasiness and his gesture to a revelation of dramatic force on the canvas; he would have left his body on the picture, if he could have (later, Rauschenberg did just that). Bacon showed man life-size on the painting's surface (something which surprised me quite a bit, because for me the smallest thing, and the largest, is the dimension of man). There, I saw myself in that dimension. Bacon, too, represents the drama of man's will to survive and to be acknowledged, as well as his frailty, impotence and weakness."

*If reflected space possessed this immense value – the capacity to fix the present, past, and future; that is, to truly contain the dimension of time – what made you go on to other experiences?*

"A new situation comes into play here that is very complex and really quite hard to deal with, because, frankly, when I look at my reflecting paintings, they have to do something for me, they have to serve a purpose. I didn't do these works for mere gratification, but to escape from a certain situation, and just looking at these paintings continues to give me a meaningful answer every time I have a problem of the same sort. I know where I have to go, to confess. There I find someone who tells me, look, it's really like this. On a working level, however, it becomes important for me to bring what was pretence in the painting into the relation between the two materials, the tissue paper of the surface and the molecules of the steel, brought together in such a way as to become reflective, and hence permeable to the eye. On the cultural and ideal level, it is clear that these relations are represented in the picture, and because I want to live, I want to detach myself from the picture, and I want the lesson I've learned from the picture to stay with me in life – which for me is always a question essentially of mind. Hence, I immediately began thinking of myself as a character who could appear both in the past, reproduced on the mirror's surface, and moment by moment in the reflection, or in the absolute adherence to the present reality, without the mirror. Here I endeavoured to see objects in a different way, as undistinguished or distinguishable, but on the level of image or contingency. In 1966 I had an exhibition in my studio which I deliberately intended to be a group show: my image disappeared as the image of an individual disappears in a group show of painters where the essential thing is not the people, but the various contingencies. Then, I was not different people at the same time, but different people every moment, in accordance with my changing needs. I moved around in the midst of those objects, an enormous quantity of phenomena that, clearly, no longer belonged to me except in that contingent instant. At this point I felt my movements as a primary element open to any subsequent situation, without giving my gestures a prefigured order. First I wanted to understand what the image was through painting; then, when I knew I wanted to enter reality, I no longer desired images of any kind."

*Hence, the overcoming of a certain logical sequence in your work, even in the concept of poetics?*

"Above all non-being; not only no longer producing images, but not being imageable."

*What you call "the bull-fighter's side-step"?*

"Yes, when you accomplish an action and, instead of going forward, you step to one side, where there is another current of energy, then moving further to the side, to another vein of energy that has already been used up. If you continue to pursue the imageing of yourself, you enter a situation of entropy: that is, you go towards cancellation and death."

*From the double of the mirror, we've passed to the double of the object, to a series of works entrusted to materials that are ephemeral and always different, until we arrive at the double of the action, that is, your theatre, street theatre, and the zoo experience. By double I mean the reflection, the ideological as opposed to the vitalistic.*

"It's clearly a unifying experience, because one never loses sight of one's relationship with the world and with what's going on in one's surroundings. If I had to make a statistical study to find out what is the best art product I could put on the market today, chances are I'd have to do work that is as figurative as possible, because everyone is used to communicating by way of images, whatever kind they might be. According to my statistics, I could not by any means do what I'm doing. But since I'm not concerned with making progress in my own regard, or in my dialogue with others, I've chosen the wrong road altogether, in terms of logic, and done things that aren't my line: acting, writing, making music, even though I'm completely tone deaf. I make beautiful music, because I work in a way that has no antecedents, no models of excellence with respect to a preordained culture or structure, and hence provides no means of judgement or comparison. It is just the indisputable absolute necessity of the moment. I've played with people who have felt this same necessity, and the communication was full, direct, and complete in every instant. It's the same way with the theatre, the gestures and movements, the same with writing. It's already side-stepping to change medium; likewise, within each medium, to do what is essential at the moment. In the end, the link comes forth of its own accord, because the various times of man go together like his organs. An organic unity is revealed in man in contradiction with a vision of pure image that is not generalized. In other words, the underlying framework comes out."

*You said earlier that today you've shifted your position with respect to the initial matter of the double. What do you mean exactly?*

"Only on a certain level. On another level things haven't shifted much at all, because I don't have many opportunities to be as I'd like to be, as I am in a different kind of tension. The work I feel compelled to do on an artistic level reaffirms, in different ways, the same thread of thought all the time, so as to keep up relations, somehow, with my neighbours. For example, the cubes provide another way of getting away from a given structure and considering that the object encloses an inevitability, a complete and total reason for being, and a truth of its own. In these cubes, I give the same repeated structure completely different meanings. This way, I think I'm able to demonstrate that we can free ourselves from a certain kind of vision. There are four cubes, 16 × 16, each of which represents a work in itself. The first one is titled *Replacement for a destroyed work*, the second is *Alternative to an unsuccessful work*, the third is *Critical action on my mica paintings* (the embodiment, that is, of my changes of mind), and the fourth is called *The title can only be transmitted orally*. The cubes are all the same, all made of opalescent Perspex. These four cubes are multiples, they are exact reproductions of the same object, 120 cubes, all the same. Thus, the consciousness of the multiple is integrated into the work itself, equality exists between the various objects, and so there is a way of witnessing a clearing away and a tension that displaces the concept of the steady state of the figure. I do this in order to carry ahead a certain sort of reasoning. If one gets everything wrong, then there isn't anything wrong after all. This liberation of thought from purely optical and phenomenological vision is necessary. Nothing in the world is an image, everything has its own structure, its own behavioural dynamics, which are continuously changed by contact with other things. Matter is continuously matched up and takes form bit by bit, every moment. But it is a transitory and non essential form if one does not have time to let one's eyes get accustomed to it, so as to overcome the sense of image. We make images for ourselves, because we think everything is still; but in living the dynamic structure of contingency one cannot obtain this phenomenological fact of the image."

*What is the role of art for you, then?*

"Art's role is the possibility man has of discovering the wonder of his existence at given moments, speeding them up to obtain a continuous sensation of revelation, without being alienated and mediated in all his endeavours. In this sense, everyone is an artist, the artists are those who tend to achieve this state at least once in life."

*Then for you the political position of art is the possibility of establishing effective communication. On this level could your "religion cube" be considered a political work?*

"Perhaps one would have to start out from the 'cubic meter of infinity': six mirrors turned towards the inside to form a cube. On the outside one sees only the back of the cube. One practically cannot see the effect produced on the inside, because one would have to deform the original structure I gave it; sticking one's nose into it means modifying a condition. When the condition has been modified, the thing is no longer the same, and that's it. One can then enter the cube only with the imagination, which is a form of image related to the past, a memory, a sensation which is never the same as the one that can occur on the inside. It appeals to memory on the one hand, and rejects any kind of experience on the other. I've been working for some time now on this abstract and elementary form of the cube, a cultural form – matter takes this form. By way of contrast, I imagined the cube in positive, and I made a series of paintings in which I painted a tiny cube at the centre of 31 panels (canvas on stretchers, 20 cm wide and 230 cm high). Then I painted the canvas white, so as to conceal the cube, as I didn't want to show any illusion of the cube in drawing, yet. On top of the three-dimensional surface of a blanket of colour, it acquires its real thickness and becomes real, even if it cannot be seen. Then I turned all the paintings around and started to put the title and my signature on the cross bars of the stretcher, of which there were two for each painting. As I couldn't give them different titles, I started writing an idea on the various cross bars, signing each one, on all the stretchers. I wrote 62 ideas, and I realized that the phrases written on the back of each panel corresponded to one cube only, the one drawn on the canvas. That is, culture, which is static, whereas every idea, born of a given circumstance, is free and dynamic. I thought this was religion: I could have made a single cube to relate all my thoughts, like the black cube, the rock of Mecca, to which all the thoughts of Islam are attributed. I wanted to think, for instance, of the obelisk in St Peter's Square, willed by one person and executed by thousands of slaves, this rock undamaged by time and carved with enormous precision to give the material an abstract form. The obelisk was brought to Rome with the further hard labour of slaves, and erected in the middle of St Peter's Square as though it represented the centre of Christianity. During the age of Christianity we had very few figurative documents, but as the power situation recovered, this obelisk was raised again. In contemplating my cube today, I think we would have to put all the world's largest steel mills to work on a hilltop, in a place suited to pilgrimage, to make an enormous cube of stainless steel, a material that corresponds to the hard stone of the past, the fruit of the labour of millions of workers of our time. The slaves today are those who make steel, mould iron, and produce automobiles on the assembly line."

*To the extent that this cube is a symbol of authority, don't you think that, in the end, you express a mystical vision of art?*

"I'm telling you about this in order to call the entire social structure into play. At that time the heads of state were religious leaders, as they are today, and the labourers were what they are today…"

*But in this case, the artist who plans the cube is a priest.*

"Maybe so. The freedom to take on any guise is a faculty one has to have if one wants to be an artist. One must not be afraid, one must always look at things from the inside; otherwise, from the outside, one is always in a position of reflection. I don't pose myself the problem of the status one can assume thinking about a thing of this sort. The artist is one who takes all possible liberties, without fear of the consequences. Freedom is full and dense where intelligence shows itself and works."

# Robert Barry
New York, 1936



*How long have you been using photographs?*

"As a matter of fact, I just used the photographs in a traditional way, to photograph my work, and then for a while I stopped using photographs, because the work was invisible. So, just a few times. Well, a few years ago I did a show in Los Angeles, and the show consisted of releasing inert gas into the atmosphere. The inert gas is colourless, it has no colour, has no odour, is completely undetectable, and for that show I couldn't photograph anything, because gas was invisible, and once it was released into the atmosphere, it just went throughout the atmosphere. Now what I did was, I photographed the sites, the places where the gas was released, and some of these photographs were published. Well, for instance I did one in the Mojave Desert, and I took a photograph, but it was just a photograph of the desert, and the information in the caption words under the photograph stated that this was the location of such and such an inert gas (like helium, for instance, or argon, or xenon, or neon – all inert gases). So, I photographed the places, but after that, I realized that really all the information was in the caption, in the words under the photograph. So then for a while I just stopped using photographs and used language instead to convey my work. In my most recent output, the slide pieces, I used photography again, but I just photographed words."

*What's the relation between your recent works (words on slides) and experiences of Visual Poetry?*

"One must see my work, or my use of language in an artistic context, rather than in a traditional poetical literary context. But I think that what's happening today is that these divisions between the arts are breaking down, and that we can have art that looks like music, or appears like music, or appears like dance, or body art – sorts of things like that. Or sculpture that looks like theatre, you know, that sort of thing. In my case, I suppose, if my work was put in a poetry magazine, it might be taken as poetry. It's not a distinction I care about, I don't really think it's a basic issue, it's art, whatever it is, it's not poetry, this or that, but it's just art, and should be taken for what it is. Anyhow, it comes out of an artistic tradition, rather than a poetic tradition."

*How do you choose words for the slides space?*

"I guess it's just a matter of choosing what I know, just like a painter chooses his colours, it's difficult to exactly say. I do try to give my works some kind of unity, so that the terms don't necessarily contradict each other."

*I'd like to know if your art is still in the zone of the object or not.*

"If you ask: is it still in the zone of the object?, I would say yes, it is, but I think we have to understand what my definition of object is. It may not be a tangible object, like this, or like this, that one can touch, but maybe the word 'entity' or something like that might be a better word to use, rather than object. But it is a certain kind of object, like our conversation could be considered a certain kind of object, a certain kind of thing. An object does not have to be static. It does function, it does change and does have a structure. In other words, I would say that there's a similarity between this chair, which might be an object, and has a function – you see, it has a use, alright? it becomes dynamic when I sit in it, alright? – and our conversation, which also has a function. You see, on a very fundamental level, these things are very similar to each other. I think that what's needed is that before we can use the word 'object', we have to have a clear definition of what both you and I mean by it."

*I think that because of the use of other doctrines (like logic or psychology) your work is more scientific than artistic.*

"No, not at all, a scientific analysis would be very bad. The difference between science and art is that science is a very objective view of reality, whereas art is a very subjective view, it is a more personalized view of reality. However, in both cases there is a certain degree of subjectivity and a certain degree of objectivity, you see. But all art incorporates other fields of knowledge, every art does, I mean. Gothic cathedrals incorporated the technology of that time, and you can't avoid it in any way, but my work is only related to art; as science, it's very bad science, it is not good at all."

*What is subjective in your work?*

"The fact that I do it, the fact that I bring my own knowledge, and my own beliefs, and the fact that I personally make the choices of the words I incorporate into any individual piece. That's what's subjective about it, or the fact that it's a result of the development of my explorations in art, and, that's it, it's my choice; that's what makes it subjective, as opposed to someone else's choice."

*What relation is there between your work and life today?*

"I don't think that anybody can help reflecting in his work what's going on today. I mean, simply because we live today. And I'm involved in the problems of today, I cannot be in another time. There are certain people who have tried to escape to another time, say people who might make abstract expressions as paintings, or do something like that. If you consciously reject that point of view about art, and you try to involve yourself in something else, in exploring what art might possibly be about, I think that you will simply have to, you cannot help but reflect the attitudes that are around today, simply because you are living today, and you are involved with the world as it is constituted today. The world presents certain issues that I have to solve today, and I've tried to recognize those problems, there are certain voids that have to be filled in, and if I can try to understand what that void is, then, you know, my art is simply a reaction to what art is about today."

*How does your work act on language?*

"I try to use the language as common a way as possible, I try to use it in a way I suppose is fairly close to a kind of conversational language, rather than an artificial jargon, or something like that. I would say that's near to the way a conversationalist would use language, and I think that's a different way of using language than, say, a technical writing. It's not technical language, it's common use language. I would say that's probably closer to how I use language."

*What do you mean by your work, what are the reasons for your work?*

"What I do is deal with words as they are used in reality, as they are really used, or as I find them. Language is fascinating to me, because it is something that everyone has, you see. It's an extension of our being, it expresses us in the things that are going on in other times, in other places, and things like that, you see. So we are no longer rooted to this time and place, but we can move to other times, and other places. Everyone has language to a certain extent, everyone has it, it's the primary way we interact with other people. Well, I certainly don't intend to change the world, to make it a better place to live in. My intention is the same as any artist's. You see, art is an exploration of reality, it's a point of view about reality, and that's what my art is about. Just another point of view about how we can look at the things of the world, and how we look at art."

*Thus words are a medium of your exploration?*

"Exactly. Words are the… language is the area that we have to pass through before we can get to the ideas, it's what I have to tack my ideas on to. Well, it may not be the clearest way of doing it, as language has many deficiencies. As Heidegger says, it separates us from animals, but it also separates us from the gods. Art is an extension of oneself out into the world; what the artist says when he presents his work is 'here I am, that's me, and this is what I think about things', you see. And in a certain sense that's the same thing people do when speaking, projecting their presence, their soul upon the world."

*So, you mean art is just a way to speak?*

"Exactly."

*Are you influenced by technological attitudes?*

"I think today there seems to be a great drive, or a great need to change things, always to discover something new, to keep expanding the frontiers of knowledge. I suppose that there are three concepts that might express how technological mentality is included in my work: a kind of systematic or analytical approach to things, the need for a background in various disciplines and the notion of necessarily not imitating the past but constantly trying new things, trying to expand. But it's truly difficult to talk about that, because it's so ingrained, it's an intimate part of my being, and I think it's impossible to separate it clearly."

*Max Bense said that technology compresses our animal space and amplifies our rational feeling. Does your work have this quality too?*

"Yes. But I don't think technology frustrates our physical space at all; I believe, on the contrary, that it expands it. Not only our space, but our awareness of things that are going on in other times, in other places, you see. So we are no longer rooted to this time and place, but we can move to other times and other places. If you have an understanding of technology, and the possibilities, and you are able to utilize those good aspects of it – then it's beneficial. But unfortunately, of course, we are all curled up in the bad aspects of it too. I think that we can intellectually deal with technology and deal with its good points also. I mean, after all, technology is the result of man's reason and logic and his knowledge and his understanding of the world. I suppose we can't do away with it."

# Alighiero Boetti
Turin, 1940 – Rome, 1994



*Among the features that distinguish your work are kleptomania and speed; a precise but easy attitude towards materials; and a vital, existential, and mental openness towards external reality.*

"As a matter of fact, all these things, which may seem very different, in time turn out to be connected by certain threads of expressive necessity. I'd like to talk to you about something that's on everybody's lips: alchemy. One of the basic qualities of alchemy is the concept of secrecy that I think is altogether lacking in certain new artists. The anonymous is totally missing, as is the everything and nothing of Borges, Socrates, Aleph. Maybe it's when the artist's narcissism becomes so exasperated that he flows into secrecy."

*In what way is your narcissism secret?*

"I'm not talking about my narcissism in particular, I just thought of this matter of alchemy and secrecy which we are generally so weak as to analyse. Now, eclecticism: there have always been people who have done a lot of different things, Madonnas, porcelain, inlaid work, dams for the Visconti, bell towers (even if it was a painter in this case, who previously had had nothing to do with bell towers)... and then, we're living at a time at which I'd like to know who is able to think straight, we're always trying to have continuous experiences. For me, for instance, the experience of the small squares, which you or someone else sees completely differently, was non-communicable and incredible, because I found myself face to face with an absolutely empty space and with a structure which one might call paternal, and with this support, that is the action of tracing that one finds also in maps. I had incredible freedom. But the first times I fell into behavioural patterns, just the same as psychoanalysis, I could make with anything. All sorts of things happened in these little squares. I wrote things that were even terrible or beautiful, secret things that later were all filled in, because the only rule was filling in without obligations of time or method, especially at first. Anyway, I ran into truly middle-class behavioural traits; for instance, the will to do things in the quickest and most rational way, which is totally extraneous to being an artist. Furthermore, with regard to waste, to not going over something that had already been done – this economy, so to speak – in the last of the series of small squares I took a pencil and never took it off the paper, without worrying about whether or not I was covering the same ground twice, and so I freed myself from this obsession, too. You can always face up to a reality (which is yours, really); the question is, how to get rid of it. These drawings, and the problem of filling them in, gave rise to a question of rhythm. I could have spent my life on the small squares. From black and white I went on to red and blue (colours that you find everywhere, on a symbolic level – hot and cold water, the blood in veins and arteries), still with that paternal support that the printed squares offered. There were infinite possibilities for variation. Then I quit, and turned to another field. The fact is that the concept of waste drives me crazy, like sunlight, which is free, completely indifferent to the fact, as a merely ocular product – in Afghanistan, for instance. Today I can no longer put up with certain features of mine that are middle-class. We still have this sense of industry and rationalization, of making a straight line, whereas our adventures have traced a sort of fret."

*Hence, you're talking about waste as a feast.*

"Yes, as an adventure, a journey. You have to go from A to B, and to follow a straight line is the quickest and most correct way. However, you can also set out on a journey, make an embroidery or a fret out of this sense of waste. I'm more and more interested in certain popular demonstrations: on the whole, all this art is middle-class, and really frightening. This is something that's always been noticed, especially by middle-class artists like me, or in music by those who draw on the popular repertory. Painters, too, feel the charms of these basic signs, like sand in a hour-glass. As regards time, it's not true that I work quickly. I've been collecting maps since 1966, and the small squares take a very long time to make, an eternity."

*I'm talking about speed in reference to technique. For example, you give the fretwork to others to do.*

"Even the small squares, which I did myself, at first, I later passed on to others as a sign to repeat (a problem of Gestalt, too), because I'd finally understood what my problem with the small squares was. Instead, I could have speculated on them, like Stella does. His drawings also come from that, from elimination, like Carl Andre. My error was often that of not having accepted the two-dimensional, conceptual side of my work (the head stuff, that is), and of having tried to do things that went beyond a purely visual fact. Formal research can be continuous, quite vivid on the level of the continuity of the present; for me it's a sort of illness, you know… When you speak of expansion, for me it's this schizophrenic concept of St Patrick drawn and quartered by four horses. The *Barbanera* for 1972, which is a leap year, says, 'You will find the need for expansion with pain'."

*Applied to you, what does this mean?*

"It means it's becoming a neurosis, an effort, a terrible tension. I can't seem to stop all these incredible possibilities. I do, I'm easily able to do, things like opening a hotel in Kabul (in private life), which in Italy is still madness. In the end I realize that it's all a venture, even to present yourself not as an artist, hence without a foundation and compelled to invent everything all over again, body and soul. For instance, over there I always wear a jacket and tie and dark glasses, and I'm very stiff and distinguished with people. It's always been my dream, to be an artist in Italy until I'm fifty and then suddenly get on a plane and go and make shoes in a village in Argentina…"

*How come? What is this born of?*

"Perhaps it's born of this schizophrenic idea that one isn't able to stay in the same place all the time, which is like the many arms of Shiva, I think."

*You know, Rimbaud quit writing poetry at a certain point and went to Africa to deal in slaves. But you're not so desperate for the check-mate of art, there's almost the bliss of this chosen dispersion you want to achieve.*

"I've certainly got nothing to do with the desperation of Rimbaud, who did the worst thing. For me creativity also means opening a hotel."

*For you, creativity is a matter of behaviour, then.*

"Not only behaviour, just doing things. In fact, I believe less and less in the idea one can live and drown and die in. If there's someone who's gone looking for lost time, I'm looking for happy coincidences. We've already mentioned blissfulness, you can see the coincidence in the small squares, in the two 'twins' of 1970, which are 49 small squares."

*What is the magical aspect of your work?*

"It's the happy coincidences. Another one I've found is made up of written numbers and letters: one, nine, seven, zero, which strangely enough makes sixteen, which is four times four. I feel happy when something like that works out. The magical aspect, you know, will come out more and more. I'm becoming a partisan to things that take a long time, as opposed to a short time. According to my little formula, mankind is divided into those who think of the short run and those who think of the long run; the former live in coincidence and the present, the latter are unable to communicate with one another. In my work the passing of time will bring me greater experience, greater consciousness, and a somewhat cosmic (but not intellectual) overall vision. Another thing that's important for the magical aspect is that I play the drums, the only instrument used by witch-doctors everywhere, because it can induce a state of trance through rhythm. Sometimes, when one plays, if one is good at it, one can levitate three feet off the ground."

*Does this happen also when you apply yourself to your works?*

"Yes, of course. Extraordinary coincidences have taken place even in the postal works, just as there are investigations solely of materials: nobody had ever really used Eternit before."

*Why is this openness to all materials important?*

"Because they still exist today, from embroidery to copper plates of exactly the same size. Perhaps everything is alright."

*In what way can your activity be defined as kleptomaniac towards the outside world?*

"In that I often pick things up from the outside. One of my favourite works is the one I did by sticking my finger into wet plaster, *The Seeing*. There, people were watching a TV show about blind people who were talking about the seeing. After a while I was struck by the fact that I belonged to 'the seeing' [Italian: '*vedente*', Translator's note] which everyone mistakes for 'the seers' [Italian: *veggente*, 'fortune-teller', Translator's note]: a slip of the tongue that provides food for thought. It's something I stole from a blind man. When I have things embroidered in Afghanistan, I steal, too."

*What do you mean, steal?*

"I really don't know, myself. Anyway, it's always a matter of taking things from reality; everything has roots in reality, no matter how shallow or scanty. When, instead, I want to do something specifically related to painting, I do postage stamps – it's just like doing a painting."

*But the postage stamps lack that element of secrecy we talked about before: a container without content.*

"Yes, what's inside these works matters little, either because there's nothing there, and then I want to show only a formal intention; or else there are some classifications, but it's just for fun."

*What's the difference between these works, which you call formal, and others, like playing the drums, having embroidery done, or handling other materials?*

"I call these works formal because I invented the form myself, and I'm very proud of the fact, because I wasn't born a sculptor or a painter. There's invention there: the practical reality of the envelope and the address replaces the dull story of painting. I'm sure that as time goes by, things will become more magical and beautiful. It's beautiful when you find an envelope with your address on it after twenty years, during which time, who knows, you might have moved a hundred thousand times…"

*So, for you the problem is almost to leave a set of tracks of your existence, through art…*

"Sure, through art and through my kids…"

*So, it's the obsession with time.*

"Yes, time is fundamental, it's the chief element of everything. Anyway, it doesn't take a lot to say so, but it's really the base: the dates, the postmarks, and the small squares are all a question of time, which is the only really magical thing there is – incredibly elastic. Everyone has his own time."

*You often use the term, schizophrenia, to describe your activity. How would you define schizophrenia?*

"As expansion or dissociation (the two twins, or when I write with two hands). If I play the drums, it is in order to be stronger than conditioning factors, than certain rhythms. It's always the same story: you have an infinity of behavioural possibilities, and you limit yourself to those two or three patterns that you have in common with everybody else. You have to reach the limit. I've thought a lot of things that, in talking about them with psychiatrists, were just right for schizophrenics – for instance, the idea of the massage that makes you feel again: in order to feel one needs the opposite. At certain times, in 1968 for example, I would have liked to do some things in an asylum. So, schizophrenia was alright for photographing these people with my Polaroid where and how they wanted, in a strong removal and bewilderment."

*Could your work be defined as a massage, in the sense that the forms help to feel things?*

"Perhaps. A project I've never carried out is a sort of yoke, a wooden tube with a circular section, with a little inward curve where you fit in, in a position of perfect equilibrium between positive and negative – in the sense that you lean on it, but at the same time it leans on you. Anyway, I always have the problem of not reflecting, of not standing still long enough to see, maybe to go ahead all the time, even if age has taught me to think things over…"

*So, your work helps you feel you're not standing still.*

"My work is adventure…"

*What is the role of your art?*

"It's one of the things I can do. I don't ask myself, particularly now, if what I do is art. I just want to live, to have adventures, and time is on my side, not against me: then a crystal-clear answer to your question will emerge."

*An artwork is art while the artist is making it, afterwards it's just an object.*

"While I'm making it I'm happy, that's all. Then it adds an understanding to things that you don't understand and that are yours alone. That way I understand more, I add knowledge, like the cerebral cortex that works in the new dimension of consciousness while maintaining the basic signs. I might not ever reach the point where I can pull the strings that are attached to everything; but if things aren't secret they get watered down."

Terry Fox
Seattle, Washington, 1943 – Cologne, 2008



*Can you tell me something about the work you did in Düsseldorf with Beuys in 1971? How did it happen?*

"I came to Düsseldorf and I wanted to do something, to make an action, and I didn't have the space. So I went to Beuys and met him the first time and he showed me all the rooms of the Academy where it was possible to make an action. Then we went to the cellar and it was wonderful there: so I decided to make my action there. He helped me with materials and things. I decided to make an action with sounds and iron pipes (like bells) in the cellar because the sound was very good there. One or two days before he asked me to do something together and he made something too. But I didn't ask him what he was going to do. His action was a kind of dream about a dead mouse he had, like a funeral for the mouse together with the sound, and fire, and ashes. Beuys too made sounds, we have a record we made of them."

*How long have you been working through actions and not by defined objects?*

"Since 1968."

*Which materials do you use most often in your performances?*

"Some materials are used every time, such as the bowl and water, candles, flowers, fish (lot of times), and other elements like light, smoke…"

*What sort of problems do you think you bring out through your performances?*

"When I make a performance I usually come to the space to have an arrangement, then I see the space and the energy in the room. I make a performance trying to energize the room: that's the main point."

*I think that the main issue in your work is transformation through time: so, what is your relation with alchemy?*

"It's because I have a history: my whole life is sickness, six months in and six months out of hospital. Transformations are the basis for what I do, but the symbols are personal and that's not the meaning for me."

*I believe there's a private space in your work, your sickness for example; in this respect this privacy, this voluntary obscurity, can be compared with alchemy.*

"What I make is something for me and something else for the person who watches. The last two or three actions I made were only for one person, or sometimes for nobody: I often make actions by myself. In public it's really strange, because it's a very private, a very intense act, but I think that for the people it's okay to see because it makes something in their memory."

*Alchemy is the passage from obscurity to light, so, again, what is the relation between your work and alchemy?*

"I try to make something that is poor into something that's total, rich. Rich in the sense of alive again, strong."

*Tell me about your work* Unity.

"The drawing was made before anything in the room and it was when I first looked at the room. I had a week before making something, and all that time Beuys had his pieces there: so I made my piece around Beuys's and the word 'unity' refers to the connection between them, between bread and fish and Beuys's work."

*Why do you use certain materials like bread, water, fire, light and fish?*

"The bound fish is me and the bread is like a possibility. I make the bread, I just cause the bread to increase, the bread moves by itself because it's a living organism. So I leave and go over there and then I make the action with the fish in the same time."

*What is the meaning in using written words, these quotations from Artaud, for example?*

"The words are just to pose the words. The sentence is used in a different sense than in Artaud."

*In your work there's always a circular movement of energy: so there's never a final point. Do you agree?*

"Because energy cannot exist in a square space, it must be circular. The light is for the attention, and the candles and curtains so that the bread can see the fish and the fish can see the bread. There's no other reason."

*Is there a relation between your performances and a kind of American culture, an Indios culture?*

"No."

*Why do you use a red band on your arm?*

"It's the opposite of the black of death, it's to make an action with life."

*How does art function compared with reality?*

"Everything is clear, I think, in these actions. What goes on in my head or mind is the only thing that isn't clear. The fact I use a band on my eyes when I touch the fish is to have another way to realize the fish, to feel the fish, another kind of more basic contact."

*Your actions are a kind of massage on reality.*

"It's just another mode of reality, another kind of reality."

*So art is another kind of reality…*

"I don't know about art, perhaps sometimes art, in the artistic system, is another kind of reality. My art is a different kind of reality because I have a different kind of life than anybody else, a different experience, I express another mode of reality."

*Your art is a way of unifying separated materials, isn't it?*

"But in a non-material way, through energy."

*So the main issue, both on a private and a public level, is always the problem of death.*

"Yes, but I don't know what I do, I'm not sure what I do, I don't see many relationships with other artists, one or two perhaps, and I don't like modern art very much. Acconci is a friend but I don't see a relationship with him. I like Beuys: our work about energy and regeneration is similar and our history is similar too."

*If your main problem is death, don't you think that to go into hospital is a direct way to fight death?*

"In a material sense, yes."

*And by performances?*

"I am not fighting against that, but I'm using it, I use death in my art."

*Your performances are a kind of magic land against death.*

"Yes, that's true, sure, but there are other things too: also against cruelty with the fish that is murdered and put in the market for money… I take him and make something else."

*So, you use reality in another meaning: don't you translate art into the space of language?*

"I bring the fish back to his real state, his pure state: his purity begins in the water, then he is murdered, and making an action is a way to return to a pure state."

*What is the political level of your work?*

"I don't know anything about politics."

*So your work is only what it is, only art?*

"It's only what it is."

*Can the labyrinth you drew on the wall be regarded as the mental measure of your work, the primary form of non-calculated energy?*

"Yes, it represents the continuity between the two pieces of the work, the unity between Beuys and me."

*So the labyrinth is the first step in your work?*

"This labyrinth is not a labyrinth where you can make a mistake, or stop, or turn around, or come back. It's a labyrinth, you have to go on."

*Can art for you be considered a way to freedom?*

"There isn't much difference between my life and what I do. My art is always the same, in the house, in the hospital, in the studio, in the gallery."

*What is the importance of Oriental culture in your work?*

"I like Indian music and I play a drum…"

*Is there any reference to Jung's thinking in your art?*

"I never read Jung."

*Do your performances give art an anthropological definition?*

"Every exhibition tries to change the memory of the persons who come into the room. The last exhibition I had before going into hospital the last six months was with objects, sort of reproduction of an experience in hospital: I showed photos of myself in hospital. So when people entered the room they thought about their experience in hospital instead of thinking of their experience in art galleries. Anyway, symbols are different for everybody, and every interpretation is correct."

# Bruce Nauman
Fort Wayne, Indiana, 1941

Los Angeles
1973

*Who executes your works?*

"I always prefer to do them myself, although from time to time I've given instructions to someone else. It's a little harder than doing them myself, I have to make the instructions quite explicit, because I have more faith in myself as executant than in others. I try to make the situation specific enough so that whoever does the works doesn't have much leeway."

*What kind of work did you do in the 1960s?*

"Works in plastic and rubber, and then, in 1965, things in fibreglass on the floor. I was still going to school at the time, and I don't think they were particularly meaningful works. I still like some of the rubber works and a couple of the fibreglass ones. In 1966 I began to notice that some interesting things were happening in sculpture, and I wasn't doing a type of work based on personal conceptions. So I quit doing that kind of things and later executed the first works with neon, and with wax. It's hard to imagine them now. They required simple operations, for instance making a mould, taking the two halves, putting them together to obtain a concave form, then reversing it. I was trying to mix up the inside and outside of a piece. One surface is smooth, and so looks like the outside; the other is rough, because this is the way the fibreglass takes form. Later on, when I did the rubber works, I used the same kind of moulds, but with softer materials. Then I did the neon work, the one in which my name was repeated and enlarged fourteen times."

*Have you changed the way you use your body in your work since then?*

"Not at all. It's just becoming a little clearer. At that time my work took the form of representations of figures of speech like 'From hand to mouth'. Now I can do dance pieces and come back to something like *Corridor of Representation* for a very simple reason. The only thing I intended to do at the time was present those objects as an extension of what I was thinking when I was in my studio. Things like the figures of speech, or making objects, and how I could put these two things together. I was bent on making objects. At that time I also executed the *Flour Arrangements*. I did them to see what would happen in a situation I wasn't familiar with. I completely cleared out my studio, so that the *Flour Arrangements* could become an activity I could work on every day, and it was also, for about a month, the only thing I allowed myself to do. Sometimes it was really hard to think of new things to do every day. Much of my later work is concerned with the same problem, for instance the movie of the two balls bouncing around my studio, or the one in which I take slow steps around the studio. Playing the violin was a more arbitrary situation, because I didn't know how. Some of the works, like the walking ones, were very logical, because that's just what I usually did in my studio. My activities were reasonably immediate and direct."

*How exactly do you use words in your works?*

"My work depends less and less on words. It has become very difficult to explain the works. Although it is easier to describe them now, it is almost impossible to say what they mean when you're inside them. Take *Corridor of Representation*, for example. It's very easy to describe the outward appearance of the work, but the experience of walking around inside it is something that can't be described. My works are always more concerned with physical or physiological responses. A couple of years ago I did a work called *Dark.* It was a steel plate with the word 'dark' written on the bottom. I don't know how important this work is, but to me it seemed seminal. The feeling of the weight of the work. I thought I had a good idea writing 'dark' underneath, because that way it could not be seen. As a matter of fact, I had also thought of the word 'silent', but this is the only word I really took into consideration. If I had to do the work over again, I probably wouldn't put the word there. Nevertheless, it seems to me that having the word 'dark' in that spot reminds one of the plate's lower surface and of what might be under there."

*How is photography used in your work?*

"I've always been interested in graphics, in prints, drawings and painting, and I painted before devoting my efforts to sculpture. I think I started using photography to document the *Flour Arrangements.* Later, I started thinking about the *Fountain* and similar works. I didn't know how to present them. I suppose if I'd known how to paint at the time, I would have done them as paintings. As a matter of fact, I think I even bought canvas and paint, but I no longer had any idea of how to set about painting. I didn't know what to do. Maybe, if I had been a good enough painter, I would have done realistic paintings. I don't know, but it seemed easier to present the works through photographs."

*Why do you use film and videotape?*

"When I was living in San Francisco, I had quite a few performances ready, that no museum or gallery was interested in showing. I could have rented a place, but I didn't want to do it that way. So I filmed the works, the one of the bouncing balls and others. Then I moved to New York, where it was more difficult to find filmmaking equipment. So I got what I needed to make videotapes, which is a much more immediate medium to work in. With the passage from film to videotape the total length increased. My idea was to run the film in loops, because these were concerned with activities in process. The first film I made, *Fishing for Asian Carp*, began when a certain activity started, and continued until this activity ended. But this process became too much like that of the movies, something that I wanted to avoid, and so I decided to record a process in action and then make a 'loop' that could run for a whole day and even for a week. Videotapes last an hour, which is enough to understand what is going on. Now I've gone back to working with movies, because I want to do some very slow motion takes. I've succeeded in renting a special movie camera for industrial use that allows me to film in slow motion, which I could not do with the videotape equipment available to amateurs. I can get almost four thousand frames per second. So far I've made four films. One is called *Bouncing Balls*, but this time with testicles instead of rubber balls. Another one is called *Black Balls*, and consists in putting a black mask on the testicles. The third is called *Make a Face*, and in the last one I begin with six feet of gauze in my mouth, which I pull out and let fall to the ground. All of these films are shot from very close up. The works of this kind that I did earlier were the holograms, *Make Faces* (1968), which came out in a very formal way when I thought of the instructions. Usually they were contorsions, stretching and extending my face. I think

I was interested in doing something extreme. It is as though, having decided to smile, there was no need to photograph it. I could simply write that I'd done it, or I could make a list of things that could be done. The holograms also raised the problem of making the subject of the piece stronger, so that people wouldn't think too much of the technical side."

*Have you done works with sound?*

"One was shown at the Guggenheim Museum in August 1969, during the exhibition *Theodoron Foundation. Nine Young Artists*. I rubbed the violin on the studio floor with the strings tuned to the notes D, E, A, D. Then, in December, I presented a work at Ileane Sonnabend, in Paris. There was a large, L-shaped partition that covered two walls of the gallery, and that incorporated a number of small speakers. I had prepared two different tapes: one was a recording of sounds of exhalation, the other of laughing alternating with sharp blows, as strokes of a hammer. The source of the sound could not be identified. It was a pretty threatening piece, especially the exhalation sounds.

*Is there any relation between some of your works and Duchamp's body moulds, or between your figures of speech and Wittgenstein's?*

"Yes, undoubtedly. On the other hand, when I had done much of that work, it was very closely related to Wittgenstein's *Philosophical Investigations*, which I was reading at the time. That work was linked with the figures of speech. I was struck by Wittgenstein's way of thinking of things, his awareness of how one thinks of things."

# Robert Ryman
Nashville, Tennessee, 1930

New York
1973

*How long have you been doing these white paintings and what is your intention?*

"The paintings that you are seeing now are very early ones, well, not too early, they were done in 1965. I can't say exactly why I chose the white. I guess because it was very neutral, you know. It was a paint to work with, where I could do something with the composition and with the properties of the paint, without going into complicated compositions of colour. I felt that I could work with that, you know, just very directly. There is never a formula, I mean, you can't say that such and such plus such and such equals the right combination. It's just a matter of taking one thing and making of it whatever I could."

*Do you use white because it is a more abstract, a more mental colour?*

"I don't know, I have not thought of it in that way; as I said before, it was just, it was simply because it was a neutral paint. It could have been black, but black is very difficult. And there was, there is no mysticism involved, there is nothing like that with the white, it's just, as I said, a neutral paint."

*Can we call your work "action painting" or not?*

"Well, you know, when you put painting on a surface there is an action involved, there is movement, there are the brush marks, or there can be, there again, there can be a very even surface with no brush marks, depending on what the issue at stake is, you know, for doing the painting. Yes, I mean, I would say that there is movement, and there is the action, as you said, but it is like that with all paintings, I think."

*There seem to be no images in your painting. Or would you say that images do exist in your work?*

"Yes, it's very true, there is an image, the image is the paint, the procedure, the brush, the way the painting is done – this actually is the image. The size of it, the thickness, the type of paint, all these things become image as soon as it is put on a wall; then it becomes an object, an image. If you mean an image like a figure or a landscape, or something like that – well, then no, of course. That isn't there, but these things are never the image, I mean, the image we are talking about. In paintings someone uses landscape, or still life, or figures, but that's really something just to begin the painting with. The painting itself is the image. Always."

*I'd like to know how you came to produce your first white painting in 1958.*

"Well, I don't know, for sure. My work has always been abstract, I mean, it has always dealt with very abstract issues. I have never worked otherwise. So, I really don't know exactly why it began that way. It just seemed the most logical way to do it, and the most direct way, and simple and… not so simple, really. I mean very complicated instead. Abstract painting, I mean, in the sense that I'm talking about, is very complicated; you become involved in so many very basic aesthetic problems, and technical problems, whereas if otherwise… if you start from the figure or the landscape, you know, that interferes to a certain extent with really getting down to the guts of the matter."

*What does "logical" mean to you?*

"Well, when I say that, it's only for myself and I'm not saying that the way I do it is the way things should be done; it only seemed the right way for me to go about it. Someone else may, you know, paint sunsets or do any number of things. What I mean, is you go about the solving of problems, of aesthetic problems, in a number of ways."

*What kind of technique do you use in your paintings?*

"They are many. Basically it has to do with putting paint, with using paint, putting it on a surface, and… seeing if I can do something with it. It's very basic, I mean, I don't really consider myself too much of, well, of an avant-garde artist. I am, maybe, I guess, but what I do, my work, involves just very simple procedures of applying paint and making something happen with it."

*What is the difference between you and action painting artists?*

"It's really difficult to compare one artist's work with another artist's work, because there are different issues involved, different procedures. Now, I think you can only compare the work of one artist, I mean one thing of his to another thing of his."

*In action painting there's the cowboy looking for free space; in your painting I find a more cultured, more mental attitude.*

"In any good painting there is a lot of thought that goes into it. There is a lot of work and a lot of thought that goes into any good work. I just have to repeat that I think any work that's, you know, solid, well, it has a lot of thought and work behind it – any painting, I mean, any art work."

*What problems do you solve or express through your art?*

"The problems are a little too complicated to go into now, but basically my work has to do with just making visual art, something that excites me, that excites me personally. Then if that happens, if I feel good about it, then maybe someone else will. If it doesn't work out that way for me, then I feel it's a failure."

*Many artists pass from object to behaviour; on the contrary, you return to painting.*

"Well, I never really returned to..."

*But you still do paint.*

"Yes, I think the only reason anyone does anything is because it's a challenge for them, it is a... very much of a challenge, it has an interest, I mean, whatever anyone does must interest him, or there would be not much point in doing it. I think that's really what it all can be. I haven't, I've never felt a need to do other things because, well, painting interests me so much."

*What is the relation between your painting and the reality in which you live?*

"Well, it is the reality; I mean, what I do is, becomes, reality, it's part of my life."

*I think that your painting is always to paint the same painting, isn't it?*

"Yes, well, it is true in a sense. All the work is the same, you know, it's the way I approach the problem of painting, of course. In another sense, every painting is different, they are not... it's not the same at all. Yes, in a sense, yes, it would be the same, in the way that maybe, you know, any artist's work is the same. Cézanne is always the same..."

*What is the meaning of painting for you? Is it useful for you?*

"It is something that I began, and there again, I guess, we just get back to the challenge, to why anyone does anything. It's difficult to say, you do things because you do, or have to do, and some people choose one thing and other people choose another, and I really don't know why I chose painting. That's something I don't think anyone can, really, know."

*Can your painting affect reality?*

"Yes, I think there is no question about it, because, I believe that if I feel I have solved the problem for myself, and if I feel good about it, and I feel light about it, then it might have value for someone else. Well, you know, you can get into the thing of art as valuable property: if someone likes something enough, they want it, they want to have it, or they want to know about it. Then it becomes, you know, art as valuable property..."

*Do you think that art is still a necessary activity for men?*

"Absolutely, certainly. But you are talking about art, and that takes us in a whole different thinking. In a sense, art is... well, you know, it's a word, and it's in a dictionary and people will look it up, and the dictionary definition is usually not very satisfactory to most people. There are many definitions of it, it can be philosophical, or you can get into the literary part of it. One definition was (I've forgotten who said this, I think some artist) that if an artist says it's art, then it's art. I like that, but of course you have a complication here... well, the rub is, if an artist says it's art, you say: well, and who is an artist? An artist is someone who makes art, so you go around and around. Now, there are other definitions of art. I brought up the point of art as valuable property, which it usually comes down to; there are millions of dollars involved in art. Museum, magazines, books, publishers, and the people who are involved in it – curators, collectors, museum staffs, scholars, art historians, critics... And teachers, art schools... you see, all of that has to do with art, and it's all because of art, whatever this thing is, there again. Artists are, of course, involved in art, they make it. But I found that usually they are not too concerned with art: they make something, they do something, they solve problems, and they work at that... Well, they make it, but they don't really care that much about it, I mean about art, because, you know, I don't think any artist, no artist says 'next week I'm going to paint a masterpiece' or 'tomorrow I'm gonna do a work of art'."

*Art helps men to live. Does art help them to die?*

"To die, yes. Well, I think, it's like anything else, it's hard work, and maybe it's a little frustrating. But artists don't die more frequently than anyone else, I guess."

*I think your work is about language, isn't it?*

"Well, not exactly. You see, what I do is a visual experience; I mean, I'm not a writer. I don't have to do with language in that sense, I'm not a musician, I don't have to do with sound, or combinations of sounds. I think it is a uniquely visual experience. Before anyone can see paintings, or experience them visually, it takes a certain amount of, you know, training of your eye and of your sensibility to that kind of approach, and that's what it's about, it's nothing mysterious."

*What do you think about Rothko's and Reinhardt's painting?*

"Well, there is no question, I think. Rothko, well… he was a major painter, a painter of first rank, first rate. He did many fantastic things and I admire, I admire his work, I mean I'm very moved by his work. And also Reinhardt, who I think was, there again, very special, a very special person."

*Do you think that Rothko's painting is similar to yours? Rothko's painting also is done to be seen.*

"Rothko was working with different issues. He was working with colour, very much with colour, and with the object, the painting. His work might have a similarity with mine in the sense that they may be both kind of romantic, if you want it. I mean, in the sense that Rothko is not a mathematician, his work has very much to do with feeling, and sensitivity. The word 'romantic' can be taken in several ways, I guess, I mean it in a good sense, in opposition to the mathematician, you know, the theorist, the person who… everything is worked out before-hand, and that's stamped out."

*In which sense do you think of yourself as a romantic artist?*

"Well, I really wouldn't put that label on myself, but I think it does have some meaning, it's because I work pretty much from my feelings. I mean I do things because of my intuition, things that I feel are right, rather than trying to prove them before. To make it more clear, I really need, I mean, it's almost essential for me that I surprise myself, you know, in what I do. If I'm surprised about it, then I know there is something happening."

*Today's technology can produce all things better than man. Why can art still have a function?*

"Art exists simply because people want it, you know, if no one wanted it, then there would still be things being done, but not many people would see them."

*Since 1958, that is the period of your first white picture, have your artistic issues changed?*

"Well, no, of course, through the years you become involved in different, in slightly different problems, but I think the... how shall I call it, the sensibility, the basic, the essential sensibility of an artist doesn't change too much. You still are yourself; you change through the years because you become more knowledgeable, and you take in more information, and so, naturally, you work changes because of that. That affects all artists. Think of Monet and the various periods in his life that he went through with his painting. I mean, they were always Monets, but, you know, he changed, he was working on different situations."

*In each picture there's a non-painted space. What is the relation between this space and the painted area?*

"Well, of course the area that doesn't have paint on it is also part of the work. It's a compositional element. There is an area with paint, then there is the surface itself, without paint: the size of the space, of the surface, well, it all makes up the painting... That's the only reason for it."

*What is the space, the white cloth of a picture for you?*

"What I mean by space is exactly the area that has been chosen to use, for use. Sometimes it's very small, sometimes it can be very large. And that's what the space is; then you have that to work with, unless you want to go off the space on to the wall. That is something which is also possible, and which has been done..."

# Ben Vautier
Naples, 1935



*Ben, what's art to you?*

"Art is a human activity, an activity whose primordial need is to give something. The driving power of the activities necessary to innovation is the assertion of the ego. Art is a purely egoistic activity, except fatally, when it serves a purpose: architecture serves to build a home. In art and painting there are no longer any specific formal limits; the only limits of art are determined by novelty."

*What's novelty to you, in art?*

"It may sound somewhat naïve to speak of novelty in art, but the word 'new' may be replaced by the fruit of a personality. One does not have a personality unless one contributes with something new; to have a personality means to be different, it's the opposite of anonymity. Novelty means the 'I' that is speaking. When you say that an artist is original, you mean that he has made an important contribution; when you say an artist has style, you mean that he has something that does not exist elsewhere: the style is the 'I'. This novelty is evidently determined, ideologically as well as psychologically, because pure novelty does not exist, anything is created with ancient elements. When Klein's blue becomes a monochrome, it's a blue that is new in art history, as compared to abstract painting, but also as compared to Giotto's blue."

*Could you say that novelty and avant-garde coincide? Does the concept of avant-garde still exist?*

"That depends on what you mean by avant-garde: if you only mean the Western phenomenon of a certain limited group of artists who live in Paris or in New York and create something new for novelty's own sake… I distinguish my personal concept of new from that of the avant-gardes, which easily becomes avant-gardism – and thus fashion. The 'new' in the avant-garde is nothing but a variant, it does not challenge anything. To be able to say that novelty corresponds to avant-garde, one must see how matters stand: one must know the artistic reality and, on the basis of this knowledge, contribute with something different instead of asserting, within the context of this artistic reality, that one has found a 'niche'.

Since nobody kicks, I want to kick, since nobody has taken Bonito Oliva by the nose I take Bonito Oliva by the nose and then one automatically claims to be part of the avant-garde: this is not avant-garde. To me, in truth, avant-garde is the phenomenon of creation."

*Is there still a need for an avant-garde?*

"The need for novelty, the need for a contribution, the need for creation is vital to man and it exists in its own right."

*I will proceed with the interview on another, more personal level, which concerns your work more closely: I want to know whether you consider that there is a poetics.*

"Poetics is the individual in a certain instant, and in spite of himself. Poetics is man in his natural state. I have never liked artificial poetry, I have always liked romantic poetry. I don't like artificiality, fiction, and today I find that, between the poetic sense of Visual Poetry and that of Beat Poetry, I prefer Beat Poetry, because it contains a true message of an individual in search of nature. I am against Visual Poetry which has lost its poetic sense, which is no longer poetry, and has simply become a plastic art, an expedient, and it is on this point that I disagree."

*I find that in the poetics of your work you make a great assertion of egotism, of the ego. Is the concept of ego, according to you, a Freudian concept?*

"On a level of knowledge, no."

*I mean on a creative level.*

"I don't know Freud well enough to tell you whether it is Freudian or not. Simply, every time I accomplish a creative deed, I ask myself for whom I am doing it, and why I am doing it, and I eliminate useless pretexts and excuses. And then if you want, on the basis of an introspective approach to my work, I see that the ego is behind it, and that I contribute with my ego on stage, in my painting, in the theatre, wherever I work I allow my ego to come forth, because in my work it is truth that matters. So I show the ego, which is usually hidden. I do not paint a painting, instead of a painting I allow my ego to come forth; the painting is just a pretext."

*So we may say that in your work the celebration of the ego proceeds in the same direction as the function of art, the political and anthropological function of art?*

"I find, as a first reply to your question, that art is a matter of ego, and I say art serves the purpose of changing the ego. But that art is blocked in the ego. I therefore believe there is a relationship between my ego, which expresses itself, and the art that attains its simplest expression."

*Yes, but why do you consider that art is blocked in the ego? Is it a historical, a political problem?*

"For the moment I think this is an unchangeable problem, that has been part of man since the beginning of time: the first man who made a painting or a machine made an egoistic gesture. To change art, we must change man. It is an almost impossible task. At present the wall of art, which makes it impossible to venture beyond, is the ego. And it is a wall that it is almost impossible to scale."

*I'm thinking about what you said: in a civilization like the Western, it may be as you say, but in primitive civilizations, for instance, it is different. I'm thinking of the graffiti in the caves of Lascaux. Art served a ritual, economic purpose then, because man traced drawings on the wall as exorcism, to catch animals to stave off starvation.*

"Art has always been a pretext. A veritable rite was performed in Lascaux; and if one creates black masks, it is to heal. But the function is secondary. When novelty appears, it doesn't matter what activity man is conducting: it is the scream of the ego. If it were simply a matter of rite or function, there would be infinite repetition – but, on the contrary, there has been differentiation. In the history of humanity, in no civilization has there been any creation without the scream of the 'I'. But there have always been decisive political factors of various kinds. In China, for instance, at a certain point the emperor used to sign the paintings of the artists, in other words it was him who was the artist, even though he had not painted the paintings. There may be political situations in which the artist has to remain clandestine, but even if he is clandestine, even if he is a prisoner, when there is creation, when the artist contributes with something that did not exist before, it is his ego coming forth. Even the creations of the mentally ill or children are egoistic gestures: no creation, no contribution can take place unless the 'I' is speaking its language."

*I want to ask you some more specific, linguistic questions about your work. For instance, the value of writing in your painting.*

"There is a lot to be said about that. To begin with, I must briefly describe how I make the paintings and the writings. It is a short story. In 1956–57 I painted abstract paintings and at the same time I wrote very long poems to my first wife. And one day Yves Klein came to see me and told me: 'Ben, the format is the same, there are written texts and drawings, there can be drawings together with written texts, it's the same'. I must mention that, at that time, written texts were poetry to me, and drawings were painting. But Yves Klein told me: 'Ben, your painting is your poetry'. I took note, and told him 'but it is a matter of letterism' and he answered 'it's not letterism because letterism is an aesthetic thing, while what matters to you is the meaning'. After that I made paintings with the word canvas written on the canvas. The meaning of those paintings was to break with painting: instead of painting a boat I wrote the word boat. In my writings I then followed two different practices: there was subjective truth, which concerned my 'I', in which I wrote 'I, Ben, am envious of Armand, I, Ben am envious of Christo', and there were objective truths, due to which I wrote 'canvas, black, beautiful, what is beauty' on the painting – in other words the objective issue. But in actual fact, when writing invades the painting and becomes canvas-writing – the first painting-writing is from 1958 – the writing *becomes* painting. It is a matter of tautology: the word red, for instance, as replacement for the colour red."

*Is there any relationship between writing by hand and the concept of egotism?*

"Well, I would say that, at a certain point, everything is related to the concept of egotism, it's always the ego that speaks, it's simply a matter of one ego which it is easy to get to speak, and another that it is hard to get to speak. If I were to have my paintings executed by a letter painter, it would be my ego speaking, saying 'I, Ben, am the first anonymous artist who makes others do the painting'. When I write by hand it's still my ego that speaks, it's me, Ben, who traces those letters: the style is the writing. At a certain point I decided that it would be more original, more egoistic, to have a letter painter do the writing for me, and that it would be a very important egoistic feat to be one of the first artists without a personal style: my style therefore consisted of not having style. And I went to a letter painter and told him: 'My good man, could you write these sentences on a canvas and give it to me?' And I made him write with simple, clear capital letters. But I realized, in the first place, that it was expensive, that it was easier to do it myself, and in the second place that it became a style in any case, because people said that Ben's letters were black capital letters, and a certain letter painting. So I decided to use my own writing, which has somehow become my distinctive feature."

*And it's all a problem of style. What influence has Duchamp wielded on your style?*

"Duchamp's influence is my influence: if I were to outline my origins, I would say that Marcel Duchamp and Dada accounts for 50 percent. I put Marcel Duchamp and Dada together: it's not the Duchamp of puns or witticisms, only the Duchamp of ready-mades and the Duchamp of certain declarations on art. That is the only Duchamp that matters for me, the others have never had any influence on me. But this Duchamp has been important because I have found it in Dada: in Dada, just like in the ready-mades, I have rediscovered the word *everything*. To continue with percentages, there is 30 percent of John Cage, while Isidore Isou accounts for about 5–10 percent, not because of the letterism but because of the issue of megalomania. This is from an artistic viewpoint, but if we analyse the influences from another point of view I would say my mother represents 50 percent and Duchamp 10 percent; and there are also other influences of a more general character, as bourgeois ideology, for 50 percent. It all depends on the starting point. But if we limit ourselves to art, I would say Cage, Duchamp, George Brecht, Isidore Isou. Ready-made is the authorization, it is the permit to make Manzoni's shit: it is a permit, an opening towards other things."

*But is it an anarchic activity, then?*

"All art is. You can, for instance, say that Malevich's activity was anarchic; I stress that novelty is provocation, when it exists; the new is an anarchic activity, in the sense of a provocation which causes a break. In my opinion ready-made stands for an important rupture, a clean cut."

*I would like to go on to another subject that is also pertinent to the general theme, but a little more specific. I will begin with a question that is very hard, and I know it is, because it is somehow like asking a person what life is. I want to ask you: what is Fluxus to you?*

"Fluxus cannot exist without Cage, and so Fluxus breaks down into 50 percent of John Cage and 50 percent of Dada, but John Cage is already Dada. We may begin by establishing what Fluxus is not. Fluxus is not abstract painting, it's not a movement that has broken with painting, it's not a matter of aesthetics – or, in other words, of beauty. Fluxus is not a question of decoration. There are two huge messages in Fluxus – indeed, there are many: there is music and 'events' and among the events there is the participation of the public, and fun. Fluxus has two or three magnificent thinkers. George Maciunas for instance, who said that if art is a matter of professionalism, Fluxus must become dilettante; and if art is elitist, then Fluxus must become non-elitist. When one listens to music, one does so with a cultural background, and one says that this Schoenberg is not so bad, but there's a little bit of Webern in it… In this way the enjoyment of music is conditioned by a need for knowledge. When Maciunas invokes amusement, he does so by saying that the primary function of art is to amuse people, and not daze them with the need to know a certain art history, and the more complex art history becomes, the more man becomes a victim of the imperialism of art history. To me, on the contrary, this is not what matters. John Cage has set the example. In Fluxus one tends to say life is art, and has to be guided back to art. Fluxus is situated in a context subsequent to Duchamp, to the extent in which, starting from John Cage, Fluxus asserts that even to extend one's hand, to greet someone, is art. In other words, Fluxus focuses on the small, imperceptible details of the world. I consider George Brecht an important figure in Fluxus because he has introduced the event. And why is the event important? Because it seems to me that to take the *Bottle Rack* and put it in the basement with a wine bottle inside is something new. But there is nothing new about taking the *Bottle Rack*, cutting it in two and hanging it in a museum. Fluxus's attempt to take the *Bottle Rack* and use it in everyday life is therefore important.

By the way, I believe that even this attempt failed, but it has been important in any case, as I do believe that all post-Duchampian situations are today, more often than not, destined to fail. Daniel Buren, for instance, is in my opinion a post-Duchampian situation or an attempt to achieve such a situation, but neither he succeeds. Also Henri Flint, for instance, is an attempt towards a post-Duchampian situation, and another failure."

*Yes, we are dealing with a declination, a conjugation. It is not a matter of venturing further, but of a repetition, a variation.*

"But it is important on a level of public opinion. Duchamp has been accepted by the general public. This was necessary, because if Duchamp had not existed, nothing else could, there would not have been any Armand, César, and the list could go on."

*What is your position, where do you place yourself in the Fluxus continent? I say continent because Fluxus is a bit like Africa, somewhat mysterious.*

"My position is very simple. I am conducting my research in a post-Duchampian situation. The post-Duchampian situations that intrigue me are different from those of Fluxus, I am interested in my situation, and my situation within Fluxus is almost ruinous because it was concluded in Rome with self-criticism and recommenced with an equally ruinous reconstruction. To change art one must change man, but I am unable to change. To change art one must change the ego, but the ego cannot be changed. An attempt to change art inevitably ends up in a cul-de-sac. My position in Fluxus is a theoretical one, in which I put the cards on the table. My cards are similar to those of Henri Flint and George Brecht and not too different from those of Robert Filiou. Duchamp said: abolish the concept of judgement; it is impossible, because in fact, if one does not judge, it means that one feels superior. I try to be natural, to rediscover my naturalness. And so all my formal attempts, such as not signing, not speaking of art, have failed. All my attempts, not only formal but also subjective, have been a failure. The limit consisted of taking art to a post-Duchampian situation."

*Can we say, then, that the art/non-art you have theorized is a new definition of art?*

"There is no non-art: non-art is another form of art. Non-art is an art that purports to make art die, and to make it disappear into life, but it doesn't work. The reason is simple: it does not work because the word art always remains. The problems of non-art, of anti-art are etymologically absurd, because as long as the word 'non' stands alone all is well, but with the word non-art, when you are told that someone is showing non-art, the exhibited piece is art, you don't exhibit non-art. When you exhibit anti-art, you are against art instead. But neither this works. Non-art is my janitor who doesn't know Duchamp, who doesn't know Cage, who knows nothing about anything; but when she knows Duchamp or Cage, it becomes art, because knowledge of the arts automatically entails an artistic frontier. It is not worthwhile to refrain from using thought, from doing something. Even body art has become an expedient."

*We may, from this point of view, continue with the question we began with: does the new, avant-garde, exist?*

"I believe most attempts to surpass Duchamp have failed, but it is already an achievement to pose the question – at least one is tackling the issue. The concept of new and avant-garde today means to pose the problem of the impossibility of a post-Duchampian situation. The solution of the problem is a challenge launched to the next generation. The problem of art is today related to philosophy, because the issue of novelty has become a problem of happiness, one of change for man. Christo can wrap up the whole world if he wants to, Gina Pane can cut herself, the important thing is that they know, from the start, that it is only an expedient. To go beyond this situation, which has already been accepted in the past, one must change man – which is impossible. Consider the art history written by Harald Szeemann, according to whom anyone who digs himself a den is a great artist. Perhaps someone makes a very intense body art. He is an artist, because he is intense. Jannis Kounellis is a great artist because he is intense."

*Does there, in your opinion, exist an international, universal art history? I know you are exploring ethnics in this moment.*

"Sure, what you are asking is a very interesting question and I sometimes fall into contradiction. My point of view is that if you make a political and ideological analysis of the artistic situation of today, you realize that would-be avant-garde art, be it Dada or Pop, is a Western and above all Anglo-Saxon, sometimes French, problem. There is another point of view, and it is the one according to which the whole world, information, mass media move very rapidly. There is therefore an interaction between ideas, and new ones move very quickly. It's a global situation. In spite of this, the world is full of different cultures and every culture has its own language, and every language corresponds to a different thought. Since novelties enrich man, novelty is good for man; the fact that many things are happening is positive. If you accept this moral premise, which is the one I prefer, that is that an infinity of things and new things are happening in the world, you must admit that a world with only one culture would be a world with few opportunities. But the fact that there are many different cultures and languages, however, does not mean that there isn't an exchange of ideas. It becomes more likely for something new to appear. I would therefore like all cultures to reach an avant-garde state soon, all cultures to find an own originality and confront one another on an international level. Mine is an ideological analysis of the situation. I consider there is a risk that the avant-garde may remain prisoner of the Anglo-Saxon world. This would be ruinous. I don't believe in the world-wide cosmopolitism of artists."

*Do you think you can exercise your egotism also in your ethnic studies?*

"Certainly!"

*And then why are you still an artist?*

"I haven't understood it yet."

*I'll ask you three questions: 1. Do you think you can exercise your egotism in your studies? 2. What is most important to you now, your study of ethnic groups or art? 3. Why are you still an artist, is it just a question of economic survival?*

"As to your first question, my answer is that I haven't understood it well. You are asking whether I can venture beyond my egotism. I'm in favour of free enterprise and private initiative at certain conditions, I don't move at the pace of Communism because I believe it is the value and contribution of individuals that make nations progress and that build ethnic realities. In my opinion, a positive ethnic reality is one where there are many egoists, many individuals who do new things."

# Nam June Paik and Charlotte Moorman
Seoul, 1932 – Miami, Florida, 2006
Little Rock, Arkansas, 1933 – New York, 1991



*First of all, I'd like to ask you how do you structure, stabilize your collaboration. For instance, describe the performance where Charlotte was nude with the two monitors and the cello. What meaning has it for you?*

CM "This seems to me the piece where Nam June Paik was going to the water, or do you mean the topless piece where I was arrested? That's a different performance. Or, maybe, you mean the *TV Bra* piece…"

*TV Bra, yes.*

CM "Well, Nam June Paik made a brassiere out of two television sets. What he did, was to put them in a Plexiglas brassiere, and then connected my cello to this video system so that when I made cello sounds I could also produce beautiful images. I could make a mechanical distortion of the video image. This is a magnificent method to be used in commercials – it makes them look so much better. I had pedals put at my right foot and my left foot, and when I made the sound I could make the connection like you do with the light switch. Paik said, in a very beautiful statement, that he had combined technology with a part of the human body, and said he had also liberated TV from the monitor asset, you know, from the chest, and configured it in one thing. But there was no nude in it."

NJP "Humanize the technology. You know, in the 1960s there was a big movement, Art & Technology; most people made more technical toils, but that's a nonsense. The problem of art and technology is how to humanize technology. What is basic is not about art and society – artists are banged out of the society anyway, that's the problem of artists. In that sense, the effort of humanizing technology, where television is the number one, is the basic reason of that piece."

*What's the value in your work of the way you use your body?*

CM "I'm nothing more than what I am, I'm a living sculpture. So, the *TV Bra* doesn't work without the living part of the piece. But the gallery that owns the *TV Bra* doesn't own me…"

NJP "It was a living sculpture, used for the first time in June 1969."

CM "The video-sculpture is in Cologne now, but the living part of the sculpture is sitting here with you! I brought the *TV Bra* to the Cologne Kunstverein in 1970 at the happening of the Fluxus show. I also wanted to bring it down to Italy, but they seemed to be afraid or something… but I was totally covered, with the largest brassiere that you can have. And in the next show Paik will put live breast into the TV picture."

*What's the difference between these performances of yours and happening?*

CM "The difference between sculpture and theatre. Everything now is mixing, so it's up to the individual person to decide what we are doing, if it's a happening or a sculpture or a dance. For instance, sometimes they call me a storyteller, sometimes they call me a composer, sometimes they call me an interpreter. So I like the observers to make their own decisions. Nam June Paik is called the Rembrandt of video."

NJP "I think that in this ephemeral society you have to put a new name to the same things all over. You had in the past centuries one name for the Baroque, one name for Rococo. Now it's under Rococo for one year, the year after you have to put a new label to it, next year still another one. But it will be the next century to decide."

*According to me, the importance of your work, as of the work of a number of other Fluxus artists, resides in interdisciplinarity.*

NJP "Fluxus has been not interdisciplinary, but non-disciplinary. So, you know, Fluxus is not one person or two. Many times I thought Fluxus was dead, but it's alive and dead at the same time. Alive because it has no name: Lao Tze said that Tao has no name, just as Fluxus has no name. Anybody can say 'I am Fluxus' and he is Fluxus. In 1965 we thought Fluxus was dead, then in Los Angeles Ken Friedman said 'I am Fluxus', so it was alive, and died one more time.

Then in England David Mayor said 'I am Fluxus' and it was alive again, without permission. In other fields you have to have the permission to get out of a contract. In Fluxus nobody is really Fluxus."

CM "George Maciunas said that what they were doing was not Fluxus."

NJP "But George is not Fluxus, everybody is Fluxus."

CM "George went to the countries, like Cologne, and he declared that what they were doing was not Fluxus and that they even were not part of it."

NJP "Everybody made it in Fluxus. In Fluxus we used to say that we were anarchists, because the anarchy worked positively. Very often an anarchistic work means negativity, but in Fluxus it worked positively because no mania and no fame were involved. It was underground, nobody cared."

CM "Another important thing that I forgot to tell you about the *TV Bra* is that Nam June Paik doesn't write scores, generally, and he does the words as the Oriental masters, by word to the student or by word to the person. There is no written score. He said you want to publish the score of the *TV Bra* but he couldn't give you one. He has discussed with me and told me what he didn't want and what he did want. But there is no written score, just in a few cases."

NJP "There is a lot of Charlotte Moorman in *TV Bra*, a lot of her creation and interpretation, a lot of her personality is in it. If I had made the *TV Bra* with any another person, it could not be the same. Charlotte's charisma is strongly involved in it."

CM "One of the first existing scores by Nam June Paik was made for the *Opera Sextronique* (Filmmakers Cinematheque, 1967), when we were both arrested in New York. We were not arrested in Germany, there was no problem when we premiered it in Aachen in 1966. Later we were arrested again at the Philadelphia College of Art, but we survived hardly enough, when we played it in 1967. The next performance was held in New York City for invited guests, no paying people, no public authorities – just the invited guests. But the funny thing is that the score became famous because the police asked for it and we gave them and they ridiculed it. The district attorney thought that this was a very silly score. It didn't look like a score to him, it was just Paik's scribbling with a few notes and they didn't even consider it real. But for us it was very unusual that we had anything written down. If you want to see, I have that score with me."

*I believe that the importance of the Fluxus artists resides in their giving to the creative experience an anthropological value, not only a linguistic one.*

NJP "Yes, the anthropological value is undoubtedly the number one. Anthropology is the study of men and mankind, so Fluxus was a man's natural phenomenon in a natural cycle. Fluxus really seemed to have been a natural cycle in the early 1960s. And then George Maciunas wrote to me and Sylvano Bussotti and Hans Helmus; but Helmus and Bussotti didn't take seriously all the Americans and didn't answer the letter, only I answered it. He wrote a bunch of new names that I had never heard before, as Dick Higgins, Alison Knowles, LaMonte Young, Emmet Williams, Simon Maurice, Bob Watts, Walter De Maria – all absolutely new names, George Brecht. Beuys not yet – he was writing from America. Also Richard Maxfield, all new names. How was this possible in the USA, when we were little known in Germany and I had just one good museum contact… So I thought it was crazy: he didn't work with any gallerist."

CM "Well, he had a gallerist."

NJP "Yes, but he was collapsed in three months. Then I found in Europe very strong people, who wanted to do that too. So, it was like the ying and the yang, it just came very easily, not contrived or managed. All seemed so natural and that was because Fluxus was the only one movement that was really international: no hegemony of New York or Paris but quite a natural phenomenon. It died out in New York but survived in Germany and Tokyo. Giuseppe Chiari was the contact man in Italy, he did it very well. There was a human quality, the most important thing in communication; we had no money but we had men. Claude Lévi-Strauss said that culture is the network of communication: I talk, you talk, but he said it. We are talking about the same thing, variations of the same thing, like telephone: you decode telephonic language and it becomes what we are talking about, a network communication. In that way I think your interpretation of Fluxus as an anthropological phenomenon is true and I never thought it that way. Thank you very much."

CM "I'd like to tell you a short part of that story because it was in 1961 or 1962 – maybe 1961, I can't remember now – that the Carnegie Hall concert of Fluxus happened and George Maciunas asked me to please help him and call the musicians I had met at Yoko Ono's concert."

NJP "Oh yes, George brought Yoko Ono and it was very important because at that time nobody knew her."

CM "So it ended that Yoko asked me to manage her concerts. I was so excited and called everybody interested, and it was a really huge thing, and we did photographs when we came down the steps… I called the musicians for her, and it was a marvellous thing, it was a whole new world for me. Just tremendous things, and Bob Watts and all these people, and Maciunas thought how brilliantly they work. In 1963 I started a Festival that I still do every year in New York. That year I started with John Cage, Marvin Feldman, Friedreich Jusky, David Tudor, Edgar Varese, Al Brown. We did six concerts. That Festival was essentially music-oriented, but for the second edition Nam June Paik came to the US and it took a completely different atmosphere: we played Stockhausen and I added jazz and films and poetry, and I met a lot of tremendous people. So, now, the Festival has a wholly different feeling, the works are the most diverse and everything is more informal. Last year was the tenth edition. Paik and Fluxus took in a whole different tone."

NJP "I already mentioned many names on the American side, but European artists like George Brecht, Beuys and Vostell and also Chiari are also very important. And Stanley Brown, very good later on. George's preference was Chiari, George liked Chiari from the beginning, very much. I heard about Giuseppe Chiari through him, he was the one who discovered him. We thought Fluxus was related to the 1960s, but we found that it went into the 1970s as well – and this was a great pleasure of course. Fluxus published also videos. *Fluxus* newspaper no. 4, reprinted later by Daniela Palazzoli, included my video stuff of 1964, with the best essay until then written on this subject, video subject; but George had some claim."

*It is my opinion that, within historical Dada, there is a group that is very near to Fluxus: it's the group of Zurich. Among them, Hugo Ball more than others shares this same anthropological approach to art. Do you agree?*

NJP "I don't know very much about Hugo Ball. He wrote about Hermann Hesse later, isn't it?"

*Maybe you don't know that, after the Cabaret Voltaire, Hugo Ball retired in a village in Switzerland and later died in the odour of sanctity.*

NJP "Serious negation: that's the very important thing, serious negation. To be alive, to live an anti-art, superior life. I don't think Fluxus was anti-art in the sense that you make, it is also life. It's everybody's dreams, because very few people realize dreams. We are pure only in a certain time of our life. For instance François Mauriac said, quoting Thérèse de Lisieux I think, that our lives in the beginning are like tall mountains, and snow, snow, the very pure snow on the mountains… But it gets down dirty and dirty and more dirty, and in the end it becomes extremely dirty water. Our life starts in a very clean virginity and becomes dirty and more dirty. The Fluxus period was very pure. And it was not only a worthy desire. I feeel that when I did Fluxus shows I presented things that were most important in my life. We all thought in a purer way at that time than now. Now we are bigger and more important; but there is a lot of pollution…"

*I believe that neither Dada nor Fluxus pursue a negation of art. Theirs is not an anarchist attitude, rather an approach founded in a new affirmation, based on the positive and not on the negative and the destructive. To think that Dada is negation of art is a big mistake. It is an alternative kind of art with a strong anthropological component. Do you agree?*

NJP "Negation of art leads to the affirmation of life. Negation is a very important part of our life. In Hegel, Marx, Lao Tze's negation and in John Cage's silence all is negative, negation is truly important. In his last book Sigmund Freud said that 'life is creation and destruction, Eros is destruction. If we have no winter we don't have any spring. And then, I'm not ashamed to destroy the piano. I'm ashamed of the people who say that it is destruction. I want to give life to the piano, once life is gone you can have a new one. I am just not natural. Being natural means to die. If we lived forever, it would be boring'. George Maciunas worked very hard because he had asthma and he thought he might die the day after."

*In the work of Nam June Paik, Kosugi, Maciunas there is a strong influence from a different kind of culture. How much of Oriental thinking is in Fluxus ?*

NJP "George was a big fan of Japan. I believe that Fluxus is simplicity, as simple as George Brecht, Maciunas's idol. When I came to the US in 1964, once I heard George say: 'The best composer in America is not John Cage, or whoever, but George Brecht: all concepts are already present in him'. Just one heart: Winter even Snow, Snow even Winter – that is very Japanese, very hai-ku. George Maciunas and George Brecht were similar in that. George Brecht couldn't make a living so he started to make over jackets, but before making over jackets he was a great artist. When he came to Europe and became a fashion creator, he went from one princess to the other and this was dangerous for his art."

*There is another possibility for Fluxus to be related to Oriental culture, and it is the dimension of time, the value of time: is it true?*

NJP "This is very interesting: tell me more about it."

*For Fluxus, time is not an abstract cultural category; it's experience, everyday experience residing in the progressive gesture of an artist.*

NJP "Everything appears together, but there exist time and space. It's the time sign that interests me. Indian philosophers say: 'Time and I'. In Kosugi's work a very important part is breathing, Yoga is time, time, Yoga is breathing, *atmen*, that in Indian Sanskrit means first 'I', and second 'breathing'. It's a time element. Atmen is also a German word meaning 'breathing', the same as in Sanskrit. Kosugi's pieces are the best ones from Japan, together with the ones of Yoko. George made an American interpretation, he made it a little funny, breathing in a big tunnel. George is at times a bit stingy, he wants to double you, he wants to make a new and better piece than yours. He had a lot of paper rolls around, so he made a new 'Kosugi' with ten paper rolls, he made an American interpretation of Kosugi…"

*There's a difference between Happening and Fluxus. Happening is still a very Western kind of interpretation, it is still theatrical and related to schizophrenia – in short, it's just a show. Fluxus features a more precise and rigorous structure instead, sort of forerunner of the art of behaviour. I feel that Nam June Paik's and Charlotte's work together features a very deep link with Oriental theatre, Japanese theatre. How do you see this relationship?*

CM "Our work is definitively theatrical. As I told you, I do a Festival in New York. And I have to label it, I don't like that but I have to label it for the press and communication and the general public, I have to categorize what we are doing. That's very hard to do for me. So I may say it is video art, Happening, art event, eatable art, plant art, air art, postcard art – and I put all these things down. Once the electricians came and I had to give them a plan for each piece. Nam June Paik brought on board three television sets, as in the *TV Cello*, a video tape recorder, tapes, and needed a certain electrical high disposal; Jackson Mac Low came on board with a video tape recorder. Jackson is considered a poet, Nam June Paik is considered a video artist. Tom Strider, the magnificent American artist, came on board and brought three TV sets and a video tape recorder and made a structure, a gorgeous piece. He is considered a sculptor. Jeff Hendricks brought TV sets, an audio tape recorder, a video tape recorder and materials of painting and pieces of wood and everything. I call him a sculptor or a painter. Poor electricians looked at this and saw that they were all using the same equipment. But I have to try to label, and the way I make my decision is considering the way they use that material. Jackson is definitely poetry-oriented whereas Jeff Hendricks is really sculpture-oriented… But it is just for the label. It's not easy at all…"

*Let's go back to the relationship with Oriental culture… There is another point which is very important and it is the attempt you made to represent the invisible, the way you have hidden yourself, which is part of the Eastern attitude. There is no physical presence like in Western culture…*

NJP "Kosugi knows how to become truly invisible and makes magnificent performances of this very condition of invisibility. When Kosugi came to New York in 1965 he made a statement, a very good statement: 'I came to New York to teach New Yorkers how to become shy…'"

*That's why I'm a little confused about Yoko Ono. Through Fluxus, she learned how to be aggressive, she became too much Westernized…*

NJP "You know, all the Fluxus people shared the same Oriental or Japanese tendency to be shy; but when they exceeded a certain limit they all became the opposite. But I feel Yoko Ono was not like that."

CM "Yoko's work has gone back now to its early qualities. Last year in my Festival she had a whole railroad car in the hall of Grand Central Station: she brought her coffer, a Plexiglas coffer, she brought a dish of emotion, a dish of tears, she brought a plate of broken promises... It was such a beautiful car and everybody said that she was back to normal, she was doing incredible work again. Now I have to take you back to Kosugi, it was so beautiful. He came in 1965 and did some of his older pieces in the Festival; but the following year he did something that was so gorgeous that I can't get over it. He said what he was going to do was to play a game, to play baseball in the park. The Festival was at Central Park, and I said, yes, you're gonna play baseball? He said yes yes yes, I'm gonna play baseball, and I made it right but I could not understand well because his English was very bad. So he and his friends worked all night over and made a piano, a ground piano out of paper, and floated this ground piano in Central Park. It was beautiful."

*Tell me more on the Festival in Central Park...*

CM "Well, Christo wanted to represent a plastic piano. Alison Knowles was in a section of the park doing *Shoes of your Choice*. For sixteen hours people came up to a microphone to tell the story of their shoes and it was incredible what you could find out about people when they start talking about their shoes. So many interesting, unusual stories about shoes. On another hill Allan Kaprow had these children building towers out of wood and plastic. Then at the end of the day he let them destroy the towers rolling down the hill. They made staff for the garbage men... At the same time Jackson Mac Low was reciting his poetry and all this was tape recorded. Richard Huelsenbeck came to the Festival and said that what we were doing was all that not completely unlike Dada, and the City of New York took it seriously – after all, they did not think we were completely crazy. Bob Watts was sitting at a table and people walked into the park and said 'you have a beautiful garden here'. He was just sitting at the table and gave people passing by instructions on how to get to a certain building to say good morning to the doorman. All these things were going on at once: some pieces were very small and some very big, some of the artists were very famous and some of them were totally unknown. And that was the year of Chiari… As for me, I did a piece giving everybody pennies, even to the policemen. They were so shocked, they did not want to take them, they thought that it was strange to get these pennies and became quite upset. Other people said: 'Oh, how wonderful, you are giving me some money'. Emmet Williams did a beautiful book that day: he went around saying 'everybody in the park!' and thousands of people came. He had his book signed by thousands of people and by the end of the Festival he had all these names, no addresses, no phone numbers, just the names. Oh, hundreds of pages of signatures… He did also all the works of Yoko, because Yoko had to leave for London that day. He did for her because he thought that it was a big honour for him. I thought it was quite dangerous instead."

NJP "Fluxus covers the whole problem of the twentieth century: how should art relate to the social structure, to the organized society (which means museums), to the oppressive nations. It means the necessary evil, you can not live without that. How to get out of these structures? Fluxus people show that at least we can do something about it, we have existed outside of the museum and did our work. It was very hard but not totally unsuccessful."

*This is a very big point: Fluxus's relationship with the social position of the twentieth-century man. Artists finally came out of museums, of galleries and structures, they severed their ties with the establishment in order to act in a much wider historical context. I think there is another one political dimension of Fluxus's artists, that is, art finally became free and liberating, also in the cultural context. It broke the barriers between Western and Eastern culture, and that anthropocentric approach according to which man is the centre of the universe, is definitely over.*

NJP "This is me, I'm a shadow of this. It is important that George Maciunas was a pure Marxist, a proto-Marxist, in the sense that Saint Paul was a proto-Christian. George Maciunas was a proto-pre-Marxist. And George has a catacomb consciousness, he hides, he hides himself."

*Would you describe last night performance authored by Kosugi, and describe Charlotte's feeling about it and the relationship between your performance and Japanese theatre?*

CM "My feeling is that it was Japanese No music, because I feel very related to the No theatre and I think Kosugi made it for me again, he gave it to me and said: 'You are going into it. Look, it's indeterminate. You can go on for two minutes or for two hours'. But when I first started doing it, I was doing it in a very American way, I was rushing around, I was doing things in an American way. Kosugi was so happy when I got very sick. I had serious surgery. Of course, he was not happy that I was sick, but happy that when I did that piece again I had to slow down, because I had such a long cut in my body. I had thirteen tumours removed from me so I had to be very slow. I was sure the performance could help to get better – I don't believe in staying still and wait. So, I started doing his piece right away when I got out of the hospital and the first time I did the piece he said to me: 'this is the first time I like the way you did it, because you slowed down'. I was so angry with myself… It's just a totally different approach. When you watch at Kosugi performing himself, the slowness he does it is so incredible, I think he takes about thirty minutes just to open his pot. It's so incredible… He did another piece for me that is very difficult and beautiful, called *Instrumental Music*. You know, when you take up the cello bow and put it on the cello and draw a note, it's very simple; but for Kosugi that wasn't simple, I had to take two minutes to reach the bow, two minutes to take the bow slowly up, two minutes to get the bow under here, two minutes to pull the bow. Two minutes to take the bow up, two minutes here, two minutes there: that requires an extreme control and that's where my background Juilliard School of Music came in very handy, because I have an excellent bow-arm. I have got a complete traditional career, and my good bow-arm makes it possible for me to make that movement last two minutes. If I had not been a student at Juilliard I couldn't have made it. I think it was ten minutes for each action – it was so long! For an American point of view it was a totally different experience, a very valuable one. The only time that something quite similar had happened to me was in October 1961: I did a concert with LaMonte Young, he asked me to play his trio and I had to find two other string players. I got a violist and violinist, I got the best bow-arms, he said. This was in the New York Jazz Hall. Whenever I hear the name of LaMonte Young I hear that only note in my ears because we played it for one hour, it was all that we played and we made arm bow changes that were just inaudible, perfect with LaMonte conducting. But the funny thing is that he wanted me to have a very fine cello, so that the resonance would be incredible. I went and borrowed it for 600 dollars. The man who gave me the cello, did it because of my traditional career, they trusted me and let me borrow this cello for the concert. But the owner came to the concert and he was horrified and he never spoke to me again. And never let me borrow a cello again. When I did Yoko's concerts it was a slow type of thing but never ever like Kosugi. Kosugi brought very important things to America."

NJP "It's very interesting that the Americans, who use to be very action-oriented and always moving, suddenly begun to appreciate slowness. This is a very import phenomenon, culturally."

*A sort of searching for rules, actually.*

NJP "Yes, but they never liked the slow things."

*Obviously, America is not just a Western country…*

NJP "That is true, there are strong influences from native American Indians and there are considerable numbers of mixed marriages, you know. I don't remember names but there are three prominent artists with a quota of Indian blood – very important artists. There is also a considerable mixture with black Americans and this has a very deep psychological impact…"

CM "I'd like you to know that in performing both our own works and works by others, we are not against museums, we are not against galleries merely out of prejudice. Some of our pieces are magnificent in a museum or a gallery, like the *TV Bra* we now play all over the world. I like, for instance, the De Marco Gallery in Edinburgh, the Kunstverein in Cologne, the Kunstverein in Stuttgart, the Cochrane Gallery in Washington. The pieces are beautiful in a gallery and are also very beautiful outside, it's really lovely. It is not that we work totally against museums, but personally when I'm doing something I enjoy having a different location. It's somehow more exciting to go to a place where I am not supposed to be."

*Yes, Duchamp uncovered this attitude fifty years ago but it also belonged to ancient Greek culture. That's what the Greeks used to call* stranein *– wrong-footing, estrangement, alienation…*

CM "But I want to say that we will go to big museums and over the galleries every year. But now I'd talk about the Festival. The first three years it was held in a concert hall. Then we got kicked out because of Allan Kaprow's *Pushball*, a magnificent piece; but we were kicked out of the concert hall. The year after we went to Central Park, out in the open air and it was wonderful. The next year we started in a ferryboat, you know the boat that goes back and forth in the water? We got there. Then we had a parade going down Central Park West, the year after I could get an island – a difficult situation, the island… then we were given the Armory of Duchamp's *Nude Descending a Staircase, no. 2*. Well, I choose the Armory because of that, because it had that tradition behind it…"

*… and when it was exhibited in the Armory Show this Duchamp's work shocked and upset President Wilson.*

CM "In the past years I got railroad trains in Grand Central Station, and this year we are going outside again and I'm trying to get the World Trade Center or the Shea Stadium where they play baseball, because in America baseball is so important."

*In my opinion, Fluxus work has a precise strategy: make life impossible, I mean today's life. This is a strategy that all art should share, this pushing life towards a condition of impossibility.*

CM "Oh, no!"

*I mean life as it is organized nowadays…*

NJP "Yes, but not for Fluxus, because they want to escape, you know."

*It's a way to organize the flight…*

NJP "Well, it's your idea, but that is a casuistry, it looks like tiny forces, like an escape."

*Yes, they are so tiny that, when they escape, nobody will notice!*

NJP and CM [laughs]

CM "Are you an artist also?"

*Me? I am an artist as far as I chose to be an art critic. A gesture of freedom for me. But yes, you're right, I started as a poet and writer ten years ago.*

NJP "You see, the subversion of the system is very important; video art is the subversion of television."

*It is a quality and not a quantity subversion. So, it is not a political gesture (or at least, it is in a very restricted way) in so far as politics are always quantitative.*

NJP "But you know what Hegel and Marx said: the increment of quantity changes the quality."

*OK it's true, but the issue at stake now is this: art as a proposal of alternative behavioural models.*

NJP "Yes, alternative television."

*No, alternative models of life – alternative as regards reality that, as you know, dies hard. Possibility against reality.*

NJP "You know that to subvert a system you have to know the system first. That's why I worked in institutional television first: to study and manipulate them. So people, this impatient left wing people, say that I'm making compromises. It's not true, I'm learning."

*Weel, I do agree that art and culture are, after all, study and analysis.*

NJP "Yes, because you have to know the complexity of a system, you cannot live alone, you live in a system and you have to go and play and see how it works. There are so many details, if you don't know details… you cannot repeat 'Allende!'. Allende means Chile, the Allende government, and we can not repeat the Allende government, it's very important that we learn something."

*Finally, a tricky question: we have said that Fluxus is a kind of anthropologic work through art, it is a gesture that always aims at totality. Whereas art is generally very partial, it is linguistically circumscribed and limited. Today you have often recalled your past, historicized your gestures, remembered dates and places. And this is a way to go back to the history of art, a quite bourgeois attitude, a limit in your approach that, on the contrary is total and not partial.*

NJP "You are completely right: I quoted that, citing François Mauriac at the beginning. Fluxus was like snow on the top of the mountains. Now we are in a sort of steppe land. In the early 1940s or maybe late 1930s water became dirty, so they were making images of dirty snow. Fluxus was a perfect idea, but it's falling. My Fluxus work is purer than what I do now. When Fluxus becomes nothing, then you have absolute Fluxus. Fluxus means going away, disappearing like through the toilet."

CM "I have to tell you: George Maciunas was very upset with my second Festival because some of the Fluxus people were in it, I and Bob Watts, Joan Jonas and Dick Higgins and all those people. So he went outside and picked it, picked my Festival, and said that Stochkausen was not seen around and even entered and picked up and down when Paik and all the others were still performing. But Alain Gainsborough did a gorgeous thing: he went out and joined the picked line and picked it himself. Then he stopped picking and came in and made his performance. He was out of Fluxus, George Maciunas was out of Fluxus. And it was wonderful what he did. Nobody from the press could understand how a performer could go out and pick. But it was so good."

NJP "Your last question is great, that is, the idea of Fluxus disappearing without entering the museums. To lie is mean. To be forgotten in a museum is a sort of lie, a mean. John Cage liked this. Sometimes I was a purist and asked him questions and he then answered: 'Oh I must have a drink!' Cicero, the Roman, said: 'Don't trust a man who says: I'm a good man. I'm a good man means just: I'm a real man'."

# Wolf Vostell
Leverkusen, Germany, 1932 – Berlin, 1998

Berlin<br>1974

*What is Berlin for you, Vostell?*

"For me Berlin is not a city, it's a phenomenon. But I have to say that it is at once a pleasant and an unpleasant phenomenon. I am like two opposite poles of electricity. One day I'm in an agreeable frame of mind and the next I feel a negative force around me, in my surroundings."

*What is the positive polarity and what is the negative polarity of this relationship with the city for you?*

"The very electrifying, very positive polarization that I experience in a situation characterized by a great deal of highly complex information, information based on different ideologies. You are certainly aware what the ideologies are in this city and you know about the difference in the sources of information. We do not like frontiers and I try to break down boundaries in art. For this I need that huge amount of information and I also have to break down that information. I believe that information is a very important aesthetic weapon. The negative polarization of Berlin for me is the lack of possibilities for expansion. I feel a bit like I'm in a cage, but at the same time this city, these people like me have a great desire for expansion and that expansion is impossible. So it is not negative for me, it is a very creative thing to want to expand."

*It seems to me that with your work you are able to grasp better than perhaps any other artist a situation, a structural element of the context where you live, the element of violence. It appears to me that your work has the property of unmasking the visible and invisible violence of the total space in which you live.*

"You are right, I try to make invisible things visible. You have to use a technique to unmask things. Masking means covering things, does it not? There is a contradiction, an antagonism. If you like, my new environment is a mask, but a mask that is unknown, a mask through which you discover a state of life that is more significant than you think. There is invisible violence, if men and minds – I am talking of men in terms of brains, of mental output – in this world cannot do what they want, then there is great violence. It is like destroying plants. I draw this analogy with plants because they die, just like thought dies when it cannot do what it wants. By this I mean that I'm aware that to be happy in life it is necessary to be able to do what the brain asks from you, it is necessary to be able to realize that dream, otherwise you just can't live. It is absolutely necessary to be able to do it. I feel it is essential for each person to be as fulfilled in his life as possible."

*I believe that your work has another quality, in the sense that violence is generally a reduction of reality, a decrease in reality. Precisely because it is founded on creativity, your work is a development of reality, an amplification of it. I would like to know whether you agree and, if so, in what sense.*

"For me, every time I go out of the house I sense everywhere a complexity of energies, in each millimeter of dust, in each millimeter of air. In all the elements I sense forms of energy. There is nothing more stimulating for me than energy and I believe that there are many forms of invisible energy, just as there is invisible violence. So it is my job to make the forms of invisible energy visible. I mean that I'm not interested in just expanding the aesthetic point of view and that of the history of art. My work is dedicated to human beings. It shows them how to do something, shows them processes, the means to increase their creativity, to live in a more creative way. I believe it is possible to learn how. In classical art you can go and see the picture, but the picture is not a process, whereas I want to produce an art of seeking that changes people's heads, that changes the way they think. That is what interests me, an art of behaviour. That's my contribution to art, my desire to wake people up so they can live a more complex, more conscious life."

*We have reached the heart of your poetics, of the issues you tackle: psycho-aesthetic energy, what the psycho-aesthetic energy in your work is. Because you have always theorized about psycho-aesthetic energy through debates, through your writings, but I would say especially through your works. What is the psycho-aesthetic energy in your work?*

"Well, 'psycho-aesthetic' work is mental work, the creative work that leads someone outside normal thinking. What I'm trying to say is that if a person lives in an uncompromising way with his awareness, that person realizes that he is aware of everything.

Then that life of awareness gives a value to each insignificant thing. For me that is psycho-aesthetics, living each second of your life with awareness. I believe that the majority of people today do not live in a conscious way, most of them live outside their own minds. And everything in the world, all the events, all the possible details of our world, have a visible or invisible connection. So someone who has an awareness of the infinite complexity and the awareness of an infinite connection lives much more intensely and has a higher quality of life than those who live a quiet life and do one thing after another. The multi-complex human being can create something new."

*In what year did you start working on psycho-aesthetic energy?*

"Well, I have to say that when I was young, in Paris – I studied in Paris in 1958 – I was interested in reading Freud and Jung. That means it is sixteen years that I have been systematically investigating the psychological literature. For seven years now I have been collaborating with an art psychologist who carries out research into my work. With him I can speak about other problems too. To take an example, in Berlin a person was very influenced by one of my Happenings. It was someone who didn't know my work at all. I believe it was the first Happening of that kind in the world, and I think you agree that a Happening like that has never taken place before. It's a creation that exists like a bacterium, like a particle of information. I told my psychologist I was convinced that a lot of people who don't know my work have now been influenced by my work, exactly because of that special piece. And he's the only one who really understands me and accepts what I say on the theoretical level. I must say that there are very few art critics or philosophers who accept this possibility."

*To me it seems that at the cultural roots of your work there is not just the Freud–Jung polarity but also the polarity with Marx, and in this sense I feel that your work has caught in a precise way the importance of that historic avant-garde movement which is Dada, especially the Dada of Berlin; a Dada that aimed on the one hand to combat the negativity of history, and on the other tried to work at the anthropological level through art. I'd like to know if you agree.*

"I'm very happy that you have noticed the connections between me and the Dada people. When I was young the first thing that made an impression on me in the history of art was the historic Dada exhibition in Düsseldorf of 1958. It was their first show in Germany after the war. It really woke us up, and though in the 1960s German art critics often said that 'Vostell was influenced by the New York School' it's not true. The source of my work is Dadaism and that exhibition in 1958 at Düsseldorf. Of course I had commenced my research before that and my technical approach did not change. You know, I read about a plane crash in *Le Figaro*. I thought that it was a process of destruction, a 'décollage'. And I started to reflect that up to then the collage had been something of Schwitters's and the like, a little thing made of paper, but I saw that word used in *Le Figaro* to describe a great human disaster, the crash of an aircraft. It was one of the gravest things after the great disasters of the war. It was the first disaster after the war, which killed 120 people. Then Dada caught my interest, and it still interests me because the Dadaists tried to create a new man. I corresponded with Haussmann, who was living in Limoges. One day he wrote to me 'In Berlin, I saw the hold that the Dada posters had back in 1923'. I replied to Haussmann: 'You know, the only movement in art that assigns Dadaism its great historical value is Fluxus, the Fluxus Happenings'. And I said too that in the 1920s there had been three striking phenomena: plane crashes, car crashes because of the German expressways and television. So I was the first artist in the world to devote myself to these phenomena, which are fundamental elements of our life today and which pose enormous problems. If you like, I anticipated aviation disasters a little in the work of art… I wrote to Haussmann that the Dadaists had not known these phenomena and that they had not worked on the phenomena of destruction and mass communication. Afterwards, Haussmann became a very close friend of mine and he changed his opinion completely, because I had convinced him. A few months ago, I told this story to Marcuse when I was with him in Bremen and he told me: 'You know what the difference is between Dada and you?' 'No', I said, and he told me: 'There was Fascism in the meantime, that's the difference'. Fascism has made our art necessary. That gives you an idea that for us it was absolutely necessary to fight against art as a pleasant product, as a fetishistic product, as a slushy product. And that is there in my own work too."

*I'd like you to describe from the viewpoint of psycho-aesthetic energy three works that I find highly exemplary: the one of the woman in a mask, the one with the automobile you did at* Contemporanea *and the work done here in Berlin where a bus has been covered with strawberry plants. I would like you to comment on this from the viewpoint of psycho-aesthetic energy.*

"The woman in the gasmask is the idea that no one is worth anything in the face of the problem of violence. I mean that faced with destruction, with violence, each person is helpless and each person has to define his own destiny. In this society, there are no institutions that can provide a solution to the problem of violence. But I would like to say that even if you are powerless you are linked with everything that happens in the world in terms of destruction. You are not free, you are obliged to confront the war in Vietnam. In the second work, created for *Contemporanea*, there is the confrontation of three forms of energy. It is not just mechanical energy that is present in each second of a person's life. There is also physiological energy, psychological energy and intellectual energy. With the third piece I wanted to make people understand that everyone always criticizes everyone else. They say: he is bad, he is worth nothing, he does nothing. But no one ever speaks of himself. The whole of society is like that. I want to create a new awareness, I want all of us to question ourselves and to realize that our forms of energy are sick. I see a negation in principle there: life is an illness."

*The principle of psycho-aesthetic energy, in my view, is the one that has also determined the methods of your work. Your works have always been processual, open, seeking to capture temporality, the time of life. This can be seen in your décollages too, for the décollages are also processual works.*

"Not made by hand, not made by the energy of many people, since this complexity is made for an ultra-complex industry."

*What in your view is the difference between your Happenings, your processual works, and the Happenings that have been staged in the US for example? I would like you to talk about it from your own perspective.*

"In general there is a great difference: at the end of the 1950s, I started to carry out actions in the street. So, in contrast with Duchamp's work, my contribution is not the *objet trouvé* but the *vie trouvée*, the found life. But the American Happenings did not begin with *vie trouvée*, they began with the theatre, the theatre of Cage and even the Happenings of Oldenburg. Kaprow's first Happening was in a gallery, whereas my first action was in a deserted Paris street. And I believe that my style of Happening is based on processes found in real life and with real people. The American Happenings, in my view, are a bit of a pantomime. They have the character of an object. My Happening is concerned with the psychological and physiological processes and responses of human beings. In general it is the object rather than the human being that dominates in American Happenings, with a few exceptions…"

*If I had to give a title to your work, I would put: "La violence trouvée".*

"Sounds very good!"

*I think that this is very important: it's true that you work on found life, but we know very well that the essence of life today in modern society is violence, and so I would speak of "found violence". I would like to know if you agree and, if so, what violence is for you.*

"I think you have found the essence in your conversation with me, an essence I myself perhaps didn't want to admit totally: I mean, the fact that everybody is afraid. It is an invisible fear. The most thriving and industrialized nations are afraid, but so are housewives, so are the strongest, the most vital people. Everyone is afraid. Of course, fear is very complex too. There are many kinds of fear: economic fear, fear of destruction. I'm not free from it either, I am afraid too. Fear is one of the forms of life's energy. And for this reason as an artist I cannot ignore this form of energy. It is necessary for me to comment on this phenomenon of my age. In this I am perhaps different from other artists, I cannot drop this theme. But if you look closely it's not just a question of violence. I have, for example, made the woman in the gasmask, I've made a comparison of violence and love, for I feel that love is one of the strongest forms of energy. Love and violence are the two most important poles for humanity. As an artist I feel obliged to carry out research on that. It's very simple."

*In our society violence arises from competition: don't you think that when you put more than one reality together, you pass from violence to peaceful coexistence?*

"I believe so, psychologically it's like that. Take the example of the accident: if you buy a car, you also buy an accident. That's how I would put it. André Citroën said: the automobile is 75 percent psychology and only 25 percent technology. I believe, in other words, that if you practice a life of awareness, you can never be surprised by violence. Another example connected with the car: if you drive a car and think about the risk, that is to say about the possibility of an accident, you react in a different way when an accident occurs, or you don't have accidents. I want to say the same thing about violence: if someone is aware of the brutality in life he does things differently, he comes up with a defense against that violence in advance. Someone who never thinks about violence is surprised by the chance event that destroys his life. And I believe that it is necessary to give society a dialectical and pacifistic idea, possibilities of behaviour that prepare it for violence, against fear, against the idiocy of life. I cannot change life, but I can give things that help humanity to change."

*For this reason I would say that your art creates models of behaviour.*

"Yes, I agree completely. I believe it is possible for society to change. Life is not going to change, there will always be brutality, violence, but if one day people were to change their behaviour, life would be different. Possibly everything that happens, all the production of the mind, will be influenced by this new mode of behaviour. But I want to say that it is not enough to think in a different way, as the Left movement does. You really have to be different, to carry out different actions, to conduct a different life, and only in that way will people understand that different actions produce a different life. Then, perhaps, life will change."

*We have talked up to now from the ethical, anthropological, ideological viewpoint. Now I would like to speak of expression, of the linguistic side of your work: what significance does the presence of paint, the brushstroke, colour have in your work?*

"Well, when I found the system of décollage, the system of a painting of process, even of mechanical process – for, if you like, décollage means producing a picture with a mechanism, with the mechanism of décollage – I didn't want to practice an academic art, create a pleasant work. My art is an act of rebellion, it is a style opposed to well-made art, opposed to handmade art. This does not mean that I don't esteem the masters of the Renaissance. I know very well how to draw, how to paint, but I want to produce an art that in aesthetic terms constitutes a rebellion. And for this reason I always utilize very inferior techniques. I carry out extensive research into very poor means and techniques, because I find that inferiority possesses a great aesthetic quality."

*If on the one hand you use inferior techniques, on the other you make use of superior tools: technology. What significance in your work do you give to the use of the television, of mechanical elements, in short, of technology?*

"What I do is to give a second reality to the television set and the car: the first reality of the car is that it allows people to make journeys. Its second reality is that it is a piece of energy, and in this sense it has no logic. And this a-logicality gives rise to other lives. For me using the automobile is the same thing as using the poster. The car is a technological complexity just as the poster is a complexity of printing. Without the complexity of industry this quality of the car would simply not exist. For me there is a reason for not making a sculpture by hand, making a bronze… I have included materials that have already been used in my work because that use signifies thousands of hours of life. So in a piece you have a lot of energy and you have very great complexity. A Cadillac is the product of a lot of energy, of lots of accidents, perhaps it has produced information in the newspapers: there is a very big complexity. I have included this interdisciplinary quality in my work. It is something very different from a handmade sculpture in the studio of an artist."

*Your work has always been the result of a process based on the event, on the action. What significance, what value does the final object that remains after the process have for you?*

"Well, the object is not just a memento of the action. I rightly draw a distinction between a sculpture that does not have a life of its own and an object that genuinely has a life. For me the photograph of an energetic environment has very little value. But the object itself has a lot of value because you can touch it. You can touch a car and you know that this car has done a hundred thousand kilometres. If you touch a model by Henry Moore, you know that Henry Moore made it in his studio, but if you touch one of his sculptures, a casting in bronze, you don't feel his creativity. The Cadillac is part of the real world, it has driven on the expressway, it has produced events. You understand, it has influenced the lives of others, it has been mobile and it is this mobility that I keep – I keep its life. A photograph does not preserve life, you can't touch it, it's not three-dimensional. This is why I go on making objects and don't content myself with writing down concepts on a piece of paper, as conceptual art does, for it is only the object that intervenes in life, that has the power of life. An idea on a piece of paper does not have the force of energy."

*In that sense your work is Fluxus…*

"Yes, in the sense that I create open processes, that I practice an art that is not comprehensible straightaway. The objects that I make and the events that I stage stay in the mind and stir thoughts in the public for months, for years. We have carried out research on this. It is a mobile imagination, whereas artists who are not Fluxus produce a static imagination. Conceptual artists produce a concept, but the concept stays there, it is not mobile. While a Happening produces aesthetic information that acts like a bacterium. A bacterium is fluctuating and invisible. Invisible fluctuation is my Fluxus contribution."

*What is Fluxus?*

"From the historical viewpoint Fluxus means: declaring that every being, every action, every production, every Happening is an artistic creation, even being here, even seeing, even breathing. All our expressions and the expressions around us are artistic phenomena. Life as artistic phenomenon, life as music. That is what Fluxus has been for me historically, the same kind of thinking that you have in music."

*What is Fluxus in this moment?*

"For me Fluxus is continuing to see life as a fluctuating river and breaking down the boundaries of conscience. Breaking the bounds of thought – that is Fluxus for me."

*What does the word Fluxus mean exactly for you Fluxus artists?*

"Fluxus is a Latin word, you know very well what it means. But for me, its a synonym for a stream, for a river. I see life as a river, but I swim against the flow, I don't swim with the river."

*So your work is a stand.*

"Yes and no. Opposition is very complex too: sometimes opposition wants to provoke something positive. I think that today the artist's obligation is not to show society his love. The problem of today is to show society as it is, to hold up a mirror to it. And that also means giving society the chance to behave in a different way because it is only when you look at yourself in the mirror that you can change.

At the end of the 1950s there was abstract art everywhere, the so-called Informel. The world wasn't looking at the elements of life. I realize that it is absolutely necessary to bring the problems of life into the work and I am unable to separate the problems of life from my aesthetic production. I am what I am is an existentialist phrase. I believe that Sartre and Kafka and Chaplin have had a greater influence on my work, more than the American literature or art of today. Without Kafka's détournement my work would be impossible. Because Kafka means the mirror, Kafka is creative, Kafka is another reality. I learned from him to see the details of life, the importance of all the details in people's behaviour, and that is an existentialist philosophy."

*On the linguistic plane estrangement is a Dadaist technique.*

"Well, Brecht used it too…"

*Yes, but in the figurative arts it was with Dadaism that estrangement was born.*

"Estrangement is the photomontage…"

*The object, Duchamp's bicycle wheel. Duchamp's urinal is estrangement.*

"Yes, but estrangement in the process. The Dadaists didn't do this process."

*The object was made by the Dadaists.*

"The big difference is that I do the process, I don't just make the object."

*We could put it like this: that the Kafkaesque spirit in your work consists in thinking that the world is widespread violence, that the only possibility of escaping violence is to remove the object from the widespread violence of life, that is to pass to the existential level, from the false totality of the world to partiality.*

"This is very interesting. What I want to do is give the object and the behaviour another 'use', even if the object is ridiculous and violence is the least possibility. You know, if I speak of the second reality, that means giving another use to the Cadillac. What I called a-logical before."

*We might say then that the title could be "La deuxième réalité, la violence trouvée".*

"Magnificent!"

*What is the importance of your work on Charlie Chaplin?*

"Most essential, because Chaplin is different. He is different from other comedians. It's not pantomime what he does. He expresses inferiority. Other comedians work on gags, Chaplin is almost the only one who gives great importance to the inferiority of life and the inferiority of objects. He has an admiration for things that for other people are *mierda*. I look for the same thing in my means and in my objects. I take inferiority and I give inferiority a quality. And that is a peaceful and humane contribution. I cannot be humane and give money to someone, but I can say: if you take a handful of sand and you look at it for an hour, you'll find a fantastic quality. It's much more substantial than having a thousand dollars in your pocket. So the difference between the research of other contemporary artists and my own – and this is very Fluxus – is that I give great importance to lost qualities. I composed this cow piece in Cologne during the Fluxus exhibition because I wanted to pay tribute to the process of birth of a cow in an art institution: I wanted to describe this process that is very normal in the world, but given little consideration in our modern society. We have lost the ability to look. Society doesn't want to see, doesn't want to know how the birth of a child, the birth of an animal takes place. There are things greater than a play, than a film. This is precisely my job as an artist, to show that simple things are the great phenomena of life."

*I would say that there is another connection between your work and the films of Charlie Chaplin: a sort of sentimental relationship with inferiority, with the humble world.*

"Yes, of course I am often criticized for that, because my private life is not a life of poverty, a life lived in the street, even if I did start from nothing. I believe that to express my sympathy for things, today I have to make use of technique. To be able to say easy things, to work with these inferior sympathies, I see no other possibility than to make use of all contemporary procedures, of television, video, the art of engineers, even the advice of psychologists. I draw on science, I draw on all the creative elements of my age. In life I'm not a down-and-out, I'm not a fighter. I can't fight in the streets, I'm not fomenting rebellion in the streets, but through my work I try to create models that allow others to liberate themselves, to have a freer life. Naturally I can't do it with words. I do it through the action and the object. It is my fate that through my experience, I want to give a model so that people can free themselves of all this inferiority."

*There is another great comic called Buster Keaton. It seems to me that Buster Keaton has a colder, more cynical, harsher relationship with reality, because reality is harsh, it is not sentimental. Don't you think so? And it seems to me for example that in the cinema Godard has understood this great lesson. Don't you think that today the relationship you have to have with reality, to struggle against reality, needs a colder attitude like Buster Keaton's, rather than Chaplin's?*

"I can make a comparison: for me Chaplin is the Happening and Buster Keaton is conceptual art, because conceptual art concerns the problem of having new projects and new ideas in life; but conceptual artists never go to the heart of things. They touch the surface. They don't say: it's my problem. They say there is a problem. While Chaplin says it's my problem, Buster Keaton says there's a problem. For me Chaplin is the greater of the two because he makes all the problems of the world his problem."

*A matter of subjectivity…*

"In this way all the miseries of the world or all the great things of the world are also his problem, while Buster Keaton, in comparison, is like conceptual art or abstract art. He excludes from his personality life, the real problems of the world. Fluxus and the Happening try to mix with the world and make things symbolic."

*At the beginning I described your work as a work on found violence. If your work is also one of opposition to the violence of the world, then we have to say that art is counter-violence as well as violence.*

"The greatest art is counter-violence. Counter-violence is creativity. I mean that these are the strongest ideas in the art of today. One uses the word 'relevant': for me Kienholz's work, for example, is relevant. Buren's work is not relevant because it is not a counter-force, whereas with Kienholz I see an ironic, melancholic, tragic counter-force. In Buren I find an exclusion. He says: that is reality and I remain Buren."

*I find that in your work in addition to the problem of violence there is, within, the issue of death.*

"Death is fear. Death is the same as fear. But I have to say that it is not just that; I find that everyone is afraid of physical death but I want to show that everyone is also afraid of mental death. And if I say that society is crazy, society is death, I mean that society is mentally dead because it is not creative enough. Even if it is dynamic and industrial, it is mentally ill. Otherwise there would not be so much violence in the world. Look at Vietnam: it never ends. This is simply because people's mental output does not match industrial production: industrial production is creative, complex, fantastic; people's mental production is impossible in its entirety. You understand what I mean? There are fantastic exceptions, among the philosophers, but I am speaking of society in general and I think that politicians cannot solve the world's problems. Only artists can provide models for the mental process; the industrial process is marvellous because industry is really avant-garde. There are two things that are always avant-garde: industry and art. Society's thinking is never avant-garde, don't you think? No, there is always a time lag, a difference. The society that makes fantastic discoveries is at the same time very poor in its organization, in life taken as a whole."

*Even though your work is a work on violence, precisely because of that sentimental component of which I spoke earlier, which is also typical of Chaplin's movies, I find that in it there is not so much a sense of tragedy but a sense of melancholy, which is different. What do you think?*

"Melancholy can be tragic too. If you look at the biographies of some of the Renaissance painters, you often read that this or that artist died of melancholy. Melancholy can be fatal."

*Dürer for example…*

"Now you understand the psychological connection, don't you? Psychology is melancholy. I want to give people a quality, I want to make them able to doubt. I don't want to show them how to believe, because believing is dangerous. Doubting is difficult, it is melancholic. But doubting leads to a greater quality than believing."

*I would say that the quality is not so much believing as hoping. The sense of tragedy stems from the lack of hope. Melancholy stems from the rejection of the present, but with an opening towards the future.*

"Yes. After melancholy can only come a positive period. After melancholy there is nothing else."

*So for you art is always political?*

"Yes, but political in a different sense: I believe that an artist is always a politician of culture, and there is this word in German, *Kulturpolitik*, which means all the political events that have something to do with culture. Generally when we speak of politics we are referring to social problems, but there are not just social problems, there are also problems of culture. Several artists – I am one of them – are working today on social and cultural problems."

*In what sense?*

"Well, if the art we do is negative, destructive, an art that is opposed to professionalism, that is against academicism, an art that is not agreeable, we are a counter-force. We oppose the production of art that society wants to have. Society doesn't want an art that is a mirror. Society wants an escapist art, an agreeable art. The two forces in the history of art are art as awakener of its viewers and art as tranquillizer, and there is a great and permanent struggle between these two forms of art. You can find it in the whole history of art and that is going to continue. I am against a tranquil art."

*But the market is society too. The market tends to treat both kinds of art in the same way and tends to absorb and accept the art that tranquillizes as well as the art that does not tranquillize.*

"That is true. The point is that the art that does not tranquillize has to constantly step up its provocation and stimulate discussion, while the art that is a tranquillizer must sell itself without creating a dialectic, without giving explanations. These are the two types of art: the topical art of rebellion which is dialectical and art which is tranquil, and therefore not dialectical."

*Yes, but on the market there is no difference.*

"The market wants to separate the two ways of being as you've already said."

*The market equates the two arts, makes them the same.*

"Currently the market is the same, but the market's desire is to separate. It is unable to do it, but it still wants to separate them. It is the same thing in a gallery: artists who create a dialectical art are separated from artists who just create a product."

*They are separate but the market functions the same way. Your work and that of Kienholz are accepted, but Buren and Kosuth's work is also absorbed.*

"My art is much more difficult, much slower, because you can't put a bus in a room. There are not yet any museums that collect environments. I can show the bus in Berlin, at Bochum, perhaps at the exhibition in Paris, but afterwards, in today's world, there is no way of preserving this piece."

*Then this art is an attempt to seize the bull by the horns, but it is not an elimination of the market.*

"No, no, not at all."

*I think that is how it should be, that the market is not completely negative, because the market, in some way, in its negativity gives a vitality to art, gives the artist the possibility to go on working.*

"You are right. I too – if you carry out an analysis – take part in a lot of market things, but if you like, I have won the battle. My art of rebellion, of inferiority, is taken to have a value. It is magnificent that you can make money with inferiority, the beauty of inferiority."

*Yes, but the market tends to turn values of quality, ideological values, into values of quantity.*

"But I am an artist who can only do two big Happenings a year, perhaps two large-scale environments. I can't do much more. My works are rare and the effect is that they are expensive. A gallery can never make a profit out of me, because I can't do many Happenings, I can't make many environments. So, there is a great difference in comparison with Kosuth and Buren, who produce thousands of pieces. It's quite another thing for me, I never work with repetition. Neither does Kienholz. Other artists repeat their ideas. Some of them have a very easy life, because they believe that quantity is important. Myself, I don't believe it."

*So your work is also founded on the uniqueness of the gesture, on the unrepeatability of the gesture.*

"Yes, this is very important. If you make a gesture, if for example, you touch someone, you know that at this moment there is a vast number of people in the world who are making the same gesture. We can say that this gesture is naturally multiplied. But there is an original qualitative gesture that is different each time, so it is a multiplication in the difference of individual gestures. I am filled with admiration for inferior things. For many people that means nothing but this multiplication of the original gestures is a very great thing."

*To conclude our conversation we could say that paradoxically your work on violence is also an attempt to reduce the distance from the world and to allow people to touch each other in a unique and personal way.*

"Yes, I believe that it is possible to overcome violence. When people take each other seriously, each carries out a self-analysis, each begins to discover himself. This discovery is a great act of love, perhaps the greatest love that two people can have. When you discover yourself there is no more violence between people for you no longer hide your problems from the other person. So if everyone tells the truth there is no more violence."

*So for you art is a laying bare?*

"Yes, a return to nakedness in order to start again, a reduction…"

*But a reduction that cannot fail to take account of history, because history has created a depth around human beings.*

"No, not a return to the past, but a return to the foundations, to the fundamental structure of creation. Then, if you like, the Happening is creation."

*So we could say in the end that art is a sort of, a kind of contagion, a transmission. We could say that art is a contagion of creativity, a transmission of psycho-aesthetic energy.*

"Art is a radio station, it is transmission by radio, it is broadcasting."

*So just as in Fluxus, art is acoustics.*

"It is life, it is acoustics, Fluxus is life and acoustics."

# Jan Dibbets
Weert, The Netherlands, 1941

Amsterdam
1975

*What relationship is there between your research and the Dutch tra-
dition of painting?*

"We already talked about this. I think when you're an artist
you are actually addressed to the art of your time. Regarding the
past I am specially interested in certain Dutch landscape art from
the seventeenth century, like Vermeer and his contemporaries. I
think they had a very clear feeling for what painting was. Since
I'm not a painter I am not directly involved. I try to make something similar to what they did with painting. I try to."

*What specific connection can be made between your work and
Vermeer's painting?*

"You are saying that I think very high of myself, but I don't
want to raise this question. I don't want to be compared to Vermeer. Maybe other people do."

*So visual perfection becomes the only goal that painting can
pursue, and thus your research too.*

"I am very much impressed of what those artists did. It's not
only optical, what's important is that they understood that seeing
goes parallel to the activity of the mind. This is something which
is very difficult to express. It's a typical problem for art, which is
well understood by artists but not literally expressed. I make it
clear in my work. It's not only a problem of giving visibility, it's
the main concern of art."

*And thus the investigation of reality. Your work is a twofold
investigation: a research on the specific means that the artist employs and another on the limits of the artistic operation, is it not?*

"I have not as high ideas of art as many people do. I think
art is not as important as many make it. I admire artists very much,
but every person, every human being is equally important to me.
Insofar I don't see the double investigation. I think art is limited,
art is an invisible situation, it's the creative part of what we see. I
think we are now in a situation of living painting, whereas in historical periods the question at stake was perfection. Anyhow, we
feel that we can do what we want, art is not a limited thing."

*It seems to me that in your work there is a continual need to represent space and represent time – time as progression and space as frontality.*

"I think time is not too much a problem of my art. I think I bring together many elements which will always be accepted as splits, as things that are not together. But I think this was done already in the seventeenth century and by the Renaissance Roman painters."

*You have created works using slide photography. The slide has a technological and a physiological trigger at one and the same time, in the sense that technological time corresponds to real time and so the temporal dimension is incorporated into the work, as for example in the one presented at the Venice Biennale.*

"I keep saying that art is a visible fact, time for me is only necessary to create something visual. So, I keep refusing to accept that time should be part of my work. I use time as I use objects as reality. From the moment I see something, I use time and I use the facts. Time is neither in your mind nor in my mind. When the world is dead, time is gone."

*In your work the use of photography, in my view, is part of the awareness that the object in the photograph is not the object itself, and therefore that the image is part of a language that is not reality.*

"Absolutely. Art has nothing to do with reality, it's a shift from what I see."

*What relationship is there between your works created with slides and your interventions of land art?*

"I think land art is just something different from painting or sculpture. The work I am doing now in my opinion goes much further, it's something different. For the work which is neither painting nor sculpture, I need the land, but this land disappears in the end result. To be more clear, it never existed as a category, it's just there. What I try to say is that the land for my work is not important, I feel it too closed to sculpture. I always had in mind this idea of painting without doing a painting. I actually know that I will never be a good painter. I'm not able to make a painting, what I do is only a thinking process and this thinking process is connected to the fact that you also want to see, to realize. My work is just a question of organization: to find a more or less good photographer, to find somebody to do the prints, somebody to gloom the pictures on aluminium, and so on. This way of doing is absolutely open and, until now, not used by anybody else. I think that art is connected to the ideas about art. Art is something you can see, but the media artists use to express themselves change, even if art has existed for thousands of years and, in a way, never changed. The philosophy is still the same, but the way or the media you choose to express yourself change. This changes are the visible fact. I think it is very relieving for an artist to know that many of his colleagues left old media behind, left traditional painting and sculpture. In the work created by new media, it is the medium itself that becomes a message. Many paintings of former centuries are so bold because there is a feeling of something more than just the painting by itself. You feel in these works an effort to go over painting, to show more than a painted subject, something over painting and over time. You can't do art without using a medium, it is like a body without blood. To make it more clear, you can be far from reality, abstract. Abstract philosophy, abstract painting. Abstract. Artists like Vermeer or Ingres, or, even more, David could have never made abstract paintings because their philosophy was not abstract. Only in the twentieth century this problem was solved."

*The photographic medium does not coincide in your work with the representation of the method, and so even the type of sensibility employed is a chilled sensibility.*

"This has always been typical of photographers. But it also depends on what you do with photographs. I mean, when you have photographs you still have a million of ways to put them together; the choice of how to assemble our material is similar to the way a painter uses colours. You have a pencil, you have a canvas, you have colours: but it's never the same, it's always different. I know what you mean but I refuse to believe it, it's too easy, I don't believe it. First of all, the photograph itself is already conditioned by your choices: where you are going, what you want to photograph, why you want to photograph. When the photograph is done, again another choice: what will I do with it. Can a photograph change the world or does it simply showcase itself? There's much more behind a photograph than just documentation. My work is never concerned by documentation."

*It seems to me that the use of the slide, of the transparency, which is repeated, even if the image inside is modified, is also an attempt to represent the mechanical eye in your work. Repetition and modification capture two important moments and two values.*

"There might be a misunderstanding. You know, I use film to make photographs but I never use it as a film, as an end in itself. I take it to the laboratory and they print photographs for me of every part of the film. Then I throw the film away and use the photographs."

*The use of photography is a way of cutting reality down to size. Then you work on dissecting it, on redoubling the reduction. Is this a way of working on the microcosm in order to refer to a vaster reality, that is to the macrocosm? A relation of referentiality through the sign and the object that represents the sign, or not?*

"Yes, it's certainly true. For me the relation is how the film uses things. The little thing that you call microcosm is not the photograph itself but the movements of the camera, an horizontal and a vertical movement. My work is generated by the turning of the camera, which is both the beginning of the whole process and its result."

*A medium only represents itself. A medium also creates a new type of sensibility for the artist. So to what extent does your work also have an anthropological value?*

"When all you can do is an entirely white or black painting, well, it is time for you to find a new medium. I use land art, film, photography, all different languages that put me into different situations. That's typical of what happens in art at this moment."

*Your references to the art of the past are right, in my view, on the level of linguistic references, but I also think that they result in a deviation with respect to what might be the function of art today. Don't you think that the function of art has changed with respect to the art of which we have spoken up to now, the art of the past?*

"I still do believe that not art, but art's function can change in time. This has nothing to do with the fact that I respect the art of the past, you can respect the drawings made 100,000 years before Christ, respect Egyptians, respect the Greeks. Today they still have the power to explain what art should be, and it's good art; and they are still there, they have not disappeared. So far, even when the social situations change, art doesn't change that much. Between Mondrian and Greek sculpture there are many differences but they also share a lot. The task of the artist inside society is to create something unchangeable. Mondrian was a product of his time as the Greek sculptors were a product of their time – but, again, they have many things in common. I could be very good at remaking a Greek painting today – but that would not be true, it would be an impossible painting. I don't think the function of art has changed that much, it's just a matter of time. It is a really impossible question, a question without an answer. It's the question of what art is; and, as we know, it is still an unsolved issue. As far as I understand, you think that art changes because it's out of function in the modern times. I can only reply that in my opinion the final solution would be that nobody makes art anymore. But as long as artists exist…"

*Your work can be defined as an investigation of the photographic method in a painterly key.*

"Let's say I try to deal with some – not many – problems of what's visible."

Douglas Huebler
*Crocodile Tears:*
*The Great Corrector*
*(Mondrian III)*, 1990
Painting: acrylic on canvas,
46 × 46 cm
Panel (photo and text):
51 × 97 cm
Courtesy Lia Rumma

Sol LeWitt
Drawings in Indian ink
on wall. Wall drawing
created on the occasion
of the exhibition at the
Galleria Alessandra Bonomo
in Rome, February 2003
Courtesy Galleria
Alessandra Bonomo, Rome

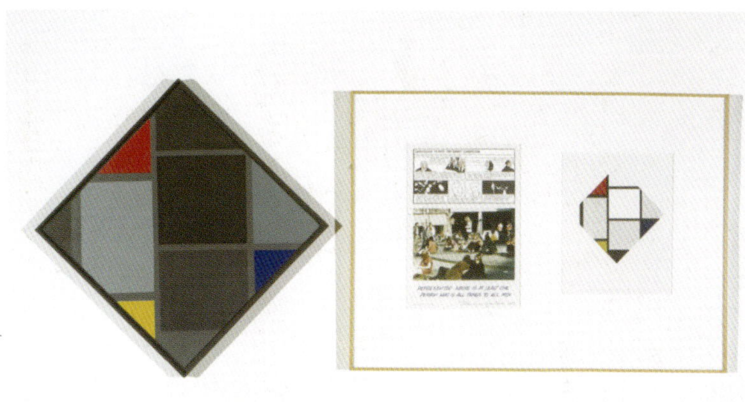

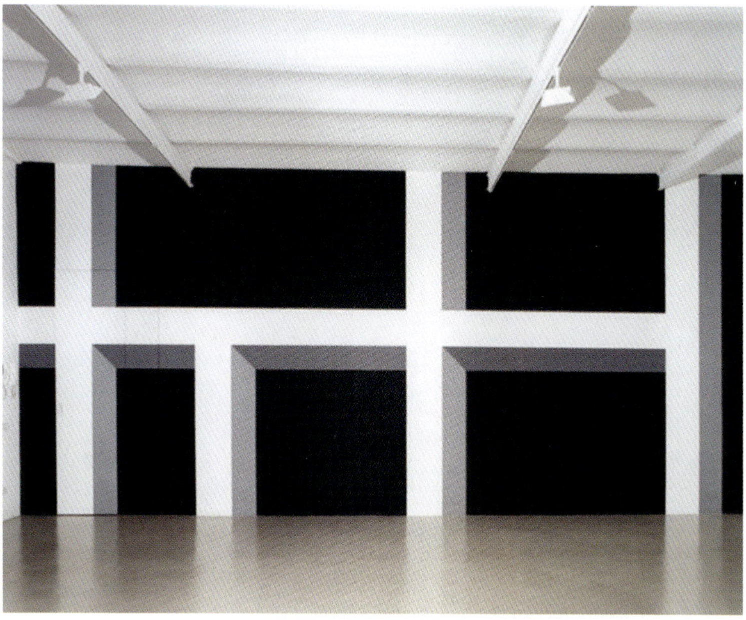

Robert Smithson
*Asphalt Rundown*, 1969
Gelatin silver print,
150 × 120 cm
Courtesy Estate of Robert
Smithson – James Cohan
Gallery

Vito Acconci
*Untitled*, 1972
Gelatin silver print,
150 × 120 cm
Courtesy Vito Acconci

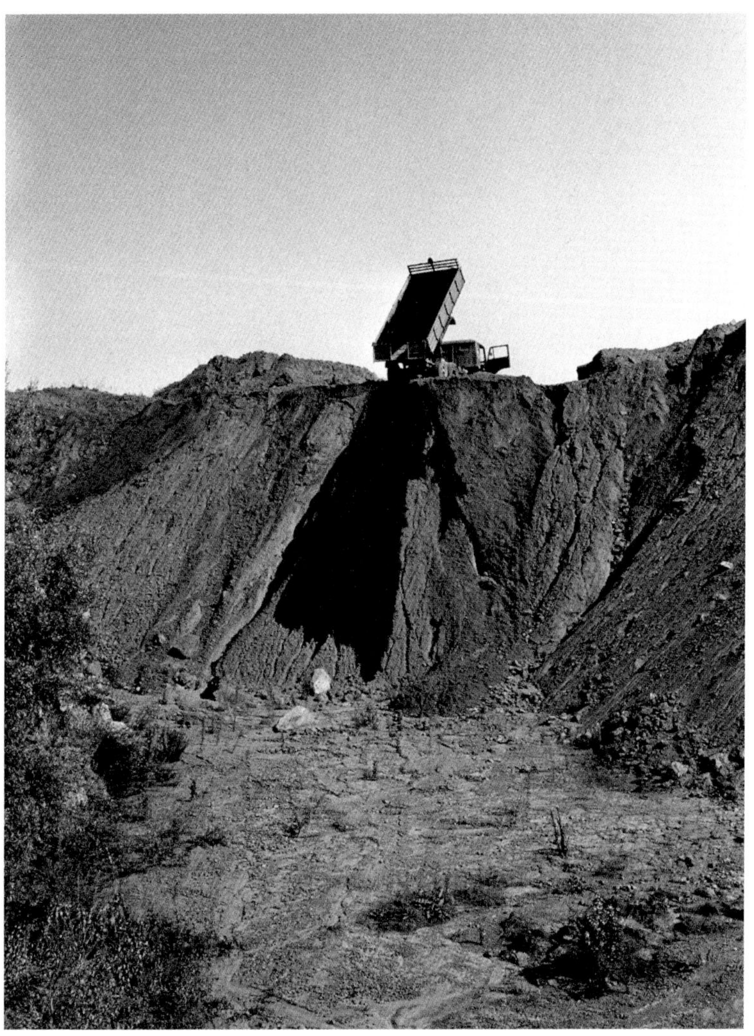

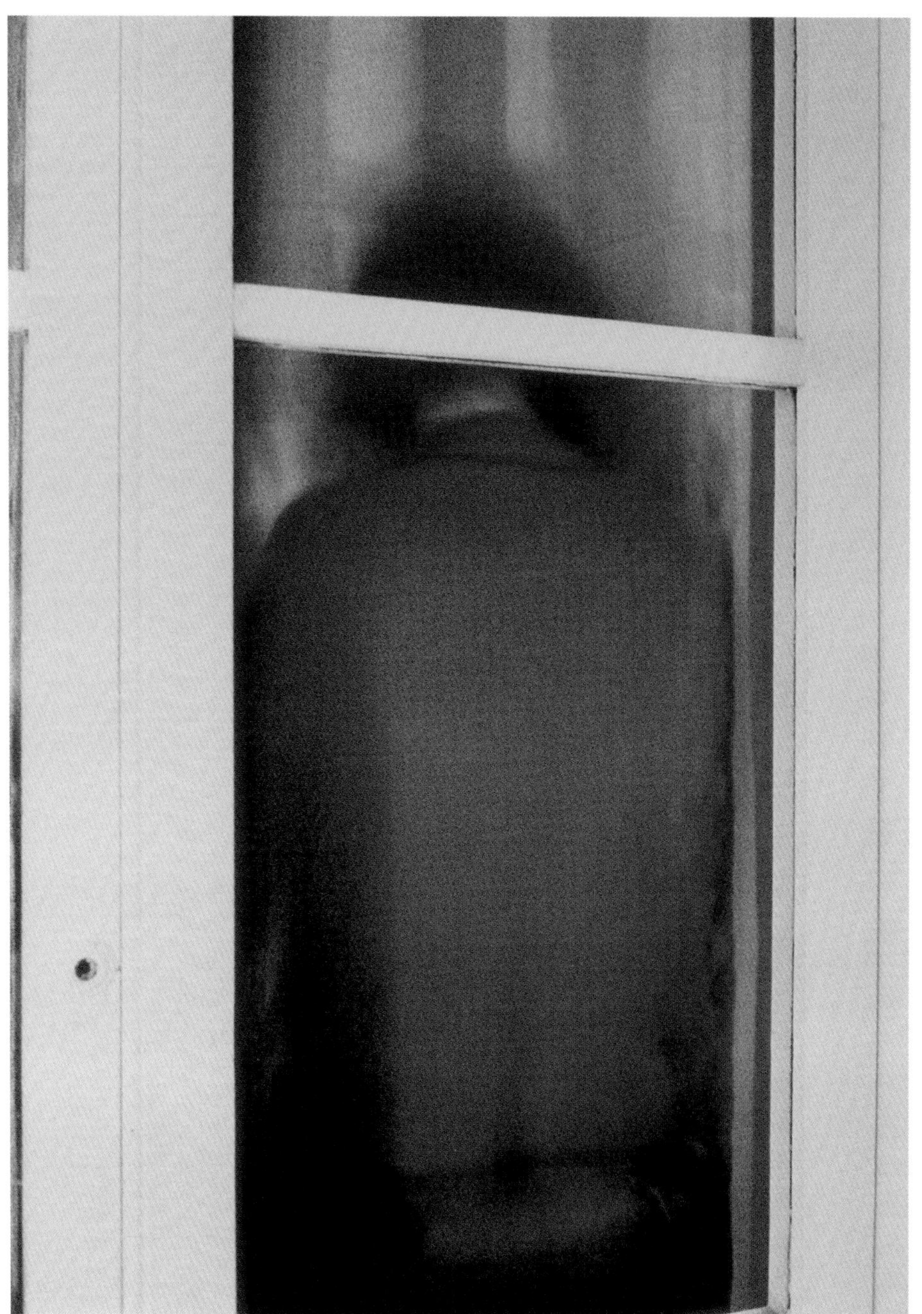

III

Joseph Beuys
*Earthquake in the Palace*, 1981
Four wooden boards,
terracotta vases, glass vases,
beeswax, an egg,
variable dimensions
Galleria Lucio Amelio
Courtesy Fondazione
Lucio Amelio

Joseph Kosuth
*Essay #13*, 1999
Photograph mounted
on aluminium, 120 × 210 cm
Courtesy Lia Rumma

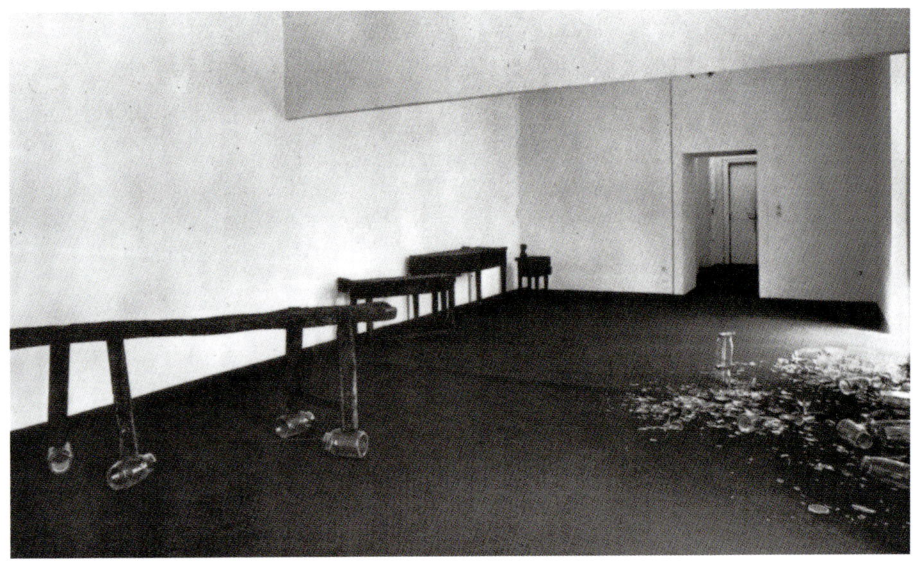

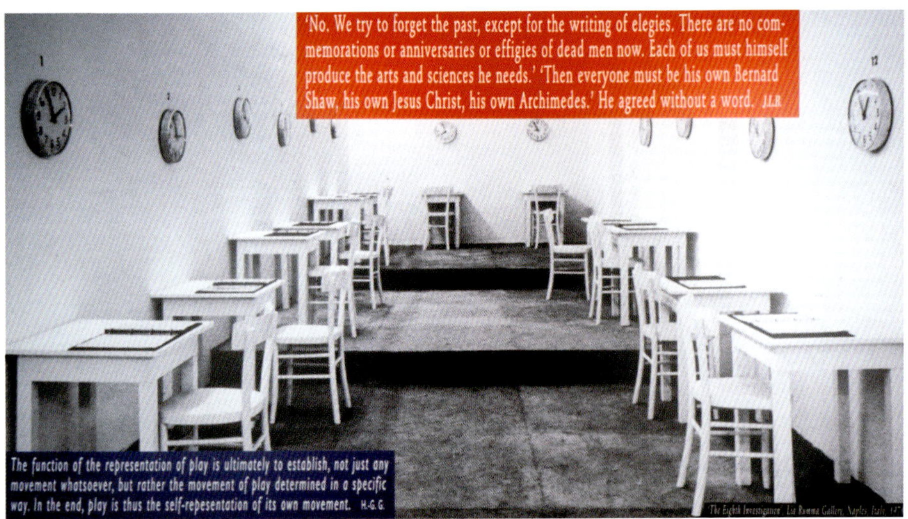

Giulio Paolini
*In ascolto (stanza
dello spettatore)*, 2005
Frames, Plexiglas,
pencil and collage on wall,
variable dimensions
Private collection
Courtesy Galleria
Alfonso Artiaco, Naples

Lawrence Weiner
*As if wrapped in cotton*
*As if sheathed in cork*
*As if buried in foam*, 2006
Language and reference
materials, variable dimensions
Private collection
Courtesy Galleria Alfonso
Artiaco, Naples

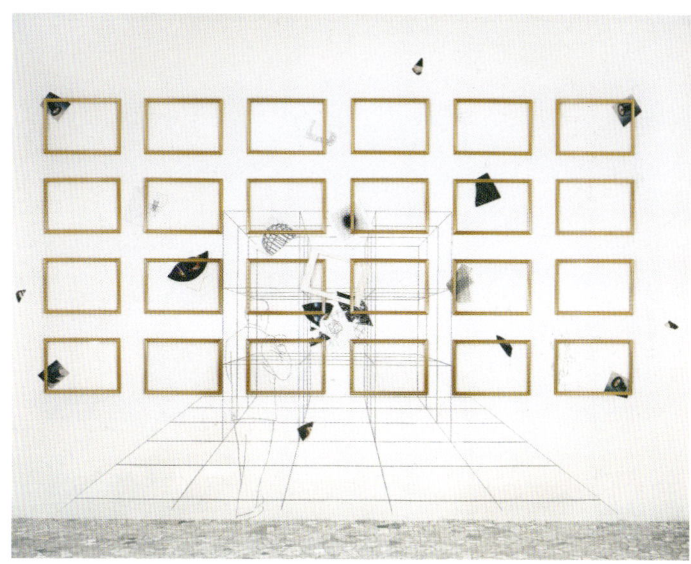

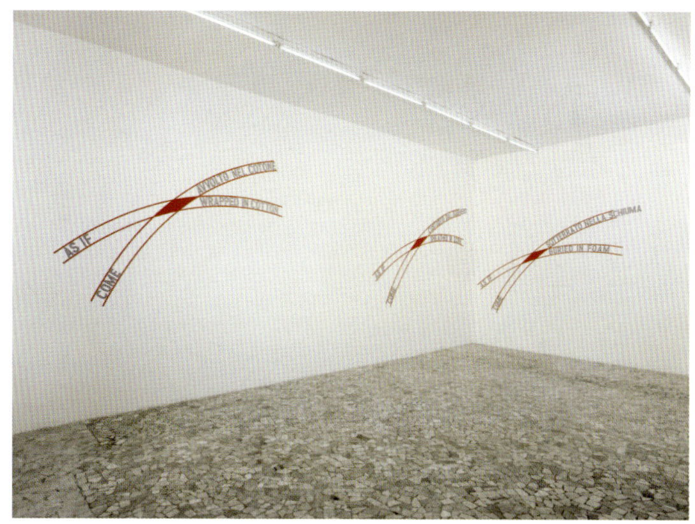

Ian Wilson interviewed
by Achille Bonito Oliva
at the Galleria Marilena
Bonomo, Bari, 1972
Courtesy Galleria Bonomo,
Bari

Carl Andre
*Aluminum Sum 21*, 2006
Aluminum
View of the installation at the PAN
(Palazzo delle Arti Napoli), Naples,
16 December 2006 – 17 March 2007
Dedication: "1986-2006: vent'anni
della Galleria Alfonso Artiaco".
Courtesy Galleria Alfonso
Artiaco, Naples

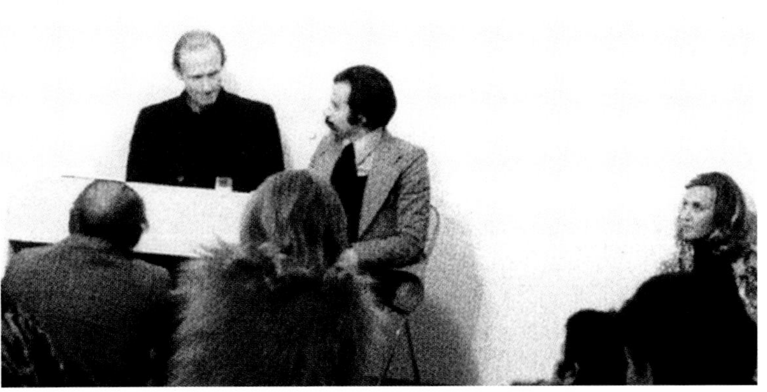

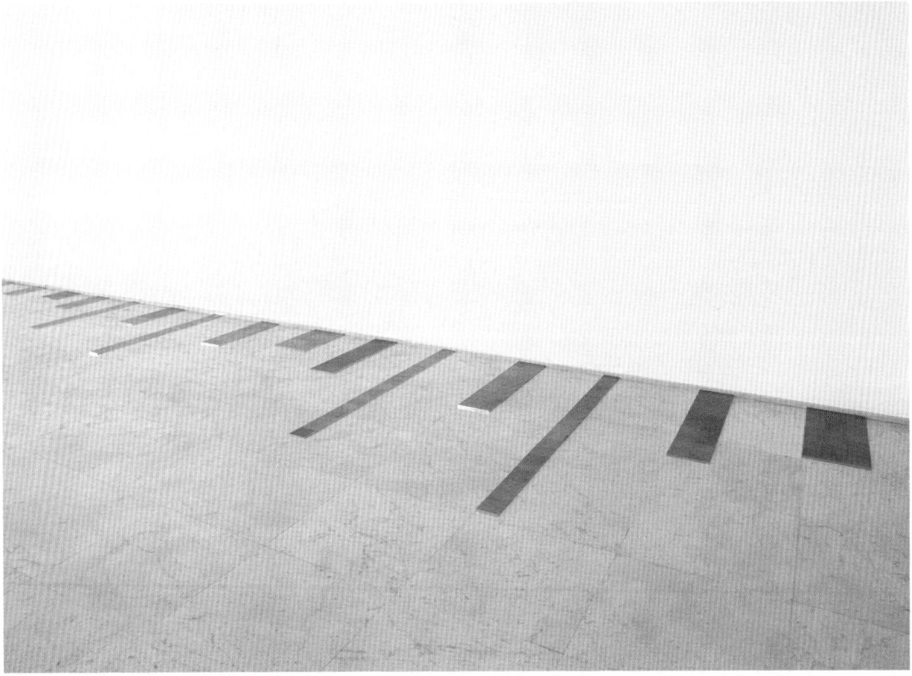

Robert Morris
*Untitled (Felt)*, 1980
Felt hung on wall,
152.4 × 122.3 cm
New York, Sonnabend
Gallery

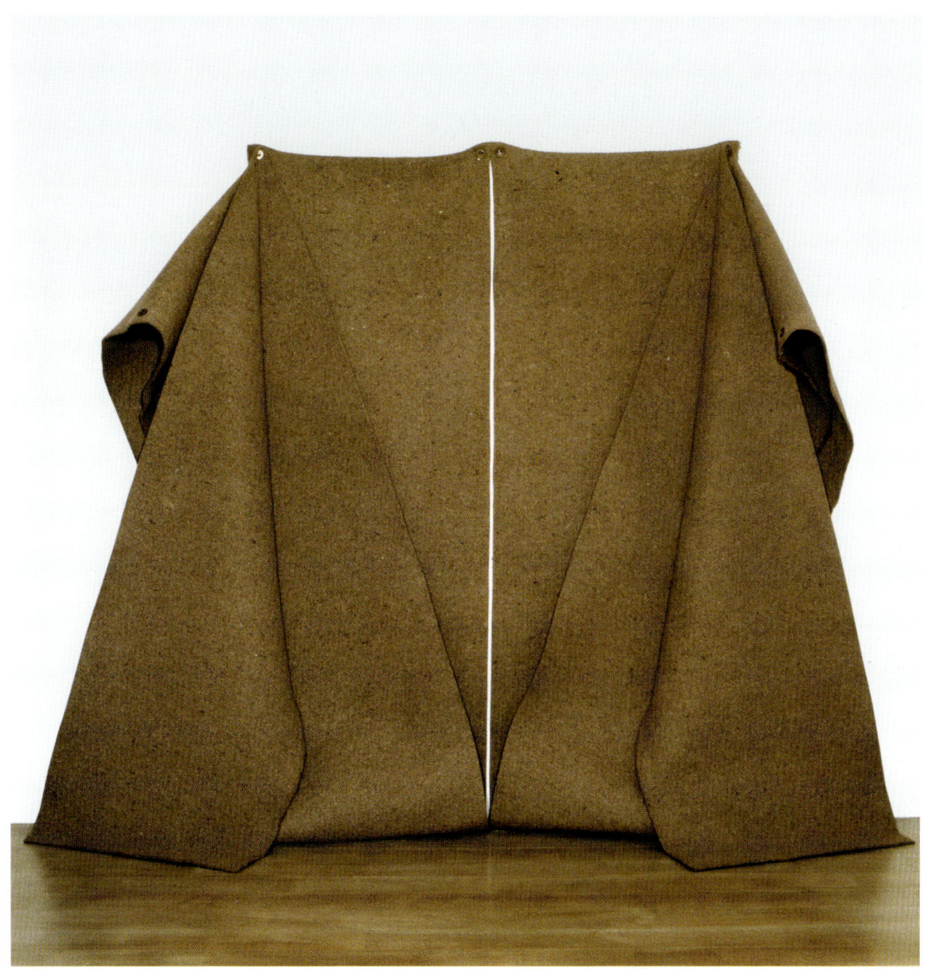

Vettor Pisani
*Camera dell'Eroe
(Venere di cioccolato)*, 1970
Installation with
chocolate-covered cast
Courtesy Cardelli
& Fontana, Sarzana

Robert Barry
*Golden Words*, 2006
Gold-coloured paint
on white wall
View of the installation
at the PAN (Palazzo
delle Arti Napoli), Naples,
16 December 2006 –
17 March 2007

Dedication: "1986-2006:
vent'anni della Galleria
Alfonso Artiaco"
Courtesy Galleria Alfonso
Artiaco, Naples

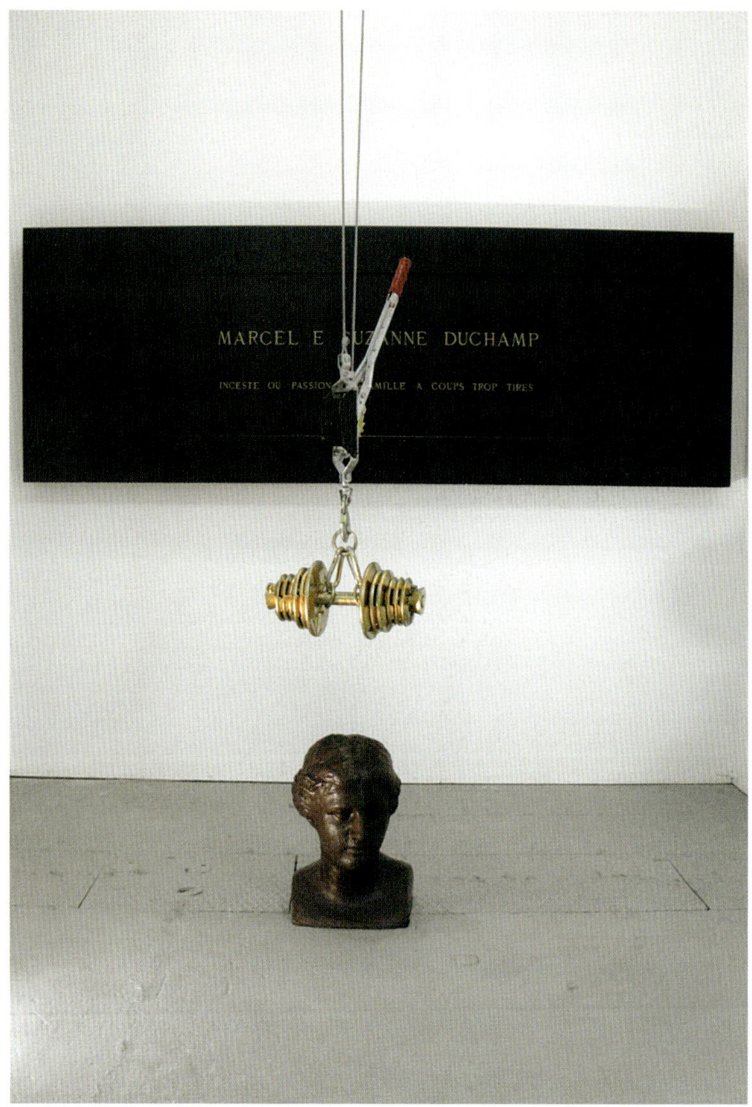

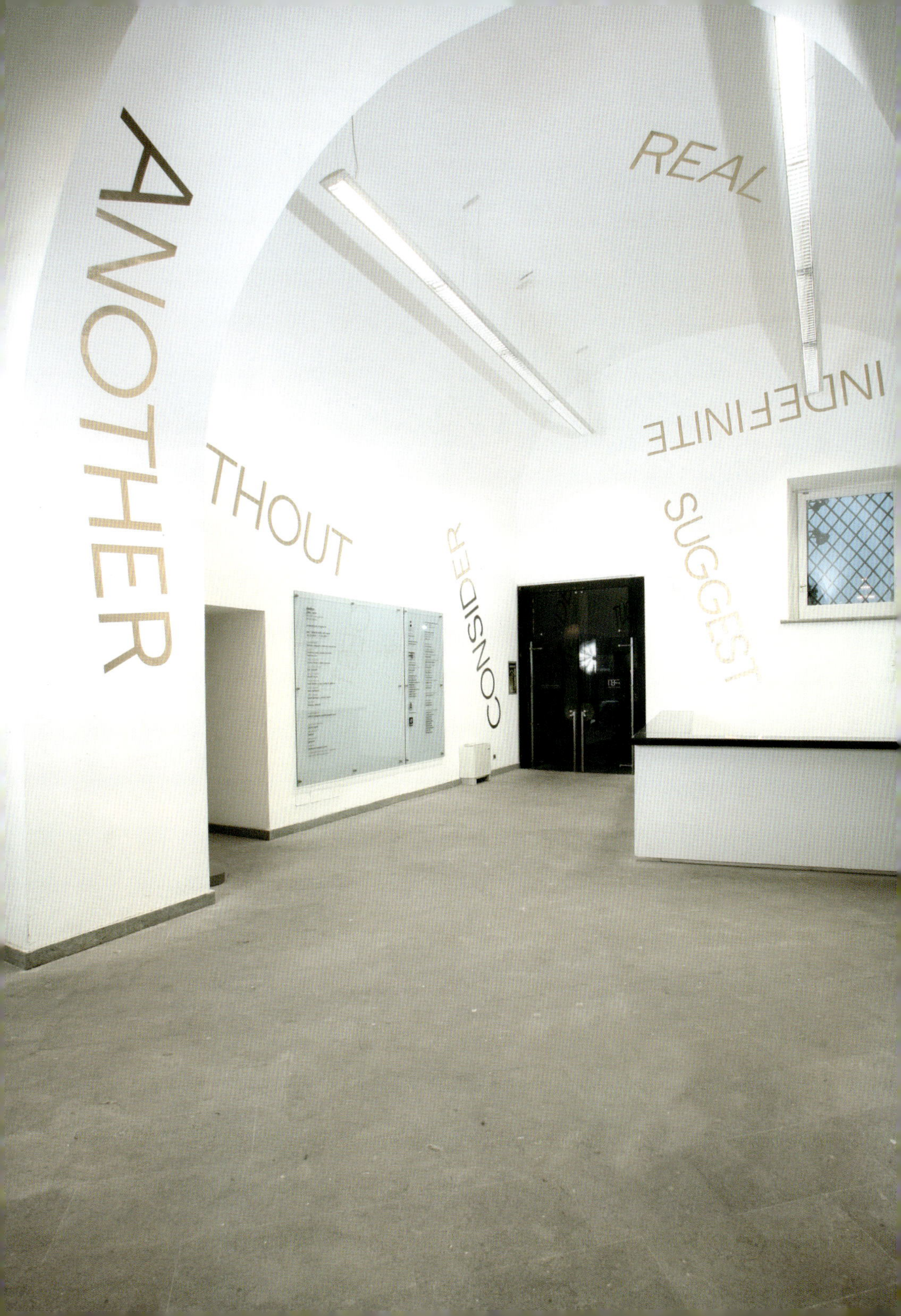

ANOTHER

REAL

INDEFINITE

THOUT

CONSIDER

SUGGEST

Alighiero Boetti
*Tutto*, 1988
Embroidery, 107 × 263 cm
Courtesy Fondazione
Alighiero e Boetti

Terry Fox
*Untitled*, 1972
Cloth, string, fishbone
and mixed media on packing
cardboard, 39 × 52 cm
Courtesy Studio Trisorio,
Naples

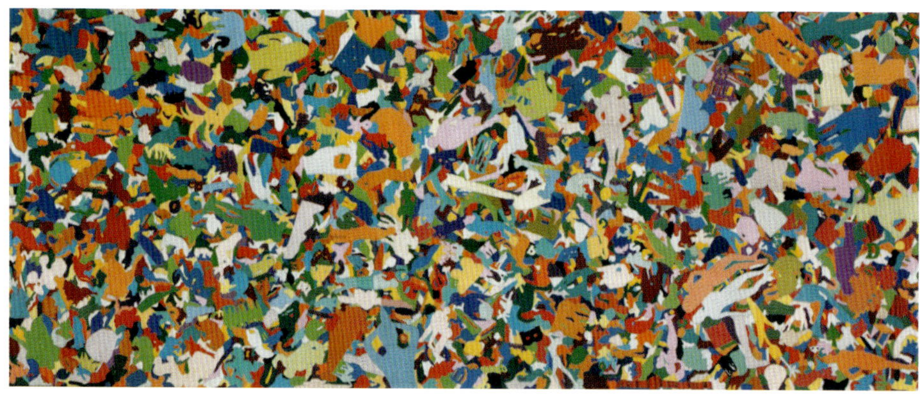

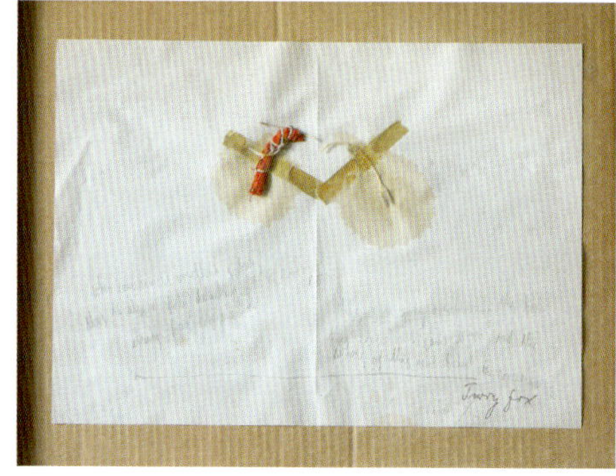

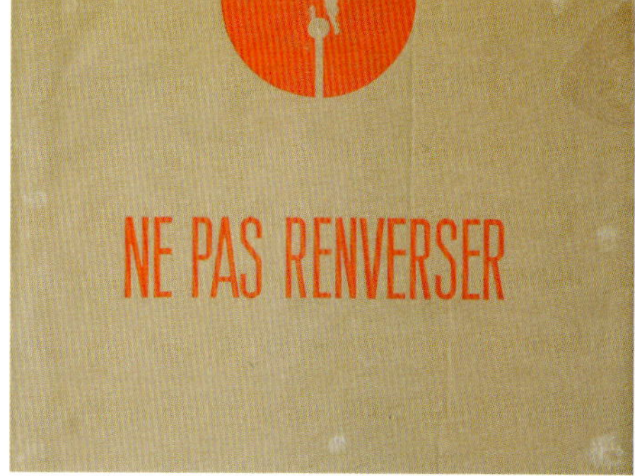

Bruce Nauman
*None Sing Neon Sign*, 1970
Neon tubing, 33 × 61 × 4 cm
Castello di Rivoli Museo
d'Arte Contemporanea,
Rivoli–Turin
(long-term loan)
Genoa, private collection
Photo by Paolo Pellion, Turin

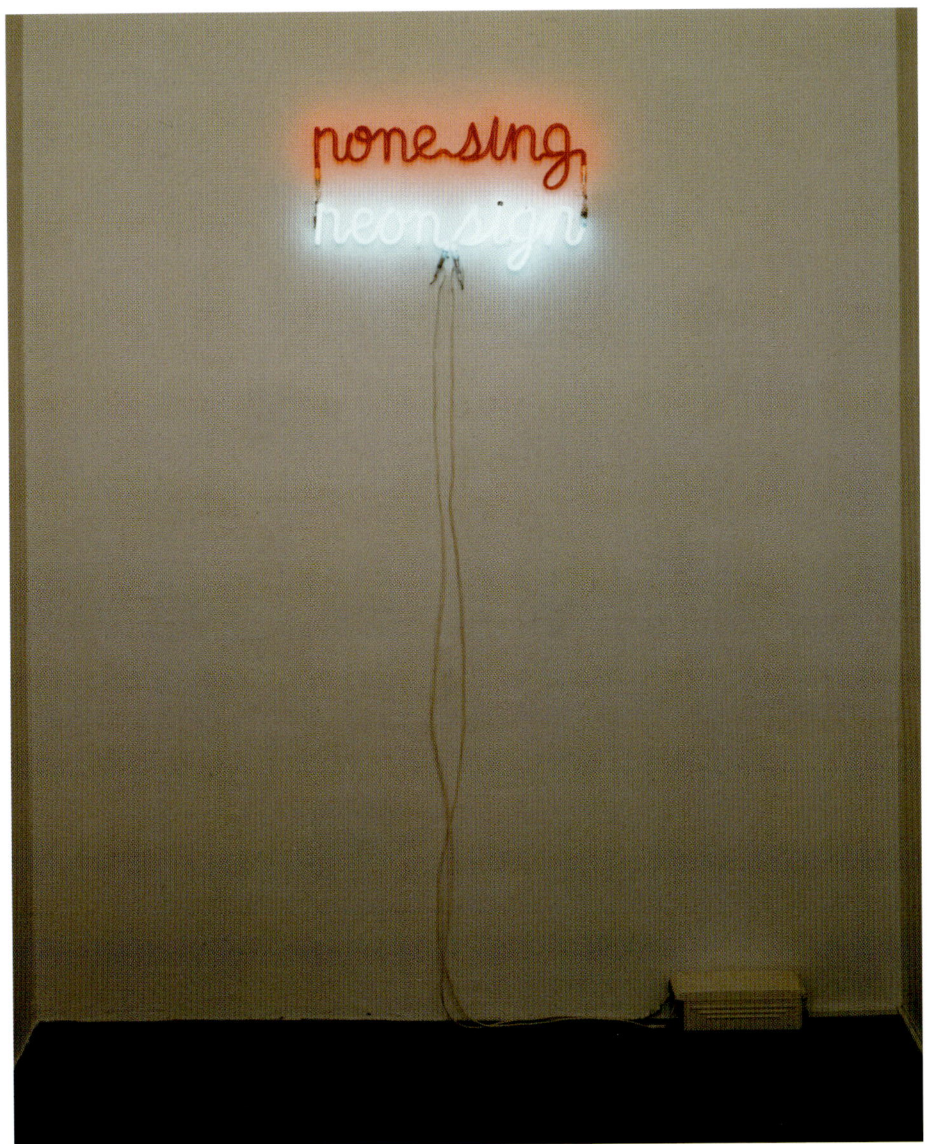

Robert Ryman
*Winsor 34*, 1966
Oil on linen canvas,
160.02 × 160.02 cm
The Greenwich
Collection Ltd.
© Robert Ryman

Ben Vautier
*Et si je me trompais*,
1975
Black letters
on white ground,
60 × 80 cm
Courtesy
Fondazione Mudima

Nam June Paik
*Beuys Paik – TV
Buddha*, 1990
Installation at the
exhibition *Le Opere
e i Giorni*, Padula
Charterhouse, 2004
Courtesy
Fondazione Mudima

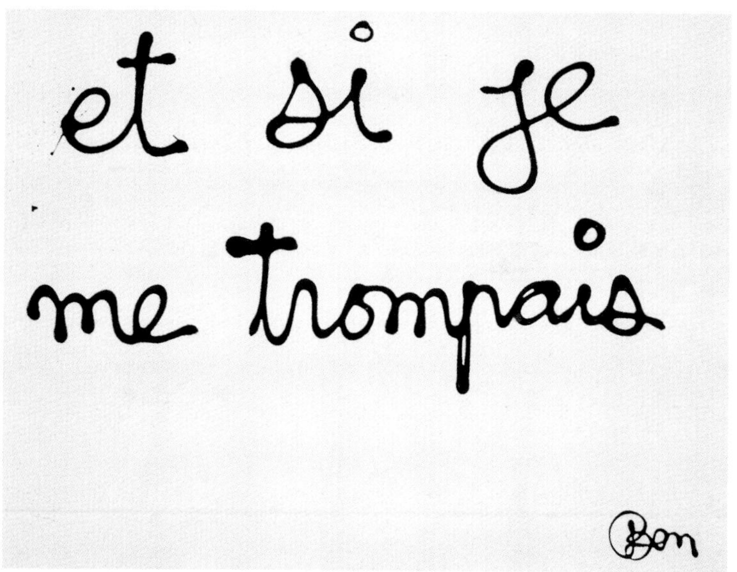

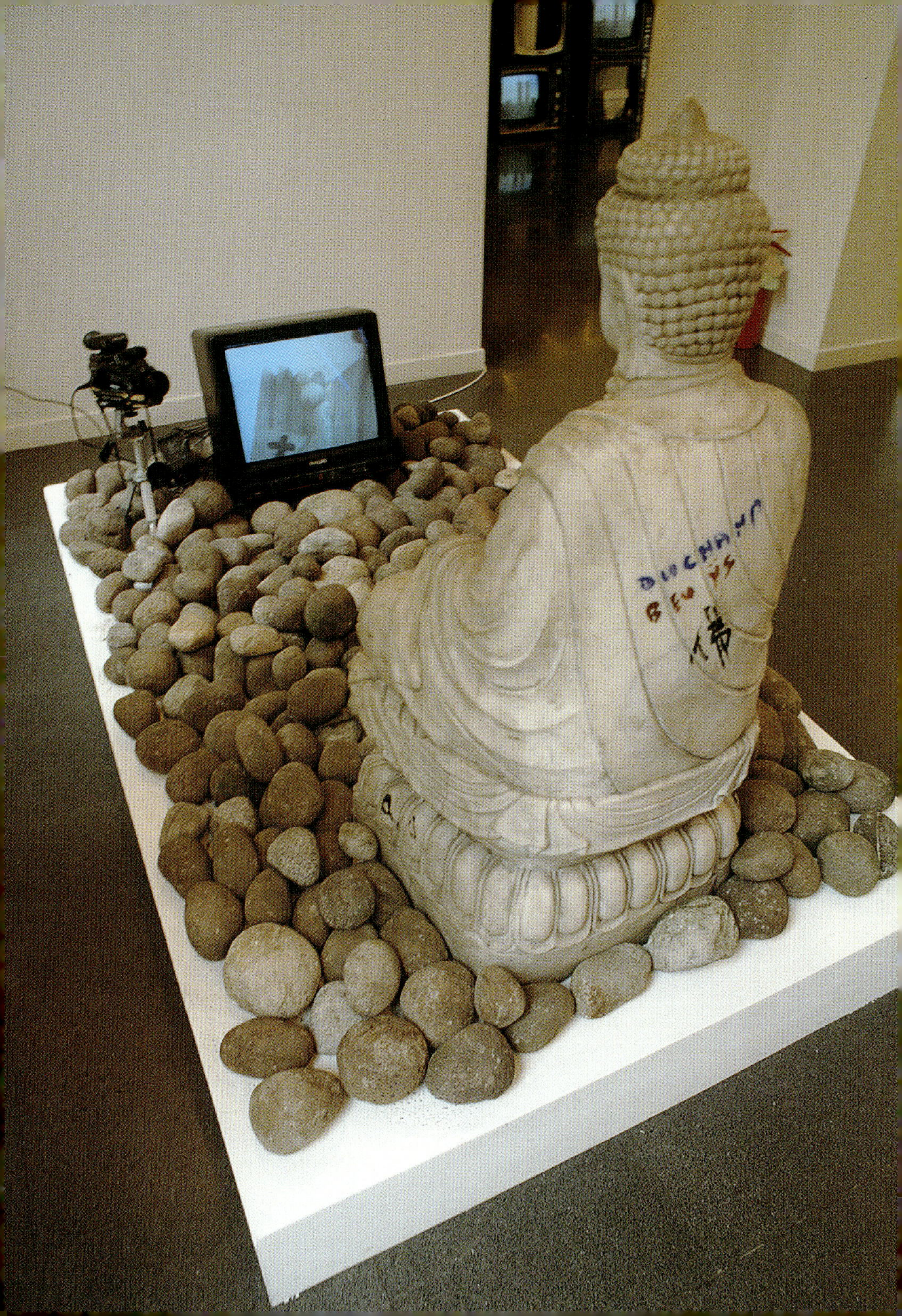

Wolf Vostell
*Fandango*, 1972
Twenty car doors with
hammers, three painted
canvases with objects,
each 130 × 180 cm
Courtesy Fondazione
Mudima

Jan Dibbets
*The Bridge of Towers*, 1980
Installation at the exhibition
*Arte nella città*
Courtesy Galleria Marilena
Bonomo, Bari

Richard Tuttle
From the *Vienna Gothic*
exhibition, 1990
Paint on balsa wood,
40 × 30 × 20 cm
Courtesy Galleria
Alessandra Bonomo, Rome

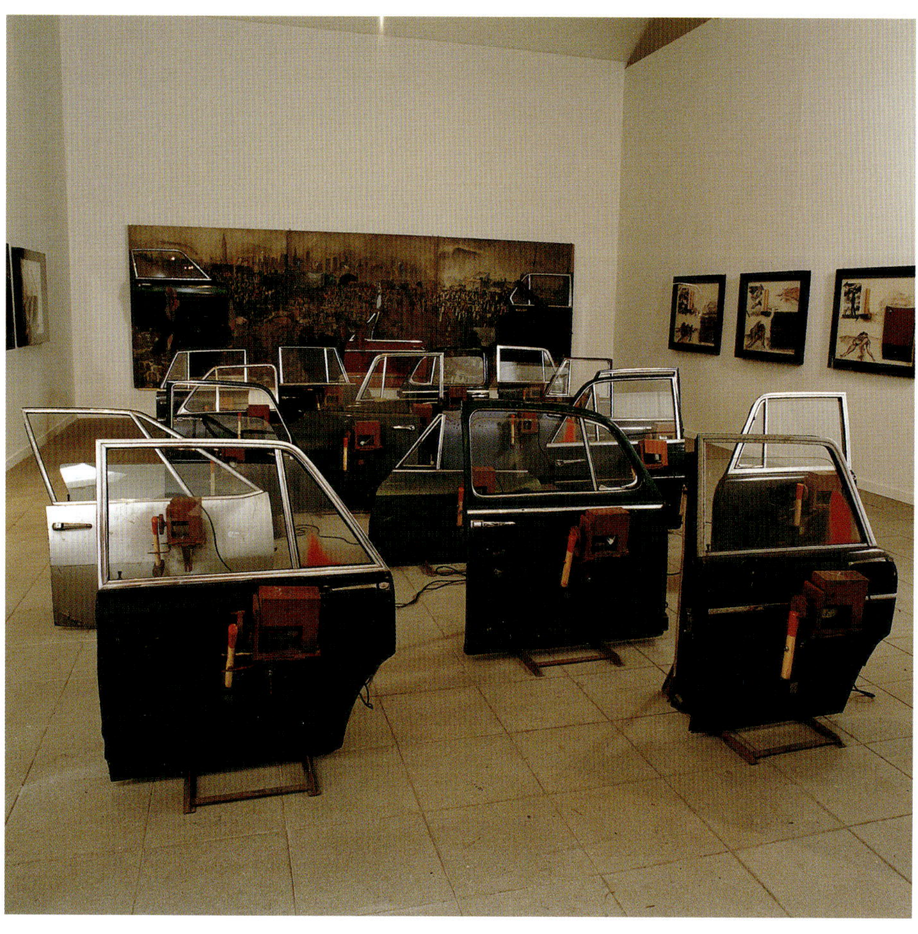

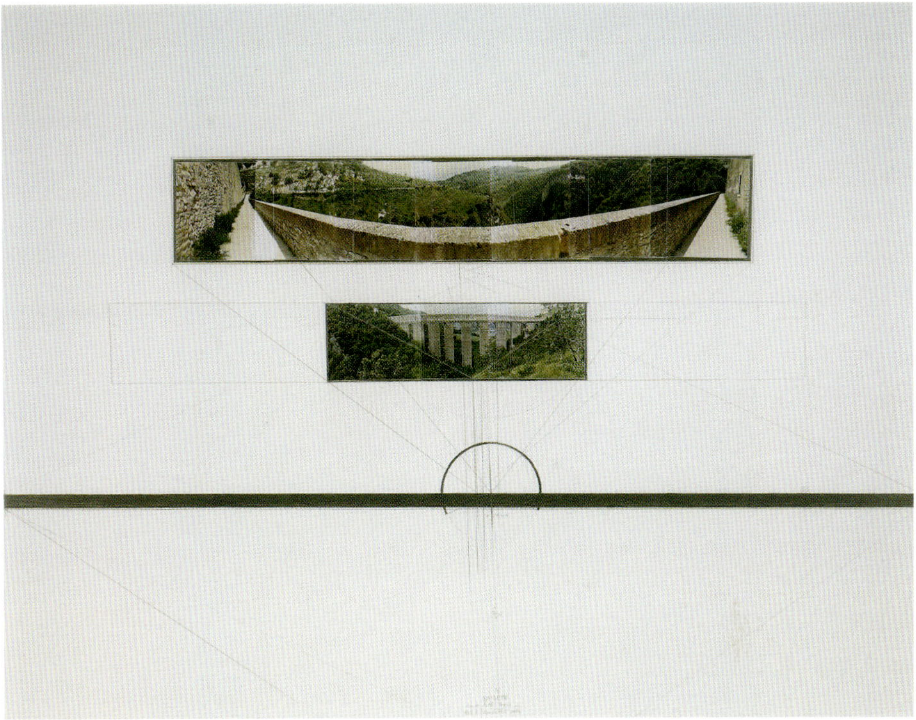

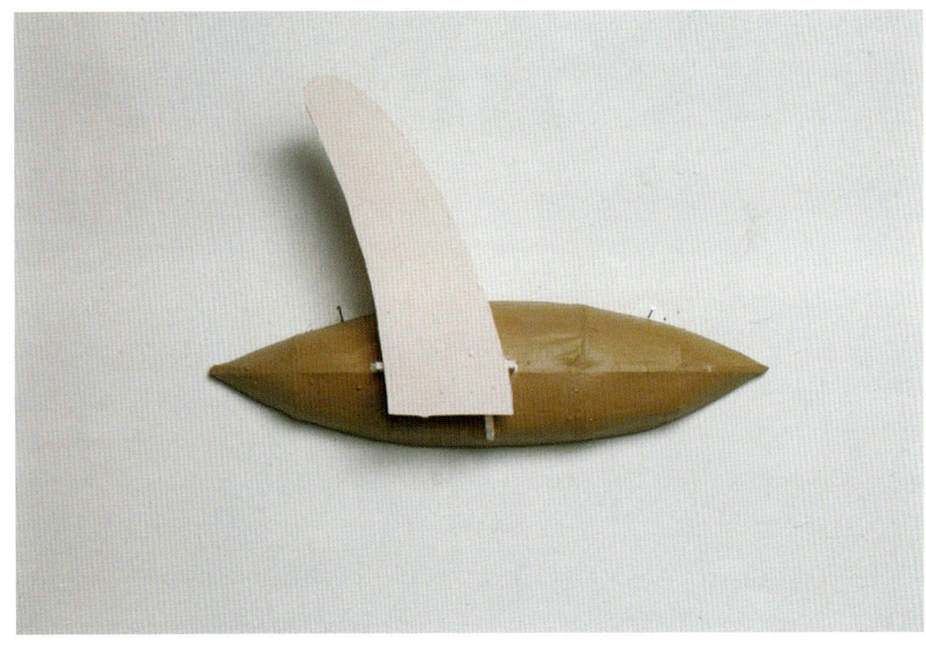

XV

Robert Watts
*Jim Dine*, 1964
Signature in
coloured neon,
50 × 130 × 20 cm
Courtesy
Fondazione
Mudima

Sandro Chia
*Ad Achille*, 1980
Oil on canvas,
120 × 90 cm

Gilbert & George
Partial view of
the exhibition
*New Testamental
Pictures*
Naples, Museo
di Capodimonte,
December 1998
Courtesy Galleria
Alfonso Artiaco,
Naples

Luciano Fabro
*The Expired*,
1968–73
Installation at the
*Contemporanea*
exhibition,
Parcheggio
di Villa Borghese,
Rome,
November 1973 –
February 1974
Courtesy Archivio
Incontri
Internazionali
d'Arte
Photo by Massimo
Piersanti

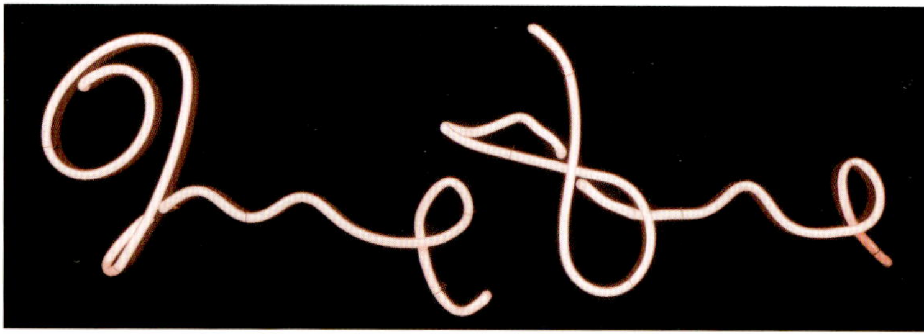

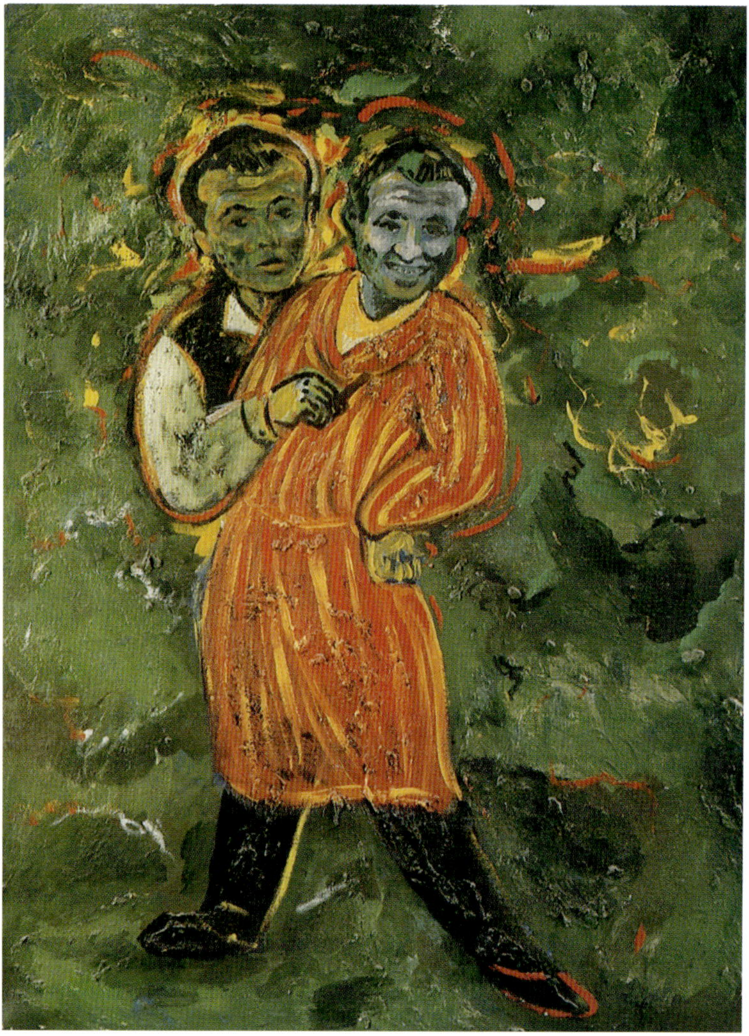

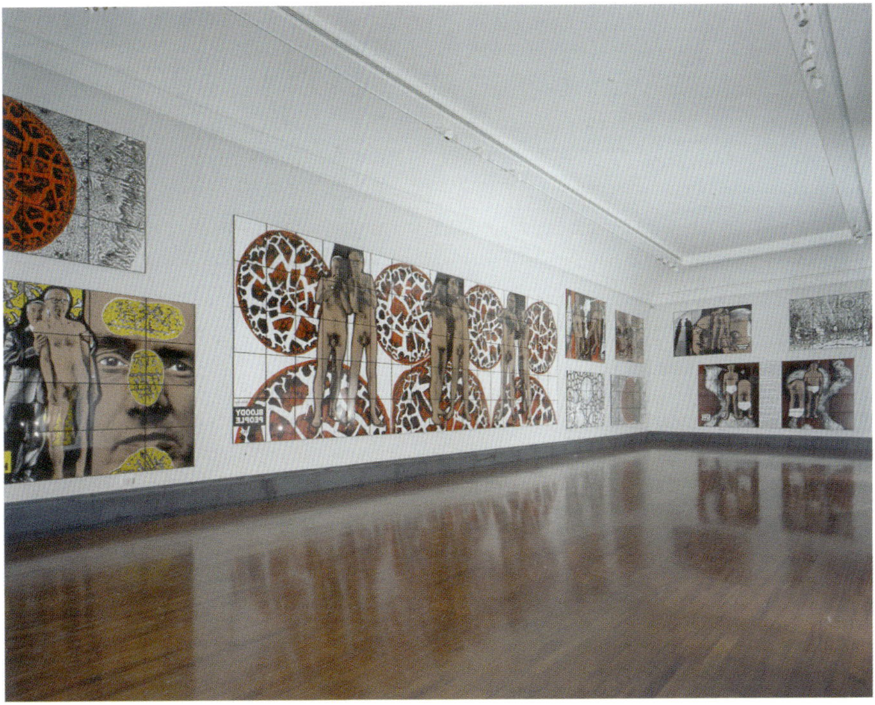

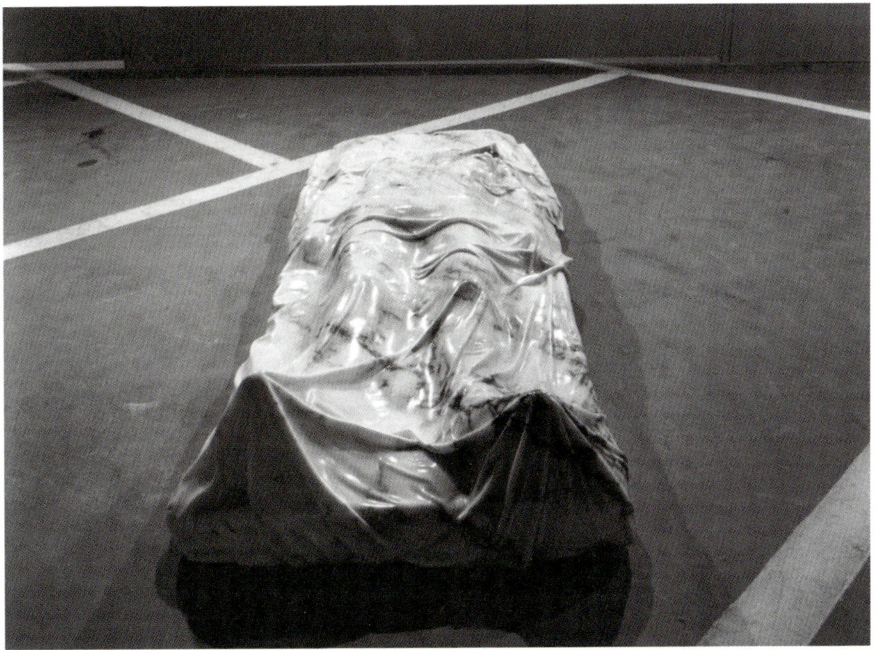

XVII

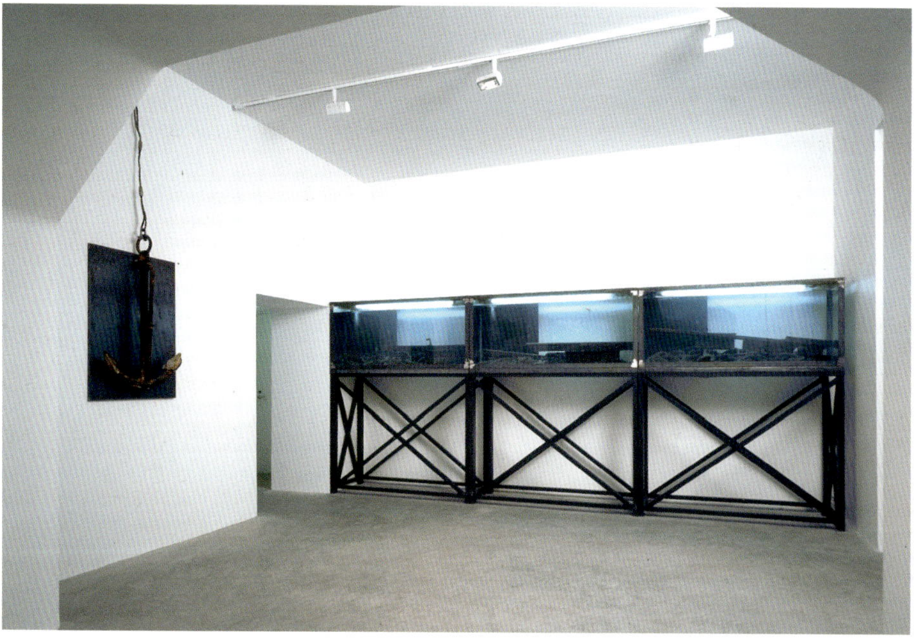

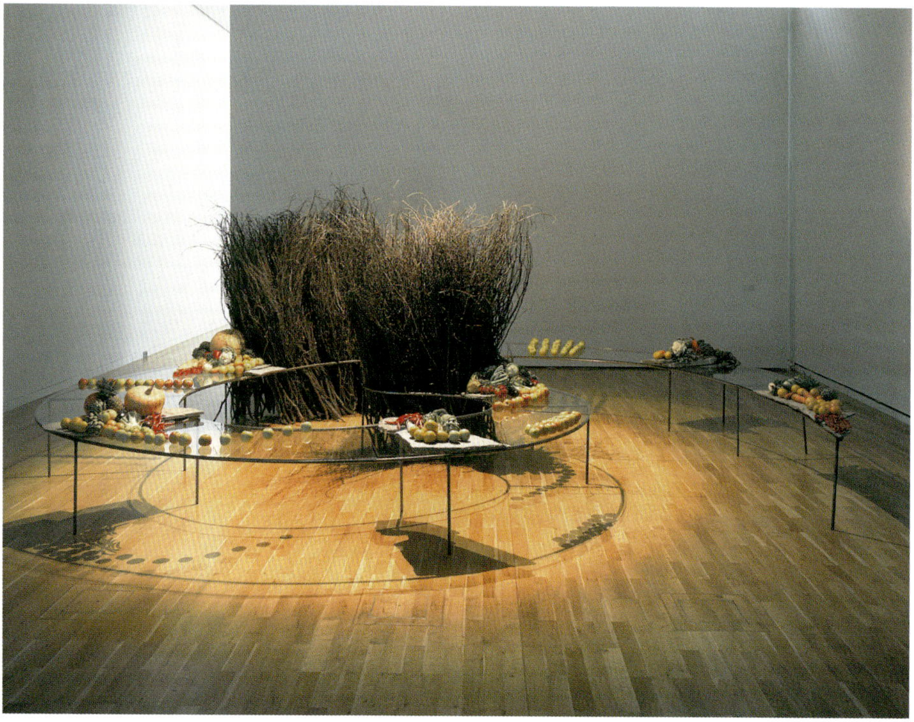

XVIII

Jannis Kounellis
Installation, November 1997
Courtesy Galleria Alfonso
Artiaco, Naples

Mario Merz
*Spiral Table for Party
of Newspapers Dated the Day
of the Party*, 1976
Circular structure in metal,
glass, stone, bundles of sticks,
fruit, diam. 630 cm
Collection Kunstmuseum
Wolfsburg
Courtesy Archivio Merz, Turin
Photo by Helge Mundt,
Wolfsburg

Niele Toroni
Partial view of the *Vedi
Napoli e poi…* exhibition
Imprints of a no. 50
paintbrush repeated at
regular intervals of 30 cm,
enamel on canvas
PAN (Palazzo delle Arti
Napoli), Naples, March 2004
Courtesy Galleria Alfonso
Artiaco, Naples

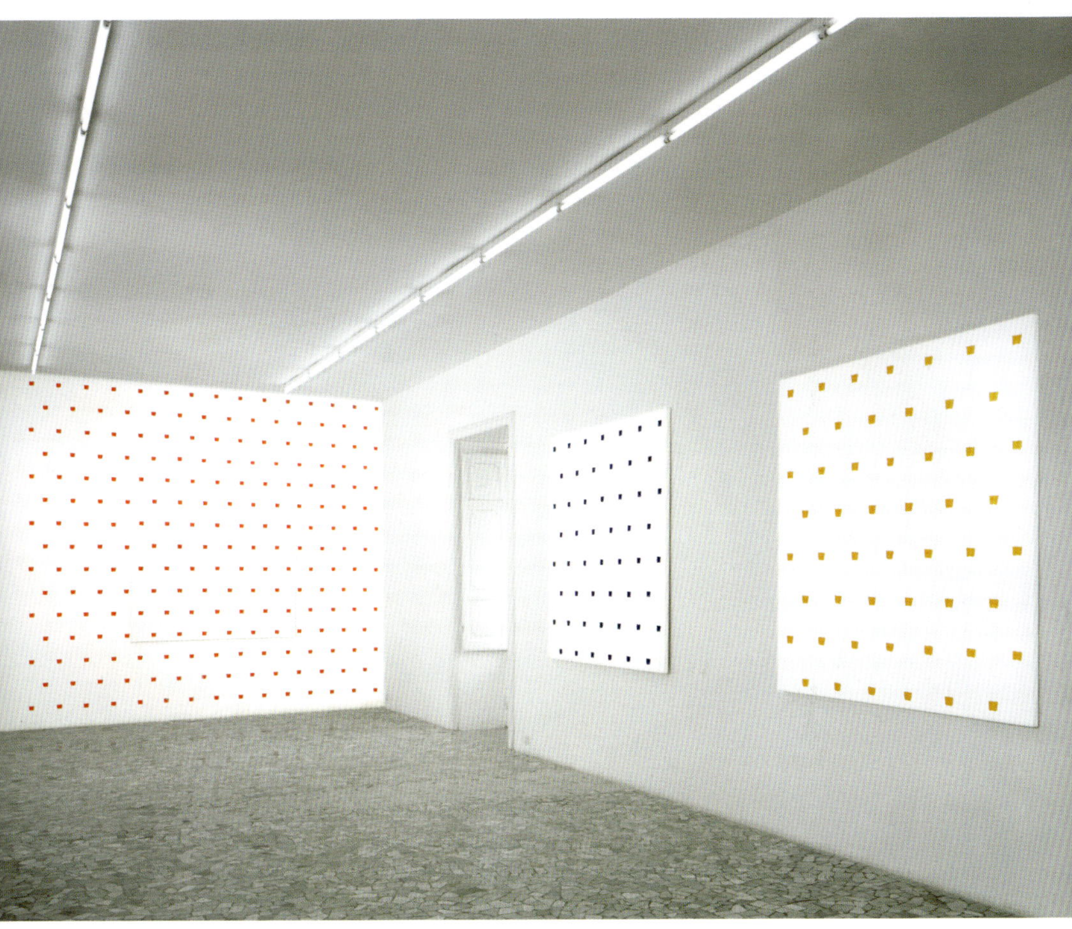

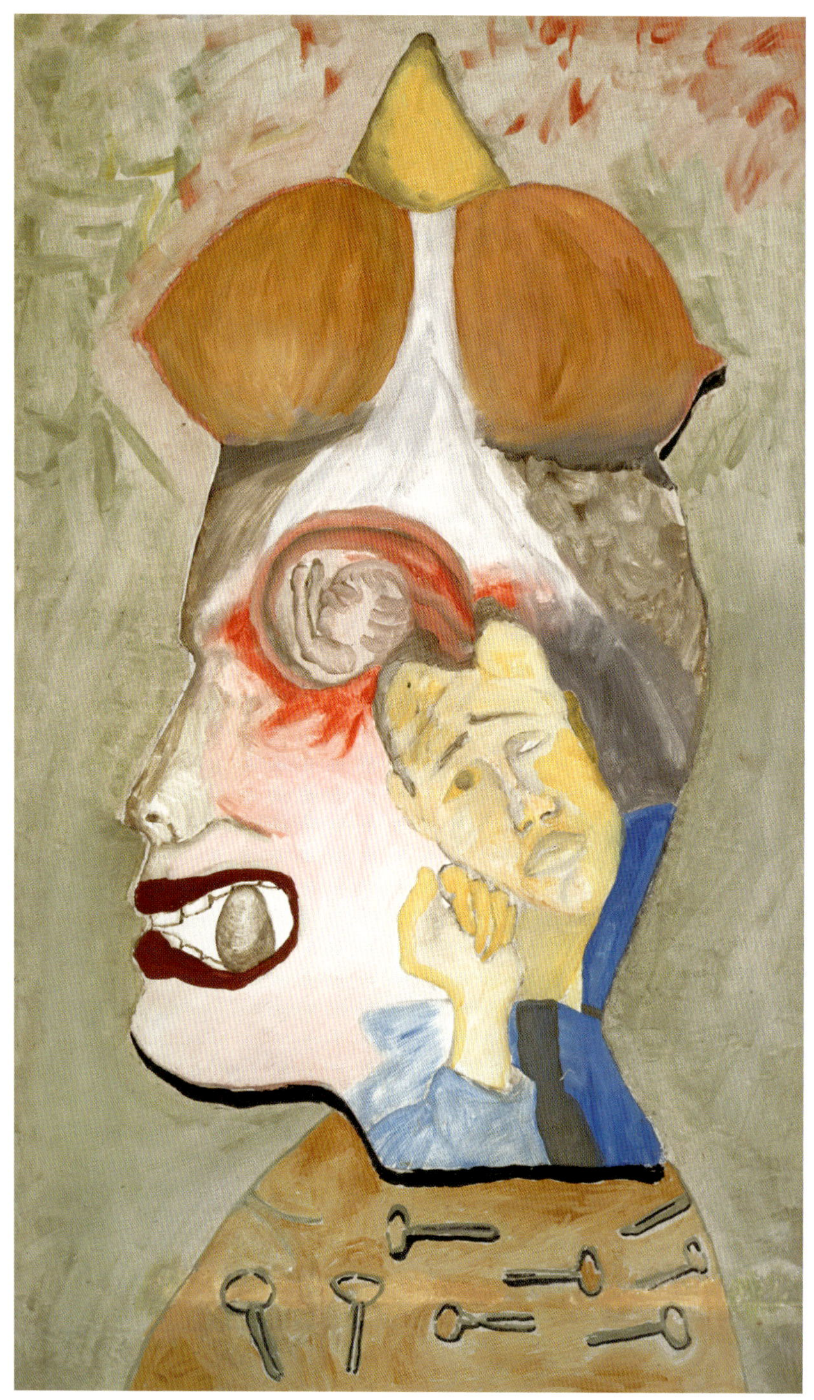

XX

Francesco Clemente
*Untitled*, 1981
Fresco, 100 × 60 cm
Courtesy E. Righi Collection

Giulio Turcato
*Rovine di Varsavia*, 1948–50
Oil on paper mounted on
canvas, 69.5 × 100 cm
Courtesy Archivio della
Scuola Romana, Rome

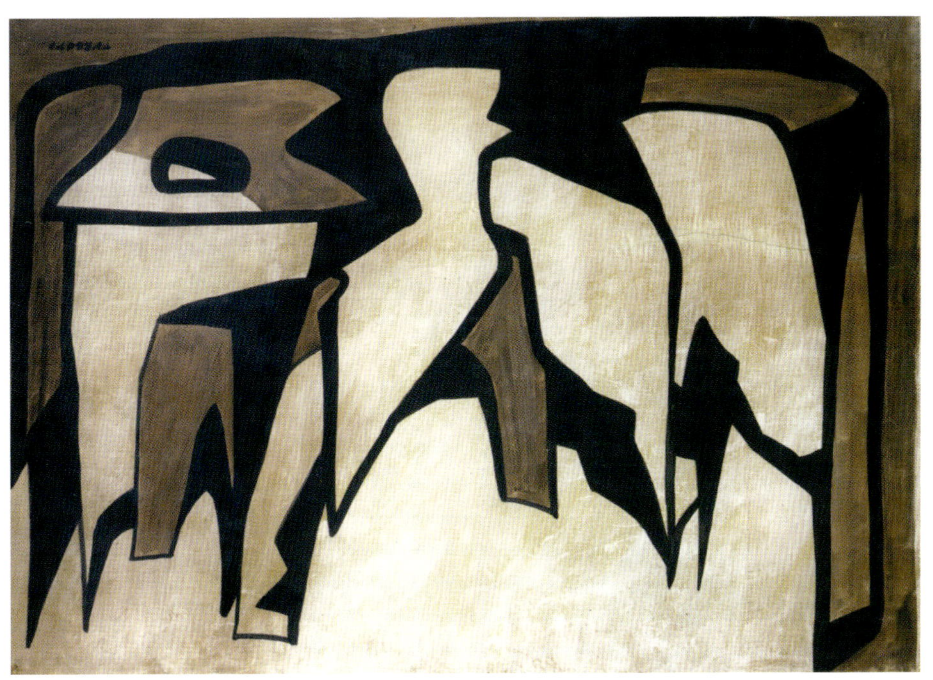

Enzo Cucchi
*I piedi di Caravaggio*, 1993
Mixed media on paper transferred
onto canvas, 227 × 577 cm
Courtesy Galleria d'Arte
Contemporanea Emilio Mazzoli,
Modena
Photo by Paolo Terzi, Modena

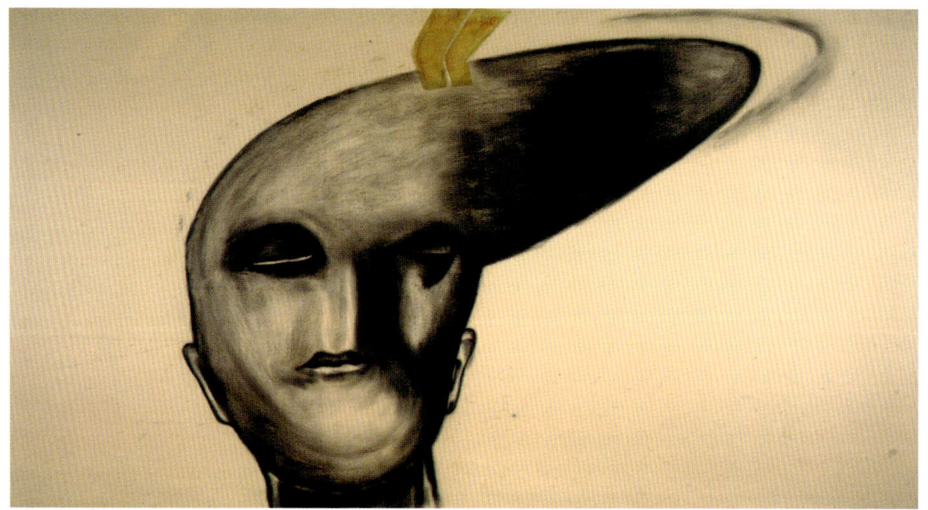

Mimmo Paladino
*Untitled*, 1996
Oil on canvas, 110 × 90 cm
Courtesy Amos Parlatini,
Modena
Photo by Amos Parlatini,
Modena

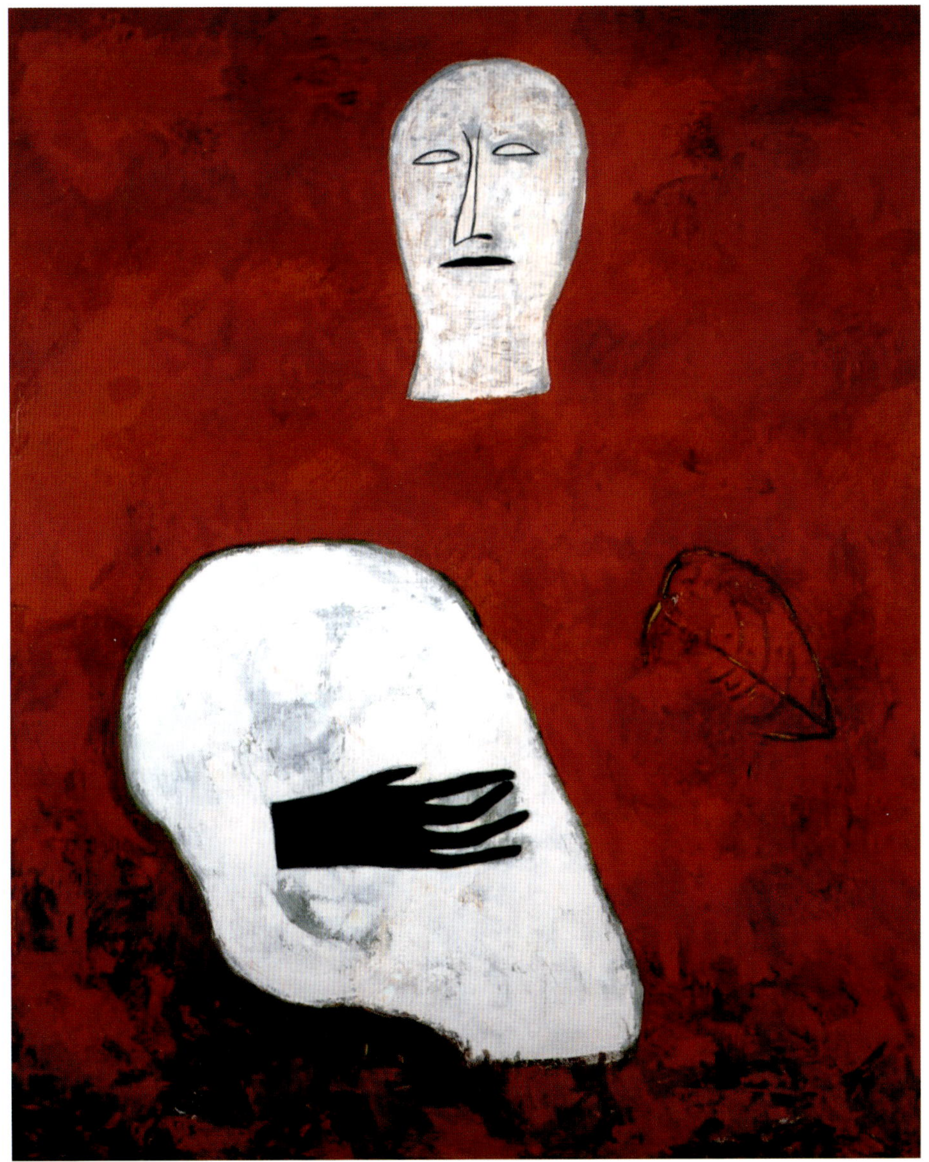

Andy Warhol
*Flowers*, 1964
From the *Contemporanea*
exhibition, Parcheggio
di Villa Borghese, Rome,
November 1973 –
February 1974
Courtesy Archivio Incontri
Internazionali d'Arte
Photo by Massimo Piersanti

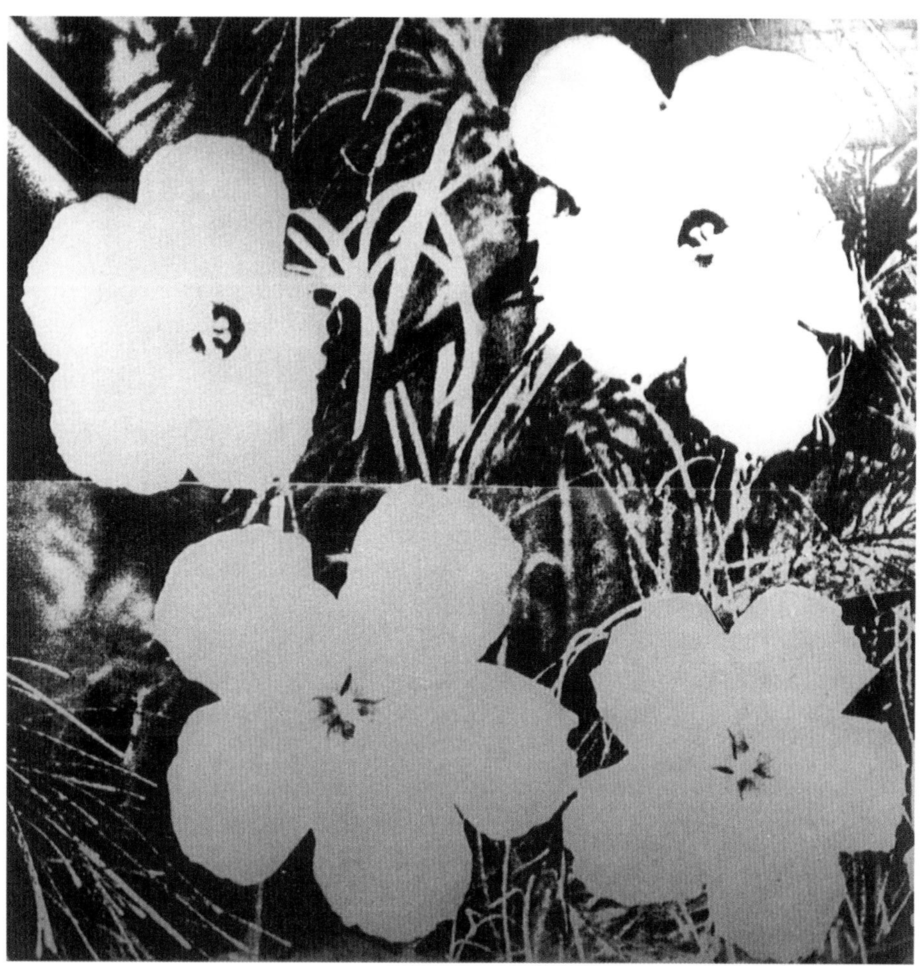

Daniel Buren
*Couleurs et ombres portées
pour une cabane éclatée
au toit pointu*, 2006
In situ work, Galleria
Continua, Beijing,
January 2006

Coloured filters, black
and white adhesive strips,
Plexiglas, plasterboard
and steel
Courtesy Galleria Continua,
San Gimignano–Beijing
Photo © Daniel Buren

Nicola De Maria
*Poesia notturna dentro il Regno
dei Fiori*, 1990
Mixed media on canvas,
200 × 300 cm
Courtesy Paolo Terzi, Modena
Photo by Paolo Terzi, Modena

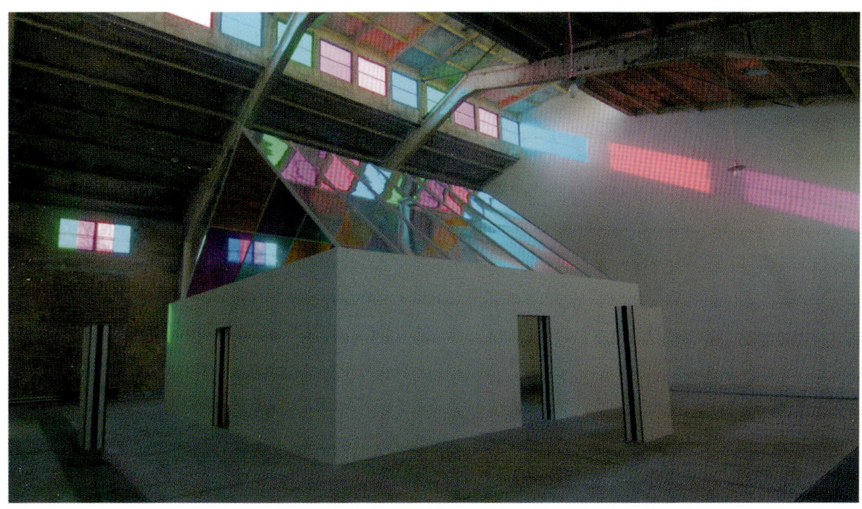

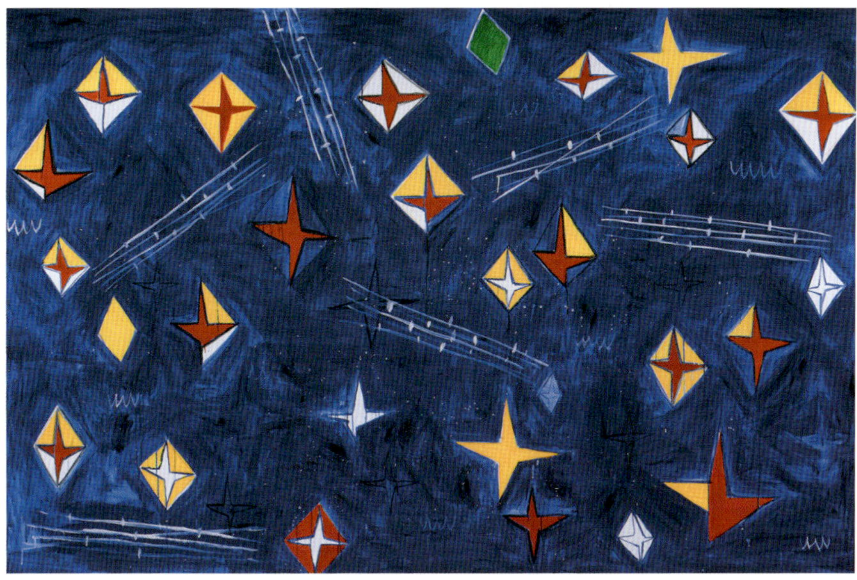

Mario Schifano
*Sand Sculpture*, 1984
Mixed media and sand
on canvas and painted
frame, 275 × 275 cm
Courtesy Archivio Mario
Schifano

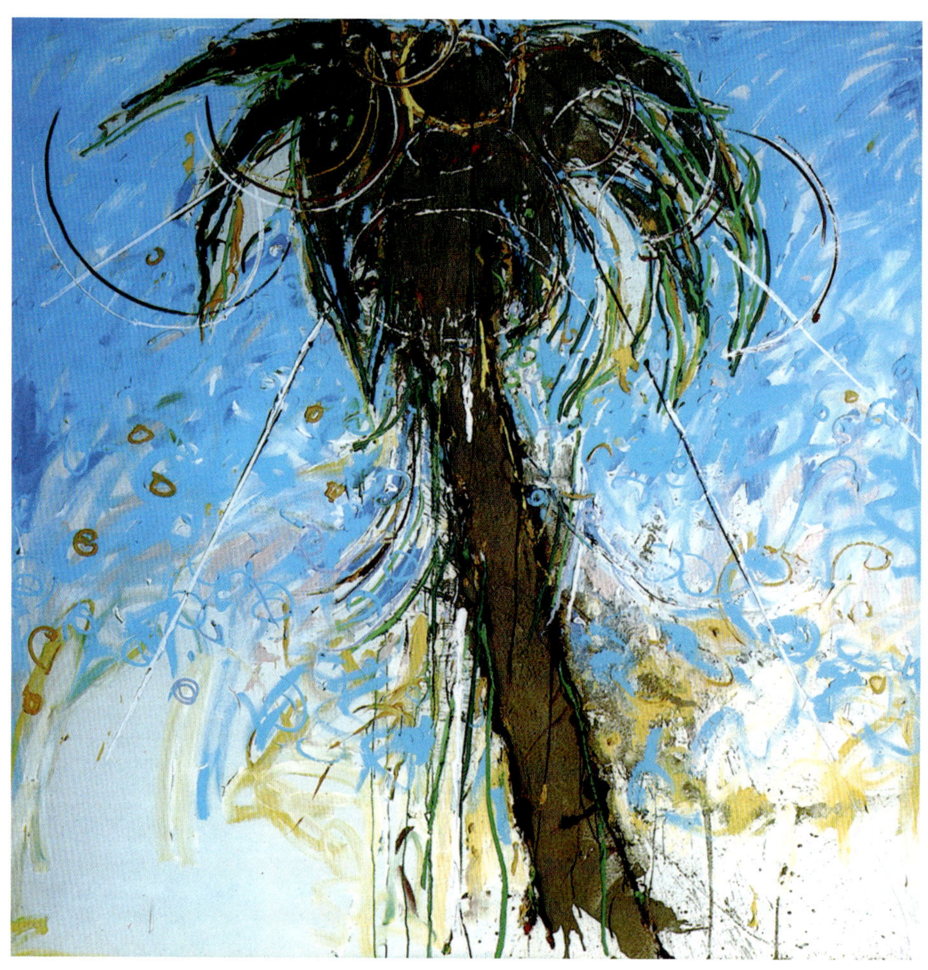

William S. Burroughs
*Wood Spirits*, 1987
Paint, collage and holes
made by a shotgun on
plywood, 40.6 × 66 cm
Courtesy Tony Shafrazi
Gallery
Photo by Ivan Dalla Tana

Gino De Dominicis
Poster of the exhibition
by Gino De Dominicis at
the Galleria L'Attico, Rome,
November 1969
Courtesy Archivio Sargentini

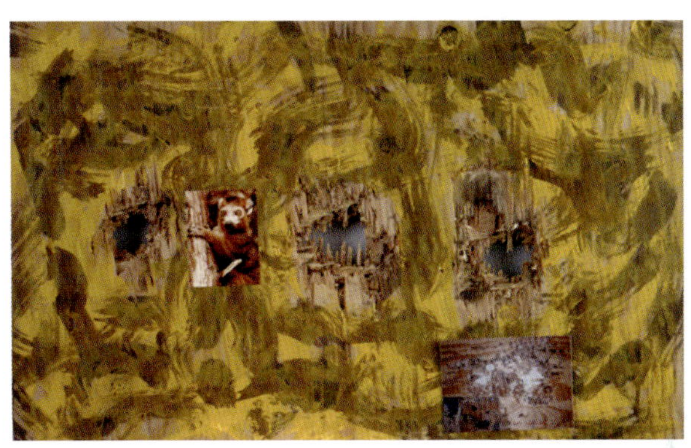

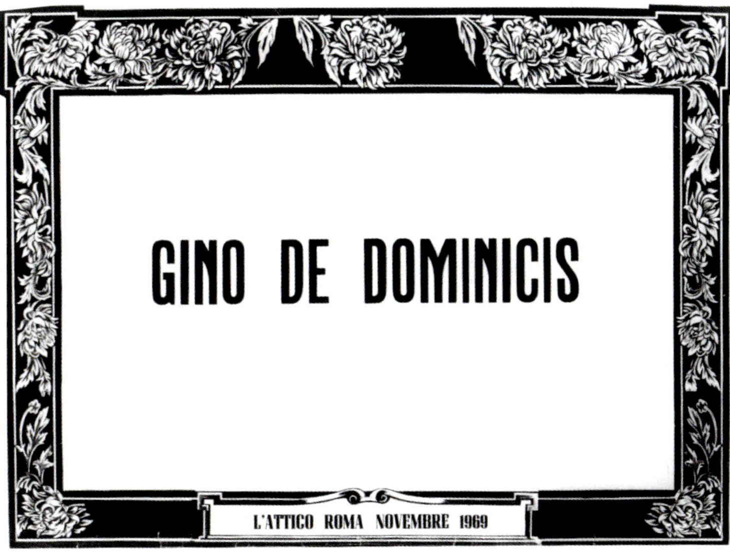

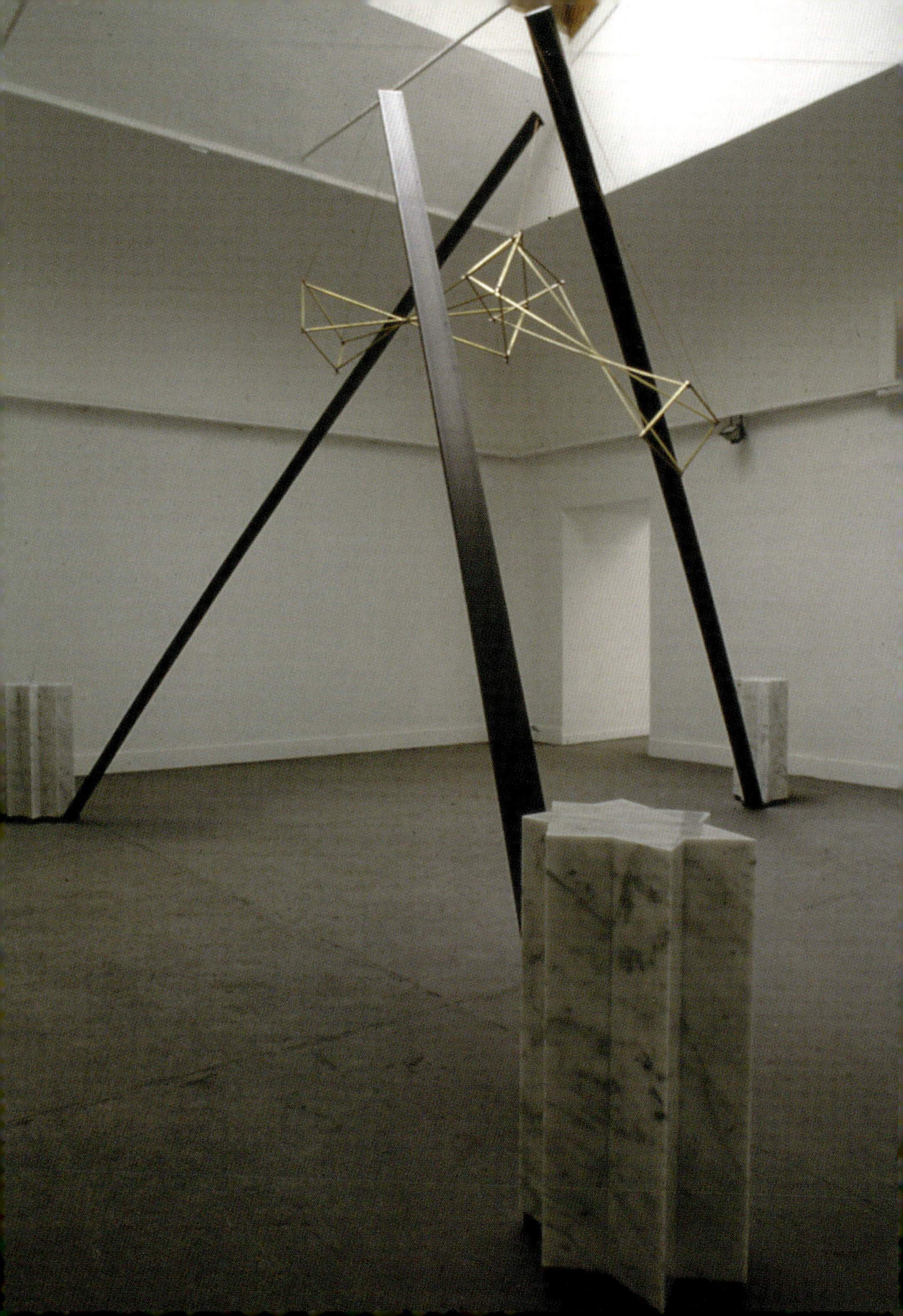

Hidetoshi Nagasawa
*Iris*, 1993
Marble, iron, brass and
copper, 550 × 500 × 500 cm
Courtesy of the artist

Louise Bourgeois
*Untitled* (*Ears*), 1998
Pink marble,
100.3 × 182 × 182.8 cm
From the *Arte all'Arte 1998*
exhibition, San Gimignano
Courtesy Associazione Arte
Continua, San Gimignano
Photo by Attilio Maranzano

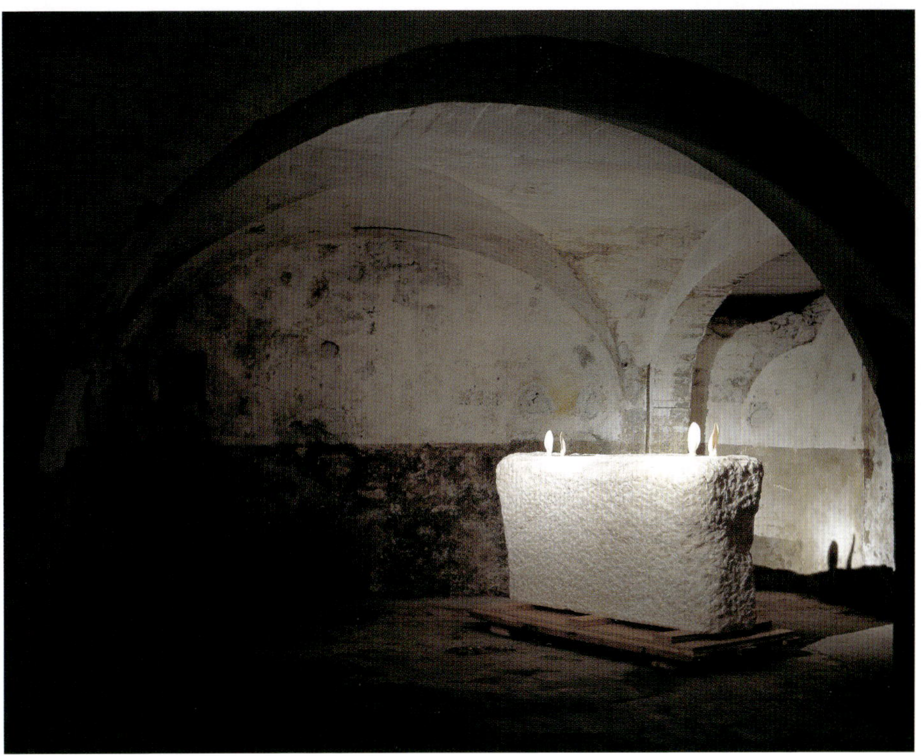

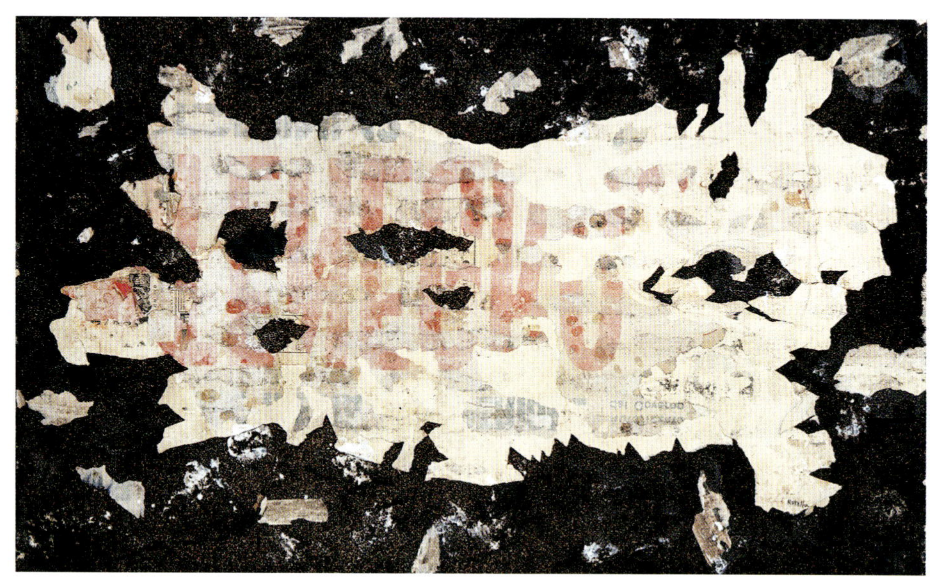

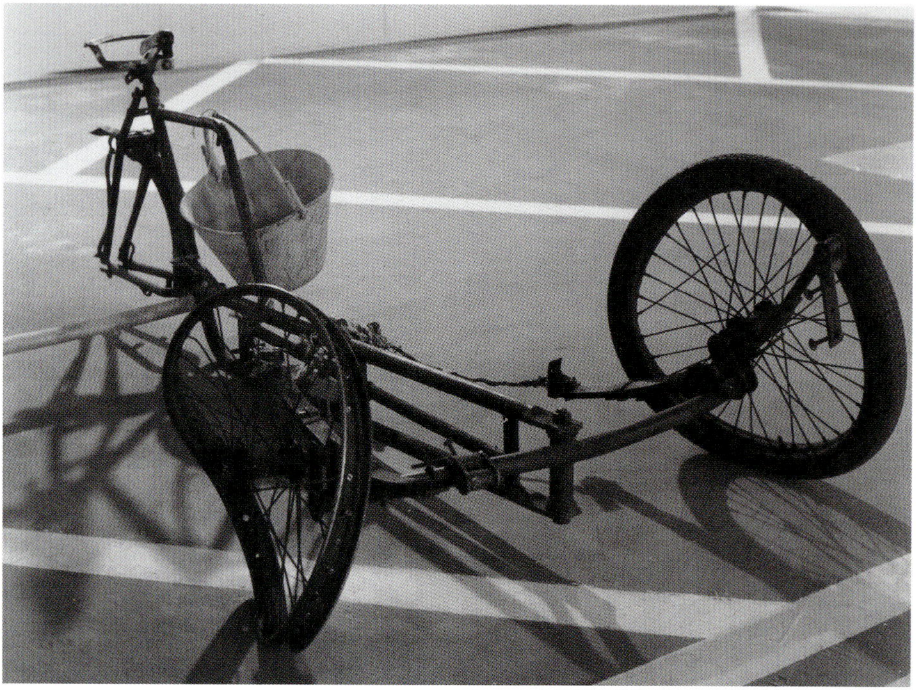

Mimmo Rotella
*Come un animale*, 1954
Back of poster, 60 × 100 cm
Private collection
Courtesy Fondazione
Mimmo Rotella
© Fondazione Mimmo
Rotella
Photo by Alessandro
Zambianchi

Robert Rauschenberg
Installation at the
*Contemporanea* exhibition,
Parcheggio di Villa
Borghese, Rome, November
1973 – February 1974
Courtesy Archivio Incontri
Internazionali d'Arte
Photo by Massimo Piersanti

Ben Jakober and Yannick Vu
*Leonardo's Horse*, 1993
Stainless steel tubing,
1,400 × 890 × 770 cm
Venice Biennale
Courtesy of the artists
Photo by Alberto Favaretto

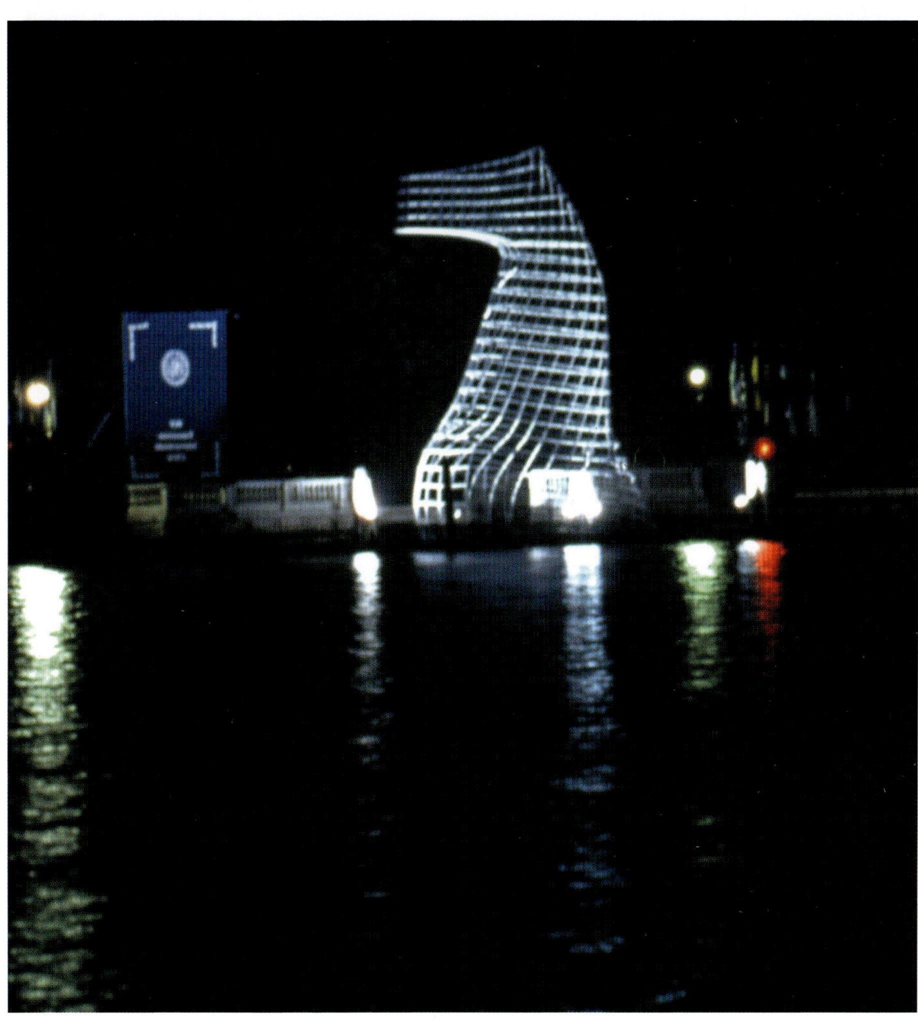

Carla Accardi
*Si dividono invano*, 2006
240 × 1,248 × 2.5 cm
Courtesy Marta Herford
Photo by Hans Schröder

Lugi Ontani
*Electric Throne*, 2006–07
Ceramic and metal,
158.1 × 69.2 × 68.6 cm
Courtesy of Luigi Ontani
and Bortolami Gallery

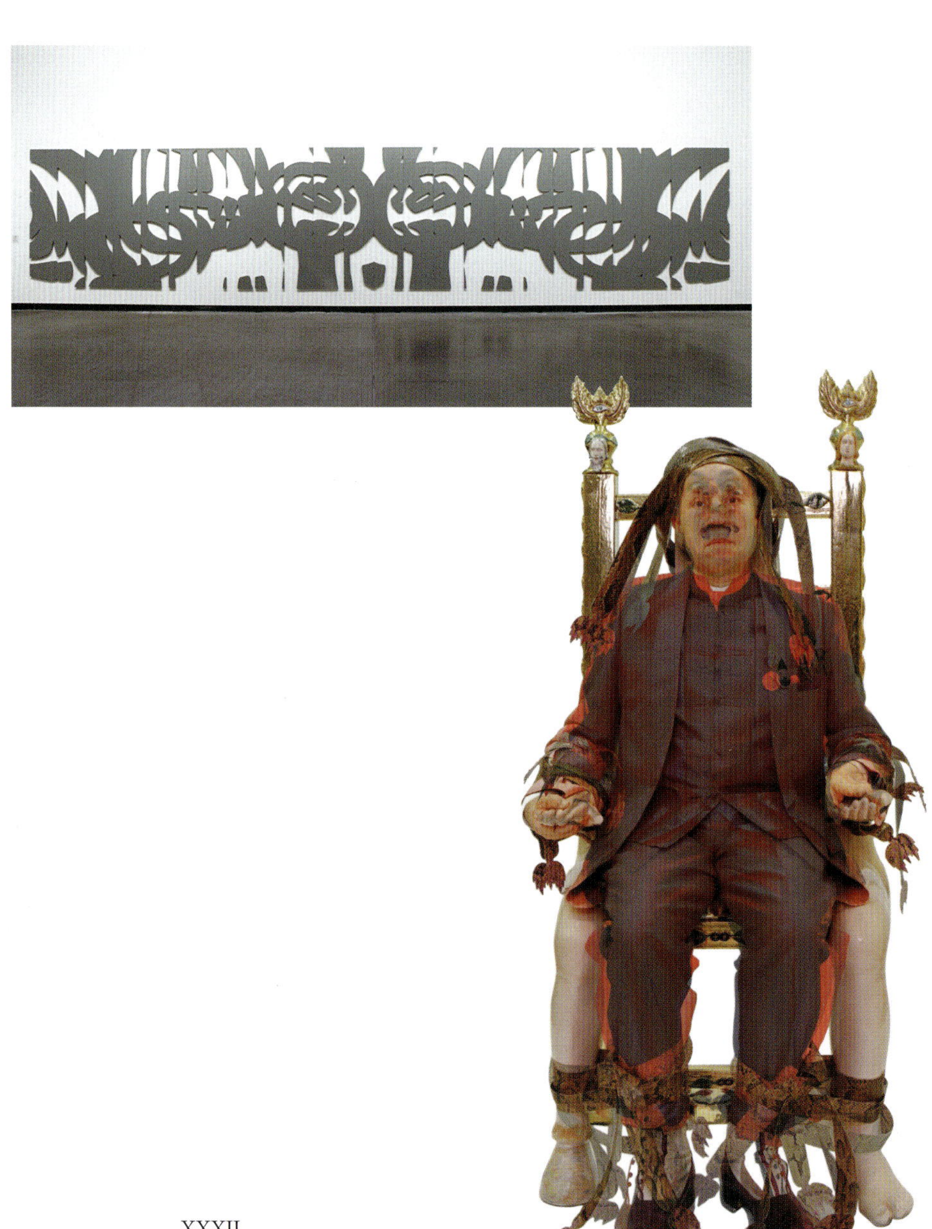

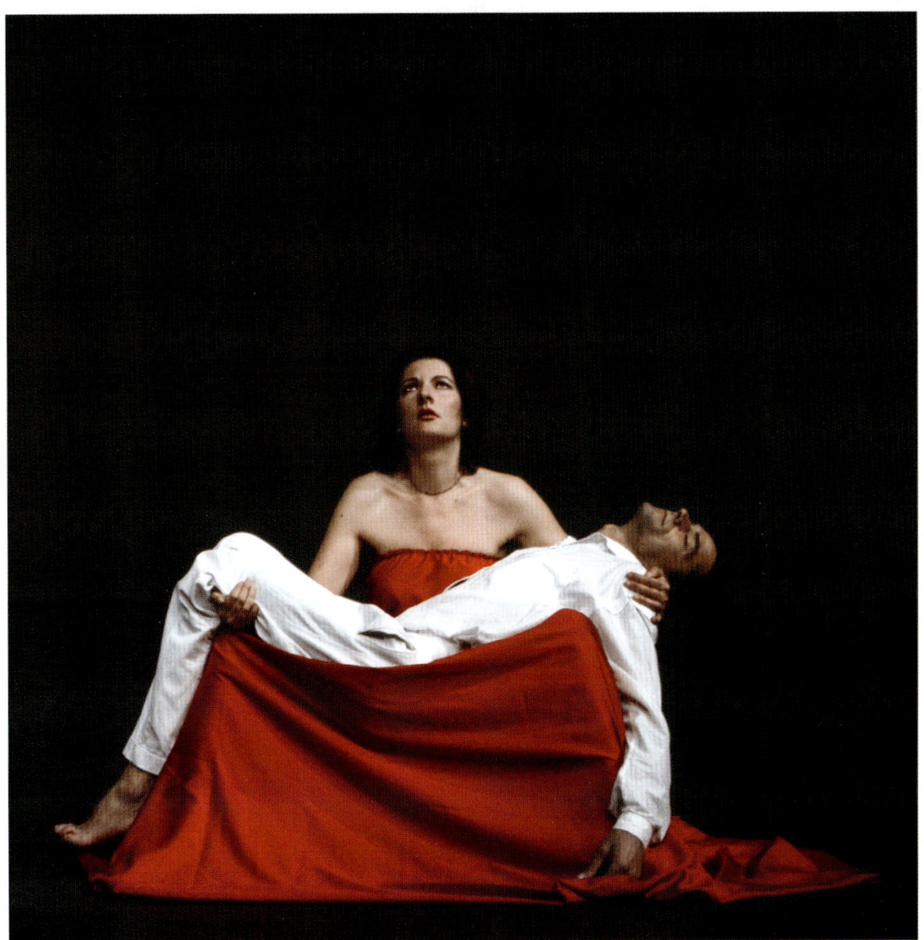

Marina Abramović
*Pietà*, 2002
From the *Anima Mundi*
performance, Theater Carré,
Amsterdam, 1983
Photograph, 180 × 180 cm
(one of three copies)
Courtesy Lia Rumma

Marc Quinn
General view of
the exhibition,
2006
Courtesy MACRO
(Museo d'Arte
Contemporanea
Roma), Rome
Photo by Giorgio
Benni

Pedro Cabrita Reis
*It's Never a
Question of
Balance*, 2006
Travertine, HEB
200 iron girders,
variable
dimensions
© Pedro Cabrita
Reis
Courtesy
Magazzino d'Arte
Moderna, Rome

Maurizio Cattelan
*A Perfect Day*,
1999
Electrostatic print
mounted on
aluminium panel,
258 × 192 cm
Courtesy Galleria
Massimo De Carlo
Photo by Armin
Linke

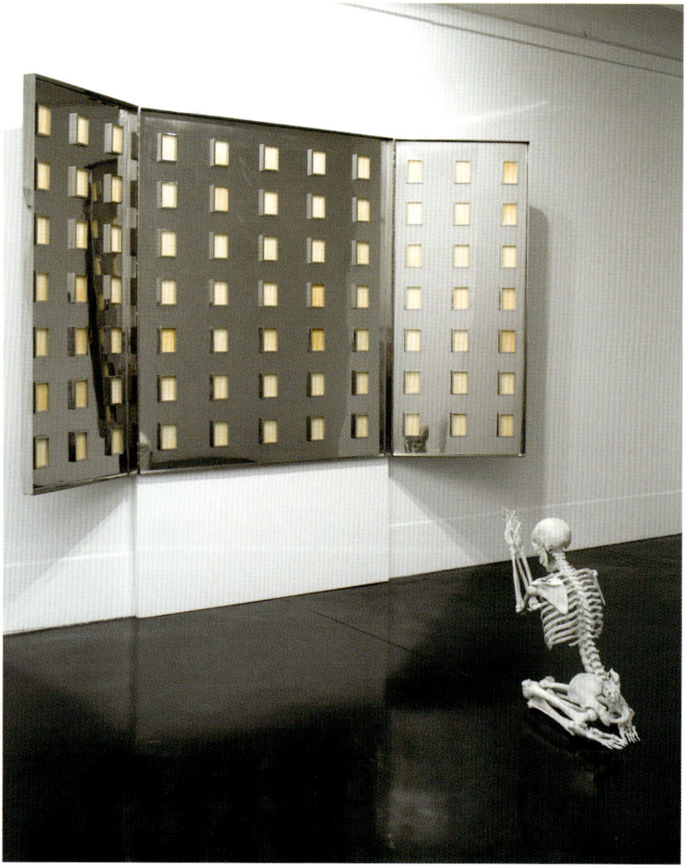

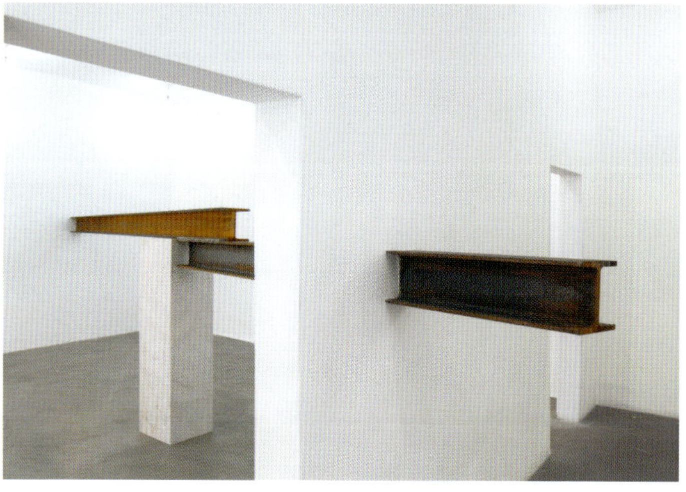

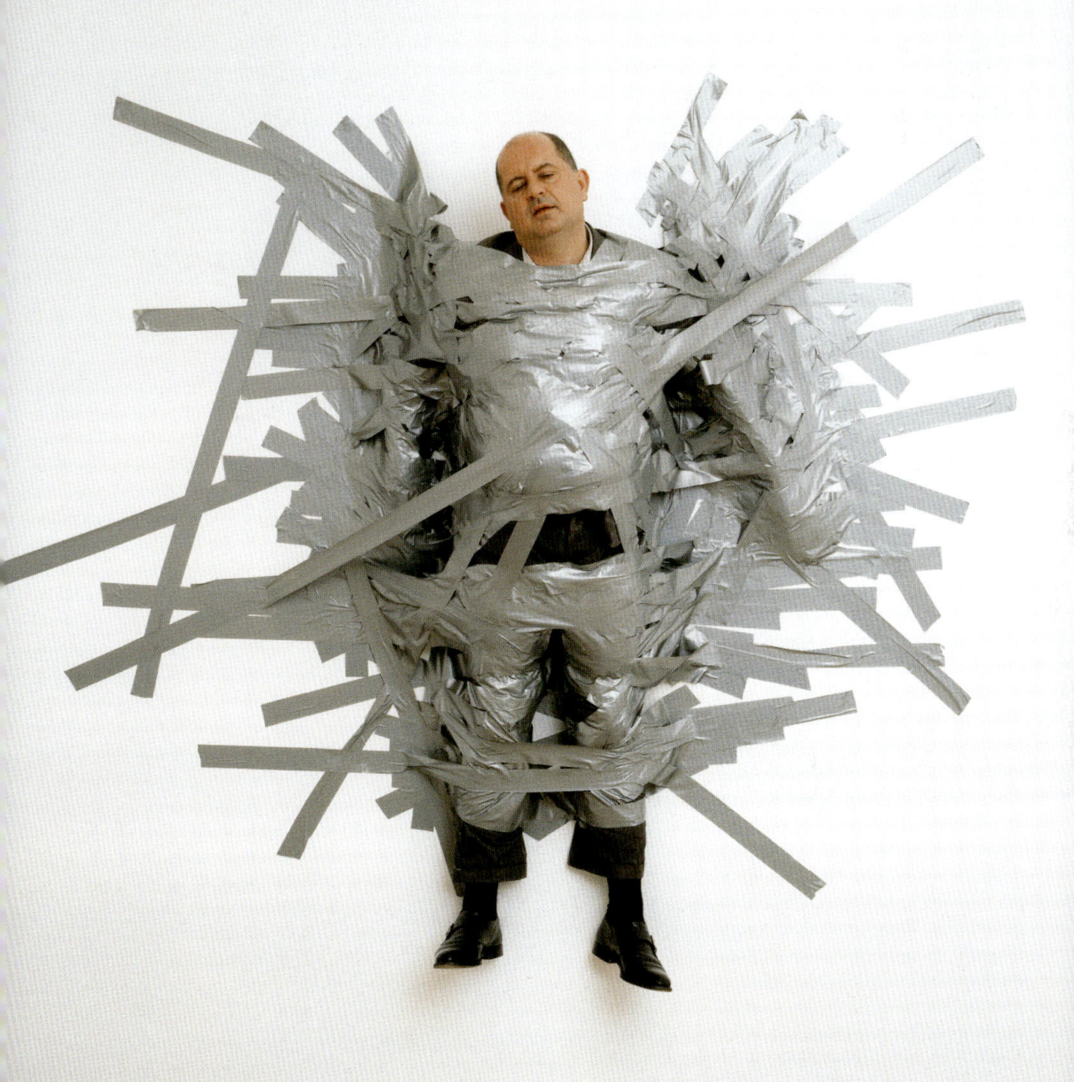

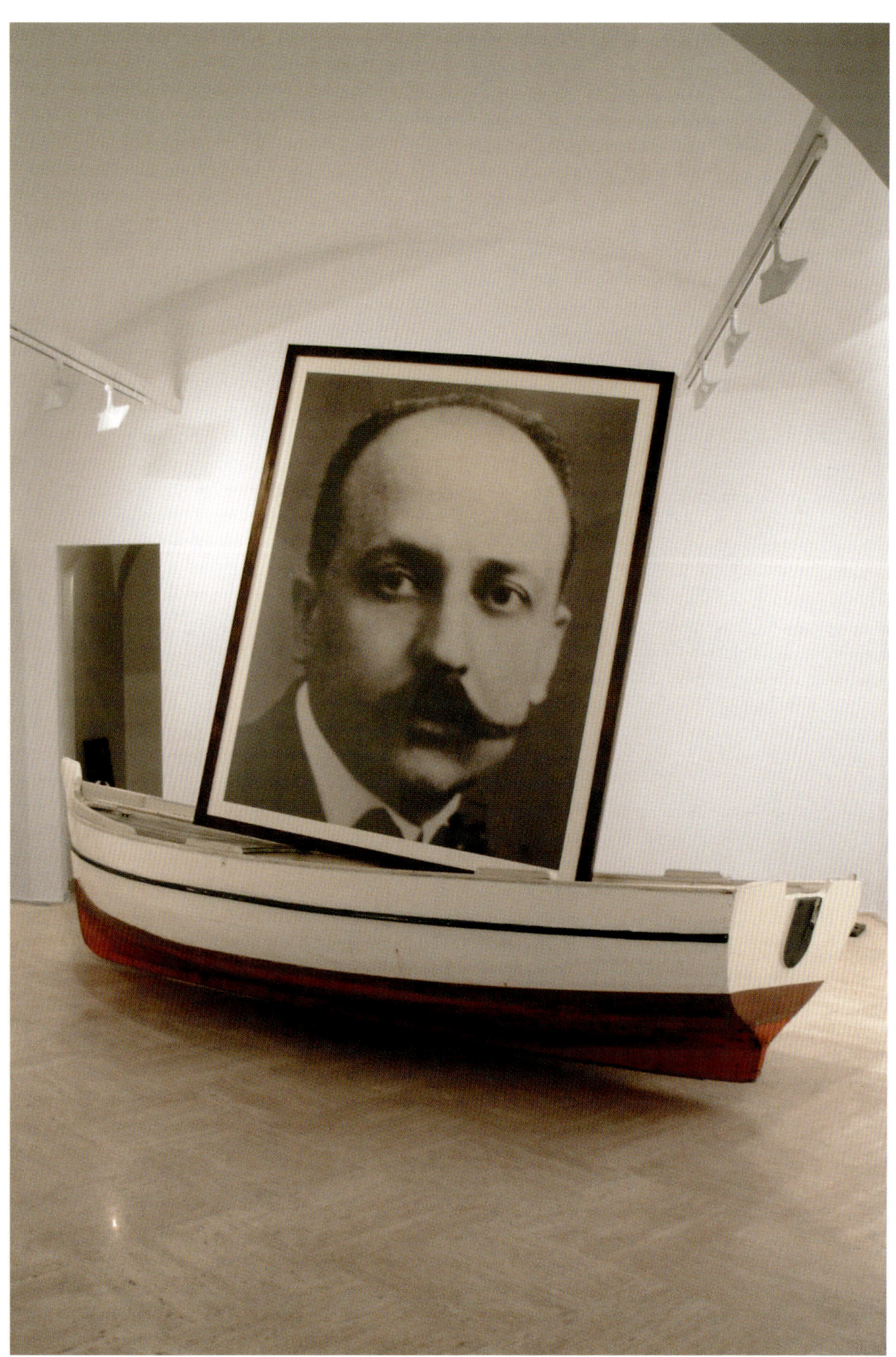

XXXVI

Braco Dimitrijević
*Marinetti*, 2006
Boat, iron, photo, frame,
300 × 400 × 143 cm
Courtesy Galleria Il Ponte
Contemporanea, Rome

Jimmie Durham
*Deposition*, 2006
Glass, metal, obsidian,
fabric, 140 × 387 × 97 cm
Courtesy RAM
(radioartemobile)
Photo by Marco Fedele
di Catrano

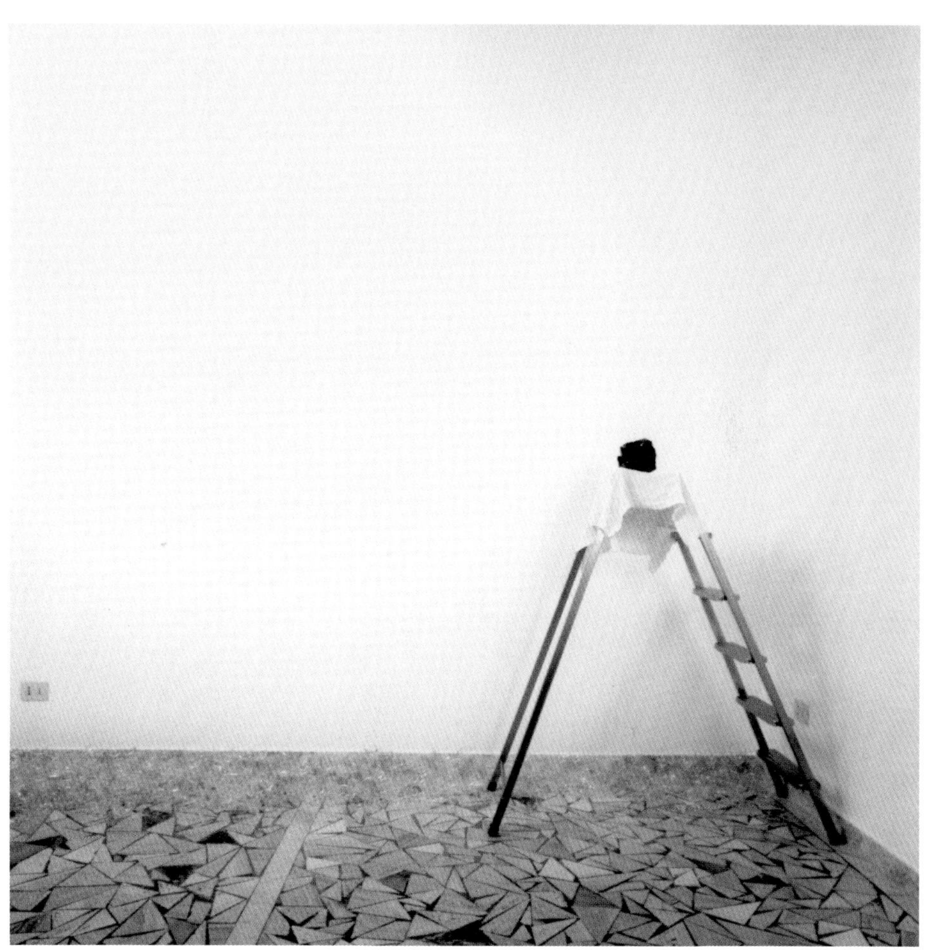

Jan Fabre
*The Decapitated Messengers of Death*
Installation at the *Intramœnia extra art – Castelli di Puglia* exhibition, Castle of Monte Sant'Angelo (Foggia)
Courtesy Jan Fabre / Angelos, Antwerp
Photo by Maurizio Abbate

Alberto Garutti
*Corale Vincenzo Bellini*
From the *Arte all'Arte 2000* exhibition, Colle Val d'Elsa
Courtesy Arte Continua, San Gimignano
Photo by Ela Bialkowska

These words inscribed on the front of the building are an integral part of the work:
"THIS BUILDING IS THE SEAT OF THE VINCENZO BELLINI CHORAL SOCIETY. MY ENCOUNTER WITH NUMEROUS RESIDENTS OF COLLE VAL D'ELSA BROUGHT TO MY NOTICE THIS PLACE, WHICH IS VERY DEAR TO THEM. I DECIDED THAT THE WORK I INTENDED TO CREATE IN THE TOWN FOR THE ARTE ALL'ARTE 2000 EXHIBITION, WOULD TAKE THE CONCRETE FORM OF THE RENOVATION OF THIS BUILDING IN NEED OF MUCH ATTENTION. ALL THE TIME AND WORK THAT HAVE GONE INTO IT HAVE HAD THE IDEAL MOTIVATION OF CONSTRUCTING AN ENCOUNTER BETWEEN ART AND THE REALITY OF LIFE IN THIS TOWN, IN AN ATTEMPT TO APPEAL TO THE FEELINGS OF THE PEOPLE WHO LIVE THERE. THIS ARTWORK IS DEDICATED TO THEM AND TO ALL THOSE WHO, WALKING BY, WILL HEAR MUSIC COMING FROM THIS HOUSE."

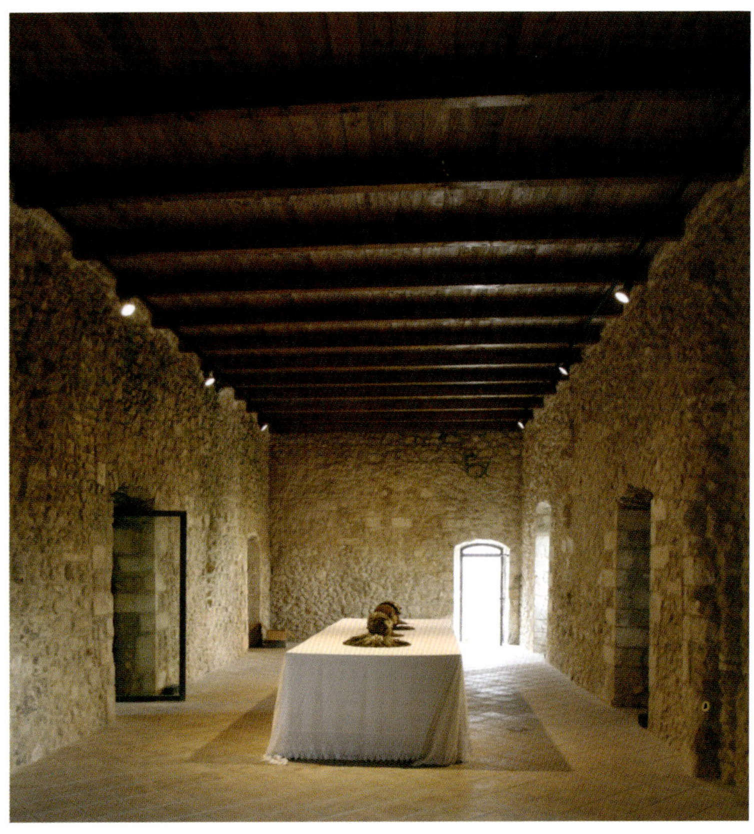

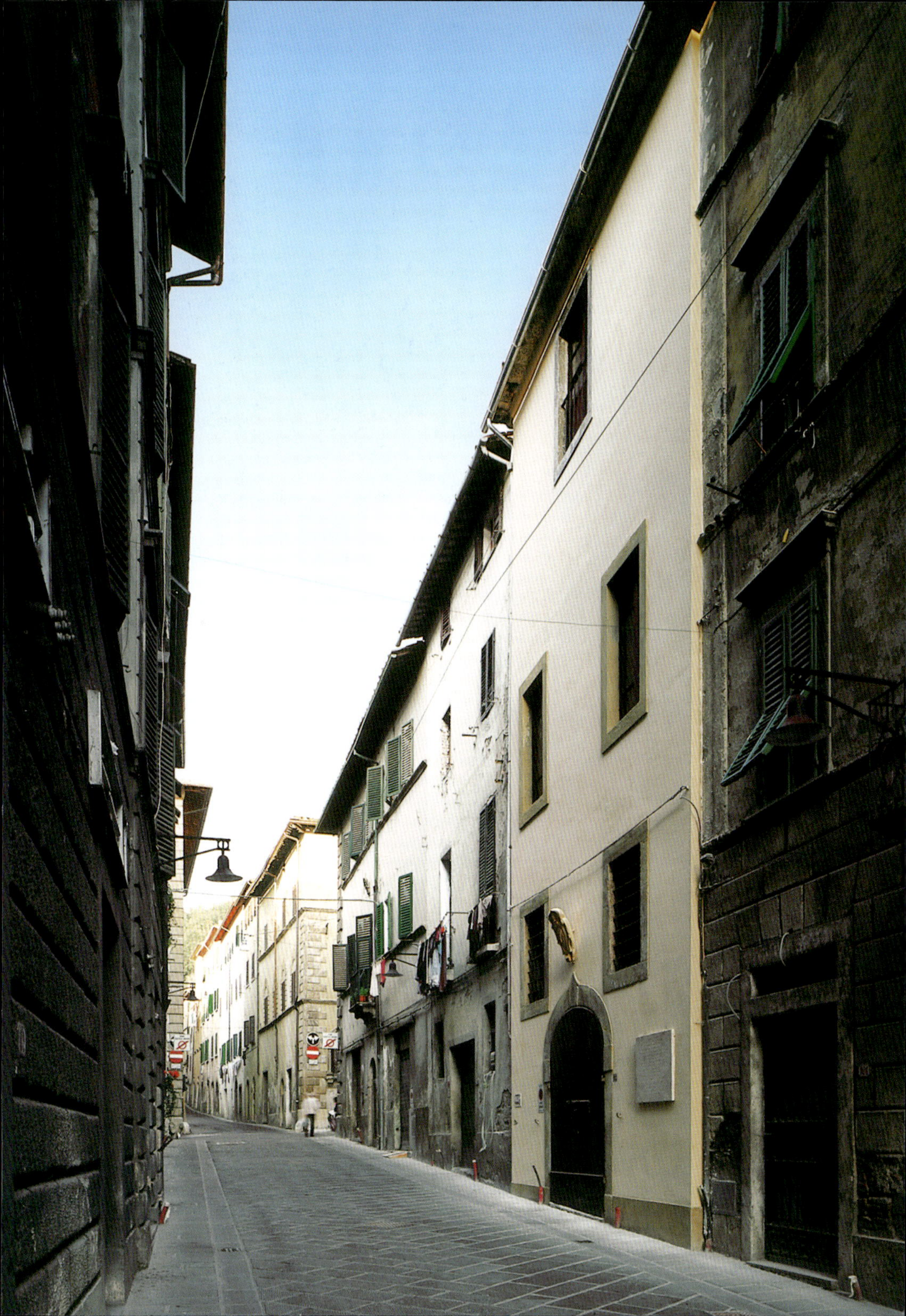

William
Kentridge
*Drawing from the
Venice Biennale
Project*, 2005
Charcoal and
pastel on paper,
120 × 160 cm
Courtesy Lia
Rumma

Fabio Mauri
*Cinema e Figura*,
1960
Gauze cloth
painted with
tempera and oil
on wood and
metal frame,
125 × 113 cm
Courtesy of the
artist

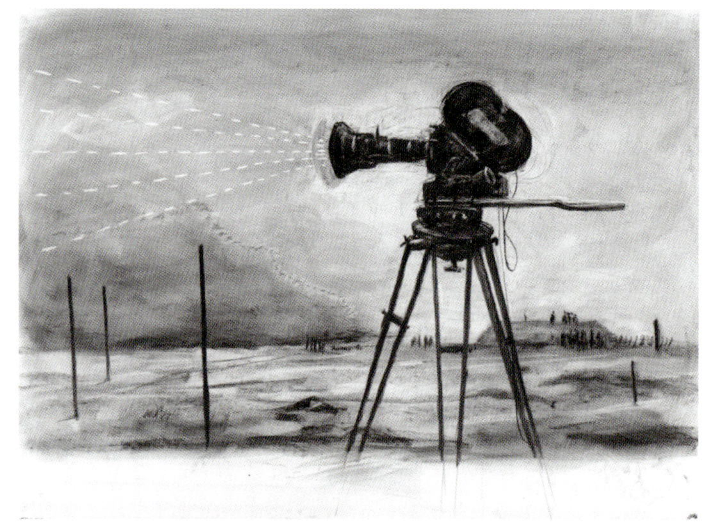

Dennis Oppenheim
View of the installation
at the Fondazione Volume!,
2006
Courtesy Fondazione
Volume!
Photo by Claudio Abate

*Overleaf*
Christian Boltanski
*Exit*, June 2006
300 items of clothing,
plastic-coated rooms,
*6 September* video, eight glass

cases containing clothes
The installation measures
1,000 square metres and was
realized at the Mattatoio,
MACRO, Rome
Photo by Giorgio Benni

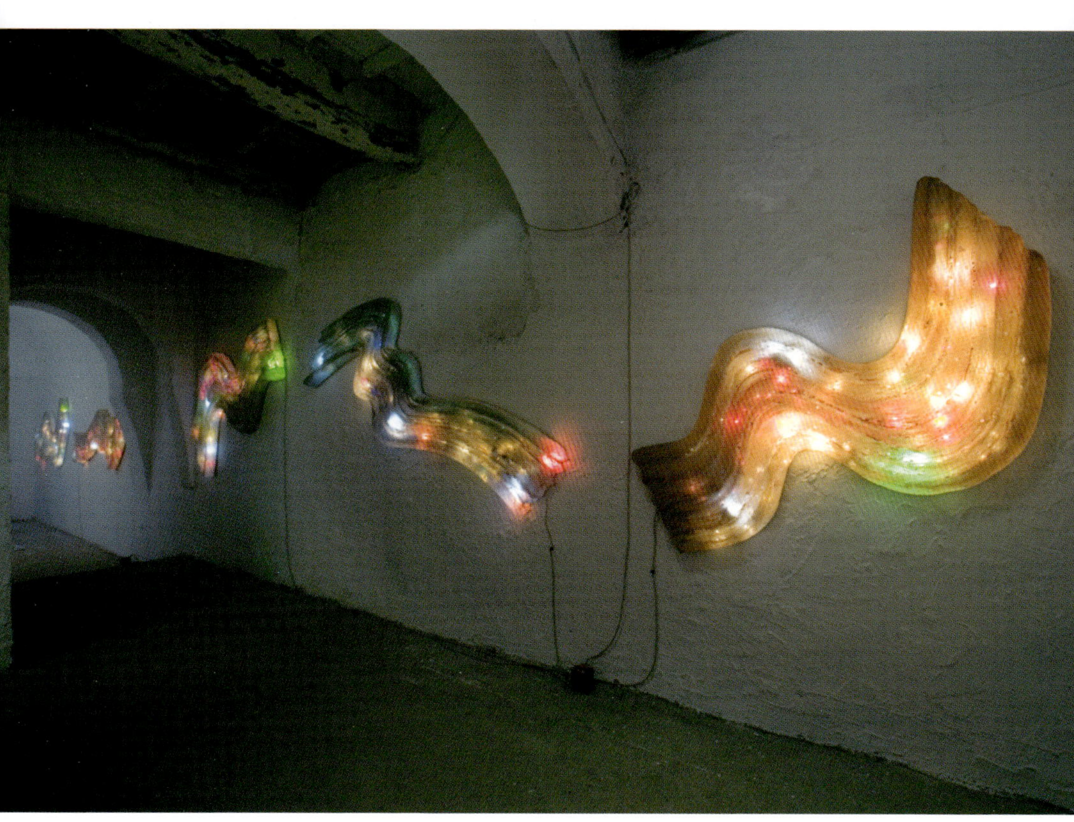

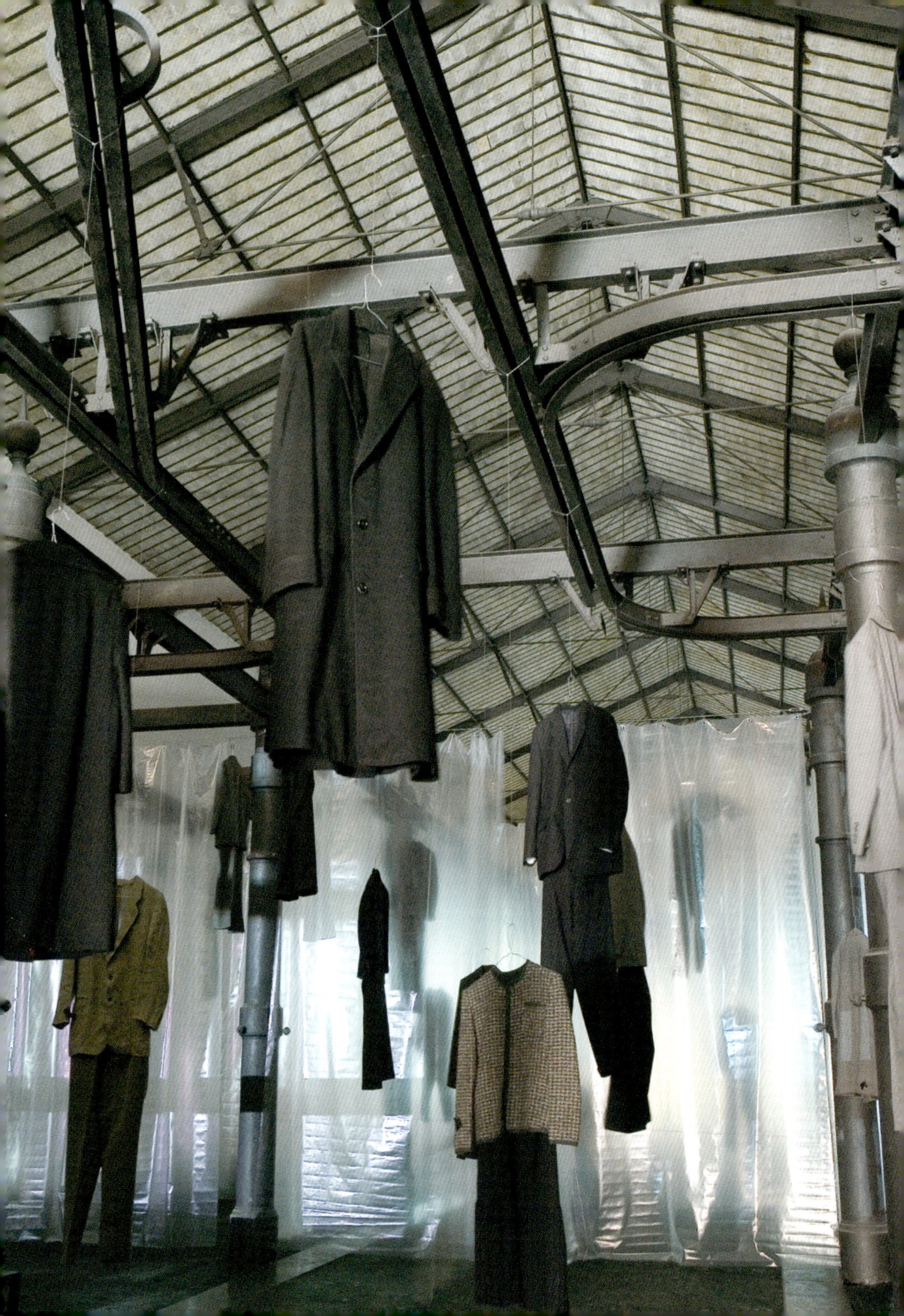

Ettore Spalletti
Installation for the Museo
di Capodimonte, Naples,
1999
Courtesy of the artist
Photo by Attilio Maranzano

Franz West
*Pancetta in Gorizia*, 2006
Aluminium, water circulating
system, 30 × 300 × 260 cm
Courtesy Zerynthia
Photo by Marco Fedele
di Catrano

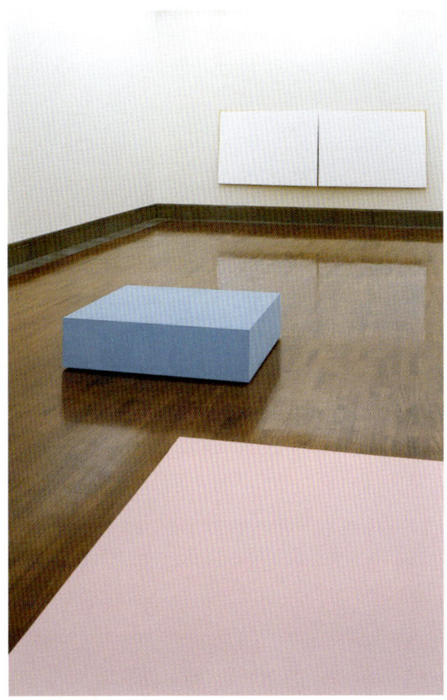

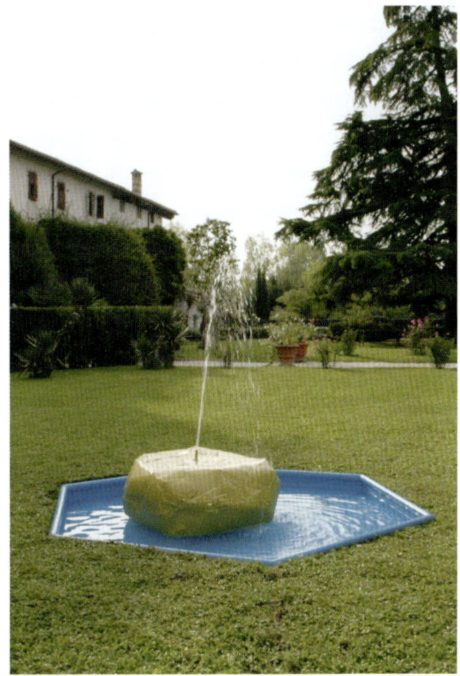

Sislej Xhafa
*Zemra*, 2007
Sculpture in
asphalt and
pigeon droppings,
170 × 140 × 10 cm
Courtesy of the
artist and Yvon
Lambert, Paris–
New York
© 2007 Sislej
Xhafa

Pier Paolo
Calzolari
*Materassino*, 1970
Mattress, lights,
freezing system,
motor,
125 × 180 × 10 cm
Courtesy Galleria
Il Ponte
Contemporanea,
Rome

Maurizio
Nannucci
*Let's Talk About
Art... Maybe*,
Edinburgh, 1993
Courtesy Galleria
Il Ponte
Contemporanea,
Rome

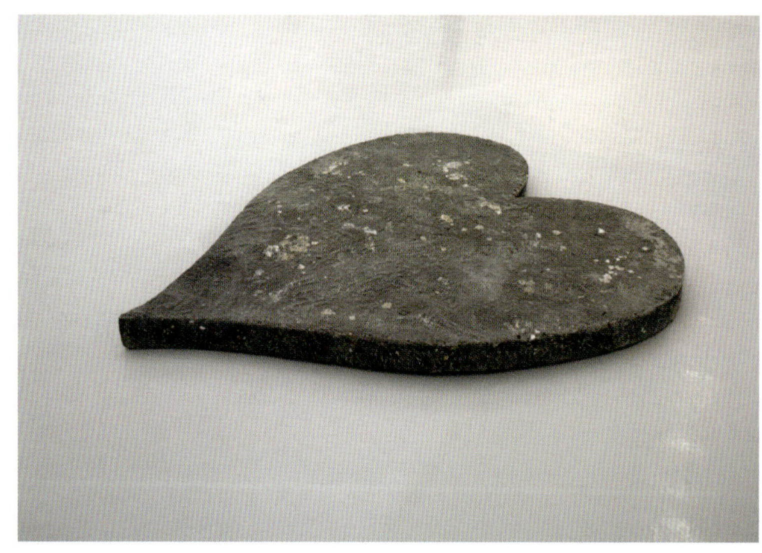

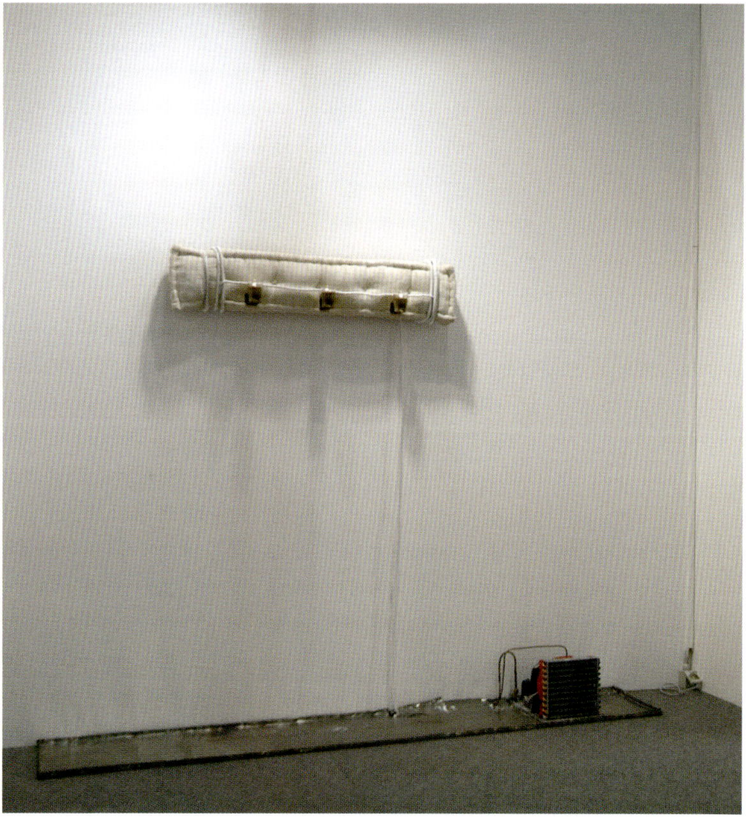

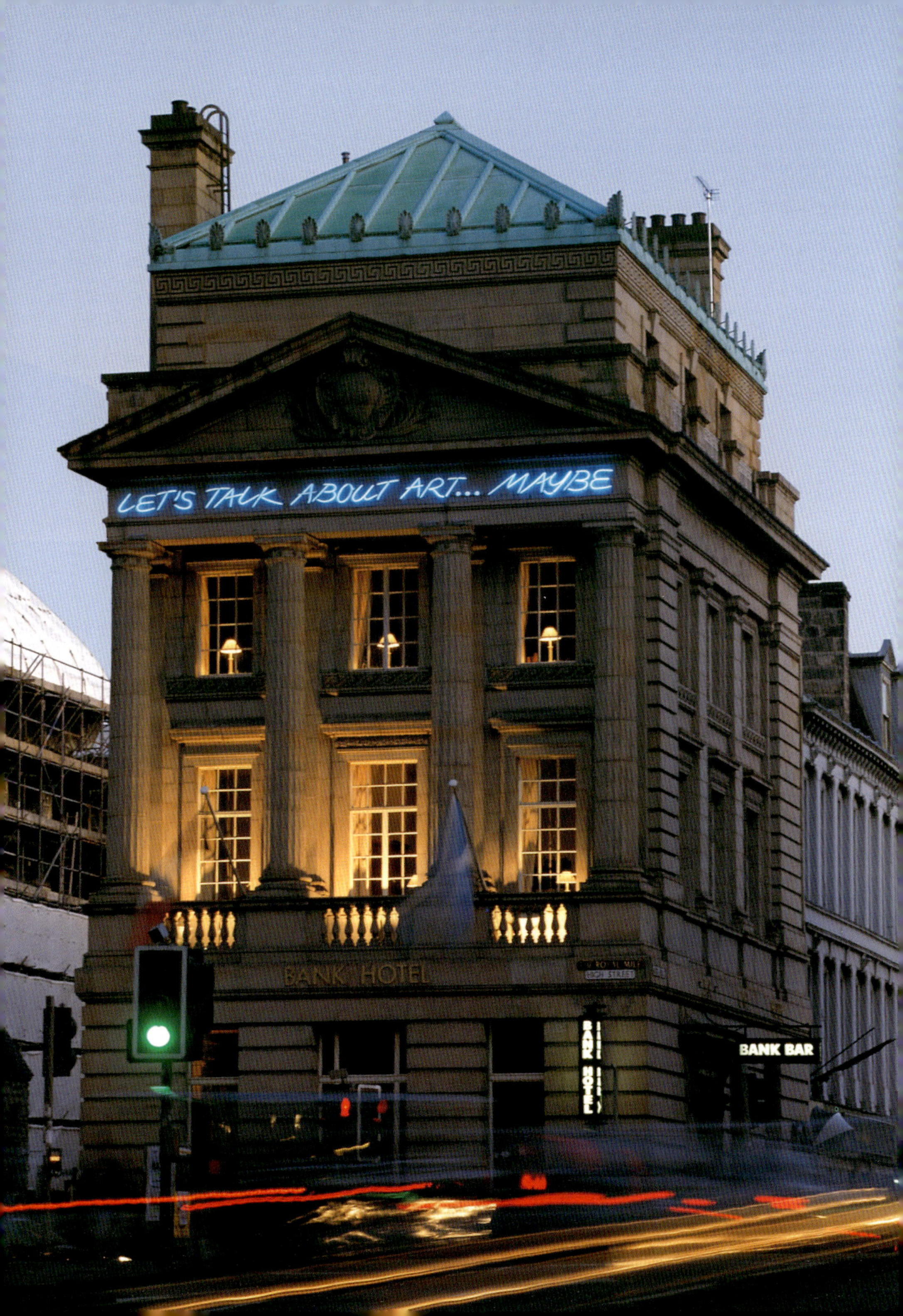

LET'S TALK ABOUT ART... MAYBE
BANK HOTEL
ROYAL MILE
HIGH STREET
BANK BAR

Gianni Piacentino
*Black Frame Vehicle with
Light Blue-Gray Triangle
Tank*, 1970–71
Painted wood and iron
tube, nickel-plated
(clear-painted) iron, painted
rubber, mahogany stand,
73.5 × 342.4 × 22 cm
(assembled in four pieces;
wheels diam. 45.7 cm)
Courtesy Galleria Il
Ponte Contemporanea,
Rome

Dan Graham
*Portal*, 1999–2004
Two-way mirror glass and
aluminium, 70 × 89 × 72.8 cm;
wooden base, 107 × 92 × 9 cm
(second exemplar of three)
Courtesy Zerynthia

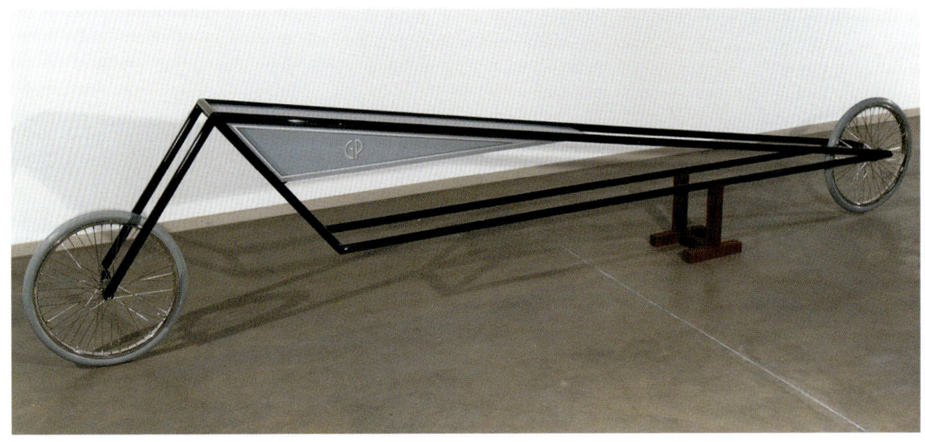

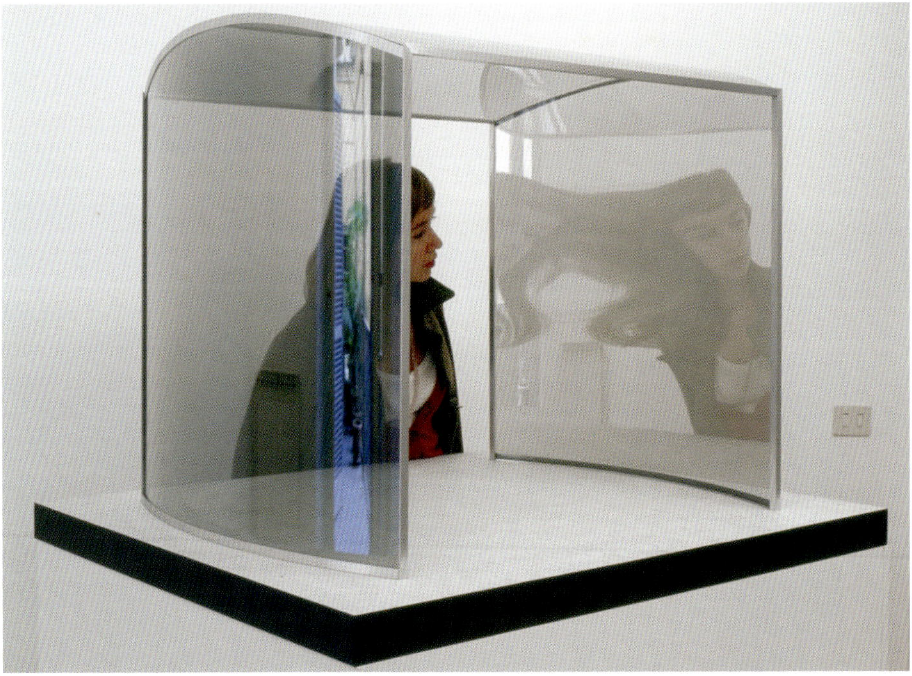

Ghada Amer
*S'il pleurait des larmes*, 2004
Environmental intervention
at the exhibition
*Le Opere e i Giorni*, Padula
Charterhouse, 2004

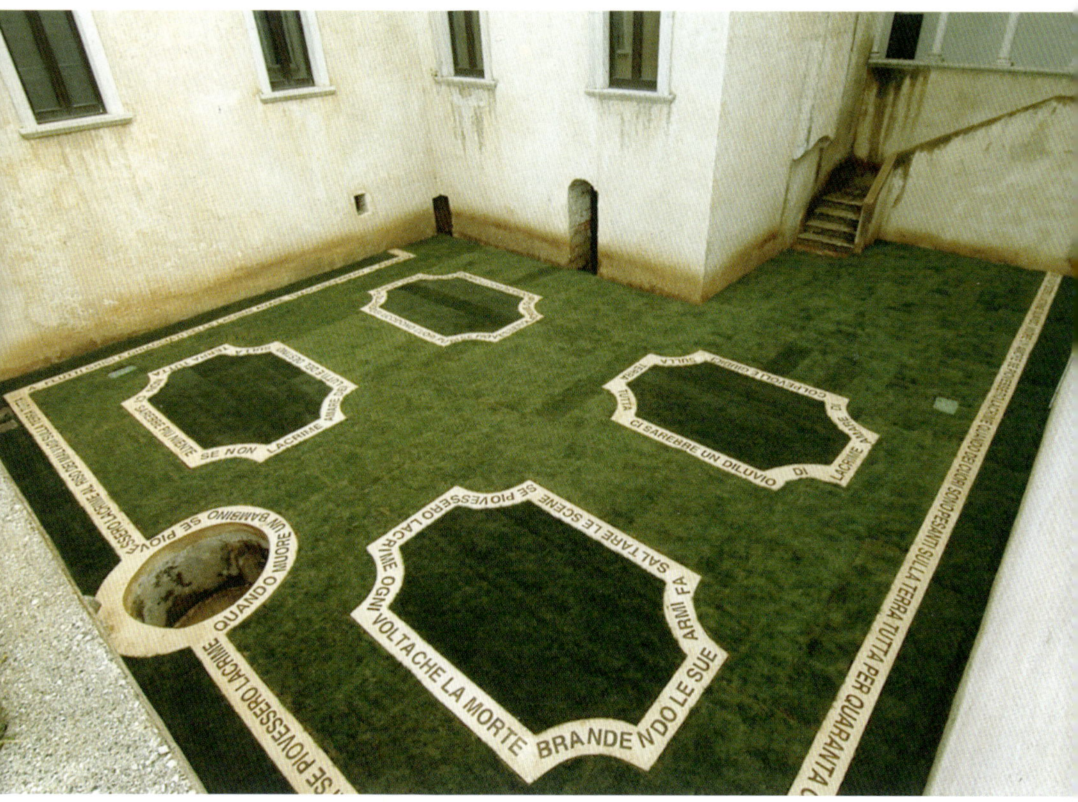


XLVII

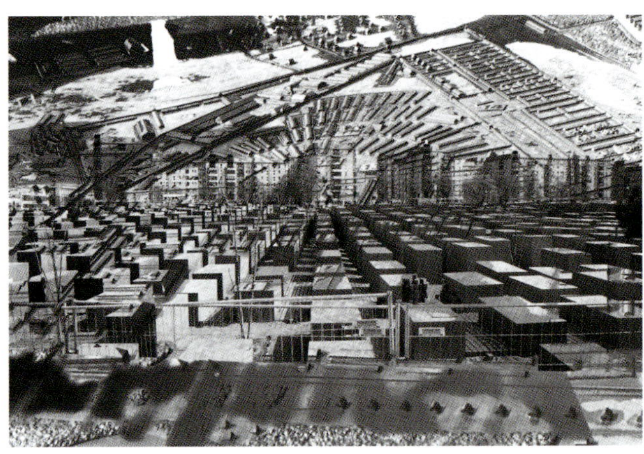

Katharina Sieverding
*Encode VII*, 2006
A/D/A process, acrylic
and steel, 125 × 190 cm
VG-Bildkunst
Courtesy Galleria Il Ponte
Contemporanea, Rome
Photo by Klaus Mettig

David Tremlett
Intervention in Line 1 of
the Naples Subway, second
exit of the Rione Alto station
Photo by Peppe Avallone

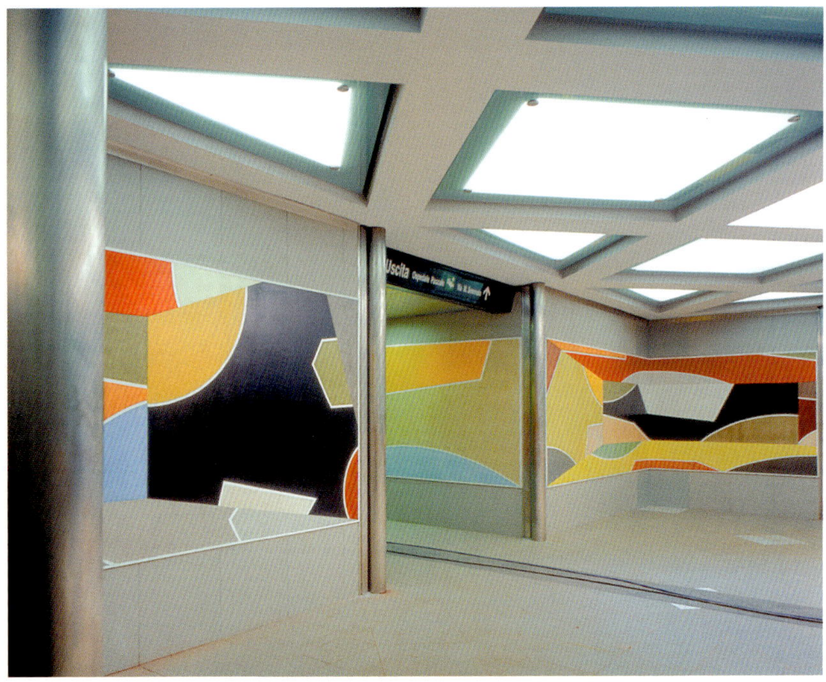

# Richard Tuttle
## Rahway, New Jersey, 1941



*It seems to me that your work generally tends to present itself as a system of relations. It is a structural work, in my opinion. I would like to know if you agree that your relationship with space is pragmatic in nature, and that the image that results is not a form, but a system of relations.*

"In terms of the structure of one of my 1975 works, perhaps before I began it I had already known that the desired structure was impossible. I feel, in a way metaphorically, that the two elements of this work, namely the paper and the line elements, have a contradictory desire or force that is guiding them in terms of the individual pieces. Perhaps one could say that the paper has a tendency to want to become circular and the lines want to become square, and for one piece then the suggestion would be a rather classical statement on squaring the circle or circling the square. However that is just one level, perhaps the level of pattern; it is not the primary motivation of the work at large, or the work in terms of self-statement. I think that the question must have an ambivalent answer, because I have yet to understand whether what I want in doing this work, is precisely inside a particular work or somehow outside the general work. But I don't want to suggest that my aim is a kind of invention of structure – it would be more accurate to say that this is the opposite of my aim, it is when the structure disappears or dissolves that I find something quite inspiring."

*Speaking of relations, I find that your work conducts an analysis not only of space, but of time as well. Although time and space are two different dimensions, they are identified here. Time and space coincide: space is the delimitation, in pencil, of the field; and the paper is the moment in time.*

"First, I would like to say something about the question of analysis. I find myself extremely interested in analysis in terms of the verbal, in terms of the speculations and the investigation in the work that I am doing, but I must emphasize that this comes after the work and is in a way in opposition to the work. I find that a work for me is something leading my intellect. I mean, I do not follow my intellect, but I am aware that my ability to receive is very much connected with my intellect. So I have proceeded to try to understand very well the nature of my intellect and its limitations and when I surrender my intellect, when I give up its 'special child', which is analysis, I proceed to step into a kind of unknown situation which I find is creative – as opposed to intellect in this case. But I don't want to overemphasize this separation, because in the work itself they go hand in hand. As for the other part of the question, about the time and space problem, I do feel that this work is for me the first time when I have made something which is a kind of a statement that time and space are the same thing. In that I feel quite strongly that my work exists between, as if, the two poles of knowledge and experience, that our experience of time and our knowledge of time are quite reversible as is our experience of place. So, I would simply ask the question then, could we not reverse the idea and say that perhaps our experience of a place is, shall we say, in our minds, circular?"

*Another thing I find very interesting in your work is the break with, the transgression of, the idea of the module. Paradoxically, your work is directed against geometry, it possesses "esprit de géometrie" without being geometric.*

"I agree with this idea. I would perhaps like to add that it is a characteristic of mine, part of my personality you might say, that I feel that if we have a problem, the only way to deal with it is to make it centralized. I feel that in twentieth-century art one of the most difficult areas is the area of sign. I think that much confusion arises about art, because it is associated with sign; my work has generally been sign-like with the hope of getting beyond that issue right from the beginning, not to find that problem coming up at some later place. In this sense the work does look like a model and it does have geometric bases, but it is exactly because these are so apparent, so obvious and so superficial in the work that I feel that once these have been set aside, as it were, we have a situation that is vastly more and more interesting."

*Going back to your earlier things, that you did, for instance, with metal wires that projected an image on the wall, I think your work is involved with research not only on the sign, but on its vir-*

*tuality too: a sign that is formed beyond matter, as a projection, a movement, an essence. In other words, matter is organized in signs.*

"I am going to answer this question in terms of a rather simple statement: it is through the signs that we find the real sign, but we need a sign to go through. Let us call them the sign of reality and the sign of appearance. There is a time when reality needs appearance and there is a time when appearance needs the real sign. In this sense it generally becomes fixed to a certain material, which has supplied a way of working; and this way of working is connected to my intention of finding a true reality or some evidence of a true reality. These two things are mutually exclusive and tend to contradict each other and, in this sense, whereas I need a material to work, I am very much against the material that I am using at any time. It is also connected with my feeling that I am not trying to make art, rather I am trying to get rid of artistic impulses. I feel that if I did not have to make art, I would know something about freedom; this intention of mine could then be stated as a desire for this freedom and yet be hopelessly tied to the material. As for this question of signs: I am not a sign-maker, although there have been structural analysts who were willing to stop with the consideration that artists are sign-makers. This is the very seat of the problem between the artist and the intellectual apprehension of what an artist does. The idea that the artist is a sign-maker of the society is clearly untrue in our civilization and I feel that the artist must take every opportunity to state the fact that his true role in society is exactly not the sign-maker and, in that sense, that signs are generally related to the material, the concrete. I feel that in my work it is necessary to have, within it, an anti-sign or anti-material emphasis."

*Insofar as your work possesses this tension towards what we might call a perfection of the sign, while repudiating geometry, it seems to me that the underlying cultural structures are Eastern as well as Western.*

"I feel that we are living in a world at this moment where we are in contact with so many cultures and so many societies, that the artist or someone who wishes to find a creative form, must certainly occupy himself with trying to understand cultures and societies and civilizations that are not necessarily his own. I have been quite interested in the Oriental world as it forms such an opposite point of view than the Western one. However, I also believe that the only thing that we Western people can know about the Orient is what we can understand about ourselves. I am not permitted to have such a full knowledge of the Japanese mind, for example, but I can know something about how this particular mind is different from my own. I also have felt a certain goal in this direction, in that we can make a kind of art that is neither East nor West, or both East and West. This would tend to enlarge one's self, bring one's self to a greater knowledge of something essential in life. So I have perused that course, among others, strange as may be. The situation has come about that if a Western person looks at a certain work of mine, they may in fact sense an affinity to the Oriental in that work, as well as an Oriental person might sense an affinity to the West. In Japan, for example, the idea of time can be communicated by a drop in the river. It is more typical in the West to think of the river as time and to look for a definition of space in another direction. This is a kind of opposition that is quite hopeless. We perhaps are characterized by an obsession to act, whereas the people in the East could be characterized by a position of waiting. I recognize and feel that the resolution of this opposition is quite necessary at this time."

*To what extent is your work related to the minimal mentality?*

"As far as my interest in simplicity – which is very good for communication – is concerned with the same ideas as a minimal existing in art, there is a relationship. I do not share the idea of minimal in terms of an end or that the minimal is enough in art. I myself am challenged by simplicity and always try to make my art simple and therefore communicable, able to be communicated, more easily, I hope."

*If I had to place your work, I would say it belongs to architecture more than to painting or sculpture.*

"Architecture is quite a free thing, we in fact do not really even know what architecture is; some people say it is the mother of the arts, some people say it is below the fine arts or it is not a fine art. This in itself is terribly interesting to a mind like mine, and perhaps that very sense of freedom that I find in architecture and do not find in painting or sculpture or drawing is more conductive to my direction. The aim is of course to communicate, and an aspect of communication is coming very close to another person. In a specific suggestion, which might be a definition, in this case, of architecture that is communicated from one mind – the author's mind – to another person, you have a very strong social *conviction* and perhaps this conviction, whereas it is not the essence of art, might be a motivation for it…"

*In my opinion there is a marked didactic quality in your work which comes out through the simplification of the instruments used and is created from the communication that art must have.*

"Here again we have a situation where there is a didactic quality in art, but for example in Western art some of the greatest examples have been extremely didactic, in the sense of being excellent propaganda for an idea that exists outside that art work. In the art of the East, I find the greatest examples are not didactic at all. Much of Western art seems to be involved in such a clear statement of a problem, in that this art tells the viewer something about himself; you find a didactic statement of the problems of life as we are aware of it in the West. I feel that art must concern itself with both sides. I do not like art which is only didactic, and finally I feel that if an artist can offer the viewer something that he can take something away from, to make a solution of his very own, in that situation he finds a kind of freedom which he does not ever experience when he is concerned with the production of a didactic system of forms… Intellectual systems can be the source of the propaganda. Malevich and Tatlin were not interested in religion, philosophy, etc. They were twentieth-century artists in that they hoped to push forward an intellectual system. *White on White* is such a great work because it is the clearest statement of the didactic quality within the system."

*So in the end what is the function of art?*

"In this question I see a kind of basic problem of something that is static and something that is dynamic. I concern myself with structural linguistics and feel quite happy and in a kind of agreement with this approach. However, I also feel some disagreement in that I find, whereas it is terribly interesting and perhaps useful at this time, that there is also another side of the question, one might say a non-structural, static side that is not accounted for. I feel as well that the potential of creativity is perhaps a unification of the static and the dynamic, it is a unification of the signifying and the signified."

*Do you believe in Reinhardt's affirmation "art as art"?*

"The conclusion of art is not the conclusion of art, to ape Ad Reinhardt's statement. I feel he would probably have agreed to such a statement. The necessity to make art is not housed in the idea of art, but is housed in the human being. As long as there are human beings on the earth, a few of them will have this necessity and perhaps what comes out of art is mostly directed to those other human beings who feel this necessity for themselves. In a way, one makes art in order to find friends. When I look at a Rembrandt or a Titian I am so happy to have a friend who supports my life, and perhaps at some time in some place someone may look at a work of mine and find something that supports their life. I expect no more than that. I have never experienced anything more than that. I just allow that as a possibility. I knew Ad Reinhardt well enough to understand his humour. He would say 'art as art' as a pointed statement from which a much less serious and more human element might derive. If I believed in anything, I would believe in what comes after such a statement as 'art as art', rather than in the statement itself. The statement's holes are mines; it is strong and simple, but my mind would like to travel some place else…"

# Robert Watts
Burlington, Vermont, 1923 – New York, 1988



*What is the difference for you between an event and a Happening?*
"Events are more like real life and they happen everyday, but in Happenings or in performances the score is planned."
*Can the performance that you are going to put on this evening be defined as an "event", and in what sense?*
"I think that the one of tonight is really a performance piece."
*It is not an event?*
"No, not so much."
*Do you work more often through the performance or through the event?*
"For this piece, I think it is an event in the sense that after it's finished people of the audience can associate it to their own lives. But both Happening and performance are more alive than theatre and drama, they are more theatrical."
*What value does the reutilization of the objects of everyday use have in your work? You have always used everyday objects in your works, objects that already existed. What value do you give to these objects?*
"I just use them for what they are, there's no other significance."
*What was it that led you to shift from a scientific activity – for you are an engineer, aren't you? – to an artistic activity?*
"Yes, I was an engineer. But at a certain point I and my work were replaced by a computer."
*So what do you expect from art and what significance do you give to your artistic experience?*
"Oh, seems we need a Bible! If the work is good, for some people in the audience it may be a revelation, an important connection in their lives. That is number one; number two is that I have to do my own revolution."
*So for you art can also be a transmission of energy.*
"Yes, energy, and ideas, and knowledge."
*So we could say that Fluxus signifies transmission of magnetic waves?*

"Electromagnetic waves, some kind of universal energy…"

*Is there a linguistic connection between your work and the experiments, for example, of John Cage?*

"Something, yes. I think we have a similar feeling about Oriental philosophy and religion. Then, in early date Cage was interested in random occurrences. In my own work I adopt random situations and use them mechanically in my performances as well as in other works."

*Going even further back, can we find a lineage that runs from Duchamp to Cage to Fluxus? What has Fluxus taken from Duchamp?*

"It has taken Duchamp's attitude towards objects and the question of giving up art in order to get something else. But for Duchamp it was kind of a joke, because he nevertheless continued his work."

*Along with this mental attitude of Duchamp's, in my view Fluxus also draws on Zen, on Oriental culture, on an Eastern dimension of time. I would like to know if you agree and to what extent this happens with you.*

"Well, I think it's an indirect influence, in the sense that we all have read about it. When we read poetry we feel something in ourselves that's similar. This happens in a very special way also with actions."

*How do these actions end up in your work?*

"Every day on my car I go out to my pond and stand two or three hours watching the fish. When I first put the fish in the pond, I watched them grow up, but now I can't eat them any more."

*I find it interesting that in your work there is not first a plan and then an action, but there is an action which is at one and the same time plan and life, events.*

"My life consists in actions."

*Western culture has accustomed us to having a plan first, then the idea and then reality as the realization of that idea. Instead, Eastern culture has taught us that reality is always richer than the abstract idea.*

"You know, what you said is the very pure situation…"

*What value do you give to the presence of the public and its participation?*

"Hope."

*Your position also seems to me a very American, Anglo-Saxon attitude towards life and the problems of art, which can be defined in one single word: pragmatism.*

"Well, I think that American work, I mean some American work including my own, is pragmatic in the sense that each time we do something it is connected with our experience."

*This suggests to me that in some way you too are a spectator among the spectators of your actions.*

"I am."

*What was the first artistic action that you did when you left computers behind?*

"In 1946 I came to New York after a period in the Navy, to study art. I studied art in the evening and worked during the day as an engineer. Then I quit my job and went to Columbia to study art history. In the university I studied primitive art: American Indian and South Pacific."

*What was your first work?*

"At the age of seven, I carved a pig out of wood."

*Then what was your second work, when you stopped being an engineer?*

"I studied painting and did watercolours and at Columbia I studied sculpture. My first work was welded sculpture."

*What meaning had for you the passage from the fixed object to the event, which is instead an active, dynamic situation?*

"I think it has to do with my early connections with Fluxus. The energy of Fluxus came from somewhere. A lot of people at the same time between 1957 and 1959 took a similar direction. I was doing large paintings à la Pollock and welded sculpture at the same time. But then I got frustrated, nothing was going right with the painting, so when I was painting with the broom, one day I just picked it up, threw it out of the room and said to myself 'c'est fini'. I can't remember the rest. Something similar happened to other artists like Alan Kaprow and George Brecht."

*How did you come into contact with Fluxus?*

"It was in 1962; George Maciunas was in Germany, working as a graphic designer and he was already organizing performances in Europe with Dan Harrison, Alison Knowles, Dick Higgins, Thomas Smith. And when Alison and Dick came back to

America they told me about George and suggested I send him some of my events. At that time he was in a hospital with asthma, so I thought to make events for George to be performed in the hospital while he was sick. This was my first connection with Maciunas. He wrote me many letters from Europe."

*What changed in your work following the encounter with Fluxus?*

"Everything and nothing. I'm always the same."

*What is Fluxus for you?*

"This is a very difficult question. It's somehow a different channel of energy. It flows in and out. It had to do with my and other people's experience in Fluxus and their energy."

*This means that according to you there is no energy in the world and therefore only art can create it, does it not? What does energy mean for you?*

"I think it's some kind of exchange, of communication. When I wrote the piece I showed last night, I already knew that there was a problem. I couldn't do what I wanted to do here, so I made a piece out of this. So it did happen last night, it was impossible to do anything; so, maybe, I knew that subconsciously. The world is full of energy of all kind, positive, negative. And if it turns to myself, I can get really all my energy, but I'm not able to know in advance what will happen. I think I picked up something when I wrote it and something was happening, the energy was coming through, but the reading was not so clear."

*So for you art is always a direct experience, is that right?*

"Even now I can relate some kind of energy."

*But this means that you cannot think about an event before having a direct relationship with the space, a physical relationship with it. How did you decide, for example, on the actions to be carried out in Italy before getting to know the spaces in Milan and Verona?*

"Well, it's very difficult. I made some changes to resolve the problem last night, when Di Maggio showed me the space. I really didn't want to do it there, but he said 'do it here'. To come down and see a place and to do a piece after is something completely different."

*But does this energy exist before the action or is it only created during the action?*

"The vibe comes down after you look at the space. Then you start feeling things about it and you create a performance from the way you feel it. It's not something planned in advance. You can't do that for a place you don't know anything about. Here I changed the whole thing this afternoon and went upon a different idea."

*Is there a difference for you between working in an enclosed structure like a gallery and working in open spaces?*

"I don't like galleries, too much control, too much artificial."

*Where does the control lie?*

"It means that I'm affected by the reason of a building. Who did it, and why..."

*To me this seems a bit like Fluxus's general attitude towards commercial structures.*

"Maybe, I just like to do things that are non-commercial. We have a bad feeling about things that are just commercial, intended only for the commercial world. Of course there is a problem of money because we have to eat. Fluxus knows very well how to make money. For instance, last year I bought something which I knew could only keep about nine months. I shouldn't have bought it, but I had the money so I bought it and now I will sell it to get the money to do an electronic sound piece. This is a very Fluxus-style way to make money."

*Fluxus is an idea, not a group.*

"Yes, it's not a group, it's an idea. It's what we talked about earlier, some kind of energy. Each person in Fluxus is a kind of planet from some different planetary system. But somehow we are all related to the public."

*In your view, is there any element of theatricality in the event or in your actions?*

"No, not for me. Ask Kaprow."

*Why?*

"Because he wants theatre."

*He likes spectacular action.*

"Allan Kaprow is in love with the Roman arena, with the lions and tigers."

*Can we say that the difference between the Happening and the event, between the Happening and your performances, is that the*

*Happening relies on accumulation – of gestures, people, situations – whereas events are not an accumulation but a progression?*

"Yeah, I think so. What kind of progression?"

*An unfolding, and, if there is, a continuity.*

"This is a very dangerous word for me."

*Why?*

"It has something to do with my own evolution, with my own way of dealing with the world, with the human being: this kind of progression."

*Even if Fluxus is an idea, don't you think that it has now become a label too? What I am trying to say is that Fluxus is the idea of a mode of conduct, whereas today it runs the risk of turning into just an artistic movement.*

"Only because the art world became more interested in Fluxus recently."

*In my opinion Fluxus has something to do with anthropology, do you agree?*

"I don't know how Fluxus could be connected with anthropology."

*As a pattern of behaviour.*

"Like sociology? No, I don't think either. Fluxus is just a little bit of that, not anthropology, these are conceptions of man. Men like to define things. I'm only talking here because I am polite."

*I've written an article for Di Maggio's magazine that will come out in a few days and that is called "Fluxus as Fluxus".*

"The more words are said about Fluxus the worse it is."

# Sandro Chia
Florence, 1946



*Where shall we begin?*

"Let me tell you a story, which we'll call mine because I'm the one who's telling it, although that doesn't mean it's my own story. A new artist comes onto the scene, but not without forgetting his part altogether (in fact, he should have sung, and could have, too, in the surprising abundance of his attitudes). On the contrary, and on the crest of a recent change, he completely ignores every obligation of part and position, and goes to take his place almost at the back of the scenes, amidst the moving mirrors and devices for various tricks. From here he begins to slide, perhaps in the direction of the scene, but to our dismay any number of directions can be postulated. This ham's entrance onto the stage is in no way connected with time and the progress of events. He does not progress, he wastes every asset the scene provides him with."

*And he isn't thrown out?*

"In the semblance of representation, rather than representing events, he lets himself be represented as an unnecessary and replaceable object in a theatre of errors. Because errors and enticements on the stage echo backstage and accumulate towards a zenith to form the splendour of a peak. The new artist, with one eye on the stage and the other on the peak, rejects passivity: he thinks. And his thought, it seems, attributes little importance to the iniquity of the scene. Nor does he fear the vortex of distillation towards a more immaculate conception, provided that he is allowed to move around on the mobile threshold of the back side, an uncommon place where, extraordinarily, thought is possible."

*In exchange, the thinking artist shoots off sparks of light and darkness in the direction of the stage, deforming himself, becoming thinner, fatter, splitting, disappearing, and reappearing. Does he come forward?*

"One can say that the manoeuvring ground, the ground for thought and the threshold of the back of the stage are a sole line of profile delimiting the unstable figure of the new artist-thinker.

173

The novelty of his participation does not lie so much in the dissipation of his part, but consists instead in questioning and answering dialectically, in thinking problematically, where thinking does not inspire happiness or freedom. Then the audience, accustomed to every contortion and to the most impudent disguises, exchanges admiring opinions of real innovation: 'This is the new pupil of a non-interpretable art, pure criticism of a reason in itself'. 'How different from the old and hard-working artist devoted to research, to the problem of problems, to conveyance by symbols. But how different, too, from the melancholia suspended towards the indifference of things and of the world'."

*What does his art consist in?*

"The clarity of his chiaroscuro art depends on certain rarities of statements: titles stated once only, and then immediately replaced. These require a certain amount of attention. In turn they promise the novelty of a point of view, but not the originality. As a matter of fact, terms of beginning, grounding, and origin are ill suited to this thinking artist, since his very presence is separate and full of gaps. It is an emission that refers only to the filled void of itself, which for this reason could be another."

*But is it recognizable?*

"It can be recognized on the basis of absence and normality: absence of style, class, or classicism, and normality of the title, which is the rule, the predicate of and the check on the pure emission in a context of strange homogeneity and narrowness between practice and theory."

*But does this madman who desires desire alone have a name?*

"Clearly, the name of this artist is an anagram of itself, or a trade name, because here, too, he has to be mobile, mortal, and masked (it is important for the attributes of the name to begin with 'm', as in 'mother'). Thus the name is transmitted in a special form, so as to avert every notion of origin or anonymity in a variety or a blank list. An example of how the artist shows himself as circumstances permit is: by mimicry. By mimicry that alludes to the jumping frog, a concatenation of smaller and larger cones. One is clearly dealing with the three-dimensional outline of a perverse and possible change that at once regards the form of form, or the form of meaning, or the mimicry of the jump. In fact, the data on the regeneration of the limbs of beetles or newts, despite their anatomical differences, follow the same basic rules of cellular interaction. These rules can be schematized by representing the limb as a cone, for instance. A curious scheme, with unusual properties: sections of this cone (beetle or newt leg) regenerate the amputated part, or duplicate the stump, depending on where the cut is made. If a fragment is capable of regenerating itself, the complementary fragment duplicates itself. Hence, we have a very strange looking cone, in many ways similar to our multiple-show philosophical theatre."

## Gilbert & George
San Martino in Badia, Bolzano, Italy, 1943
Plymouth, Devon, Great Britain, 1942

London
1976

*Can you explain the "red sculptures", the use of red on your faces and hands?*

"We have been doing red photopieces. We like the subject of the red. Red has so many meanings: love, violence… Red has a great aesthetic influence in old China and also in new China. It is a colour to which one must be attentive. We like all the meanings of the red; when you look in the dictionary all the meanings are there – red things as subject: red roses. For us red is not a colour, it is like blood. We have red and black."

*You use also gold?*

"Yes on the faces – it was gold with silver, bronze… But gold is not a colour, it has some meaning like red, like black."

*I remember that your first living sculptures of 1969 had colours that were related to nature, whereas the red of the "red sculptures" has non-natural political and psychological connotations.*

"It is true, it is not natural at all. It is completely only meaning. Not very political considerations, but yes, of course, red is also the colour of fighting."

*This Red Sculpture show is divided into moments. How many are there?*

"Nine sections with a beginning and an end."

*That makes eleven moments. There are words and verbal commands that make the living sculptures move. What kind of progression is there between one phrase and another?*

"There is always the same use of the same tape every time. Each session represents an aspect or a detail of our life."

*Is there any special reference between your works?*

"They are subjects in which we have been involved. For example, we did a series of works on *Human Bondage*, all sorts. We put them together and we did it. When we are doing it we even try to feel it."

*What are the nine sections, phrases, or propositions called again?*

"First the title, *The Red Sculpture*; then comes *Human*

*Bondage and Dark Shadow, Ready, Cherry Blossoms, Bad Forces and Broken Heart, Coming, Wooden Air, Bloody Life and Dusty Corners, Gone, Red Boxes,* and *The Red Sculpture*."

*What is the relation between the phrases, the propositions and gestures, and the movements you perform on this small stage?*

"They represent the physical equivalent of these words."

*The movements are slowed down quite a bit, though. They're very slow, very small minimal movements. Why?*

"Because in this way they mean much more, they are more descriptive. We like to make it as clear as possible: it is like writing something very, very slowly, carefully for someone to understand us. It is what we are in general, but more framed up, so that people can see it more easily, can see better what we are."

*Ever since you started doing the living sculptures, you've used a suit that is always more or less the same.*

"Yes, it is the same suit."

*I remember when I saw the first living sculpture there was music and your faces were covered with a sort of blue bronze gold. It was very colourful.*

"It was powder."

*It lasted eight hours, the whole time the place was open… Your early work was done in direct relation to the people who came and went. Why do you now ask that the audience sit still and not move?*

"It is just a different form of sculpture. This one has a beginning and an end…"

*It's like a book, people have to stay put and see the beginning and the end.*

"Well, let's say that it is a question of form."

*What is the logic behind the timing of this work? Because there's a timing here in the sense of rhythm, rather than duration…*

"It is a formalized work, like when we do a book. There is a beginning and an end at every page. The opposite of a movie. Every aspect of life is given in the sculpture the same tension, the same frame. As in a microscope: you put the next slide and it is a fly or something else, but it is the same cycle of life."

*It is the opposite of a movie, because everything is already in focus in a movie. It's interesting that here, as in a microscope, things have to be brought to focus, then the image takes form little by little. I mean, there is no narrative as such. Each part is like putting a microscope up to an object and then bringing it to focus.*

"It is the same as in our photopieces."

*What relation is there between Gilbert and George in each sequence? Are the movements synchronized, is there a mirror-image relationship?*

"The same relation exists between us and the sculpture that exists between two people in human life. We do the same movements, but we are still different. The work shows the similarities and the differences."

*I would like to ask some technical questions about your work. Although surely similar in their difference and different in a sort of resemblance, do both living sculptures, Gilbert and George, always respond in the same way to the words that come off the tape?*

"The work simply is based on a system. All the pieces we do are based on systems. One needs a form to put something on paper, or in photographs, or in books. First we find a form to explain ourselves, then we do it."

*What is the purpose of this little stand, or stage? It's just like the base of a sculpture...*

"It is very simple: they can see us better. We like it because it is a frame."

*Each section, each phrase of this work corresponds to some of your preceding works. All nine of them. Right?*

"At the time we made the sculpture, summer 1975, these were the main nine categories we could break our life into, our experience. It is a frame, a context, such as one has in normal life: one has a day, another has a house. They are groupings, categories."

*Essentially you're saying that every section of this work corresponds to moments of your past work, and these moments correspond to moments in your lives. But now I would like some sort of linguistic explanation, because these phrases are still slightly complicated. For instance, what does* Human Bondage *and* Dark Shadows *mean, exactly?*

"We just took the truth from our life, there was no other possibility. It is all biographical anyway, we can't make anything up. We just took a reading from our life at the time of making the sculpture, that is what we found in our life."

*Right. But, again, what exactly does this phrase mean, in your life and in your work? As I see, there aren't any dark shadows in the second section…*

"That's not important. They are metaphorical phrases."

*Let's move on to the second moment,* Ready. *Does this, too, correspond to a moment in your lives at which you were "ready"?*

"Ready in the general sense."

*And what about* Cherry Blossoms?

"This is a very famous title for us, it has a lot of meanings. The Japanese use the same term for young soldiers, because they are the first to come. The cherry blossoms are the first flowers to appear, the young soldiers are the first to volunteer."

*So, can we say that in the* Cherry Blossoms *section you go through the motions of looking for flowers on the ground? Is it possible to look at it this way?*

"Well, in the *Ready* section we could be looking at the blossoms on a tree. In *Cherry Blossoms* we are just looking at the earth. Everything overlaps in life, so also within the sculpture there are overlaps."

*What general relation is there between phrases and movements?*

"We show our feeling about *Cherry Blossoms*. They are the first ones to fade away, like young soldiers who are the first ones to be killed."

*Are the gestures always an illustration of the phrase, or are they emotional responses to the phrase?*

"Half and half. It takes us half a year or even a year sometimes to prepare each new movement."

*Well, I think this is not a formalization of movement, it is a work of emotion. After you had been doing these things for years, you found a formal parallelism to your work in certain ways of being, acting, and moving in the Oriental films of Ku Fu, which you find very amusing. If you think of what certain actors have done and how they move, there are some strange equivalencies.*

"Yes, we were influenced. You can certainly see similarities, because we really like those films."

*It's a slowness, a slackening of the pace of things. There is a timing in the living sculptures that absolutely is not Western.*

"The sculpture is not slow, it is the natural time for a sculpture. It would be inaccurate to say it is slow."

*So, where is the Oriental influence we are talking about?*

"You see, we are influenced by a lot of things. It could be an English gentleman. Or it could be a Shakespearean actor."

*OK, but one thing is certain: it is not a naturalistic time.*

"Of course: it is the time of sculpture."

# Luciano Fabro
Turin, 1936 – Milan, 2007



*Contemporary art generally starts out from an initial state of in-completeness. It promises something that it can't give in the beginning, because it can't work by itself. Do your works give a sense of fullness, or do they follow this sort of rule of the initial incompleteness of contemporary art?*

"I find that contemporary art for the most part is reductive, except in a few cases that aren't particularly well understood. Up until the eighteenth century art unwound itself rather like a polyp that extends its tentacles a little bit in every direction. But in the nineteenth century with the advent of the middle class, specialization, and the specific use of the best in one detail, one tried to achieve reduction by creating a kind of dissociation. Reduction in the work of the artist helped guarantee the viewer a dissociation of his own, to understand a detail and to be able to identify with or talk about that detail. One of my expectations, ambitions, or desires has been to reverse this situation: that is, instead of reducing the field of inquiry, which in the end always tends to be identified with the ego, I wanted to throw it open to the entire refraction of the impression, of the urgings. Just as things are visible in the round, so that our knowledge of them in the last analysis is a matter of 'the more we go round them, the more we learn'. So I thought I would try to do something similar with my works. I hope my explanation hasn't been too chaotic."

*In what sense, for instance, do you say your works give a sense of fullness?*

"This term is valid within the limits of the current mood towards art. Perhaps at another moment or in another civilization, in another context, my works would not give this impression of fullness. However, there is a tendency with regard to contemporary art to polarize meaning and attention, and to circumscribe the field of inquiry. When one goes out of bounds it feels like, well, too much sugar: that is, one acquires a palate for delicacies only, and risks to lose the taste for more substantial things."

*It seems to me that you have always tried to shift art from significance to the signifier. Let's take one of your works, which is already quite radical in itself: a gallery floor just covered by a layer of newspaper. What relation can you establish, for instance, between this work and your definition, or at least the clues you give, when you say your works give this sense of fullness?*

"This piece came at the end of a series of works concerning the experience that exists between viewer, artist and artwork. The same theme inspired the *Hole*, too, which preceded this piece by five years, so I'd had a chance to think things over… In this work I kind of wanted to catch the viewer, whom I called the guest, by the tail. This guest expects to see, and to remain detached from what he sees, to have a sort of tourist's attitude towards art. So, I did this work, which really doesn't even belong to what might be called the specific field of art, but, naturally, can be considered an artistic provocation. I took part of the regular floor – it was a pretty simple gallery, like an apartment, so I could even make reference to situations familiar to the visitor – and I cleaned it, waxed it, and covered it with newspaper. But the work is not complete as such, it has to be coupled with a caption, a piece of precise information. In this caption I said that the enjoyment, the reading of this work, consisted solely – not substantially or also, but *solely* – in the operation itself. That is, in order to enjoy this work it was necessary to clean and cover it; in other words, the work consisted solely in working on it (after all, it's something that many people do, housewives do it), solely in this preserving, this keeping a thing the best one can, as I remember people doing in my hometown, when they cleaned the floors and then covered them, at least the first day, so they wouldn't get dirty… There was this clean feeling, which, however, couldn't be put to the test, because that first day or two or three that it was covered with paper so it wouldn't get dirty, nobody actually saw the clean floor. Nevertheless, there was this way of considering the work and preserving it, not as ostentation, but as something almost private, an attempt to assure that something that might have cost a day's work, didn't go up in smoke."

*I was thinking of another statement of yours: "The artist today must re-educate the senses for the sake of the intellect". The de-*

*scription you just gave us of your work with the newspaper, this reference to a domestic situation – even an anthropological situation, I would say, this going back to the memory of facts that belong to your personal history, helps us understand how this coupling of the sensorial with the intellectual is one of your systematic ways of working. You never work on one thing or another, but always on an alternation of seemingly contradictory elements. At a moment like this, in which there's a lot of talk about conceptual art, you quite rightly call attention to the existence of a sensorial whole. The self-referential tenor of the linguistic tools that are used is invariably linked with the pleasure in really attaining an impact, a relationship with the images in which even the material has an importance of its own. Elsewhere you say: "To prevent the discovery in oneself of a state of nature, and to simulate agreement with one's own artifice, is commonly called hypocrisy; whereas art is that artifice which corresponds to the state of nature. A comic example of simulation is the dissemination of artworks in which a photographer photographs a photographer to make a photograph that represents a photograph to be photographed, accompanied by 300 lines that re-explain the rediscovery of photography". As a matter of fact, you systematically avoid – and this is what I meant when I spoke earlier of a strategy of shifting and overturning – working with symmetrical elements. In this connection I would like to call attention to a work you did for an exhibition I curated in 1973,* Contemporanea. *The work is* The Deceased, *a marble sculpture that rejects the idea of art's perpetual search for new subjects, languages and materials.*

"I really don't prefer any one material, but then I don't think any artist does, really. Each case is different, and one adopts the material that is best suited to the task at hand. I used marble because I could count on a certain evocative capacity marble has: nothing historical or cultural, but an indirect quality. What I mean is, this sort of material, precisely because it has been used so much, lets the attention shift to certain changes. What's more, it is a particularly warm medium. In fact, the same object had to be made in plaster first, it *was* made in plaster: there's quite a difference between plaster and marble. I think marble was used for so many centuries not so much because it had been used in the centuries before, but because artists saw that it lent itself to a certain mode of expression, facilitating a certain kind of approach. This sculpture consists of a cloth draped over a body, except that at a certain point, at the height of the shoulders, the body should emerge from the cloth, or the sheet, but doesn't, not because that part has been removed but because beginning at the end that is covered better, at the feet, I mean, as one slowly proceeds towards the head there is a continuous degradation of the structure, so that when one gets to the end of the sheet, the physical structure one expects to find underneath is no longer there. I mean, one notices it isn't there; but it wasn't there before, either. The work was studied to make it look as though the body beneath the cloth had disappeared, passed away, passed *out*, leaving only the self-supporting sheet. What is left, what gives one the idea that the body is underneath, is only the sheet, propped up to stay in place. If you remove the feet the sheet stays up just the same. But describing a work is always a bit embarrassing, and then one is never able to explain things the way they really are. *The Deceased* was conceived and the first trials were made at the same time as *Tamerlan*, which is much smaller and much nicer. That they were done at the same time is important, for there is a correlation between the two moments. *Tamerlan* has not a face, or even an invented mask, but the outside of a mould. You see, to make a mould from a face, plaster is poured onto the face itself. The features, of course, are impressed on the inside, but I reproduced the outside. And the two straws: what do they stand for? If you take the cast of a living person, even the most cooperative model has to breathe, and so you give him two straws so he can go on breathing throughout the operation, which takes ten minutes or so. The two straws mean that the person is alive. This face has nothing in common with invented or symbolic masks. It has the same make-up and shows the same kind of approach as the mould. What is different is that you see it from the other side; that is, instead of looking at the image, you see what lies behind it. Although you can't really *see* it, you might make out a face behind the mask, but at the same time the image that's in front of it is embarrassing. So there is a continuous give and take, a negation of the visual impression in favour of a reading that takes you further. In *The Deceased* the sheet refers to the body. The only legible thing, however, is the sheet. Hence, a dichotomy is established between the purely visual reading – and it's no coincidence that I made this point precisely at a time when it seemed that the only possible culture, or at least that which was most popular and defensible, was visual culture – and the cognitive reading. A visual reading, of course, gives the sheet. A cognitive reading gives rise to the question, 'what is the sheet or the mask hiding, and why does it correspond with the real image to which it refers?'"

*You not only speak of visual language, you also maintain that the image brings about something else. Hence, a cognitive relationship that utilizes, but does not stop at, the image, is really possible.*

"What I'm trying to do is track down the substance in reality at an inherent level where I really can't decide anything, I can only check if a thing coincides with certain data inherent in reality, or not. If it doesn't, I throw the thing away, because there is no reason for it to occupy space. If on the other hand I have the impression that it does, then I keep it on reserve."

*This provides for an ethical component in your work, in fact. I'd like to quote one more statement of yours: "The work of the artist is always moral. Even when a painter brings a colour back to its purity, as when he puts a shadow in the proper place". This seems like just the epitaph…*

"Yes. I didn't want to make too much of morality, as a sort of messiah that must necessarily bring about a revolution; anyway, this revolution has to involve millions of people…"

*The consciousness of the immanence of art, of the relativity of the work of the artist, denies its ethics. This is very important.*

"Consciousness of the quality, not the relativity; that is, of the quality regardless of the relativity…"

# Jannis Kounellis
Piraeus, Greece, 1936



*Can your work be considered in an ideological sense?*

"What a shame that we cannot make politics in interviews!"

*Why not?*

"I'm not talking about politics as ideology, but rather politics as behaviour. It is easy to say that Marat is Marat, that David was a Jacobin, that he made Marat and did all those things; or that someone else is a communist. But talking about ideology in a sphere which isn't that of its content is an extensive topic. Sure, politics is worth art, but how much and how? It's worth art because making art in this dimension is dialectical. But at the bottom of this there is a consideration, the birth of Impressionism. The birth of Impressionism is an ideology in itself which describes a situation which politically, ideologically, as a structure, has already been achieved."

*In your opinion, is there a general ideology of art, and what is this ideology?*

"But the ideology of the artist, the ideology of art that is, does not exist in itself, because art is an expression. Not all artists have the same ideology in fact, not even the people who do the same things have the same ideology. So this is important."

*What is the critical vision of your work?*

"The critical vision is the reason for birth, the reason that is born is the critical vision, not of my work that is, but of any work."

*But to what degree is your work critical? I'd really like to understand this.*

"It's really very difficult to answer the question to what degree a work is critical, how a work presents itself. It presents itself in a critical way, as far as it is critical. Critical because it arises from a critical relationship. Using horses, in fact, is a critical relationship, but not just this…"

*So for you a work is critical when it places two elements in a dialectic?*

"A work is not critical only for this, it is critical for many reasons. The base of the word is true for many artists, but absolutely not for me."

*This critical thought which is then displayed in an artistic form has a function, not just on the spectator but on you too. Art for you, that is, your work, has a liberating function.*

"All art is liberating, whatever it is… that's why we do it, because if not I don't understand why one should be an artist."

*But do you think art alone can liberate reality?*

"It isn't possible to liberate reality alone, and this for a number of reasons, because art doesn't have the same instruments as politics. Art always proposes a utopian way to be achieved, it is not true that it can modify reality on its own, this would really be a Utopia."

*So art proposes alternative models, a different way of behaviour?*

"It is difficult to say models, because that immediately leads to the artist and what he does as an example, and that is a humanistic position. It's like that too, but art is more freed from humanism because humanism always has a precise end while art is transcendent – if it doesn't transcend it isn't art."

*Couldn't this transcendence be the ideological aspect of art?*

"Art in itself doesn't have an ideology, it can't possibly have one. Art has a history, and since it has a history it represents ideologies; that is, each time it is displayed with an ideology, but it's not ideology in itself."

*A constant of European art, or of a certain recent kind of European art, is that of always considering the artistic gesture, imagination, not as an improvisation, but always as a relationship and a series of relations with the culture of the past. Does this kind of relation exist in your work too?*

"As far as I'm concerned, I like Masaccio very much, because I think he's a great revolutionary. As for Rembrandt and the other artists, I like all of this, not because it increases the variety but because it increases the profundity; that is, as I see it today. Naturally enough from a physical point of view, Rembrandt represents many things, he also represents a certain bourgeoisie, not as a representative of course, but as a painter. I like Goya too, and other things as well: Piero della Francesca, the ancient Greeks. All this has a single denominator."

*It seems to me that all your work always tends to re-establish for you, or for the spectator, the totality; that is, it rediscovers even the lost links, it re-establishes an anthropological condition that reality does not allow us, and it also seems to me that the way in which you tend to reaffirm this totality is the rite. It seems to me that in your work there is usually a ritual. Do you agree?*

"Yes, but we need ideas. How can we relive an ancient rite? We can't make it come back to life any more because we have lost the signs, the common run that is, because the rite is common, and precisely that rite is tied to a certain type of community."

*In point of fact I think that your work tends to establish a community experience, not an individual one. The paintings sung and played, the fire, a series of elements, that is, pour out in the moment in which the spectators are all together in front of the work, and so the work is not a dumb object that can be experienced individually in any moment, but it is alive in so far as it lets itself be taken by the entire community. In this sense the rite is the way – I think – of re-establishing a kind of concentrated community, a reading which is no longer solitary, but where the spectators can find a contact between each other again. Can we say that your work tends to produce a communitary ecstasy?*

"Do you think so? I don't understand when they talk about ecstasy, I don't understand if this is a defect for me, why they say 'ecstasy', this is the term they use: understand people who talk to you, when they say poetry, that is, they mean one thing but I mean something quite different."

*What do you mean by poetry?*

"Poetry is the story of creation, that's what I mean by poetry. And creating in any case is poetry. Here there's an idyllic image of poetry, almost heavenly… But the *value* of poetry is very vast, not what is meant by poetry. So when you talk to me about ecstasy, I don't know what that ecstasy is."

*OK, let's talk about your work then.*

"It's a work that has its own particular time, that's all."

*A work where the two times correspond, don't they? The time in which, for example, the violinist plays your painting necessarily corresponds to the time in which the spectators participate and experience this work.*

"Yes, but this too is an evaluation of the role of the artists and what they produce. I don't know, in the fourteenth century there was a certain type of artist, his presence was much more… social. So we must also consider the gallery as an environment; the gallery was a shop at the beginning, but it was found to be also a point of fruition. So its characteristics are already different from the gallery in the nineteenth century, which only sold these things. It's a certain kind of painting, precisely because everything is tied to ideology."

*So in your opinion the rite of art is the possibility or the attempt to make art social once again?*

"Yes, in my opinion this is the height of being social. I'm not able to view the artist as a private being."

*In your work, and this is true even if we go right back to the early paintings with the letters, there is the continual attempt to lighten the weight of the object by introducing an impalpable element, that of music, which in your more recent works has become, I would say, quite an important part of your creation. So then, the introduction of the musical element. If we carry on the theme we were talking about earlier, that is the constant introduction of a dialectical element, what value does it have?*

"First of all, we need to see what kind of music we are talking about, because there's a kind of music that gives you an image which is determining and figurative. I think that it isn't true that there is an abstract music because it gives us precise references which are like words – everything, that is, is tied to the image. Then there are different properties, the use, that is, that one makes of music: I use it as a painter, I don't like music as a musician that is, I like it as a painter."

*Earlier I used the word "poetry" about your work because it seems to me that you always have the intention of never defining anything by means of your work, but always alluding, producing, that is, allusive works. In this sense, if music is allusive in that it is an impalpable element, it seems to me that the word "poetics" can correspond, not to the qualitative value of your work in which all the successful pieces are poetical, as we said before, but rather to a sort of condition above your work itself.*

"Before you said 'impalpable', something extensive but which doesn't escape you, it is defined. This is a consideration: if you say that there is a kind of flat, horizontal civilization and the other is vertical, naturally everyone of us interprets one part of these activities, so this is more impalpable because it's not that it's more possible, but it's wider. Anarchy is the ability to understand and not make judgements, so it is an opening because a judgement is a limitation with precise interests. Of course a judgement is very often revolutionary."

*Contemporary artistic experiences tend to present the themes of death, paralysis and immobility. Your work, on the other hand, in so far as it is based on dialectics is, I think, a work that tends to represent not paralysis but movement, not death or immobility but life and expansion.*

"I wouldn't say that the work is based on illuminism. It's you, that is, who base yourself on illuminism."

*In what sense?*

"Illuminism is the product of all our Western culture and it has provided the basis on which the entire bourgeois revolution, and the Marxist one too, has based itself. When I think about the horses, I am very pleased that it was like the cover of a book by Voltaire."

*As a good illuminist, you also know that art alone is not sufficient to underturn the world.*

"No, it's clear that it's not sufficient. But art gives expression to a certain world. It isn't sufficient to underturn the world, I'd say rather that art provides energy."

# Mario Merz
Milan, 1925 – Turin, 2003

Turin
1977

*Mario, you've raised a problem which concerns the whole of contemporary art, and by means of which the knotty relationship of 'art and politics' is tackled – the problem of iconography. What do you mean by iconography?*

"The problem of iconography can be seen from two points of view: it would seem that iconography is the product of a society, a heap of men put together, and from the positivist or rational point of view this idea could even be valid. But in reality I think that iconography is not a product but simply the very expression of life, so that men produce iconography in the moment that they live, human life is iconography in itself. So it isn't what is generally thought, what unfortunately many think today, that it is a derivation of the bourgeois category of the last century, according to which we have an iconography in so far as we are a society. Even disintegrating societies have an iconography, so in reality iconography isn't a product but is the very life of man. I remember that I've always seen the paintings of the great masters of the past in reproductions – I've rarely seen the real paintings. A reproduction allows you to see a painting by Cézanne 70 × 50 cm as if it were a painting by Tintoretto that is 12 metres long. So, in reality, the reproduction reproduces the same thing, it gives you the iconographical dimension, but it doesn't give you the truth of iconography, it gives you an iconography which is different from what the painting itself really is. All artists have the basic mania of thinking that they are the iconographic experts of the society. Renato Guttuso still thinks that he is the iconographic expert of a new society in revolution. Many American artists I've talked to believe that giving a conceptual product means taking on the responsibility of understanding that a sentence, or a thought, is an iconographical product. In my opinion they are right up to the limit in which that iconographical product is, let's say, a coin of exchange for everyone; but they totally lose the moment of truth when they think that this is a new iconography for America."

*To what degree is your work iconographical?*

"From time to time my work is iconographical, but it does not set out from iconography. From time to time, that is, it becomes iconography in that it is inserted in contexts which are already iconographical. Take for example architecture: be it a gallery, or a private space, or a public space like a museum – these are iconographical spaces that have already been determined in other periods. So when my product penetrates one of these previous products, it becomes iconographical out of symbiosis I'd say. In fact, many of my works are a struggle between what I make and what existed before, and in the best examples this becomes a dialectical note."

*What's the meaning of the number for you?*

"I've used the number to get out of iconography which, it seemed to me, was always presenting itself. So the number, in my opinion, is this way of getting out, it's an exit not an entrance. The number automatically leads you out of the iconographical concept that too often is presented, almost like ghosts. I believe today that everyone can have iconographical ghosts, they can have the ghost of Goya just like they can have the ghost of Titian, they can have much more ancient ghosts or the ghost of a child's drawing, or else the ghost of a technical drawing. They are all ghosts in my opinion."

*You mentioned architecture…*

"I think architecture is inevitably iconographical, and at the same time it's a vital necessity. So when it's a vital necessity it's supreme iconography, it adheres completely, that is, to the complete iconography of life. Today, however, since the product of architecture is basically an inferior product since people live more in the streets than they did before and they spend a lot of time in the bars and in public places, then there's no longer this courtly relationship between what is the environment in which you live and the person who lives in this environment. It's the product that represents the property: everyone seeks to create for themselves an environment as favourable as possible for themselves and their own life."

*What part does the concept of proliferation play in your work?*

"Proliferation is a means of exit since it means self-understanding. Proliferation, that is, is naturally a simplification of everything I'm saying here, so on the one hand it could be taken, as some have done, to be an iconographical product. But in my opinion it's really more a method, a thing, that is, that clears the ground of the ghosts I talked about before. Clearing the ground means not having any more, it would be like saying: in reality what use has proliferation been to me?

I haven't invented anything; the law of Fibonacci is practically elementary arithmetic, but it's interesting in that it isn't present-day arithmetic but an arithmetic that comes from the past and proposes strange modernizations like the relationships between arithmetic and biology."

*Is proliferation a political concept?*

"Inevitably, I suppose, because the very proliferation of the individual on the face of the earth is a political concept. If we were still about ten million people in Europe, we would certainly have different politics. The fact that we are thousands of millions on the face of the earth shows that our understanding changes with our own number. We are the numerous ancestors, hugely numerous; we are new ancestors, that's it, that's how we can consider ourselves. I am anti-historical in this sense, I'm against historicism because historicism is always provocative saying that we are the end of a process, while what I say is that we are the ancestors, and that's quite different, it's the beginning of a process, not the end…"

*What can you tell me about the other forms of your work, like the igloo and the dome?*

"It's possible to make an igloo according to where you end up, where you find yourself, and with the materials that you have at hand. I've used the relationship between the dome and other domes, like architects do, because it is known that it is necessary to take into consideration the dilation of the construction materials. There are cracks called dilation joints, that are joints or cracks. In this case it was a circular crack, I used the circular crack to work with. I used, that is, something that was my immediate precedent, but it was precedent in the social relationship in that the object that we had in front of us, that I had in front of me in that moment, was practically the place where I had to make the exhibition. Since the igloo is a simple form, the simple form penetrates much more easily than forms that are too complex, within iconographies that are already solemnized as are the environments, or as a piazza could be. I could even make an igloo in a field of potatoes, or I could savagely go to a place where there are still trees and forests and fields. In the so-called nature one could create iconographical movements that bear in mind, for example, the number of people and so the inhabitability of certain places, or their un-inhabitability. When you are in front of a totally iconographical product like, for example, the Gothic cathedral (just to mention one that's close to us), you see that it's easier to connect a product of that type than an eighteenth-century product, or above all a seventeenth-century one, where the arts are separated from each other and are trickles – no longer this great river which, iconographically, is superior. The igloo is an attempt to summarize, to say that it is architecture (because the igloo is basically architecture), but it's also a sculpture, it's also a painting in the sense, I think, not of the traditional three arts, but something that is a synthesis over and above the three arts – the igloo was my first intuition of this.

The igloo is a small structure. It's small in that it's solemnly small, because if you let yourself flow, let's say, then you make a metaphysical product: the tapir, for example, makes a metaphysical product, it makes its house, that is to say that the house of the tapir is architecture. But it's architecture and sculpture, in that it's the metaphysics of the house. The igloo in reality is a solemn product, even if it's small, and the solemnity of its psychical being means that it can be really connected with architecture, even if it's an architecture that you can put inside a room. Architecture materially transforms itself according to the organic unit of the number and not according to the previous preparatory will. In synthesis, you can think one thing, that I'm an anti-Bauhaus. The social component of Bauhaus was important; the component and the means with which Bauhaus worked are means which, in reality, are drawn from previous situations, they are means of fortune in my opinion, they are means by which the rational positivistic ideology of the nineteenth century, for example, had the greatest weight. The means are not tied to the social idea which, instead, is formidable. So it was easy to forget Bauhaus in order to go and seek something else or to go towards an organic architecture or even an architecture of the pre-scientific peoples, or pre-technical, pre-technological. That's why architecture today finds itself in almost a paralyzing mess. I'm sorry to say it, but I wouldn't like even to talk about architecture but rather about social art, that is about life. I can say 'architecture' but it's a negative term in my opinion, it's the negative term of a positive state, it's a term that should become negative in this moment, out of a state of necessity. All those who use a too automatic descriptiveness of the life we live today are a few artists, because they have few opportunities of moving away from this limit of deference towards iconography, which is typical of the non-artist. Too much objectivity creates a foundering of the imaginative possibilities of man."

*How do you relate to the history of art?*

"Today we should really completely abandon the history of art, because everything the history of art has created is a nineteenth-century product, the antiquated cataloguing of history. There are very few artists today, and at the same time there are very many artists, that is to say there is an enormous number of artists who, since they naturally have the objectuality of our life, create the enormous quantity of number of people who would like to give themselves up to the continuation of this objectivity. But in reality it should be the opposite, the real artist today, that is, eliminates the objectuality or the ghost of the objectivity itself.

For example, even the difficult placement, the difficult cataloguing, the difficult co-existence between critic and artist is precisely this, it derives, that is, from this fact, it derives from the fact that the critic often dedicates himself, just like the artist, to controlling the objectuality already taken place, and this control paralyzes it."

*What can you tell me about your relationship with nature?*

"Still life, in so far as it is nature, is alive. I made a table that wasn't an object, even if it then became an object, because the table represented for me the raising up of the earth. There is an analysis of the table that derives from an analysis that goes back in time, since I think the first table was the altar on which the first butcher on the earth killed an animal, let's say he provoked the first social shock. Then the table was distributed at length in history and today, in my opinion, the moment has come to project it into the

195

future. Going around the different cities, I've realized that the most explosive thing from the point of view of the colour and the form is nature itself – it's the product that the farmer brings on his lorry and sells on the stall that we find twenty meters outside our front door. So I put that product on the table, it's the product of nature. But the product of nature must be directed within history – that is to say, it isn't the product of nature, because even a bundle of sticks is the product of nature, but it's unfastened from nature and fastened in history. That's why I've done these works, because there's the thought that you always work on a totally fixed object, so in the future it will have its objectivity; but it will be placed objectively without basically that excess of energy which we carry today.

There then, this is the condition of art today. Of course I'm an artist, I'm not a sociologist or a revolutionary. It's precisely because I'm an artist in this way that I'm revolutionary."

*The natural element is extrapolated from a system of relationships…*

"On the one hand I could have put the fruit that you find on sale on the stalls, and it would have meant basically not being enough of an artist. The fact is that there was the idea of creating precisely the right quality of colour and the right quality of sculpture of the various products of the earth put together, so I thought that certainly Caravaggio, when he distinguished still life, put living nature on a table in a certain way in order to paint it, not in another way, in any old way. This fact of not placing things in any old way provides the possibility in the future of being an architect, because the architect justifies the positions of his own product."

*Isn't the recovery of still life iconographical?*

"I suppose it's iconography projected, I think it's projected into the future, in that I haven't thought about the still life of the past, we stay with still life for itself."

*How has Marisa participated?*

"A great analytical capacity, that's typical of Marisa, Marisa moves a thing and puts it in a better place, i's a colouristic method. For example, I had placed pieces of glass and stones, and she moved things from time to time: these islands of fruit and nature are placed so that they reflect in the glass and have the supporting systems of stone and so, in terms of sculpture and architectonically, are very, very present. It's rather like ikebana. Ikebana creates, the ikebana that in Japan is considered an art is the ability, let's say, that instead of presenting the object, the object is deformed with the scissors of the artist in such a way that it takes on fantastic aspects that it didn't have before. It's rather like drawing. The real drawer goes right inside, eliminating, that is, certain things and exalting others, he creates language… ikebana: the masters of ikebana are effectively masters of advanced language."

*To what degree do you place art and politics, to what degree can art today intervene in a reality like our own?*

"I'd answer like this: art intervenes in that we live a condition that, precisely because it is really lived, ends up being exemplary, but not exemplary, in my opinion, as a product which has already been perfected, but as product-information. So it's our life itself as artists that is exemplary. We need to get out of the duality, on the one hand art and on the other life, and get back to a synthesis of art and life – that is to say, life itself is practically our iconography. This would be the conclusion, and it goes back to what I was saying at the beginning."

# Niele Toroni
Muralto, Locarno, Switzerland, 1937

Paris
1977

*I would first of all like to ask you if you think that your work falls into the realm of painting.*

"I think that it undoubtedly falls into the realm of painting. In January 1967 this work was seen by the public, and this for me is the interesting thing. It was a work that four of us did jointly: Buren, Parmentier, Mosset and I, the result of a study on painting, on what kind of work would still be done, as long as it was still painting. More simply, the elements I use are those used for painting, i. e. a brush, some colours that I buy. I don't think it is interesting to try to classify me. This idea of putting things into boxes has always existed."

*But when I speak of trends, I don't mean groups or temporary situations; I mean cultural trends, I mean the possibility of tying your work into a history of culture, a history of art. From what linguistic matrices does your work stem from and how do you apply the grammar of painting. I feel that in your case painting breaks up into its grammatical and structural elements.*

"You are right and it is much more interesting when somebody sees and discovers this work. I am always afraid that comments, whether spoken or written, subsequently become an alibi in order to give a different importance to this work, which I intended to be rather simple and clear; although not completely so since it should involve anyone who wants to look at it. That's why I have practically never written anything, or only a few lines now and then. As far as my own history is concerned, I suppose that one should go back to people like Cézanne, although I would prefer to go straight to Pollock. I think that Pollock's work is very important and I don't know whether this has been fully understood yet. The essential thing is the relation between the artist who works and the surface that he covers. There are still painters who feel the need to fill a space, to take it for themselves. This can go beyond the *chassis* or the paper, and I think that explains Pollock's importance. Wherever he goes he takes everything – that is the way I see it. I have thought a lot about this, and I think this is more important than his technique or his aesthetics, even though the latter seems to be the main thing to others. He had this need to fill his own space, without fooling around, and this is the most important thing, though it has sometimes been forgotten. There has been a return to 'beautiful' painting, to mere aesthetic games. This was true in America, but Pollock was still the best. In the other case, in a completely different situation, there was Klein and the problem of monochrome. Here again there was this need to fill a space, and the place, that of painting, in a rather brutal and simple way. I always thought that there was an ambiguity in these works, which could easily be seen as feelings and beauty. It is from all this that I started out this method of 'traces' with a no. 50 brush. You take a brush, 5 cm wide, and you apply it every 30 cm. You have thus filled the space in a rather neutral way, you have covered it and not covered it. At the beginning we worked in public, to show people that it was a sort of everyday work. But I think it was good, it was a kind of desacralization of the profession. Today I would do things a little differently. There is something more in the work I do today. To go back to your question, that may be the starting point. Before the 'traces', I spent a year repainting the squares on linoleum for kitchens. Big white and yellow squares that I painted and repainted. Not very many people have seen them. I did not want to do more, to reinvent a form, I only wanted to paint. So every day, from morning to night, I repainted the linoleum, trying to stick to the squares."

*Is painting a form of physical production for you? Is it work, and if so how?*

"As long as I do something it is work; I do it like you do a job. That is the interesting thing: others could do it too, they could get the same results. Because this requires minimal ability, all you have to know is how to put colour on a brush and apply it. But these are not probably the most essential or important things, they are possible demonstrations that I always shift onto the work. When I say work I mean the piece that can be seen, the work in both senses, what you can see has been done. It is clear that painting is not only that, it is the part that afterwards becomes the individual history of each one in front of this thing to look at. Basically this minimization to the technical means used came also from the fact that I did not want to show things of mine or give lessons to people. I wanted to leave the viewer before something that he sees or does not see, for him to be active and not be obliged to digest, as is usually the case, the bravura piece of someone – who could also be someone big – with his own experiences, but which concern him before they concern the others. Always using these basic materials: the brush, the colour. I believe that at that point there was also a work of reflection, there were lots of new things and new movements. One example that I think is still meaningful: take a heart, there was a painted heart, I can't remember by whom, there was the heart in neon, then there was someone who simply wrote the word heart. But I don't care, in the long run all they communicate is heart, whether painted or called by name: only the form changed. Formally what changed was only the way of giving it to you: everybody looking at it reacts to everything that the word heart carries with it. And this was not concerned with a specific problem of painting, maybe it was interesting in other fields, but for me it was less so because I wanted to see where I could go, how I could go with painting. Doing something. Trying to remain within the limits of a specific field. Now I am interested in seeing this possible relationship, when you leave the specific area of painting; because you take into account other elements, other things that for me add up to painting; for others – well, I don't know."

*And what is it that makes it possible to consider your work as art? Your intervention, what you do to a canvas, to the wall…*

"Yes, of course, the galleries, the museums, the well-known circuit; you know them as I do. After all it is always the same thirty people that you see in France, in Germany, in Italy. There might be a possibility today, perhaps it is only a hope; there are young artists who are a little more interested in all this. But the problem is whether they are interested precisely because they want to stay 'inside'… It is a serious problem; there is this discrepancy between a work done in the context of a given reality and what it becomes after. There are people who do interesting things, serious work, but their work is mutilated because the system keeps a hold on it. Since the system is very strong it makes these works meaningless and they become the pieces you find in the museum and that's it."

*In your work you have shifted from pictorial space, a finite surface, to the wall, the floor. Where does this extension, the escape of the sign from the canonical space of painting, come from, and where does it lead?*

"It comes from this will to break out; you can do it by not exhibiting in the galleries. At one point this was fashionable, but what was the use? You do something outside of the specialized places, but then you invite the 25 specialized people to come and see what you have done, because if you don't your work does not exist. So I thought that I might show that it could be done outside, as you rightly said, of the canonical spaces. The question of size is also interesting. It is something that I have always concerned myself with. I don't know whether you remember, but some years ago I did a few pieces (I am still doing some) on rolls of oil cloth ten meters long, which I painted in a long corridor and it was interesting because you could show just the length that could fit into the place where it was being shown. If the wall was four meters long you could see four meters of it; if the wall was three meters long you could see three meters. If there was a place that people did not walk on, you could also unroll it on the floor. To go back to what we were saying before, it was a way of taking a stand vis-à-vis this filling up of a canvas or a given surface. That was all more or less painting was about, and it seemed that you could not do anything else. The point was to try and give a work some form of autonomy and that's why I mentioned neutrality. The neutrality of the strokes and of the distance between the strokes produced that kind of visual neutrality that made it possible to shorten or lengthen the work. Obviously it was not the same thing whether you had two meters or whether you had five, but at the start the piece was always the same. Another interesting thing is the piece I painted on the floor. It was only possible because the floor was white. I generally work on a white background. This piece refers to another across the room, which is on canvas and of the same colour. It will remain while the first will disappear because the more people walk on it, the more it will become uniformally grey. There is also the question of how long the show will last; the works on the walls or on the floor will disappear after three or four weeks because obviously the galleries have to be cleaned. The second piece begins on canvas and continues on the wall. I felt I would be clearer, I would almost say didactic – though that is a dirty word that nobody wants to use nowadays – because it made it possible to give a reading of something that is never limited by the usual frame. For me it's evident that even if it's a canvas or a sheet of paper of a given size, the work can expand, although sometimes you have to extend it physically. This touches on broader problems than simply this need to break out of defined structures, in which things get caught and finally negated."

*One could then say that your own emotional preferences and your own subjectivity play a part in choosing a colour.*

"I think that is always true, and that is why I try to use a great many colours. One could, over the years, analyse and see. It's always the same old story: you put names in a hat and you draw one – there is no such a thing as random choice. Obviously when I do a piece for a specific place, I may prefer to choose my own colour. But I use them all so as to avoid making one more important than the others. You are right to say that colour is important. There are people who say: I like the blue painting better than the others. I tried to make the point at White Wide Space, where I had shown ten pieces of ten different colours on sheets of paper of the same size. Since the size was the same, the only difference was the colour. Some preferred one or the other, and I too probably had my preferences; but then it was my problem, just as it was other guys' problem. I left them free to make a choice different from mine. Sometimes there are certain reasons for choosing a colour: I am thinking of something that I believe you saw in Milan. There were going to be elections in Italy two weeks later and so I did something which I called *Red or Black* because that was the decision that the electors had to take two weeks later. This is one of the possibilities you have with this method: there was one violently red piece and a black one. In this case the colour was used for what it represents as a symbol, for its history as a colour."

*Do you believe that art is a method?*

"I don't know. When I talk about method of work, I am talking about my method of intervention, which I always define as being 'traces with a no. 50 brush, repeated at regular intervals of 30 cm'. This is how I can be either inside or outside the art community… I don't know whether art is good or bad, what I do know is that at a certain point it becomes a method…"

*In what sense?*

"For instance, today it could be an interesting method of investigating things that have happened, things that you have done, the history of culture. Sometimes I get the feeling that it is only a way to escape… But it is true that if I weren't me, if I didn't have what I have behind me, I would have done something different. When the four of us got together at the start, we had very few things in common. The experience did not last very long. We were four very different people, with different ideas, a different past, but we had something in common. Buren, Parmentier, Mosset and I: we didn't do the same thing, but there was at least this need to minimize, though what one saw was objectively very different: there was the subjectivity of each one of us."

*Would you say that your work is political?*

"My intention is to show things that involve the people who want to look at them. But at the same time that are not too demanding, so that people who walk by can also not see them or can simply laugh. Anyway something that conveys some form of knowledge of yourself or of others; it is positive because it implies an effort. Therefore it is political."

Francesco Clemente
Naples, 1952



*Does the body have nine holes, or ten?*

"Yes, no tradition is persuasive. At the same time, everything seems traditional, conventional. A new culture will be made, for instance, by whomever will be able to take in all the air he needs to live in one breath, and spend his life in a single, sweet sigh."

*Is the holy cross two straight lines that come into sight of each other, seen by a third subject standing on this side of them?*

"In other words, who sees the cross that's there? I don't. We weave together questions and answers that belong to the experience of another, but of whom? I don't want to move from one place to another in town, I want to move the places."

*Will a Chippendale chair ever crouch down on a Biedermaier, or vice-versa?*

"Furniture and paintings are gracefully arranged in an interior that they never decided on. The painters I know personally are the ones I love. The others matter to me only because the economics they have produced works in my interest or against it. Thus, art is an unreliable institution or a tradition of knowledge, depending on the chemistry that regulates my days."

*Is popular art possible?*

"Popular for the suspicious passer-by who listens to us, for the informer. Polar for whomever is tired of the West and there is no East where he can go or stay."

*Number Ten: do this and this.*

"In the end none of this matters, because we know it already. But not even artists on their last legs say it, because arms don't acknowledge them. The commandments make one smile if the person who makes them can also fall victim to them. We go away omnipotent, alone or in pairs, non-artists or artists. We go away, but only for a little while, naturally."

*Conclusion: but couldn't you say it all at once, without talking in pieces?*

"The luxury I desire takes away my intelligence. Or else,

all at once: 'When I called a work *Barbarous Paintings* I was thinking of the Barbarians as the protagonists of a place without enemies…'. Suggested title for the glossary or the follow-up of this interview: 'The last Thule first, how unbearable'."

# Giulio Turcato
## Mantua, 1912 – Rome, 1995

Rome
1981

*The painter does not dream, he paints… in the sense that your paintings and the images that spring from them seem to allow no suspicions other than their fragrance, power, and ability to act as a flash of lightning, occasionally soft, that strikes the inner eye of the viewer, not just the explicit outer eye… in this sense your paintings stand at the juncture of the abstract and the figural, in the very midst of a series of processes that ends on what I call the painting's skin, on the surface. The surface is that horizontal viewpoint from which you balance signs, languages and material in such a way that they become the skin of the painting. To reach this end you employ a very original and peculiar process, I think… a passage from de-concentration to concentration, from dispersion to precision, from an attitude that may be considered rampant to one of convergence on a point. If I had to find a paragon for your process, I would describe it as the opposite of the ripples that form when you throw a stone into a pond. When you throw a stone into still, deep water, it produces concentric rings of larger and larger diameter. Your work functions instead like a circle that begins with a broad circumference, and is suddenly sewn up, zipped shut, to form a single point. The originality of this process lies in the fact that the centre can also be the external boundary, that it is not necessary to wait for a conclusion, or for the outer circles to fade away in order to reach that lightning moment of the result. This is also the power and originality of your work, the continuous passage from an initial lack of attention to a subsequent precise concentration – that of the work. It is a passage that is never made along regular roads, but that follows instead an irregular, anomalous path like that which leads from mumbling to articulate speech.*

"In these interpretations based on relations and comparisons you have set forth your critical method, which consists in looking at what happens to a painter first… That is not easy, because it has to be discovered… to the extent that a sign, a form, something will figuratively establish or define the premise. I make my painterly vision into an abstract formalism. Although the first step towards this mode of being is spontaneous, what comes later is an analysis of how the forms themselves will be realized. Painting has always been grounded in psychology, but in modern painting the psychological factor has a broader meaning, because it derives from introspection and hence proceeds, in a more intimate transformation, towards speculation. It cannot be explained in expressive terms, for the forms change depending on how we look at ourselves, and so can give rise to an infinite number of visions… It is a chain reaction. In this respect I think abstract painting makes a universal statement and has cosmic importance, because figurative painting involves a deformation of the representation of man, nature, and things: this cannot be infinite because it is always tied to the scheme of nature and the visible… In abstract painting, form is not tied to any framework. It is free to project itself, hence it can be guided, collected and transformed in any number of ways which, naturally, have to be apprehended by the painter… not as a psychological copy, but as an aesthetic and expressive transformation of the visions and forms of the mind."

*What is the reality of forms?*

"First we go to school, then each of us goes his own way, but this is not the beginning: there is the choice of what to do, of a mode of being and of self-expression. This mode is not ascetic, philosophical, or transcendental. It is a metaphor of the sign, of drawing, painting, and the achievement of a certain synthesis of the world we live in as perceived by an inner sense that is more than just visual. Although the execution is very important, the vision is what will be transferred to the painting, the object, the environment, and so forth… in order to move others, who are naturally incapable of this metamorphosis. This is how things happen formally… The Romantics found a very simple solution in drama and the chiaroscuro, as in Delacroix – but Tintoretto had already begun. After Cézanne, making a quick synthesis of what can be explained, the mind and a new feeling moved in painting. Gradually, as society began to have doubts about how to interpret things, the painter immersed himself in an introspective analysis, an analysis of himself and of his emotions, not to find out whether he was crazier than he thought, but to create an expressive form that was not only abstract… what's the word… mellifluous… ephemeral but intelligent. Then what happened was as in a dark room, with movements of colour and light…

and when everything became clear, modern painting was born. This process is not easy to understand, especially for politicians: it is the way experimentation goes. Neither vain nor hypnotic, it is something that is acquired through a series of events cautiously produced by a special person who is a certain kind of painter."

*I look at this painting, which is quite beautiful by the way, and the painting becomes a dreamer. It becomes a subject rather than an object, it becomes an interlocutor, a sort of reservoir of images. In this respect I think painting is never abstract or figural, because it is a reservoir, a sort of well whose bottom we can never see and will never really know. You can immerse yourself in it, and look deeper and deeper, and if your eyesight is sharp enough you might even reach the bottom, or you might stop first, you might have some ghosts to hold on to, let's say. The painter doesn't dream, he paints. It's the painting that dreams…*

"It isn't the painting, but the painting's formalism that makes the interlocutor dream… The painter, in transposing what he thinks into what he paints, sometimes gets lost, but in this symbiosis he rediscovers the itinerary of his vision through his own formalism… Naturally, I'm speaking of a painter who possesses specific qualities and belongs to an artistic current based on a timeless faith… These are almost initiations in which one needs an education, a self-education I'd say. In this respect there is an uninterrupted line connecting the cave man to our own time… in abstract painting as in a certain kind of figural painting, so that at a certain moment one sees how a painter by means of the sign succeeds in identifying his visions, the forms that others have not been able to express."

*And what do you think you have identified with your painting?*

"I see it when I've finished it. I can't tell you beforehand, because I've only imagined it. I say the painting can still be a message… I don't know… let's take two classic, even commonplace examples: Leonardo's *Mona Lisa* and Giorgione's *Tempest*. Well, beauty of course… there are others who have produced that… let's call it beauty, as the critics have termed it. But there's something in these works which goes further, which people are not always aware of, especially because it might be vague, represented as an image, an accomplishment… The Renaissance, I think, was the first painterly form to free the arts from a dependency, whereas the Gothic is connected to an ecclesiastical situation, just as the communists don't realize that socialist realism is tied to a diktat… In reality it has already been upstaged by nineteenth-century French humanitarian and sociological painting, Millet and others… and by photography, and that's a fact. They are elastic… there instead it's really fixed, there's nothing you can do about it. On the other hand, the images made by painters are a sort of photo film of what can happen not with photography but with a metaphor of the sensibility of a certain age, of a certain way of seeing interpreted by everyone in his or her subconscious, but of course always through the painter who makes this image, an idea of the passage through the ages of a way of seeing and feeling."

*In your painting, the way of feeling is a way of thinking. Feeling is the method of your thought…*

"It is a sort of rationality that is inherent to this way of feeling, but clearly understood as invariably a product of intuitive knowledge and even of invention."

*How do you distinguish between intuition and invention?*

"Well, intuition presupposes invention, it's what gives strength to the formal passage of creative execution, to what will be concrete."

*Let's go back to our opening statement, then. The painter does not dream, he paints. It's the painting that dreams, or painting in general that dreams, painting as an active subject which, in addition to letting itself be pierced by the sensitive eye of the viewer, penetrates the viewer in turn. It is a sort of symbiosis, a bilateral relationship, an exchange, a marriage. In short, painting, and your paintings in particular, allow exclusively for two-sided dialogues. One interlocutor at a time can stand in front of a painting… your paintings are made for solitary conversations.*

"Painting is enigmatic, it needs in-depth analysis and a suitable cultural knowledge of how an artist produces his images. But a deep comprehension of what he proposes con also spring from intuition."

*How do you realize that a painting is finished?*

"It's like a clock… although it's not so rational and precise as that, one realizes that there's no going beyond a certain point, that the charge has a limit."

*For the viewer the process works the other way: if for the artist*

*– and for you – the clock stops once the result has been attained, in the eye of the observer the clock accelerates. The work, the painting, produces an acceleration of sensitivity.*

"A painting, an artwork in general, the manufactured article, let's say, is a hope… a hope in an imperceptible, hidden release that takes place between the two issuing sensibilities. The viewer proceeds with caution because he expects a surprise. The painter invented it, and the critic accepts it… it is not easy to speak of the critic in a historical sense, because in the Renaissance, for instance, Vasari's was the first real analysis… but he was satisfied with a description of the artwork, saying that it was good or bad according to his standards of judgement, whereas later on critics tried to penetrate the psychology of the artist. The important thing is that it not be easy to show what ordinary painting is, because this would disconcert the viewer, it would be a betrayal in his regard."

*Painting… your paintings… Thus, painting dreams, but this doesn't mean surrealism: just abandoning oneself to the currents of that inner action which painting produces, because clearly the dream produced by your paintings, which are sensual but cultural, is one in which nothing is automatic. It is a dream that activates processes of intuitive knowledge. Your paintings produce a strange dream state consisting in a moment of acute awareness; they are keen vigils, not at all like daydreams, not like sleep. Extremely keen awareness, the capacity to sharpen – through paint, images, the sign, colour: processes in which the nerve of sensibility is at work, in addition to the intellect, intelligence, and clearness of thought. Our awareness is sharpened because your paintings give strength and breadth, they reconnect things that are ordinarily disjoined – reason and sensitivity, the rational and the emotional.*

"I would say imagination, a specific imagination that suggests what we see and what we cannot see, but what we see should give us an idea of what we cannot see. The painter can't explain it but the audience, in my opinion, when it looks at a painting, the wall, a drawing, with its signs, shades, and what is capable of being understood, might not understand…"

*So, the painter doesn't dream, the painter paints. Painting dreams, what is painting? But painting, we've said, doesn't have a soundtrack, in the sense that it is not made of words. But what is the soundtrack of this dream we call painting? It's colour and the sign... In short, painting tends to broaden our sensibility, concentrating everything on a sensory quality which is that of vision. What then does this dream, painting, possess, beyond the light, the image, the visible; and what is it hiding?*

"I have imagined the colours beyond the spectrum, colours that can't be seen, but are perceived with the effect of matching even the furthest extremes, colours invented because they are wandering in the earth's aura and beyond. Monet changes colour in the water lily paintings as a function of the sunlight, and it becomes abstract rarefaction. My research concerns the light in movement in the painting so that what it reflects will be progressively unstable in a dynamic relationship of signs and space."

*The painter doesn't dream, he paints... the painting dreams... and it is not a dream painting... The painting dreams to the extent that it becomes an emanating object, a thinking subject... painting becomes the subject that emanates images – but what images? We have said that painting has no soundtrack, in the sense that it does not appeal to heedful ears, but to watchful eyes; and so, painting concentrates its soundtrack in the sign and in colour. What do the sign and colour express? The unspeakable, among other things... So, painting dreams the unspeakable, what cannot be said, in that painting does not have words. What it can express, in sign and colour, is what words lack...*

"Figurative painting itself isn't entirely plausible or comprehensible. Figuration sometimes hides arcane meanings – indecent, we might say, so much so that certain pictorial scenes of the Middle Ages, the Renaissance, and even our own day have been interpreted well, as it were, by a figuration, a sort of theatre of gazes, as in Masaccio, or a more mysterious type of representation, as in Piero della Francesca. But we come to the conclusion that not all painting, even figurative – I've just mentioned the more famous examples – can be apprehended. The meaning remains enigmatic; and if we take the point further, Oriental or cave paintings, we do perceive the genius of primitive man, his creative power; we are amazed by the beauty, but we do not know how to explain it... It's not true that everything can be understood. There is a subconscious energy that enters into the figurative and non-figurative sign that we still don't know how to explain."

# Enzo Cucchi
Morro d'Alba, Ancona, Italy, 1949

Rome
1982

*What is the dream of painting?*

"It was probably because he wanted to escape from the gods that the sacred baboon told me in a dream... I was strolling in the countryside and alongside a river, and I thought about how the horses hurtle between two smooth banks without any noise at all. On the hillsides some houses are falling into ruin; the mysterious breath of a horse stopped me getting closer to the entrance. A troubled place, a pit; there I found a gathering of painters' thoughts. They had impaled the day and night equipment on the claws of black roosters. The banks of Italian painters... the same decorative mistakes as always... penetrated by the bourgeoisie; a state of drowsiness, of relish during the day in the visible world. But of course this doesn't exist in the daylight world... In our Italian towns they are gourmets, manufacturers of luxury objects, hotel managers. So I continued my walk and came across roosters that fly away from any doubts about our origins. Flights like this are important for the twentieth century; they are spiritual demonstrations, since they are distinguished from any earthly tastes... In the sky one has the impression of a gigantic, revolving form; over these years I've seen many images rise up again as in a storm... bourgeois tastes have been removed, that small country which is Italy has been assailed not once but twice in a century. Today the Italians Dino Campana and Medardo Rosso have been buried in the small cemetery, with their spirits that had become entangled. I went to visit them in a dream. The entrance was so nearly closed that it was a struggle to get through. In this stroll along my path I don't remember meeting books, intellectuals, gifts and other such things..."

*How do you place yourself in relation to the history of painting?*

"I feel like a survivor in painting, a hero. I'm one of the few survivors in the history of painting, in the sense that I've survived the war and the destruction. In the sense that I'm a healthy carrier. Of course, it's clear that I've been 'kissed by God'. It's not even on my own merits. That's the way it is, that's all. My painting comes out of me like a natural emanation… even though every painter passes through the body of other painters, of the great painters, all the great painters of the past. Of course, because we must only go back in time. Going forward doesn't mean anything in painting. We could begin by eliminating the impressionists: we should get rid of them all apart from a few good paintings, some by Monet, some by Van Gogh… All the rest is really bad painting, real crap. Then, going back to Delacroix, you then get to Titian, and El Greco who's really extraordinary… Not to mention Masaccio or Piero della Francesca who both take your breath away! There then, as far as I'm concerned these are the truly great painters, the ones that I feel inside me."

*So is history a feeling of continuity?*

"I feel like a soldier returning from the Great Modern War. I feel like I've been enlisted in the great, tiny army of painters. From time immemorial. Because the continuity, the fluidity of the idea of painting is a river that never stops flowing. It's not something that you can detach or separate from the rest and say: 'this is modern and this is old'. The problem is always the same – that of talent. That's why I feel that today I'm just painting pictures that the world needs – the world, that is, not people."

*Is this what spurs you on to paint?*

"I began to paint so that I could use my brushes to create a new world; the only world which could excite me, astound me, surprise me. Yes, it was an irrepressible need for wonder that led me to painting. This need then became a preposterous vice, an intense desire. For it isn't true that I go to the studio out of love for painting in itself. The things I use to paint with are horrible: they smell, they soil and make you dirty… think about the oils, the thinners and colours… it's all stuff that disgusts me. But I can't do without it. It's a problem of being obsessed. It's the need to astound myself that drives me here, to this room, among the canvases and the colours."

*So art and life are separated?*

"Painting is one thing, life is something else. After all, don't forget that Titian was a usurer for his living. His direct contact with everyday things was to lend money at interest. His painting was in another dimension. It's only in this century that we tend to confuse the individual with the artist. The artist is a completely different person because his work is exclusively tied to talent. And talent can live alongside the usurer, the bandit and the ordinary criminal… Because talent isn't tied to any kind of moral quality. On the contrary, it must be completely devoid of it. It must have a zero level of sensitivity with respect to the normal things of everyday life, secular things in a certain sense. Talent is amoral. It doesn't need virtue, nor does it need moral qualities."

*Why is your painting one of images?*

"It's all to do with iconography. America is the most representative synthesis of the present weakness in the world. As always, in moments of great weakness the world needs iconography, images, icons, don't you think so? At this point, they've viewed Italian artists like the Madonna! So they seek the Madonna, the image, something they can cling to. There, that's what I think is the real meaning of the success of the Transavantgarde in America. It's a success that is tied to the fact that we're healthy carriers of images! Because the way we express ourselves with images is a natural situation or condition for us in Italy… It's clear that up to some time ago this anxiety, this thirst for images didn't exist."

*So the world needs painting?*

"We talk about painting of all the species in a world made up of only one species. And here it occurs to us that painting concerns a small spot of earth in the rest of the world where a particular human species has refined this taste which now has become the painting that we know and *feel.* This place is this small strip of the Mediterranean that contains all our feeling along with it, the impurities. And then what is a drawing? In order to learn all these themes the best way is a strange conversation with all the things that live in this place. Is this place free, enlightened? For the young painters it's a hallucinating, incredible place, especially at night time; tie up alongside and so draw nearer… Painters are rare on these coasts that are as slippery as a sleigh."

# Mimmo Paladino
Paduli, Benevento, Italy, 1948

Naples
1982

*What did the revival in the mid-1970s of the outdatedness of painting mean for you?*

"Above anything else it meant a kind of tremor that ran through this idea of the revival of painting. As you well know, I materialized this revival in just one painting and then, after abandoning not so much the idea as the tremor, I concentrated myself in a dimension of continual movement between an idea that was certainly still tied to a conceptual approach and, naturally enough, the fixed idea that continued more silently underground with the drawings. For a very long time I didn't ever exhibit my drawings – I didn't see them as the planning or preparatory stage of the work, but rather as an underground stream that could flow beneath this enormous energy that materialized from time to time in strips of walls, spatial situations, ephemeral works. This idea of painting, as I was telling you, materialized with a great tremor in just one small picture which was then abandoned as a project in process."

*Can you describe this painting to me?*

"It was a painting titled *Silenzioso* [silent, noiseless] and it linked back to other of my works which had the same title with the subtitle 'retired in order to paint a picture'. The subtitle at the bottom is, in a certain sense, the picture's unconscious as an expression of my existential dimension at that moment, that of being quite distant from the circumstances of art."

*What were the distinctive features of this painting?*

"Its physical characteristics were those of a real oil painting, the recovery of a tool that I was using for the first time. The recovery of a tool, of the brush that is, and oils and canvas, a small, vertical canvas about 50 × 70 cm. In this way there was an image, an allusive image that didn't recount anything. It recounted an interior, vaguely in the style of Matisse as a chromatic solution, with a transparent character, like a phantom hovering between strange measuring instruments or strange pieces of furniture. The structure was rather architectonic and balanced, so everything was in proportion with the thing next to it, and every colour was in harmony or out of harmony with the colour next to it. The idea was really and truly to stay there for a week and paint a picture without having an expressive idea of the work but rather thinking about its slow spreading and a slow designing of the structure of the painting."

*But in this case, as you said, the introduction of the subtitle is important, the introduction of what you rightly call the unconscious part of the creative work. So what was the sense of "retiring to your painting?"*

"Retiring is like the withdrawal of the monk in retreat, far from the uproar of the world, the uproar of ideology, from the power of a work of art in the world. So, I repeat, it's probably an attitude which one assumes, certainly not as an ideological fact, but rather as a sensation, as a tremor with respect to work. There's probably been this strange coincidence – it wasn't a choice but quite precisely a historical coincidence, that of thinking of this kind of poetic enclosure. It's an attitude that I've never ceased to like."

*This poetic enclosure means, naturally enough, the revival of a subjective need that, as we well know, had been penalized by the art of the 1960s and the early 1970s. This return to the individual, and in your case I'd say to a private ego, to the individual's everyday emotions: what kind of linguistic outlet has this return found in your work?*

"This first attempt, this first awareness of the possibility of painting in seclusion dried up in the end, or at least it was satisfied in a single painting. Then in reality what continued to live internally were the circumstances of art and the situations which could still be linked up to an art situation that was no longer this utopian grasp of the world but probably a poetic grasp of the physical space – in my case a gallery, a wall, a more overall situation of involvement – but with this underground flow of poetics, the poetics (as you said) of everyday things: the garden is more mysterious than the wood, the things you find on the table and the relation between them probably provoke more mystery than those which you can find in a city or in the world, a strange microcosm, pieces of the world, the city, the universe. When I used to prepare short circuits between an abstract wall and a figurative painting, to tell the truth it was still probably within the atmosphere (as I was telling you), not of visualizing but of conceptualizing the aftermath of art as a process. But there was the intention of getting closer and closer to the individual, and not being the maker-protagonist of this individual any more."

*In the very moment that you drew together and placed alongside the abstract and the figurative, it seems to me that you introduced two characteristics, cultural nomadism and stylistic eclecticism. I'd like to know what you mean by nomadism and stylistic eclecticism.*

"At this time certainly, and thanks also to your focus on what we were doing at that time, I probably agree very much with what you say – the idea, that is, of nomadism, the idea of moving. Then I reflect on my own dimension at that time, and the idea of those strange short circuits I was telling you about. To tell the truth, it was this continual need not to be able to identify with a single form of language any more. I spoke about the passive hero and the negative hero, in reality the anti-hero. This figure of the anti-hero was much clearer to me, a hero also as the passive creator of the problem of creativity, and so the fact of being dominated daily by the use of language. At the same time there was an incapacity, but a subtle pleasure which was also perverse: the fact of not being graspable and, at the same time, so incapable of producing an amount of work with a recognizable form of language and style. That's why I spoke of a passive hero."

*The return to the classical spirit of the work, closing the image within the frame or including the frame within the painting, in any case placing the painting on the wall again – what kind of movement has all this provoked in your work?*

"The fact of using a frame has probably a very precise meaning: that of using minor art – which as an idea is very close to that of the monk in retreat who has absolutely no intention of taking the leading part in the situation – but being the creator of the work, even with the decoration and the frame. There's probably also the sense of wanting to cross the frontiers, but this is probably something that isn't very true of me."

*Your sensitivity still continues to operate poised between the abstract and the figurative. The abstract part has been replaced by decoration. Do you think that painting the frame is the part that offsets the abstract element to be found previously in the work?*

"This doesn't always happen – it only happens in a few works or else when there's a relation between what's roughly speaking the sculptural part (and consequently this kind of relief) and the architectural part of the work. The intentions are a little different – with the abstract wall and the figurative painting I really wanted to provoke a shock, but a shock that was purely didactic. In these latter works, on the other hand, there's the painted frame or there's the sculpture that emerges from the painting, there's the decoration which at times is internal as well because there are signs you can't interpret within the work, there's this passivity of the decorator in that he wants to paint a scene which isn't a representation but a second level, a scenario. I could paint it myself, just like anyone else could paint it – I prefer to paint it myself, like a medieval painter who paints this dark, obscure chapel."

*The medieval artist as a complete artist who manages to maintain a high-level skill in painting and a minor artisan skill which is manual and decorative. The medieval painter is such in the very moment in which he paints the Madonna or Christ in the foreground, but also when he humbly paints the background.*

"Of course, and it isn't an attitude that calls for virtuosity either. In point of fact, this virtuosity doesn't exist, and very often my paintings are cracked so I'm not so interested in retrieving the artisan skills of painting as in putting them into practice. So there's probably complete passivity, complete negativity, but complete protagonism (that is, I accept all this within the work). A domestic hero, certainly; but one who makes paintings. Really and truly the hero, and so the creator."

*What's the difference in your idea of protagonism with respect to this?*

"My idea of protagonism is that of really being a protagonist, the creator of work, with the awareness that this work means falling over and being contaminated time and time again. It's for this reason probably that the quotations I can accept or use are always poetic in nature or coincidental, so I think of Twombly and Schifano. As far as previous art is concerned, I have to acknowledge the geographical distance and the equal distance of a certain North American kind of culturally and technologically advanced world (and also North Italian, all things considered). The whole of Arte Povera revolved around a technological problem which was typical of the North of Italy, and it permitted the underground development of the Transavantgarde, just like a volcano below the ashes which grows and grows and in the end can only explode in a certain way. It enabled this slow accumulation of energy (it is not by chance that we find ourselves in telluric, earthquake lands), this slow accumulation of energy that, in my case, could only explode in this painting, the single painting of this period and others. For example, I remember an exhibition of Sandro Chia, perhaps one of the most beautiful ever done – it was so totally reeling and rickety that it could only have been the work of a Tuscan artist. I mean, these are things that perhaps you interpret better now, but at that time, some years ago, you felt that this idea to create this image didn't exist but there was all of this emotional intensity, and then you understand that he was born there, he lives there, he's understood certain things. He acted on the basis of that culture, but not so much thinking of a geographical area that was distant from a problem that, sure, was Italian, but was North American in its intention; so that perhaps this is the true meaning of this work. Francesco Clemente has lived more in India than in Rome and knows perfectly well – there are very precise indications – more than anyone else he's the one who makes his own roots the reason for his work. Perhaps this is probably the most apparent indication that characterizes both my work and that of the others, even if, I repeat, I probably don't want to restrict this question of a geographical poetic situation as the matrix of my work with a sort of equation."

*There's also a northern element in your work.*

"Yes, and precisely at the level, in my opinion, of a historical referent. You know very well that I used to live in a geographical area which had nothing to do with the Mediterranean, or at least it had some of the cultural clues of the Mediterranean but with historical and natural characteristics which were northern and Longobardic but not mild in nature either, bleak nature, foggy and gloomy – so, okay, a southern artist, but from the more mysterious, gloomy south. That's why in Brazil, or, if you like, in certain aspects of northern culture as well, I find poetic sensations that belong to me, so I can paint a completely black picture just as I can paint a totally sunny picture. This is a twofold nature that I keep finding in my work, and in my sensitivity too. That is to say, I realize I'm really, at times extremely, taken up between my desire to be sparkling and shrewd and ironic, but at the same time a feeling of sadness comes down on me. In a certain sense this is my peculiarity, so my work is like this. I like to think of it as a co-incidence – that is, my painting and my work were moving in a certain way and there has been a historical coincidence. I still don't understand the meaning of this very well."

# Andy Warhol
Pittsburgh, Pennsylvania, 1928 – New York, 1987



*The images in your paintings are always taken from a stereotype. They are never an invention of your imagination. Why?*

"All paintings are directly or indirectly inspired by things or people around us. I guess this is what you call a stereotype. The selection of the images is the most important and it is the fruit of the imagination. I generally take a photograph, or a painting and it's just easier that way. I try to do the easiest one so that everyone can understand and relate to what I try to express."

*Is there any difference between an image taken from advertising and one taken from the history of art?*

"They are both images. One relates to products, the other to people, or historical events. Both are means of communication. The advertising is more intriguing. In fact, I buy old magazines and use them just for the advertising. Even when I watch television, I like advertising better than the film or the programme being shown. The other day somebody thought I wanted to do commercials. They really brought down 4,000 commercials and I watched most of them on our TV set. I view advertising as an artistic expression of our times. I watch advertising just as much as I go to museums."

*Why de Chirico?*

"I always admired de Chirico. He inspired so many painters. The retrospective at the MoMA was great and showed what a greater painter he was. I met him in Venice so many times and I thought I loved his work so much. I love his art and then the idea he repeated the same paintings over and over again. I like that idea a lot, so I thought it would be great to do it."

*De Chirico, too, repeated images from his earlier metaphysical paintings. Is there any difference with your work?*

"De Chirico repeated the same images throughout his life. I believe he did it not only because people and dealers asked him to, but because he liked it and viewed repetition as a way of expressing himself. This is probably what we have in common... The difference? What he repeated regularly, year after year, I repeat the same day in the same painting."

*Can we define your work as metaphysical industrial art?*

"I guess metaphysical means out of the physical reality. The content of most works of art may be metaphysical, but my paintings are very real… People always understand them. Is there any difference between realism and surrealism? Are my paintings real? Yes. Are they metaphysical? I do not know. I like the idea of industrial art. Paint is made industrially – so are the brushes, or the canvases. Everything is made industrially today. All the tools we use to create images are made industrially. I do my paintings half mechanically, but I wish I could do it all mechanically."

*De Chirico worked on the myth… You work on the modern myth. Is there any difference between the two?*

"I like the myth used by de Chirico. His images are myth and that's why I used them to express my feelings. He also used Greek mythology… I like that. I'm doing a Greek head of Alexander. I miss de Chirico every time I go to Europe. I used to see him in Venice a lot. I took some Polaroids of him every time I saw him in Venice. I don't know where these photographs are. They are from all the years and I just throw them in the box."

*Why did you select these images of de Chirico?*

"I guess they are among those he repeated the most through his life. Did you see the catalogue of the MoMA? Aren't the two pages reproducing the *Muse inquietanti* great? How did he repeat the same images? Did he project the same image on the canvas? Maybe he did it by dividing the canvas in sections… he could have used a silk-screen! Maybe he was not familiar with this technique."

*Art, by definition, is unique and non-repeatable. Your paintings often multiply and repeat the same image. Why?*

"And what about Morandi? Didn't he repeat himself? Most artists repeat themselves throughout their lives. Isn't life a repetition of events?"

*The reason for selecting de Chirico is cultural or sentimental too?*

"Every time I saw de Chirico's paintings I felt so close to him. Every time I saw him I felt I had known him forever. I think he felt the same way… Once he made the remark that we both had white hair!"

*De Chirico always felt free to repeat the same image. What are your reasons for repeating the same images?*

"I just said it… I like to do the same thing over and over again. Every time I go out and someone is being elected president or mayor or something, they stick their images all over the walls and I always think I do those too… I always think it's my work. It's a way of expressing oneself. All my images are the same but very different at the same time: they change with the light of colours, with the times and moods. After all, isn't life a series of images that change as they repeat themselves?"

# Daniel Buren
Boulogne-Billancourt, Paris, 1938

Paris
1983

*What do you want to convey by your repetitive work on lined paper?*

"First of all, and straight off, I have to say that there does not exist any work at all – whether repetitive or otherwise – that's carried out on lined paper. These sheets of paper, just like fabrics, are only the means and not the end. If we want to take an example from the art world, it's just as stupid to say that Cézanne's works are made up of the brushes and colours that have enabled him to paint this or that picture, that Pollock's work is a food can with a hole in it, or that Michelangelo's work is a graving tool, as it is to say that Daniel Buren's work is represented by vertical lines. Now I want to talk about the instruments I use to work with, since everyone can see them once the work is completed – something that isn't always possible, by the way, as far as the artists I've just mentioned are concerned. So for about seven years now I've been using two tools chiefly, excluding all the other instruments and forms. On the one hand I use white and coloured vertical-lined fabrics on which I do a particular painting, generally with white acrylic painting over the two white external lines. Then, once the fabrics are painted, I present them in a special way appropriate to each context (these fabrics can be cut up and sewn together, they can take any external form you like, they can even be mounted before being painted). On the other hand, I use white and coloured sheets of paper (which are identical to the fabrics as far as the spacing of the lines is concerned), or else I've recently started using transparent coloured sheets glued onto different kinds of supports – shop windows, walls, advertising boards, public buildings, etc. – according to the different moments chosen and the meaning in question. In this connection we can add that if I've chosen such a form as the means – such a work instrument – it's certainly not because I want to talk about the weather or some metaphysical problem. There's no formal difference for a superficial observer between fabric and paper. But for a more careful observer there are not only visual differences owing to the structure of the instrument used, but also (and above all) differences of meaning. For this reason the use of one instrument or another depends on the context in which they are to be found. Theoretically their use is so specific (dictated by the place chosen to develop a specific argument) that it becomes impossible to substitute one for the other (even if this would be possible technically) without changing the sense of the argument undertaken as well. We can already see that the very instruments chosen as well (which have formally been the same for seven years), express different things according to the different materials used. So saying that my work consists of drawing vertical lines is not only fundamentally mistaken, since throughout my life I've never either made, or drawn or painted vertical lines, but it also shows that those who have limited themselves to this superficial aspect of my work don't even know how to distinguish between paper and fabric or transparent plastic, something that says a lot about their superficiality, ignorance and blindness.

After this short digression, we can say that formally the 'instrument' used thus appears relatively neutral or even banal. In point of fact this neutrality of form is also understood in relation, let's say, to other more interesting forms, since the neutrality 'in itself' is nothing more than an idealist's pure fantasy. This formal banality or impersonality does not mean that the intention (the way, that is, in which this material is utilized) is banal or even neutral. On the contrary, this banal form will enable us with an enormous intensity – an intensity which is at times so brutal that it becomes almost unbearable (cf. the episode of the Guggenheim Museum in New York) – to reveal the places where it is 'inserted', their political, aesthetic, ideological, economic meanings which generally are accurately hidden not just by the system (galleries, museums, critics, art historians…) but also, and above all, by the 'system' of the club of the artists themselves who have lots of things to say and recount. The result of this is that all too soon the work absorbs all one's attention, attention is concentrated, that is, on whoever has made it, and this leads to the interruption, the definitive limitation of the link between this work and its context (whether historical, geographical or political), just the same thing that happens in the history of art. We can add that this banal form, when set up and constructed, generally makes the other 'exemplary' works collapse in their true area, i.e. in the most evident banality. We should add that if we grasp the relation between the context and the work carried out in such a way – that is, the work that has done everything possible to cancel the context – then it is clear that it is art that collapses, and radically too. This is something that is perceived and fought against by the system made up of all the artists together, and it provides support for the system in which these artists waste their time.

In my work I use the 'qualities' of the materials described above, materials whose main feature is that of being formally impersonal and particularly adaptable, and which, moreover, don't express anything apart from what they actually are, so as to be able to confront from time to time all the different places with which the above materials will be compared and so reveal them first of all in the way in which they will be then revealed by the context itself. To be more precise, in fact, it is the place and the materials placed in it which simultaneously form what we can define the 'work', and although there exists an infinity of possible places, billions of places that could be used, spaces, places that exist independently, needless to say, of the work that I could carry out there, yet there is no single work that does not call for a specific place in order to exist, that is in order to be seen.

I'd like to take advantage of this occasion to come back to a fallacious interpretation which was generally given at the time of my first exhibitions, and which concerned the formal description of the material used. It's true that from 1967 onwards I've often accompanied my work with descriptions like 'Alternating white and coloured vertical lines can be seen, which are nothing more than alternating white and coloured vertical lines which lead back to alternating white and coloured vertical stripes which are nothing more than…'. But I certainly haven't done this in order to justify the work as a complete entity in itself, just wanting to say that A = A and so fall back to the admiration of myself reflected to infinity. What I've wanted to do is to use such a tautology in order to see in an overall sense, that is, so as to no longer be clouded by the 'work' as a complete entity, but to see it, instead, as part of a whole, or rather of a unity, something which, as we can easily see, is quite different. So a formal, over-abundant description, almost completely exhaustive, of the 'object' used means insisting, on the one hand, on the fact that, in itself, such an object doesn't say anything more, and can't say anything more, than what it is (the description almost exactly corresponds to what is seen – and here we could add the exact width of the lines, the quality of the material), and, on the other hand, that if A = A this doesn't tell us anything about what A is and it's necessary that we look 'elsewhere' to grasp its meaning. This also means that if we don't even consider what I previously defined as being my work, but only the material used as the finished work (painting, sculpture, object, or anything else you want), we cannot say anything more than what it is, than what the material is – that is the axiom A = A or, if you like: zero. It's precisely this 'zero', this initial axiom, that is taken by the critic as the end in itself so as to try and ridicule a work against which, effectively, he has no idea at all what to do. And in point of fact, since my work can't be grasped in this way, if we reduce it to such a description this means not talking about it. The means alone doesn't exist. That's what A = A means.

What must be done instead is beginning a discussion in a different area: the relationship, that is, created between A and where it is to be found. It's an enormous area that at times includes history, politics, science, economics, ideology, form, object, topology, philosophy… according to the aspect or aspects under consideration. We can understand that, to do this, the formal aspect of the object or the means used should be the least expressive possible, or at least it should only express what I once called neutrality, a word which I later preferred to substitute with banality or impersonality. My insistence from the very start on the fact that the means chosen does not express anything in itself was meant to be a cry of alarm — BE CAREFUL! We are no longer dealing with a painting or an object in the sense usually given to a work of art, whatever it may be. As for the 'repetitiveness' of the work, we would need to be very clear about the sense in which this is carried out exactly. As far as what I produce is concerned, from its origins (November 1965) until December 1966 (a period in which I developed these 'paintings' in my studio and not in public), repetition was almost mechanic and formal. From then, from when that is, I work in public, I can easily state that there has not been one single repetition, but rather a sequence of unique 'events' brought about by means of the same material used in a systematic way. From January 1967 onwards there has no longer been the exhibition of a work that had already been previously 'exhibited'. The work presented to the public is always done in a special way and, since it is made up of the material used *plus* the place in which it is used, even if we admit that the same means can be used in another place, the work will inevitably reveal itself to be different since, as I've just said, the work is where the 'lined material' is exhibited and seen, and this obviously includes the place. This is one of the reasons why the work only exists in the moment in which it is seen; moreover, it should be seen in the precise place for which it was conceived and shown, as that place and the material used together make up the work and the two cannot be separated. Since the context (topological, political, social) is always different, I can maintain that the work carried out and then shown is always different and not repetitive in the strictest sense of the word. On the contrary, I can maintain that art in general, beneath the appearance of constant formal differences, is basically repetitive. The voluntary repetition of the means used is clearly a function of a difference, since the apparent, formal differences of art, from one work to another and even from one period to another, confirm this repetition."

*To what degree is your work artistic?*

"I know that if I don't say first of all that what I'm doing is art, then this means insisting on the intrinsic qualities of the work in question – and all this requires a certain degree of effort from the public. But if I say right off: it's certainly that, whether you accept it or not, I as an artist say that my work is art, then this means asking the public once again to accept it just as it is, without any discussion, or to reject it, again without discussion, so that the whole problem is reduced to a matter of taste. As far as this is concerned, a number of artists have fallen into the trap of defining art, some more successfully than others. There's one whose definition has recently had success, the American Donald Judd. He's said that art is whatever an artist decides it is. It's a head-spinning, seducing answer, but what is he saying in point of fact? First of all the impression is given that if everyone, just as he pleases, can define his own work as art, this means that we find ourselves in the realm of absolute freedom, with the condition, of course, that each one has already been previously defined an artist. Defined by whom? How? These are questions that this answer naturally doesn't satisfy. But there's worse to come: if an artist can define his own work as art, he can naturally say the same about the work of another artist. So we can already see that only the artists can establish among themselves what art is. Let's go back to the initial axiom. If the artist takes upon himself the right to say that what he's doing is art, this means that he knows when what he's doing isn't art. If we follow the previous example we can say that he also knows when another artist produces something that isn't art and he can say so. What happens in this case? Well, it's really simple. On the basic of the power conferred on him by the system, an artist has the right not just to call his own work art and accept the work of others as artistic in the same way if that's the case, but also, and above all when he has some degree of authority, he can make use of his power and order that the work of so-and-so (who hasn't got enough power to make himself important) isn't art and he can have the work relegated into oblivion. What Judd says seems innocent enough and in point of fact it represents precisely what happens in the taking-over of power within the capitalist system. There too there is an exorbitant level of power that is almost absolute and impossible to control. So we can understand why many artists have taken up Judd's expression, including themselves in the ranks of the lucky elect!"

*To what degree is your work political?*

"Every work, whatever it is, is political, all the more so a work of art. This means that every artistic work, over and beyond what its author thinks of it, has a political meaning and in this sense artistic production as a whole is perfectly reactionary. It certainly won't only be by proclaiming one's membership in one or another group or by quoting (rightly or wrongly) Marx, Lenin or Mao, that this situation can be changed. My work tends to dismantle the mechanisms that produce it, and so, if correctly carried out, it can turn upside down the artistic and fundamentally conservative power that is perpetuated by the artists themselves. In this sense the most evident political action of my work consists in its critical aspect. Constantly critical in relation to itself and in relation to the context, whether cultural or formal, according to the places in which it is carried out and according to the precise points that it touches upon in a given moment and a given place. It's also political in the sense that it contests the right of the professional artist to the power that he continues to accept and with which he's been invested by the bourgeois society which controls it. It's an extensive power that prevents anyone who isn't an 'artist' from expressing himself. In the first place such an art can only perpetuate itself – due to the consensus of the artists – by suffocating any possibility of popular art. Class struggle exists in artistic creation as well, and this will become more and more evident."

*What are the constant elements and what are the variations from one work to another?*

"By and large the constants in my work are at least on two levels. On the one hand there's the formal constant of the instrument being used, and on the other there's the constant of the concept, that is the answer to different questions posed, and more than once, in a field (the artistic field) which is apparently unstable but which, in the facts, is fundamentally apathetic and needs to be shaken up – something that's never been done. If we schematize even the differences between one work and another, they are again on two levels. The first is represented by the formal differences given by the state of the work in a determinate context, and the second by the differences as a result of the place and, above all, the time considered, as well as the specific question posed in a specific moment and which will direct the work towards determinate considerations. The essential question would be that about art at every level, including the political one; an overall question from which a whole series of other questions springs about form, weight, point of view, context, questions regarding economics, sociology, etc. All these questions mean that in the face of every proposition a problem is posed which is different from the previous one; it is here that we find the differences between one work and another – numerous and unforeseeable differences – and not in the use of white or coloured lined paper or material with the same pattern. We shouldn't forget that if the work formally disappears at the end of the exhibition, it can definitely cancel itself out not so much by disappearing as by its remaking in the same place with the same material and the same colour but in a different moment. And this will cancel out at the very least everything that could still preserve the traces of a certain gesturality."

*One constant in your work is also the diversity which you propose by exhibiting your lines in the cultural space of the art gallery and, at the same time, in the anonymous space of the city. Can you explain the ties and the differences here?*

"When I work officially with a gallery, I always deliberately arrange it that I make use of the gallery in the strictest sense of the word, above all not to give the impression that I'm playing with words but also in order not to distract the visitor from the gallery. I don't want to give the impression – which besides would be very wrong indeed – that nothing happens in the gallery anymore and that it's become necessary to go outside if we want to see what's happening to art. What I think could be interesting, on the other hand, is if we say that the gallery doesn't stir up interest anymore in its present form (although it still continues to use art), and if we say it turning art inside-out like a glove and showing in an absolutely clear way that the work in question is just as possible internally as it is externally. By 'internally' I mean the topological position of the gallery limited by its walls, and by 'externally' everything to be found outside the gallery walls. I should say at once that, whether internally or externally, the work in point of fact inevitably remains within the same system. At least for now. There's nothing at all revolutionary, either as a gesture or as an intention, in the presentation of the work outside the specialized spaces. We need to understand this very well if we want to grasp the spirit with which the work I 'sign' is undertaken. One of the perceptive differences between internal and external is just this: that the work placed inside can be seen by those who visit the gallery while it's possible that the work outside is not seen at all. For example, when the work is inside a gallery it immediately appears a priori as an artistic product, even (we could go so far to say) before it's looked at. Whatever people think about it, they'll talk about it in artistic terms, even if it's just to run it down. In the street, even if you manage to 'see' it, it's not so sure that it will appear as an artistic work. I believe that it's precisely this dialectic between the object in the gallery or in the museum and the object outside any sort of place defined a priori as artistic which poses in a real sense the problem of the location of such a work. Paradoxically we can even say that if the work exists each time in one or more specific, determinate places, in itself it doesn't have any precise place of its own. Any work of art exhibited in a precise context (a gallery or a museum) is subjected to that specific 'setting' just as my work is, except that one pretends not to take this into consideration. In point of fact, as far as a work of art in general is concerned, we can hardly ever speak of this subjection if we don't want to risk seeing the work disappear completely in such a contest. All the work of an art critic, of art history and the artist himself generally consists of focalizing interest on what is represented within the object itself, without paying the slightest attention to the place where the exhibition is taking place. In my work, on the other hand, the location of the exhibition and the 'instrument' of the work presented form an inseparable whole, so much so that an instrument with an identical form and colour (sheets of paper with white or coloured lines) doesn't convey or mean the same thing at all if it's exhibited in the street or in a museum. The two works are completely different from each other, so much so that, rather than the instrument exhibited being the centre of interest, at that point it's the gallery itself that appears for what it is. And it's precisely at that point that one realizes that the gallery, in the majority of cases, has become a sort of shop window constructed just so as to sell different gadgets. The possibility I have in my work of, without distinction and according to the circumstances, using the city, the street or the gallery and the museum cancels out the cultural location or puts it back into perspective. It cancels it out in the sense that it ceases to be a single and despotic place, and it puts it back into perspective in the sense that it makes us politically aware that that place is not at all such a neutral place as everyone has been trying so hard to make us believe. The meaning of the work is given by the place where it's carried out."

*There's also a contradiction, given that the "stripe" exhibited in the gallery has an advantage over the one exhibited anonymously in the city where nothing marks its presence or consecrates your signs.*

"It's precisely this contradiction that gives rise to the dialectic."

*Your work perpetuates the destruction of the object in order to focus on the idea, but one has the impression that it can also perpetuate – and dangerously at that – the idea of art.*

"Let me ask you a question then: what is art? What is this idea of art?"

*What's the connection between the impersonality of your work and the condition of the workers? I'm asking you this because I think it's right that since we can't define the personality of what a worker does, the artist too should expropriate himself and put aside any subjective and sentimental attitudes with respect to his own work.*

"The aim of the artistic work should be just as necessary as it is if, for example, you call a plumber to fix a dripping tap and the latter – whoever he is (unless he doesn't know his job at all) – fixes it quite independently of his state of mind. I'd like to find this same need and ability in the artistic system, but on the contrary the interest that we usually find among artists is quite different: if you've got a problem of a dripping tap, they'll come and fix your telephone."

*Don't you think that it's just this which explains why artists' attitudes remain metaphorical, and that this leads us back, basically, to a reality that's mimed?*

"I don't know if it's so much the attitude of the artist because his attitude interests me only relatively; but I'm sure that it's his work or work-product which is very often metaphorical. Here too we need to agree about what we mean by the word 'metaphor'. You can't take away from anyone a priori the right, setting out from a given work, to associate images with this work, images which will create metaphors. This doesn't mean that the work is metaphorical in itself. A fundamental question we should ask ourselves is this: can art do without metaphor? And in this case, are we always dealing with art?"

*Continuing this metaphor, could I say that your work too presents itself as the death of subjectivity, an intentional castration of the artist who renounces his own inner nature in order to adopt an objective attitude? In this case, and in your work, death means paralyzing the capacity to produce different objects and images, the capacity to represent one's own inner nature.*

"This question should have a very precise answer. That is to say, at the level of the artistic sphere, the sphere of so-called free expression of certain privileged individuals. Let's try and avoid getting confused by thinking that my work intends to castrate the expression of individuals who already can't express themselves in any way as they would like, that is as artists. I've got a theory as far as this is concerned: with their subjectivity the artists prevent other individuals from expressing themselves; the work of other artists castrates the possible production of non-artists. So, perhaps, my work castrates other artists' work, in view of the liberalization of the work whatever it may be, of the other individuals, of all the individuals. The artist should no longer be what bourgeois society wants him to be, that is the image of freedom in the midst of general alienation. Art isn't free – on the contrary, if we start seriously asking ourselves what art is it would seem that it follows very precise rules, norms and even laws which have been valid for centuries and almost unchangeable. What's left to do is to understand if such laws can still be justified today and if they should be respected. For example, what will happen if we break these laws? What already happens now? Who will the policemen and the magistrates of the artistic world be, who are they already? This is one of the many things that my work reveals or will do so in the future."

# Nicola De Maria
Foglianise, Benevento, Italy, 1954

Turin
1983

*Your painting is the production of a field of intensity. What is the value of your creative process?*
"I send my heart to have an exhibition."
*What value do you assign to fragments?*
"Every day I paint a small canvas, and it becomes a new world."
*What value do you assign to abstraction in your work?*
"little birds in the room
blast tower
1917 cities offer women
sadness in the planet
angelic little house
in the child's eye
waves in the room
I live here
I'm Nicola – I'm a painter of little houses
day of the new century
journey in the word of flowers in the painter
smoke
landscape without fox
night trees rebel against the houses
Soviet Russia
Nicola: rays from his forehead, beasts under his shirt
angels that protect my work
shiny eyes, blue hands
daily hotel
all-year faults
night thought
rose at the window
Greek lyrics
sea poem
I'm a happy runner
castaways
you
1981 billions of painters from China

touch the stars
trains at the sea, ships on land
my room flying with me inside
Nietzsche
voices
autumn songs
destiny
on the bridge between love and hate
rain of paintings
my story is a miracle of times
too old
rebel poets in the metropolis
Asiatic African
EE AA motorized spatial enterprises in the sky and on the
hills of my city
red is the colour of magic
tonight the stars are hailstones
diamond women
dead painters
earthquake of the soul
heart
days of the new century
scents
giants of the desert (trams)
winter accident
listen to me
I'm Nicola – I have three hands to paint better with
room in San Francisco
summer
gold + passions + paradise."
*What relation is there between art and music?*
"Listen, Achille, listen: it's the sound of brushes in the realm
of flowers. Listen, listen: it's the same sound as ocean currents and
mountain brooks. One can dance in my work."

*Sign and colour are your expressive tools, which tend to es-
tablish an architecture of sensibility. Is there an idea of total art
behind your art?*
"Yes, Achille, there is."

*Is there a moral temperature in art?*

"Artists are radioactive; they even go and buy a carton of milk, they're good and generous men, capable of destroying the city's anguish.

Artists exist somewhere in the suburbs, they seek a new humanism in the new beauty, and they rebel against the idea of bombs. I repeat they're good and generous men, they destroy the city's anxiety. Achille, you recognize them by the aura that accompanies them, over their heads."

# Mario Schifano
Homs, Libya, 1934 – Rome, 1998



*Your painting has the grace of the Italian artistic tradition. The evolution of your work is up-to-date exactly because it lacks any linear progress, any mechanical development or predictable evolutionism. You have shot films, made collages, and Polaroids, but you have also elaborated a kind of painting whose source of inspiration has been the visual aspect of the television image. When you passed from the monochrome abstract paintings at the beginning of the 1960s to figurative painting, you worked on a sense of the fragment, of the detail, of the particular, your figuration played again with images associated with some kind of vital frailty. You have always escaped any ideological or dogmatic view of art and of the artist in our contemporary reality.*

"My relationship with photography is parallel to my relationship with painting, in its connection to the human figure, in that it resembles the human figure. Nothing is more similar to human beings, their behaviours and their reactions, identities, violence, sweetness, love, than photography, cinema, television. Everything, including cinema, is mediated by all that. I made 16mm short films which were shown in several film festivals, it was a trilogy: *Satellite, Umano non umano* and *Trapianto, consunzione e morte*. Then I made videos, but what most surprises me is that now I cannot stand them any more. Painting takes all my time now and is my whole way of life. Back in 1968, cinema was a way of life – the life of a variety of behaviour."

*And now you have returned to painting…*

"In these last five years, starting with the *Orti botanici*, I have begun working on something that could make me enjoy painting, its softness and sensuousness, its mute richness, because colours are infinite. I use colours without ever reworking them; it is a privilege that I have allowed myself these last years. I had an exhibition in Venice entitled *Naturale sconosciuto*, in the sense that no sign, no flower, not even leaves or grass nor vegetables look like anything existing in nature. At one point there was a connection with a group of young painters who work between Italy and the

States – your Transavantgarde. I felt their strength, I saw how it is when you work in a group in which each protects the other, even without really being friends. This exhibition of mine closes a cycle. I will work on a kind of painting that renounces a lot, and is full of different intentions. I see that as a natural phenomenon, even though I do not believe in talent as a gratuitous matter of fact; I mean, we have technology now and other important factors. In these works I have experienced every possible pleasure in different ways of painting. I work and think with great ease, I understand that work stems from another instinct, another potentiality, another possibility."

*Potentiality is the speed of gestures that corresponds to an inner, psychic and deeply sentimental speed. True?*

"Sometime in my work nature has appeared as synthetic, anaemic, almost livid. Instead, in the Gibellina paintings, in Sicily, beside colour, there is also a strong sense of warmth. Many artists have left works at Nuova Gibellina. I have left there ten paintings dedicated to one of the Sicilian winds, the Scirocco. I sensed almost a kind of psychic participation. Working in front of many people is not easy. Human work is expressed by energy, fatigue, sacrifice; but a painter's work is not a question of sacrifice, it is a question of privilege, in which you are free to invent at your ease. I have invented as I liked, but actually I have also made sacrifices."

*When we speak of nomadism, we must remember that you have experimented with many expressive means. From the beginning of the 1960s until the 1980s, you produced monochromes, Cokes, details of Italian landscapes, car accidents, re-visitations of Futurism, television sets, the laboratories. In the period of laboratories, you always used the presence of a reproducible image that you managed to make tangible, I mean, the presence of automation in technology. But let's start with a title:* Divulgare, *to divulge.*

"Yes, let's start there and let's stay there, in the sense that I represent a case of intertwining languages, between photography and television. A way of preserving a steady rate of experimentation. I would like, and I apologize for the comparison, to draw a parallel between Dante's *volgare* Italian and my language, which has to be traced back precisely to the 1970s."

*Doesn't that sound a little excessive?*

"No, since the desire to divulge – stemming from *volgare* – is exactly the same, that is, to pass through the everyday inflation of a language in progress, submitted to a continuous contamination and vital distortion. The spoken Italian of the thirteenth century, of Dante's Florence, is like my 'tele-verbal' language at this turn of the century."

*Don't you think there is a risk of producing a mimetic language?*

"I don't think so. What is at stake here is the conquest of a real language. An artist photographs, detects an image and refounds it, according to a sequence that renders it more communicative and that at the same time makes contemplation more complex. Speed and delay. This is the true effect of art, when it works."

*And does it work in your case?*

"In my case, we certainly have a result. My new imagery includes the common daily accidents of an instant-language, a flexible, fragmented, self-evident and synthetic language. Exactly like the language of television. I use it in such a way that what is figurative becomes abstract, and the abstract becomes allusive. A dinosaur looks like an airplane taking off as seen on television news; continents establish a peculiar short circuit through closeness and distance, which clearly do not correspond to geography but to an artistic sensibility."

*There exists a didactic level, or I should say, a pedagogy of art. Art as explained to children: that is my catch-word. The self-evidence of image, the artificial and playful strength of colour, the oddity of combinations, the use of sequences dealing with everyday life, the fragmentation and the cutting. In your opinion, does art have a function?*

"Maybe yours is an excessive question if you think that my work is always intended for a social destination of the art product, without any sense of prudishness or morality. All of my works, made of characters, brains, dinosaurs, children, babies, spiders, spinning tops, time signals, continents, naval vessels and sugar bars, become a huge map of our new way of seeing."

*Maybe a globe….*

"A globe in the sense of a circular retrieval of all images which appear and disappear in the instant of electronic communication.

My work becomes the catalogue of our future memory storage of these images. A work in cultural anthropology, which employs art to raise the attention of a codified world. Here the code is caught and released in the divulgation of a new language."

*Then what could we say from this point of view?*

"First of all, we can say that I am a real 'painting-machine', a psychosomatic complex system, with a calling for painting – its follower, with no chance of escape. I never turn away from what I am painting or have painted. I do not contemplate what I have done and therefore I do not undergo with my work a process of satisfaction or dissatisfaction: it is up to the market and to the art collector to select among the huge amount of my production. It is interesting to note that in this case the art system finds its own endorsement, assigning to an expert, such as a critic, a dealer, or a collector, the task of choosing within a horizontal production of images. And this is how we realize how many components interplay in my work, and somehow in my private life as well: speed, focus on technology, reproduction of images, the contemplative dimension of the city, music, advertising, photography, movies. This is an attitude that has a typical Italian model as its background, close to Futurism for its cultural tension. I think it's obvious that my images are inexhaustible, a kind of storage from which we can pull up anything. Certainly my painting passes through a process of chilling down, of conceptualization: it is the mechanical eye of the camera, of photography, of the Polaroid. This is the point when I start to paint, although through the strokes of a quick painting that indicates a hard-wired emotional state. Actually my emotional state is always filtered by a process of chilling down, which is one of the fundamental moments of my personal elaboration."

*An image reserve as an Indian reservation…*

"More or less. I have a whole image reservation; it is as though my thoughts were possible only as iconographies, as if they could be heard only through the concreteness of the image and not through the abstractions of pure thinking. It is from this reservation, as well as through inattention – in the sense of Benjamin's definition of the perception modes typical of a culture overwhelmed by images – that I reach a productive attention, a personally elaborated image."

*It seems to me to be a kind of alternating cold&warm current.*

"I think my work has often been interpreted in a conventional way, in connection with the American situation, incorrectly homogenizing what I do with pop art. That would make me nothing more than a European version of the hegemonic model of American pop. That is clearly a critical mistake: whereas the US pop art made outright reference to everyday objects and to the world of merchandise, for me, a Catholic-Apostolic-Roman artist, the references came from cultured images and quotations of linguistic and iconographic fragments of the past, which had for me the same value as a hamburger or a coke. Another common misunderstanding is to consider me a romantic artist, creator of life and language, an artist caught in the catastrophe of his production, in the elitist and private processes, which the cultural gossip turns into something emblematic. Both these attitudes are very wrong: maybe the best approach is to see how much of my life and my vital and cultural energy has managed to become a language, communication."

*What you say sounds perfectly fitting for the Schifano of the early 1960s...*

"The late 1950s was the birth of Informel. A group of young artists including myself, Paolini, Festa and others emptied and reset the surface of the painting, on which there had long been too much matter. Ours is a surface filled with subjectivity, where this starting afresh means retrieving serenity and creating a new, vital elaboration of the surface itself. Painters like me should be recognized as those who have reacted to Informel and the framework of my paintings of that time is a sort of screen, of protection that draws back to a linguistic universe focused on the alteration of the surface."

*This is an intuitive, unconscious response. In my opinion consciousness is a condition of the work, not of the artist: it is the work that must show maturity, and what is most important is to be able to contextualize it in its own time. In the time when artists organized that starting afresh, your work, for example, was a responsive work, a conscious work. By defining you as a "total artist", I also underline the technological elements that nourish your work. I see you as an instance of absolute nomadism.*

"A synthetic phenomenon, I would say, capable of incorporating in the specific language of images a series of elements and quotations coming from other linguistic and technological universes. Somehow I am an electronic-village artist: through television sets, Polaroids, the camera, records, I travel all around the world at a speed that my body could never manage. I can simultaneously be in a state of contemplation and action. On the one hand, I step out of my time when I consider the revolution that has made everything a simulacrum of itself; on the other hand I focus on my uniqueness, my staying still, preserving my roots. I am a complicated artist. In my thirties I speeded up my knowledge of art, forcing myself to become a sort of settled nomad, through a deliberate use of the information system. A complex and simple phenomenon at the same time, due to that excessive improvement of my complexity."

*It is exactly my consciousness of this complexity that brings me closer to artists, but also makes me autonomous. I am very fond of a concept I developed in one of my books ten years ago: art as a source of catastrophes. A catastrophe is the eruption of motion onto the tectonic equilibrium of language. Our communication today is subject to the enormous power of images and of theoretical thinking, which tears off and discards our normal exchange, producing a split. And this split is not just a laceration, but also a reconstruction. It is a trace, a scar. If we talk of chaos we enhance that notion of catastrophe and declare that art or theoretical thinking are only productions of organized chaos, according to a method. This is the reason why chaos, as a consequence of alarm, is essential, in that it recovers the paramount movement of creation.*

"Art is not the answer to the problems of the world, it is a question about the world. Art is complication, it makes life difficult. Art is not a condominium by-law, it is isolation, but it's capable of producing social networks through communication."

*Compared to the work of art, the figure of the artist is sort of biological error; artists die, they decline, they are hungry and thirsty, they have the same problems of every human being of their time. But the artwork has its own consciousness, which separates it from its maker. This means that the artwork is that production of chaos or catastrophe capable of breaking the balanced structure of cultur-*

*al conventions. Therefore I find myself justified in accusing art and culture of irresponsibility. The utopia of the historical avant-garde is the idea that art can act upon the world and change it. From this derives the ethical stance involving experimentation with new languages and new techniques aimed at affecting things. The logical outcome is a theory of total art, of the confluence of languages. But in reality the promises of the avant-garde have been kept only by technology: videoclip. The surface of our present society of the spectacle is only an ideal synthesis of theatre and architecture, cinema, photography, scene design, visual arts, all played at high speed. A final emblem of Schifano could be this: "from art to videoclip, from videoclip to art." A round trip between life and art.*

"I like it…"

# William S. Burroughs
St. Louis, Missouri, 1914 – Lawrence, Kansas, 1997



*What is the connection between the literary technique of cut-up and your paintings?*

"The cut-up technique was not my idea, but Brion Gysin's. He was the inventor of the cut-up style that later on, after the Second World War, was applied to writing. In 1959 Gysin began his first experiments with collage, regarding writing as fifty years behind the visual arts. Every time you look out of a window or walk down the street, your awareness is pervaded by random factors… you wander around the neighbourhood and carefully observe what you see. Then you go back and write down what you remember. You will have a jumble of fragmentary images: a man cut in two by a car, for example, and so on. When Brion and I experimented with the collage style in writing we took pages of text, cut them up and rearranged the fragments. These early works were then published in *Minutes to Go* in Paris in 1959. So today I'm reapplying to visual art a style already used in writing. In this passage, however, changes have taken place. First of all I do not cut up paintings with scissors, but often use the camera. I look at a painting and pick a part that I think has turned out well, photograph it and then insert this image into other works, sometimes putting it in the foreground and painting around it or leaving a blank space for images that I select later, or again mounting them on a surface painted in advance. The selection, in this case, is a conscious process, but randomness has been introduced into the original compositions. Life is a cut-up. The concept of a writer or a painter who creates in a timeless space is indefinable."

*Your pictorial works are a three-dimensional interplay of painting and writing. In this sense do they create a third artistic genre?*

"Three-dimensional as far as my works on wood are concerned, very distant from writing in comparison with the works on paper… The majority of my paintings tell stories. Coming as I do from literature, the story always tends to dominate in my paintings. Yet I never know what story I'm telling until the work is finished, unlike with my novels. And most of the times even the title

I find afterwards. When I write it is as if I were watching a film in my mind that I then try to produce in words on paper. I can only see and understand what I am writing. Obviously the cut-up technique introduces a factor of chance. But in painting I see with my hands and I may not know what they are seeing. Many of my paintings are clearly illustrative of my passage from writing to figurative art. *Burn Unit*, for example, is drawn from a passage in my novel *The Western Lands*. And many other paintings describe *The Land of the Dead*, which is a leitmotiv in that book. But a painting tells a very different story from a novel: seen from various perspectives, under different lights and at different distances, against changing backgrounds. You simultaneously see a truck falling off a broken bridge and the driver's face disappearing... There is no satisfactory and complete way of representing simultaneous events on written pages."

*Can your works be defined as three-dimensional writing that occupies a real space?*

"I'm not sure whether I can define my paintings as writing, in any acceptable sense of the word."

*How important is chance in the creative process?*

"As I've already said, chance plays a vital role in my paintings. Obviously this is true for many painters. Jackson Pollock pours paint and lets it run over the canvas to create unpredictable and random forms, even though Pollock claims that every drip, every splash is a product of pure intention (and I believe the same for my paintings); but at the same time he himself considers chance to play a very important role in the creative process. If random factors are strictly excluded the painting can degenerate into a sterile and lifeless copy.

There are many ways of introducing chance into a work. Dripping, marbleizing, painting with the fingers, using plants or pieces of string as brushes and, finally, randomly (and intentionally) a gunshot that strikes a pressurized can of spray-paint and creates an explosion of colour across the surface of the work. And then you can use random forms of recognizable objects, houses, trees, cars, faces, guns... as I do."

*What is the relationship between your works and Eastern culture?*

"My Eastern culture is minimal. It was Brion Gysin who taught me what I know of the art of painting through studies he had made of Arabic and Japanese calligraphy. So my style is a clear and deliberate imitation of Brion's."

*What connection do your works have with the automatic techniques of surrealism and the gestural ones of action painting?*

"I've never had any success with what is called automatic writing, I can't help knowing what I am writing. With paintings on the other hand I never know what I'm painting until I've finished. It's not that I go into any sort of trance, but I strive to empty my mind of any preconceived idea. I try to put little of myself into both writing and painting."

# Gino De Dominicis
Ancona, Italy, 1947 – Rome, 1998



*I'm going to propose having a conversation where you have to answer either yes or no. Indeed the Gospel warns us that there are no alternatives. Even though the Bible states "In the beginning there was the Word", you believe in the supremacy of the image over the word. Let's respect our roles right from the start: I am the written word and you are the image that is always silent but eloquent. I will ask you questions using words and you will answer with a gesture, a motion of the head. Nod if the answer is yes and shake your head if the answer is no. This will take place in the presence of a witness, Umberto Scrocca. Is that okay?*

[Yes.]

*Do you remember one evening in 1971 when, at Termini railway station in Rome, Sargentini and Pisani, yourself and I were waiting for the train from Florence that was bringing the first copy of my first book* Il territorio magico *with your ball captured on the rebound?*

[Yes.]

*Is art a noun that doesn't require adjectives?*

[Yes.]

*Is your art always figurative?*

[Yes.]

*Is the black-edged invitation to your first exhibition (1969) at the Galleria L'Attico in Rome a visiting card for eternal life?*

[No.]

*Do you remember when we celebrated going beyond the second principle of thermodynamics, otherwise known as entropy, in Palazzo Taverna, Rome in 1972?*

[Yes.]

*Is the artist a biological error compared to his work?*

[No.]

*Does death exist?*

[No.]

*Is your attempt to fly, published for the Paris Biennale held in 1971, just the image of an attempt?*

[No.]

*Is making squares in water rather than circles a bit like walking on water as described in the Gospels? Is it the request for a miracle?*

[No.]

*Is art a metaphor?*

[No.]

*Is a work of art a means of opposing time conventions?*

[Yes.]

*Does time exist?*

[No.]

*Does the concept of entropy actually exist, in terms of what can be inferred scientifically from the second principle of thermodynamics?*

[No.]

*Is your art older than the art of the past?*

[Yes.]

*Is your laughing Madonna a response to the smile of the* Mona Lisa*?*

[No.]

*Does the history of art exist?*

[No.]

*In your view, in the work* Il giovane e il vecchio [The young man and the old man]*, do the subjects invert their own identity? Is the young man, who was born afterwards, therefore older than the other man, since he has more time behind him?*

[Yes.]

*At the Paris Biennale of 1971, you replied to my invitation with a performance at the preview, wearing the mask of an old man and a sign with the words "What's death got to do with it?" Is art an advertisement against the limits of life?*

[Yes.]

*In the exhibition* Contemporanea *held in 1973 in the car-park of Villa Borghese in Rome, your room contained various works:* Oroscopo [Horoscope]*,* Gemelli [Gemini] *and even the skeleton with roller skates. Time versus motionless space. Is this the meaning?*

[Yes.]

*Does the work of art defeat time in its horizontal convention of the condensation of a moment?*

[Yes.]

*Does space exist?*

[No.]

*Is this the origin of your invisible objects?*

[Yes.]

*Does the gravitational weight of the body exist?*

[No.]

*Does logical, progressive time exist?*

[No.]

*Is immortality therefore achievable by suspending the conventional dimension of time?*

[Yes.]

*Can immortality be defined as a body that does not grow old?*

[Yes.]

*Is biology a limitation?*

[Yes.]

*Can art overcome it?*

[Yes.]

*Does historical memory exist? Is it a mistake?*

[Yes.]

*Is the instantaneous perception of the world possible?*

[Yes.]

*Are space and time therefore dimensions that can be surpassed?*

[Yes.]

*Is it necessary to leave space?*

[Yes.]

*Do the two men hanging from the wall of Palazzo Taverna in Rome represent an attempt to achieve this?*

[Yes.]

*Is it a question of thought preserving the body?*

[Yes.]

*Is art therapeutic?*

[Yes.]

*Your work* Il tempo, lo sbaglio, lo spazio *[Time, the mistake, space] of 1970 presents a skeleton of a man and of a dog with roller skates. Is this a response to death?*

[Yes.]

*At the Venice Biennale of 1972 you presented a work featuring a person with Down syndrome sitting on a chair. For his special perception of time and space, was it a way of overcoming space-time conventions?*

[Yes.]

*Is your interest in the Sumerians just cultural?*

[No.]

*Does Gilgamesh indicate the link between past and present?*

[Yes.]

*Does he represent the strength of mind that breaks the equilibrium between space and time?*

[Yes.]

*In 1971 you presented a sign of art that was a combination of different symbols (the cross and the swastika, indicators of the immortality of the soul and the race). Does this sign refer to the immortality of the body?*

[Yes.]

*Is this the reason why you use dates that are so distant from each other, as 33AD/1919–71?*

[Yes.]

*Does the overlapping of symbols destroy historical time and the temporal distance of dates?*

[Yes.]

*Does history exist?*

[No.]

*If history doesn't exist, is art always contemporary?*

[Yes.]

*Is there a difference between a precariously balanced pole, the first drawing, laughter, the "we are drawing pins", painted figures, rock, a cage, the big skeleton, the hen, the inverted perspective of Piazza del Popolo, fried mozzarella?"*

[No.]

*Are your works all living beings?*

[Yes.]

*Living in the sense that they have reached physical immortality?*

[Yes.]

*Without any special pretensions?*

[No.]

# Hidetoshi Nagasawa
Tonei, Manchuria, Japan, 1940

Milan
1993

*A journey from East to West. From Japan to Italy, through Asia and Europe. What made you come all this way?*

"I reached Italy in 1967. I started from Japan on a bicycle, and in a year and a half I arrived in Italy after crossing the countries of Asia: Thailand, Malaysia, Singapore, India, Pakistan, Afghanistan. When I arrived in Istanbul, Turkey, I had reached the goal of my journey. But after hearing Mozart's music I asked myself, 'what is this music?'. You know, after a year and a half of listening to Indian and Middle-Eastern music all the time, I was intrigued by the music of the West."

*You have chosen the contemplative dimension of slowness for your journey. Why not by foot, then, why a bicycle?*

"I did not choose to use a bicycle for this journey out of any passion for bikes. I only chose the bicycle after I had decided to make the journey. It would have been ideal to cover the route by foot, but it would have taken at least three years. And so for comfort, I chose the bicycle to travel through all those Asiatic countries. When I arrived in Milan I had run out of money, and someone stole my bicycle. I stopped here."

*You chose an area on the outskirts of Milan, a place where a lot of artists were based in that period.*

"As soon as I had found an atelier north of Milan, on the edge of town, in Sesto San Giovanni, I immediately began working. The neighbourhood was the district of artists, there were about forty, including Luciano Fabro, Castellani, Nigro… a great number. I have been very lucky, also for this reason, I immediately got to know the milieu of young artists in Milan. We had no money, but we used to have a big party every night at that time: we had a lot of fun."

*Tell me about the materials, about how you have discovered them, and how to use them in art.*

"I began to work with different materials in 1969: copper, brass and marble. There is no philosophy underlying my choice of materials. When we work, we usually first look for an idea, we don't start from the material. And when you find the idea, you begin to look for a suitable material. When I make sculptures it is clear that I think in three dimensions. The material may be heavy or light, but it must be possible to touch it, to see it."

*Yes, but you are a tactile artist who works on the part of the material that cannot be seen.*

"I go further than that: I pay most attention to the part that is not visible. You don't see it, but it is there."

*Are you a diurnal or nocturnal artist?*

"My day usually begins in the late afternoon, not in the morning. Mornings don't work for me. Towards afternoon, with a glass of wine, I begin to search for ideas. The right moment is when one gets sleepy, that is to say, the moment of half-sleep."

*A dreamy, sleepwalking artist, a nighthawk?*

"In that moment, not always, but sometimes, I manage to enter another world. We all live in two worlds, this three-dimensional and material world of ours, which we are familiar with, and another world, where there is nothing material. It does exist, but you cannot see it. When you manage to find your own balance within the two related worlds, many things may result, also new ideas, a great many ideas. Then you choose one or two of them, otherwise you'll go mad. The morning, when I wake up, I have to choose the ideas of the night before. I cannot say which moment is real: the morning when I wake up and choose the ideas, or the night, while I sleep, when I try to enter the other world…"

# Mimmo Rotella
Catanzaro, Italy, 1918 – Milan, 2006

Paris
1994

*From southern Italy to Rome to northern Italy and on to France and finally the United States. The nomadic artist…*

"I remember that I left Calabria when I was seventeen because I wanted to be an artist and that wasn't on the cards in the south. So I decided to emigrate to northern or central Italy. First I was in Rome, and later in France. From Rome I went to Paris and then to the States; afterwards I returned to France, and finally to Italy, to Milan, where I had found a studio."

*You have however always chosen to work in big cities.*

"For a modern artist it's important to stay in the big cities, because that's where the sources of inspiration are. For me, for example, the tattered posters on the walls were a true revelation. In the big cities there's a more complete choice of tattered posters. There's the political scene, the television scene and above all the cinema scene. In fact my first show in 1962 in Paris was called *Cinecittà*.

*In Paris you became part of the Nouveau Réalisme movement…*

"I went to Paris because the theorist of Nouveau Réalisme, art critic Pierre Restany, had invited me to be part of the group, since the philosophy of the new realists contemplated my form of art, décollage. It was appropriation, the choice of an image or of an object. I had a conceptual relationship with Arman who made accumulations of objects, with César who crushed cars and then made them into sculptures, with Christo who wrapped monuments and other things. And then obviously there were Jean Tinguely, Niki de Saint Phalle and Gérard Deschamps. In all, there were thirteen of us new realists."

*This was the period in which you invented the "coverings".*

"Yes, at the time I invented the coverings, that is the posters covered in monochrome paper to underscore the fact that the advertising was dated. I also appropriated big hoardings that had been covered awaiting a new message. I called them coverings, the English called them blanks and the French *oblitération*. I took over the posters and painted over, erased them, or added new symbols."

*This is the technique of overpainting on décollage.*

"Yes, this technique is called overpainting on *décollage* and it's what I'm doing now. I work, I paint, on tattered posters and I paint over them the symbols that I see on the walls of the city or on the underground. It's the fusion of painting with *décollage*. There are political symbols, even symbols that are somewhat esoteric; there's a bit of everything, even protest symbols. Today in art we have to convey a message, as I believe was also the case in the past; but now it's truer than ever because we have racism and neo-fascism, and so it's right that we should rebel, that we should convey this message."

*You frequently work in big dimensions. Marcel Duchamp said that if a work of art doesn't generate a shock there's no point in it existing.*

"I can express myself well on both small and large scale. Perhaps I see the walls of the city more in the large dimensions. As a matter of fact, I've worked on a large scale with metal advertising hoardings, acting on the strips of torn posters that I saw on the walls of the big cities. I have also used big formats, for example 6 metres wide by 3 metres high. The city is there. It's just that with the mass media bombarding us we are no longer capable of generating provoking messages. Small wonder that Marcel Duchamp speaks of the need for the shock."

# Robert Rauschenberg
## Port Arthur, Texas, 1925

New York
1995

*You came to Rome the first time with Cy Twombly. What do you remember of your encounter with Italy?*

"After landing at Palermo, I found myself – owing to a series of circumstances – swindled out of all my money. Once we got to Rome, Cy spent my half of the study grant indulging his genuine passion for marble heads. We had a great time going round the flea markets where they sold Etruscan objects and wandering in the environs of Rome looking for what were known to be Etruscan places."

*They say that you visited some artists' studios. How did your meeting with Alberto Burri go?*

"I went to Burri's studio on Via Margutta. He was friendly and hospitable. A few weeks later I found out that he was ill. At that moment I was making the *Feticci personali* [Personal fetishes] and had convinced myself that they had magical powers. So I went back to my studio and prepared one for Burri, with the aim of curing him. Two weeks later he came to my house with the smallest painting he had ever made, in exchange for the work I had given him. That picture is still one of my most precious possessions."

*Then you left for Morocco. On your return, the same year, you held your first exhibition outside the United States, to be precise at Gaspero del Corso's Obelisco gallery. How was it received?*

"I didn't have enough money to go back to the United States, and I didn't want to turn to the embassy. So I took a bundle of the things I had done in Italy and North Africa to Gaspero del Corso, at the Galleria l'Obelisco, and asked him if he would be willing to exhibit them. He immediately said yes. To his great surprise, we sold just enough to allow me to go back to America. In that period a new gallery had been set up in Florence that showed only modern art. Their most important critic came to see an exhibition of works by Cy Twombly and Robert Rauschenberg. He observed that it was a beautiful day, emphasized the greatness of the art in the Uffizi, and then launched an attack on my work in particular: he said that it was psychological trash and that it should be thrown in the Arno. I took him at his word. The next day Cy and I got a nice picnic together and went down the Arno until we came to a quiet place, where I tied stones to the works that were left and threw them in the Arno. Then I went back to the gallery and left a note for the critic, in which I said that I had followed his advice, but that I hoped he would be less drastic in his criticisms towards other young artists."

*You're like Pope John Paul II, you travel a lot. And now you're back in Rome at last. How come?*

"In September 1989 they asked me to hold an exhibition at a gallery in Rome and I accepted with pleasure. I liked the idea of showing in Rome again and of going back to Rome after so many years. But I said that first I had to finish my American tour, which concluded with the big exhibition in Washington. And in the meantime I worked on creating these ten works for my one-man show in Rome."

*Is art of use to those who make it or those who receive it?*

"The best art has its origin in the artist's spirit. It is this spirit that then travels towards the person who receives it."

*You tell the story of the plumber who came to your home to do some repairs and then came back the next Sunday with his family to see your works, which had stirred his curiosity. Should art make people curious or fill them with awe?*

"Curiosity makes you aware, and capable of questioning your own life."

# Ben Jakober and Yannick Vu
Vienna, 1930
Montfort-l'Amaury, France, 1942

Palma de Mallorca
1996

*A book is always the space of cohabitation of the image with the word. In our particular case this book is a very special space in which three artists live: Ben Jakober, Yannick Vu, and a third artist, the fruit of a spiritual, cultural and creative marriage: Jakober+Vu. A cohabitation between "three artists", whose evidently different personalities are the fruit of interaction between their differences. The first question to be asked, in the case of an artist's creation is the choice of materials. In Ben Jakober's case we have an artist who is interested in the modernity of the materials and in the ways in which he can restore or deliver an archaic overtone to this modernity. Yannick Vu on the contrary is not worried by this quality of modernity but by the expressive and spiritual power of her images. We can say that between Jakober and Vu there is another marriage, between sculpture and painting, between Western technological euphoria and equilibrium, indifference towards the materials and a need for art always to be like a reservoir in which ideas lie and ferment. You come from separate, different backgrounds and converge in a sort of Agora of common space in which the work of art merges into a unique form. I would like to ask Ben Jakober the reason for his preference for sculpture. Why do you prefer the third dimension?*

BJ "For me the third dimension is more sensual and represents the world in a more realistic way, without transposition."

*In Yannick it seems to me that there is a longing to displace the false third dimension of the world into a kind of balanced interior bi-dimension. Why did you start painting?*

YV "Probably by a kind of mimetism because my father was a painter. Then I lived with Domenico Gnoli in a true painters' world where painting was the daily dimension."

*Ben, I see that from the very beginning in your work you have had the maturity to "cool" the modernity of the materials, always referring yourself to an antique idea of sculpture nearly to the point of moving towards an archaeological taste: helmets, or the use of certain materials like stone. For you, sculpture has been the result of an urge to bring the contemporary materials back to the past.*

*What was your relationship with the story of the twentieth-century's avant-garde?*

BJ "I am rather anachronistic. Because I'm self-taught, I followed things from afar; maybe they didn't influence me because my innocence protected me. Maybe it wasn't a question of choice – of rejecting one thing voluntarily, but rather to be driven by some sort of ingenuity…"

*Do you remember (and then we will ask Yannick the same question) when did you make your first artistic work? Can you make a short description of this moment, of this epiphany?*

BJ "I started with what was called land art by building two dams in the mountains. I made them in Mallorca with one armed dynamiter. The concept was that the water line of the freshwater basin I had created would merge with the line of the horizon on the sea."

*What year was it?*

BJ "That was in 1969. Then I left matters there for a bit. Meanwhile Yannick was painting. In fact I started again making what one calls 'pieces', sculptures, in 1980 using polyurethane, a material the French sculptor César was also employing at about the same time to make his expansions. His, I think, were out of control, whereas mine were controlled in the sense that I used the material with a particular end in sight. I mean, I knew exactly where I wanted to go. I called this series *Slop Art* because of its informality. Thus this series, which was a bit ironic, very impertinent – tongues which stuck out of polyurethane masks, clouds with arms jutting out making obscene gestures from all over the world, things more or less irreverent – this was the line of my earliest work."

*So, Yannick, when you realized your first work, certainly bi-dimensional, drawing or painting, in which kind of spirit did you confront it?*

YV "I started by sheer necessity when I could hardly talk. At the beginning I could only draw the head's outline… I could also draw the eyes but not the nose and the mouth, so I asked my brother to help me because it was extremely important for me then to draw a complete head. In a way, I was looking for collaboration right from the beginning."

*But when did you make your first work with an artistic intention?*

YV "I really don't remember. I started to paint very early. It seemed to me natural and necessary to paint, and then to show my work."

*Did you go to art school?*

YV "No, I didn't. We talked about it but my father was against academies. However, I always painted… At fourteen I had acquired what one could call a certain skill. I stopped painting later when I was with Domenico and I felt a sort of impossibility to progress in my own expression. But otherwise I always painted."

*Ben, in your creative adventure there is one thing that fascinates me, which is also a fundamental element in my critical poetics from the moment I started to work. For some connection I think about André Malraux, an intellectual whom I estimate a lot because he went through a total life. I would like to know how much your nomadism and the idea of exploring the world affected your art, before you became an artist. I believe that you have been an explorer of life, and that's why I think about Malraux travelling around the world. Do you think that in your case there is an explorer identity? Can you talk about your nomadism?*

BJ "Yes. In fact I am an example of the wandering Jew. Born in Vienna of Hungarian parents, I was brought up in England, lived the formative years in France and then settled in Spain where perhaps my family came from in the first place. When I was hardly twenty years old my father sent me to India and Pakistan. It was an unforgettable eye-opening experience."

*We can say that Ben is a space explorer and on the contrary Yannick is a time explorer. I believe that Yannick has developed an interior nomadism, a nomadism that has to do with time rather than space. Do you recognize yourself in such a definition? If yes, would you support it with your memories?*

YV "When I was a child, my father used to talk to me about a dimension of time and things that didn't correspond at all to what we were living in the West. He always described the Vietnam he had left in 1929 and I could perceive it with an extraordinary depth, derived of experiences that I could never know, which almost came from another century. And with Domenico, whose father was an art historian also culturally belonging to a bygone era, I later discovered the great Western culture. I believe that this relation, so natural, with the past made a profound impression on me."

*Let us say that your nomadism has been more cultural than geographic.*

YV "Yes, a kind of transmission of time through words, writing, memory, the desire always to go back to the beginning of things, a sort of wandering, an unlimited quest of a sense of history."

*I realize something else from what you say: for a normal Western artist there is always the problem of protagonism. For many years you have lived in a position of "laterality" rather than "frontality" and explicit protagonism. Why?*

YV "Because of insecurity. It was much easier. I think that there is more suffering when one is alone and expresses oneself through a unique language all of his own. I believe that this is a necessarily more painful experiment, maybe richer, but out of which one doesn't emerge without damage sometimes. Also there might be more to it in the sense that the Oriental soul tends naturally towards a collective dimension, and that would explain my tendency to oscillate between the individual and the collective."

*Ben, what does it mean for you the transfer of a form into a material, bronze, iron, metal, or the transfer to a metallic structure, a bone structure like the hand of a man?*

BJ "Metal is the second stage if you like. In fact, in this case I took the bones of an ox to make this giant hand, then after analysing Gray's Anatomy I added the other elements to complete the correct reading of a hand. In the last stage I transferred the bones to bronze to fix them, passing from disassociated elements to a coherent whole that thus became permanent instead of remaining ephemeral."

*According to you, what relation is there between your work and Duchamp's ready-made?*

BJ "The permission one gives oneself in certain cases to incorporate and use elements which already exist. But mine are considerably modified, that is to say they cannot be left in their primitive state, they must be reworked, deformed if you will. It's like mayonnaise: I don't want to see the oil and the egg when it's finished. I want there to be a yellow substance which contains the different elements which were used, mixed to give rise to something new, something different."

*Yannick, you instead start right away with another type of transfer: living creatures' physiognomies in the portrait, the self-portrait. What does the portrait mean to you?*

YV "For me the most important part of the human body is the head. It is the essence of identity."

*Being your sensitivity chiefly Oriental, why do you realize figurative portraits when the figurative iconography is more typically Western than Eastern? Why this need of the figure?*

YV "It depends on the duality of my personality which is half Eastern, half Western. And in any case the figure is not so absent from the Oriental iconography."

*Why this preference for the infantile figure?*

YV "It is a direct relationship with a period of my life. I have done that kind of work during a time that perhaps corresponds to a cycle of maximum creativity (maternal as well), let us say between the age of twenty to thirty-five. Then I moved on to something else."

*In your painting, it seems to me that there is an element of "fixity" which in my opinion corresponds to a state of nearly melancholic contemplation. True?*

YV "Yes, this element does exist. I think that my personality was more melancholic when I was younger; now I am more at peace with myself and this is the result of an introspection carried out between the child that I was and I was not and the person I have become."

*So while for Yannick the creative experience corresponds to an introspective value, in Ben's case it is a work that exteriorizes, a work that is elaboration, dynamism, objectivity, it is depersonalization. This is a characteristic of Anglo-Saxon culture which likes privacy, which separates art from life. Do you identify with this?*

BJ "Although I was born in Eastern Europe and brought up in England, in fact I started to really develop when I moved to France. I was thus able to undo this British education and make a sort of interior revolution against the notion that the Anglo-Saxons have of things. I decidedly put myself into a Latin situation.

Especially so when I started to work, particularly so as I was in the south. I absorbed the Mediterranean atmosphere, rebutting the constraints of the more rigid English system, although I hope I've retained a certain Anglo-Saxon sense of humour."

*I feel that a sort of opposite path marks the difference between your respective approaches: you tend to materialize abstract concepts with heavy materials, whereas Yannick dematerializes the physicality of the human being through portrait.*

BJ "But isn't this complementarity precisely the object of our collaboration?"

YV "One can differentiate between two forms of thought. One expresses itself through words, which is verbal; and the other expresses itself through images. I think that it is the latter, much faster than the oral one that dominated my work at the beginning. That is why the notion of time was at once frozen and deep, immobile and thick (as when you talk about fixity, of a moment which seems to extend itself into a length of time that excludes any kind of movement) outside language, outside the possibility of relating the experience."

*Ben, at a certain point you moved to the greater dimension, got out of the chamber sculpture, of the small dimension and invaded the exterior space practically recovering the memory of land art, of the work that defies the dimension of the great space of history, of the great public space. What caused that transition?*

BJ "First of all I would like to say that, yes, we have done some monumental work but I think never anything that menaces people, always on a proper scale with man. The libraries are only two metres high. This helmet is lying on the ground and one can go inside it, go around it, it doesn't menace you, there are no sharp angles. When we were asked to do a large sculpture for the first time we tackled the problem together. This was *Le Vase de Soissons*, a commission for a property at Maucreux by a lake in France. This sculpture is not menacing either, it was four metres high, about double human size, and one could pass in between its four elements. Those were round surfaces, quite voluptuous forms."

*Ben always worked to give body to concept. Yannick, when did you come to sculpture?*

YV "When I saw my father doing those heads, I felt a kind of atavistic urge to explore this dimension. It interested me because the subject became object and also for the sheer pleasure of transforming mud into shapes."

*In your opinion what does it add to painting?*

YV "I see it in the context of the 'head' conceived as a recipient of ideas, but open, because my sculpted heads are open. It is the part of the body with more apertures: seven out of a total of ten if one counts the belly button that closes itself. We can talk about the relation between the interior and the exterior form. It seems to me that sculpture is more in communication with the world, the environment, that it occupies space and creates its own dimension. There is no need for walls, houses, roofs…"

*Ben,* La Copa *first, then Paolo Uccello's* Il Mazzocchio *are works that you have done on your own. At what time did you start to look for references in the history of art and why?*

BJ "Gradually working and living in art I emerged from the period of apprenticeship which corresponded to visceral and spontaneous things. I looked more and more at documents and when I saw those drawings by Paolo Uccello, they truly hit me. It seemed absolutely necessary to try and make them with new materials, contemporary materials, in three dimensions. The first idea was to make *La Copa de Paolo Uccello* with tubular scaffolding that is used in the building trade. Finally, for technical reasons the tubes had to be welded. This led to the *Mazzocchio*, where again the inspiration was Paolo Uccello. This is when we started to work with computers, not as an end but as a means of transforming a drawing of the past, to make studies for something to be built today."

*In your work I find a search for symmetry, harmony, proportion; maybe that is what makes it necessary for you to refer to the Italian Renaissance. Why harmony, and why Paolo Uccello?*

BJ "The discovery of perspective in painting was a revolution. Using the studies that the masters of the Renaissance left and transforming them with a computer is, I think, another similar step forward."

*I think that you have used sculpture to give body to your need to restore an idea of symmetry to things, which is perhaps what the world of today doesn't have.*

BJ "Yes, that's right. *Leonardo's Horse* is of course symmetrical. This is not a geometric but rather an organic symmetry. It is most interesting that while Paolo Uccello's drawings were absolutely clear, Leonardo's rendering for the cage he had prepared to contain the ceramic shell for his horse's head for the Sforza was a little deceiving in the same way as his mirror image writing, because when you look at the image you see the base as from above but when you look at the neck you seem to be looking from below. It was your request, Achille, for a sculpture measuring fourteen metres on the lagoon that put us on the road to monumental pieces."

*Yannick, it seems to me that Ben is always after an idea of symmetry in his work, and that instead you are looking for a concept of "harmony" through art. Does this interior longing for harmony have solely an aesthetic function for you or has it also an ethical meaning?*

YV "Also ethical, in the sense that art has a redeeming power, for me it is a vital thing because through art you can reach a dimension unexplainable and unattainable by any other means."

*So, for you, what is the function of art? Has it a therapeutic capacity, in the sense that it can trigger self-improvement?*

YV "One cannot dissociate it from a way of being, of living, of interpreting the world. It has nothing to do with morals; I don't think that art should be moral. For me it is not its function, it is not a religion, there is no dogma. It is something personal that can be shared with everybody, it is effectively always trying to surpass, to go on discovering, to question what seems acquired. It is an absolute requirement, a problem of conscience or rather of trying to understand the multiple meanings of life. It doesn't interpret good and evil; it's just about 'being'."

*When you talk about harmony in your case, do you think that harmony is the representation of a balance, or is it instead an attempt to correct the world? So, for you, is art corrective or expansive?*

YV "I don't think it is corrective. Art doesn't correct or denounce. Rather it anticipates."

*So what is harmony for you?*

YV "It is an interior notion, a very personal one; every person has a different sense of harmony."

*If you transfer it into your work, in which way do you do it?*

YV "I think it is like reaching a certain space – not a void, but fullness, which is outside of passions."

*Therefore harmony is a condition that includes spirit and excludes matter?*

YV "No, harmony cannot exclude matter… Because there is no spirit without matter."

*And so, what is art?*

"It's the equilibrium between the two."

*Let's talk about the common part now, and we come to the point where we talk about a "third artist", who is no more Ben Jakober, no more Yannick Vu, but Jakober+Vu.*

YV "What you say is absolutely right, because in any participation, one can admit that there is one who is stronger than the other and can impose more his or her personality – let's say that one can marginalize the other. In our case I think it is different. It didn't happen like that. Perhaps in the works we are doing together I could effectively think that I assimilate myself into Ben's language, and that I have engaged in one of his discourses; but when I work on my own, for instance in the drawings, I realize, that no, it's not like that, that Yannick Vu still exists. It is true that there is also that third person of whom I am a part, but Yannick Vu still exists, and Ben Jakober still exists. It is simply when, on the conceptual level, we are together and we have a project that a new energy surges and it is that third person. A symbiosis. Or perhaps it has become more than that, because symbiosis could mean regression. At the beginning it was a more painful admission for one or the other; this new territory was a little slippery, which of course could seem more attractive but also could be dangerous."

*But talk about yourself, Ben will talk later. I want to know your feeling.*

YV "For me, in part, it was a great liberation, because this desire to work with the other goes back a long, long way… I think that we always had a dialogue about our work. That may seem obvious but our work was separate. I had a certain territory and Ben had another one. Sometimes if I did a step in one direction following an idea that was personal, but which seemed to coincide with his domain, I felt I had to restrain myself from going into that direction which seemed attractive, natural. It could create conflicts, it was not very easy... Of course there were collaborations of ideas, and so on, but it was not something that was official, it was an unofficial thing in the couple. And one day, it had the chance to come out into the open. This moment for me was a liberation because I felt relieved. I think that I gained a lot, maybe even our relationship benefited from it, since we were no longer hedging on parallel paths but could go on together. I found it positive, a form of maturity, if you like, not only in our work, but also as far as feelings were concerned."

*And you Ben?*

BJ "We are complementary but with interchangeable roles. Sometimes I have an idea and Yannick gives it form and sees to the execution, at other times she has the idea and I have the technical means to realize it. One can be one or the other: we are interchangeable. Besides being more satisfying, this avoids a lot of problems: yes, because if it were not so (if one were always the executant and the other the conceiver of ideas), it would sooner or later turn into frustration for one or the other. And just because there is this permanent ambiguity, there is mutual satisfaction and the durability of the collaboration. You are a little bit responsible of all this, because of the invitation to participate jointly in the Biennale."

*But you started before, didn't you?*

YV "Yes, but not systematically; we only collaborated occasionally. I think it gives us a great strength and enables us to confront new stages, new forms."

BJ "After the death of our daughter I made on my own the series called *Cruxigrams*. Yannick joined in when we started to work on the Chapel. Her death brought us towards a sort of – I hardly dare pronounce it – spirituality; but let's say that in trying to grasp a sense of the sacred we started to approach things differently. This misfortune, which befell us, gave us a creative force of a new kind and of a new form that has united us in our work and in our life."

*In which way does this common work hide or exalt Ben?*

BJ "We have a permanent dialogue. Often I suggest something

and Yannick imposes a sort of veto. But if the idea is strong enough when considered in all its forms, this veto is transformed into something positive and takes a new direction. There is no need to pretend to try and outdo the other – it's the work of a team. It's like a tennis ball rebounding on each side of the court and each time it comes back, one hopes, with an improvement or at least a mutation. It's this exchange which gives rise to the finished work."

*Yours is the story of a couple, of a man and a woman, and therefore of a space in which your personalities can relate to each other, through eroticism and sexuality: concepts that also enter artistic creation. Normally one says that art sublimates sexuality, concentrates eroticism into a space in which the form becomes the physical incarnation, that you realize in a kind of family in which the children are concretely the works of art. Yannick, what part does sexuality play in this creation in which not by chance you are a man and a woman, a husband and a wife and therefore the interaction of two different magnetic fields?*

YV "In our case it is often a mental proposition which could be an amorous or a seductive one. And in the woman's role I say no; but it is not a no which means no, it's a no that wants to go further, it is a form of feminine coquetry, and it goes on. So we know that the amorous dialogue about the work of art has just started, and at that moment the tone will rise, not like in an argument but on another level. The exchange continues and it is a little bit like the ritual of the *corteggiamento*, which finally culminates in an idea. Then, one has to make this work; the realization is quite another thing. But generally it happens like that, in the most unexpected moments."

*So Ben, does a constructive concept of "fight" exist in the creative relationship?*

BJ "In certain cases the birth is easier than in others. Some births are quite difficult and one sets the problem aside, works on other matters, then comes back to the subject and finds a solution. It's never arm wrestling nor a matter of the ego that must be satisfied by being right."

*I don't believe you Ben, this is hypocritical… It is not possible. Sexuality has its importance in the creation of art, and so there are some drives so elementary that they are unavoidable.*

BJ "Yannick and I have different opinions on that. I believe that the sexual drive is parallel to creativity. Yannick – although I don't want to put words into her mouth – believes that it's reticence which gives a stronger creative force."

YV "Yes, but because I am a woman and you are a man, it's logical."

*This is exactly the description of a sexual drive stemming from different identities. Does this play work on mandatory roles, masculine/feminine, or are the roles interchangeable?*

YV "Any artist has a feminine part and a masculine one, and I think that I too, have a strong masculine personality, of independence, while not denying my femininity."

*I think that the work of art, as Leonardo has taught us with the* Mona Lisa, *has an androgynous character, having a masculine part and a feminine one, and henceforth is enclosed in an androgynous structure. How is the collaboration between two androgynous figures triggered?*

YV "The androgynous becomes hermaphrodite because both are feminine and masculine."

*One can say that it is a problem of "positions".*

YV "Like the snail! I think that this is really a valid analogy."

*Let's talk about the works that were featured in public events, like the 1993 Venice Biennale with* Leonardo's Horse. La Dimora dei Corpi Gravi, *a homage to Masaccio, is a theme I proposed for the exhibitions in which you took part. In which way was your collaboration born?*

BJ "The two things are very different because in one you gave free rein, in the other you said fourteen metres on the water. We had previously worked on this Leonardo project but we had never really gone far enough, we only had a first model that was really not satisfying. But going on from there we collaborated intensely, because interpreting Leonardo's drawings is a complex process. It's not just a question of transposition but more of interpretation. Yannick made a clay model which allowed us to reconstruct the real form. I then made this in metal. There was an incessant to-ing and fro-ing. On the other hand, the participation in the homage to Masaccio was more complex because the theme was more or less open – although certain artists simply attached their work to this theme. For us it was an exchange of ideas until we were able to separate the body from the image, in a way that allowed the work to be realized."

*Yes, but why the horse in particular? Generally sculpture works on volume. In the case of* Leonardo's Horse *you have worked on a kind of paradox: transparency. Why?*

BJ "Because in the case of the trilogy, *La Copa de Paolo Uccello, Leonardo's Horse* and *Il Mazzocchio*, every iron bar, in fact, represents a pencil line. That's where there is a translation, the update of something. Every iron element having a diameter of five centimetres, corresponded to a pencil line drawn by the Renaissance masters."

*What kind of short circuit caused an image of the past, Leonardo's, being processed by a modern tool like the computer?*

BJ "It seemed a logical way to use technology as a mathematical help. One of Leonardo's fundamental ideas was that mathematics was the very basis of everything – art or science. So we naturally thought that this image was a virtual one and that to work on the computer was to restore the Leonardesque concept by adapting it to today's means."

*Do you think that the intrinsic virtuality of Leonardo's drawing can be considered the basis of a work of that kind? Metaphorically speaking, according to you, had Leonardo already computerized his image?*

BJ "Metaphorically, yes and no, because Leonardo had this rather perverse side, as in his mirror writing which people could not read easily; there is also this false perspective. Leonardo presented this as a purely technical study, but that isn't the case, he always let himself be carried away into another dimension. That's why he's the greatest, because even a leaf, a leg, a sketch of a cannon becomes a work of art in itself. And this study, which he claimed from the outset to be technical, becomes a marvel. We were faithful to this alliance of art and technology, in that we used advanced methods to make the plans. This allowed us to call upon, not what is termed in America 'fabricators for the arts' (who often have a subjective approach), but those who could make the enlargement using computers disks. On these disks each element, every angle is predetermined in such a way that this sculpture

270

could be realized even by welders in a naval yard who knew nothing of art, but who could nevertheless reproduce exactly what we had drawn. Now we also consistently use the computer to simulate the implant of sculptures into photographs of sites where we have to intervene, in order to give an exact rendering of the final result."

*Now let's talk about the work chosen for the São Paulo Biennale. This work, called* Game of Suffering and Hope, *presents strong visual and powerfully sonorous characteristics that transmit the idea of target, precision, violence: death and danger. The spectator/watcher is involved and becomes the spectator/victim of this kind of potential aggression of sound and fury.*

YV "We are not conscious of the fact that we are armoured and prepared to face and especially to get used to and accept the effects of violence."

*I think that in your work there is always the staging of an organizing principle that belongs to modern society. This is evident in a work about museums that you staged in Palma de Mallorca, then in Bristol at Arnolfini and later in Vienna, where you made the system of communication between museums evident and formalized.*

BJ "This work was a reflection on the museum and was first installed in 1991. It showed simultaneously the videos of exhibitions that were being held at exactly the same moment in ten museums around the world. It was perhaps the precursor of the simultaneous images transmitted over the Internet today, only five years later."

*We arrive at the last image, the one on the book's cover, which presents the island of Mallorca, seen as if it were from the air, an image where it is possible to see smoke columns rising towards the sky. This image seems to synthesize the body of the common work of art, it represents the theatre of your creative communion and again puts in evidence the specific and collective elements of your creativity: the earth, the fertile element which represents femininity; technology, the element of the masculine transformation; fire, smoke and the aerial, spiritual aspect of the creative adventure that you are sharing. Now let's talk about the work called* Jalousie, *which will be shown at the Pièce Unique gallery, where you use the ex-*

*hibition space in a smart way and somehow emphasize the "store front" quality of the space. Against the window you place a structure made of knives in the form of jalousies or Venetian blinds, typically Arabic architectonic fixtures used to protect, to hide and allow observation from only one side. This is an ambiguous work, because it is a mobile structure, in that the elements open and close. One could say that it synthesizes the ambiguity of a real emotional and creative relationship, made of opening and closure, of life and death. What do you think?*

BJ "This work has quite a strong connection with the representational painting of the past. One could easily imagine, especially if pushing things to the extreme, that it has to do with *Judith and Holophernes* or *Saint John the Baptist and Salome*. Finally the knife remains and the body once again disappears. Again, we are in that line of ambiguity where the human form becomes abstract. There is the added element that the surface is highly polished and the mirror effect allows the people on the outside to see themselves."

JV "I find that this interpretation you give is right, Ben, of these decapitation scenes, of castration, either in the Freudian discourse or in the hermeneutic one of religious iconography – *Judith and Holophernes, Saint John the Baptist and Salome*. That is also the elemental problem, not only in religion, but also between man and woman: the castrating woman and man's fear of castration."

*The knife represents an instrument of fight which is certainly not being used to coexist, but to eliminate the other. So the knife is an element of contact, but also of alienation. Could we say that the knife is equally the emblem of creation? Could we say that you are the most intimate enemies?*

[Laughs from Yannick]

BJ "This brings us back to what I said before about the extreme fear of castration which is epitomized by the eyes spying through the jalousie-knives."

YV "The weapon will be very polished, which gives the mirror effect so that the people outside will see themselves reflected in it. And the ambiguity: if there is a mirror, there is also narcissism and wounding... Suffering in order to understand."

*Reflection and decomposition, an image at once multiplied and fragmented which conveys movement and eroticism, which according to Freudian interpretation signifies the sexual act. We can affirm that the work symbolizes the arch of vital-existential experience of your relationship and also the definitive transformation of ambivalence: opening vs. closure, life vs. death, space vs. time. That is, the eternal movement of life.*

# Louise Bourgeois
Paris, 1911



*You are an exemplary case in the history of contemporary art. Your creative development has succeeded in carrying along within it your own biography, condensing it in the final form of the work. Is the work the only communicative means available for the artist or can one also speak through the various forms of behaviour of one's life?*

"My work is the only communication I have with the world. It is the only way I know and the only one I care to know. Communication implies there is a sender and a receiver. I am the sender and what the receiver thinks is not my problem. I say what I have to say and *advienne que pourra*."

*Your work has always affirmed the identity of the artist. Does your sculpture, which is never monumental, offer a reading of the past or does it establish a dialogue with the present through a viewing public that recognizes the intensity and subjectivity of its creator?*

"My works are the story of my past which is compulsively related today."

*Your work implies various perceptual planes, the visual and the auditory. Can we say that in the first case the new sculptures and the film offer a view of the present while the sound installation is an evocation of the past, of your childhood?*

"I welcome the auditory. Music relates to the unconscious more easily than the visual. Initially the visual plane was the most important one, then the auditory one gradually filtered into my work, because sometimes I work trying to sleep. These sound elements are not necessarily musical, but might be the songs of the night, or the traffic of people arguing in the street."

*An artist's life consists not only of creation but also of daily creativity, passions, exchanges, clashes, arguments and conversations. How do your Sunday salons affect your pattern of life?*

"Sunday salons are the day I am personally absent, but I listen attentively to each one of those present. I never show my work."

*What difference is there between your "American" Sunday salons and the European and French ones of your early training and adolescence?*

"There were never any salons in my youth."

*Is conversing just a question of finding socially interesting or politically correct topics? Or does it also involve, beyond the word, the discovery of the body of the other, the pause, silence, simple humour or even incomprehension?*

"I am very aware and I want to be very aware for The Other. It is my form of respect. The most effective either way is the eyes. The eyes never lie."

*Creation is a solitary act, conversation is a collective act. How do history and social concerns influence your work as an artist?*

"History enters through the media and imposes itself on your life. History has a delayed effect on my work, a post-traumatic effect."

*You have always attributed great importance to everyday life and family passions, which were also recorded in the diary you lost on a train when you were 12 years old. That diary was found again in 1996. What impression did it make on you to read it again 72 years later? Can time flow in a dual perspective, first forward and now backward?*

"Montaigne said: '*connais-toi toi-même*'. The more you know about yourself, good and bad, the better it is. When I reread my diaries – which I usually don't do – I see the consistencies of who I am."

*Your work is never the elaboration of a bereavement, rather it manages to bring aspects of a problematic, hidden past into the present of form. Is art always constructive?*

"My art solves my problems. My problems change and they get smaller and smaller. *Le mot pitié m'a apaisée.* When I feel positive towards others I feel *exaucée.*"

*One of Nietzsche's concepts affirms the importance of destruction in order to be able to build. Art is a linguistic catastrophe that de-constructs any convention in order to then offer its own renewal of things. Is your own creative procedure like this?*

"I've always said my art is like the pruning of a tree."

*One of your books is entitled* Destruction du père / Reconstruction du père. *This seems to allude to the problem of authority and the emancipation from it. Is art a means of existential emancipation?*

"You make peace and forgive. To forgive enables you to forget and go forth. My art is a reconstruction of myself."

*Does art emancipate only the artist who creates the work or also the viewing public that contemplates it? Do you think your works are also an instrument of social emancipation?*

"I am not that pretentious."

*I believe all your artistic output is an exemplary chain of works aimed at a cosmopolitan public, without sexual difference. Does the artist have a sex and can we consider the artwork androgynous?*

"You know, all my art deals with the problems that occur before gender."

*The artist is a biological mistake in relation to the artwork. The artist lives and dies like every other human being, while a work of art is immortal. Is it still possible to talk about the immortality of art?*

"The problem with history does not interest me."

*Does your work develop a view of art as a generator of energy or is it also a process of awareness? Does art touch both the body and the mind?*

"My art is both energy and awareness, both mind and body."

*You represent a radical conjunction between European and American culture. Can we consider your work as a multicultural rocket launched beyond the year 2000?*

"All my subjects are universal."

## Carla Accardi
Trapani, Italy, 1924

Rome
2005

*Herein lives the painting of Carla Accardi. Unique knighthood not of Work but for Work, carried out within the world of art. A work that has renewed painting and has transformed the environment in which we all live. Accardi began in 1947 in the Gruppo Forma: an historical group, defined "heroic", that brought abstract art to Italy. Carla has worked at subtraction rather than addition; a strange anti-baroque Mediterranean artist. What, for you, is subtraction in painting?*

"I take pleasure in taking away superimpositions, exaggerations, but above all creating, discovering the blank spaces."

*You come from an island, Sicily, from Trapani. In this island emptiness and fullness have always been in dialogue. A dialogue that owes to odd and particularly happy contaminations between Western culture and Islamic art.*

"It is difficult to understand what ancient Sicily was like. First the Normans, then the Arabs… this makes it something mysterious indeed."

*Also the Bourbons…*

"Of course, also the Bourbons."

*The Bourbons who "took away" from the people. They, like you, "subtracted". Yet at the same time they also added with the Baroque a sort of horror vacui that was filled with forms and figures.*

"But as I was born in this century I have always tended towards minimalism. I have always liked simplifying."

*Minimalism… but you're not a taciturn woman.*

"No, I'm not…"

*In what way are you a minimalist artist?*

"I used to like renewing."

*In fact this is a modern studio, there's even a phone… Do you know there was a game between Picasso and Matisse, they used to appreciate each other very much and when Picasso had a telephone installed in his home he deliberately made Matisse answer to show him that it was possible to speak to someone not physically present in the same room.*

"No, what I mean is that when I started I didn't even want to paint on an easel because for me it was a thing of the past."

*So even when you were younger you were a rebel.*

"Yes, a little bit."

*And when did you fall into temptation, with abstract art?*

"I was in Florence at the Academy, but I didn't like it and after two months I gave up. In the meantime I met Sanfilippo who told me he had friends in Rome, so I wrote to my parents telling them that I was leaving the Academy and I was going to Rome, where I met Consagra and the others."

*This group was an assault team, in the best sense of the word, because it cleared away much rhetoric from artistic discussion. For example, the rhetoric that saw art as "political commitment". It must have been tiring…*

"Yes, we were up against Renato Guttuso. He said to us once, 'Is this what you want to do?' And he drew a scribble. Yes, we had this wish, that of doing abstraction."

*You say you loved abstraction and you had a minimalist mentality, which is "subtraction". Can you tell me how you created this painting that has become a museum piece? What is its title?*

"I don't know."

*What title does this one have? Your usual narcissism: it only has your signature.*

"No title, a pure fruit of fantasy."

*And when have you freed yourself from the reality of things?*

"I went to the countryside where I used to do landscapes. I had just started painting. I sat down and painted an abstract painting. I started to cry."

*But why did you paint abstract? For novelty or because you could not paint landscapes any more?*

"Because I had decided that's what I was going to do!"

*But seriously… did they take you to the doctor… You didn't tell anyone about this episode. Who did you tell?*

"I told the other guys."

*And who were these other guys?*

"Consagra, Sanfilippo, Dorazio and Turcato who was older than us and whose studio was near Guttuso's."

*Turcato was the most Dada of the group.*

"Yes, he was."

*Your painting is a sign that is conjugated in space and has invaded even the exterior. For example, where does the idea of transparency come from?*

"I came to transparency after having discovered this material and also because I wanted to go against the usual regulative habits of painting; this material allowed me to annul painting almost entirely."

*Paradoxically enough, you became figurative with transparency. You did not need to paint things, but with this transparency you could simply place them in the field of vision of the spectator. Is your sign organic? Where does it come from?*

"I don't know… It's a mystery. Fantasy, perhaps. I set to work and this is what comes out."

*Your work has a high level of eroticism.*

"Yes, perhaps. Maybe because I am a woman."

*Did you have any difficulty to impose yourself as a woman painter in the 1950s?*

"In the history of art, as well as in the history of humanity the presence of women is minimal because civilization was born chiefly from wars, and wars were made by men."

*Women made children, weaved… like Penelope. Could we say that she, like you, was an artist who "destructuralized"? Was this idea of "subtraction", as represented by Penelope, already included in the Odyssey? Have you subtracted something from life by being an artist?*

"In the beginning I gave up the love for a man, with whom I'm still in touch, choosing instead to stay with Sanfilippo, a person with whom I shared a passion for art and who opened up doors for me as a painter. Then for ten years I didn't sell a single painting and my work was teaching in schools."

*Yes, but later then everything "loosened".*

"Yes, but some difficulties remain, for example the art market that imposes the lowest prices for the work of women artists."

*How do you explain it?*

"It's an ancient, atavistic part of humanity."

*Superstition…*

"I don't know if it's superstition. Maybe man has shown proof of more initiative."

*Talking about nature... as if it were Leonardo asking you... Is painting a mental thing?*

"It's a material thing because, for example, we love colours; but yes, it's also a mental thing."

*In your opinion which painting is more abstract: this one from 1951 or this one from 2005?*

"In my opinion, the 2005 one is more abstract because I simplified even more."

*So abstraction for you is the conquest of simplicity and not simplification.*

"Yes, that's right."

*Obviously you have always disowned the easel, you've never accepted it, but the architect's desk comes in handy.*

"Do you know why? Because I used to have a much bigger table that hurt my back... my twelfth vertebrae is out of place."

*Just as a pianist can get a cramp, you've got painter's abstraction.*

"I've always tried new things."

*Does your language have the ability to proliferate anything else from it?*

"Multiplication..."

*But is geometry male or female?*

"What kind of a question is that? In the past everything was male."

*So what do we do now?*

"Nothing, we go on living and see what happens."

*When this great battle started that freed Italian art from the rhetoric of commitment, of political commitment, what did artistic autonomy mean to you?*

"This is an important point. Even though we loved the left, we were in conflict with the artists and leaders of the Italian Communist Party. They didn't accept abstraction because it could not be understood by the workers."

*I know of a meeting between your group and Visconti. How did this come about?*

"Visconti invited us to dinner. We were all about twenty-three, twenty-four-year-old, much younger than all the others invited. There we met Picasso. A legend."

*Picasso had a very active vision…*

"He was an exceptional man, a great artist who nevertheless did not influence me much."

*Are these the "summer" pictures you do at Forte dei Marmi? Would you do one now, in front of me?*

"Sure, why not?"

*Now I'd like to speak about the adventure of the hand. Is yours guided by the mind or by gesture?*

"By the mind, or by the rhythm of spaces."

*Like a musical score.*

"Yes, it can be compared to music, a music that in the end I never listen to."

*Well, you make it… What does the geometry of the curved line signify in your work?*

"I don't know how to say it. I also work with fractures, I break signs… like now, you see? There, now I've done something like that."

*Let me see. In reality you like detail and the whole at the same time.*

"Yes, well done, that's right."

*You like Matisse but you also you also like Tobey. You like detail. But in your opinion does that depend on your being a woman, in the anthropological sense? I mean, you love detail, but you also have a vision of the whole.*

"Who knows? Maybe…"

*Carla Accardi, Tancredi, Sanfilippo at Peggy Guggenheim's home in Venice with a beautiful painting by Léger behind them. You see, the artist disappears but the work remains. Here we have one of your pieces from 1947 entitled* Scomposizione [Decomposition] *that marked your entrance into the Gruppo Forma. We also have one of your latest works of 2005 and, scattered around your studio, your paintings from the 1950s, 1960s, 1970s, 1980s and the "transparencies"… I truly feel like I'm in the garden of painting. Carla, you have sown. Do you realize? You have been a direct cultivator. I can feel the richness of your painting, contrary to a lot of male Italian abstract art, which was repressed, depressed and with straight geometric lines closer to the minimalists, both American and European. I say you are a a great Mediterranean artist. What do you think about this idea of the Mediterranean?*

"I don't know. Years ago I stayed in Morocco a while…"

*Didn't you have a boyfriend in Morocco?*

"Yes, that's right, a young man who came to Rome from Morocco."

*What did you take in from Morocco?*

"I was interested in that non-European culture, but also in the light, that light… I don't know, I'm a bit instinctive."

*Yes, I know. But what does it mean, being a Mediterranean artist?*

"I do not like categories. Artists see themselves as individuals. Each with his or her own story."

*Yes, but twentieth-century art is the fruit of mixture, contamination and intertwining.*

"It certainly is. Art is made out of contacts that overcome distance thanks to the ease, nowadays, of communication. There has been a change due to the new means of communication. Before artists worked in their environment. People didn't move around a lot."

*Lastly, this garden of images that covers your production from the end of the 1940s to the beginning of the third millennium makes us float in a sea of enamel painting… yet you confirm the idea of form, something which is very Italian.*

"Yes, that's right."

*You pretend to work in asymmetry, disproportion, shifting… But in fact you take us into the spaces of harmony, of concentration.*

# Luigi Ontani
Montovolo di Grizzana Morandi, Bologna, 1943

Rome
2005

*Greetings, NarciJudas of art.*

"ABO: the critic-triptych…"

*That's great! Shock critic more than art critic.[1] Am I in a house here, or more of a "theatre of mortal remains"[2]?*

"This room expresses a redundancy, which is my wish of flying in art. So, each room is a digression of sorts, and is also my way of tricking myself into feeling, cut off from the world and withdrawing into myself in order to create an oasis – an oasis not only of thought, but also of spirit, an oasis that allows me some room to breathe."

*But how many people actually live in this house?*

"There are echoes of Sibilla Aleramo[3] and then there are a lot of other identities; it's like a veritable voyage of identities."

*But that one, there, is Napoleon. It strikes me as a familiar face, or rather, I'd say it's more his clothing that's so familiar.*

"They're like attempts at some conscious, relative folly, according to the commonplace idea of the simulacrum – so, why not Napoleon?"

*NarciJudas, you've made a real work of this whole place, and I'd say your titles are solid enough to bear the weight of all the masks your work wears.*

*"Narci" comes from that drive, that ecological engine that is the sheer narcissism that produces your art, and I add "Judas" in the sense that you know the positive meaning I attribute to betrayal. So the real question is this – and it's a question that could be replaced by an exclamation: "Luigi, take the mask off!" Just how many masks have you donned since 1972, the year you started doing these things in Bologna?*

"Oh, it was earlier… since the 1960s."

*Earlier?*

"Yes. There was a rituality that began as play, with the playful consciousness of pleonastic objects, and through this kind of behaviour I came to realize that poses – specifically, fixed poses – could be the thing that I then…"

*… developed.*

"Exactly, that was my adventure. Also because the mask, more than being a cross-dressing of sorts, is the very simplicity of my own physiognomy, and is therefore also a sort of projection, of intention. The temptation is to don the mask of an historical figure, a character from old legends, a mythological figure."

*And so you're not an artist with a human face.*

"Well, it's certainly a *filtered* humanness, mitigated, full of manner and affectation, well aware of the fact that there is no such thing as everyday, quotidian desire. I set some distance between myself and what people usually consider as life; I make an absurd parody of this fragile balance between art and life, because I'm not at all interested in everyday things, that's why I flaunt something that is nevertheless – at least, I hope – always a simulacrum of art."

*But let's just say that you dip into the so-called everyday things that are neither, as we're well aware, the daily paper, nor are they some other place; they're the here and now, even in clothing, which becomes, I think, a stylistic armour of sorts that goes along with you. The clothing, with this approach so laden with deep references, creates a break, an intermission between you and the mask. So we could say that you're also a kinetic artist, a living sculpture, an untouchable sculpture that isn't up for sale – and that's another interesting part of it, the non-commercial aspect of your work.*

"I've always applied my own caption, setting it in the form of a *tableaux vivant*, precisely in order to draw a…"

*… a limit?*

"Yes, a limit, such that it wouldn't just be a performance, a bodily gymnastics, an existential gymnastics."

*I've come to understand over time, I've done some self-analysis. Then I followed a path that parallels the one you've taken as an artist, but mine led through the theoretical realms of the Transavantgarde movement, because your work, in effect, is such an individualized, individual, and solitary oeuvre that it can't really be limited to any group, it doesn't do group tours, also because that would make it anachronistic. You, Luigi Ontani, dressed like this, couldn't go travelling abroad alongside Chia, Cucchi, Clemente, Paladino and De Maria. You go to America all alone, like Christopher*

*Colombus. But now I'm seeing another iconographic illusion, that of being able to wear the entire world, in a way.*

"That's a temptation I've experienced with these masks."

*Oh, alright, I'll climb aboard your same train…*

"Masks are born of a collaboration, of a hybridization, of a relationship with the ideal artisans, be they in Bali or in Japan, in Mexico, in Burkina Faso, in the Upper Volta, in Tyrol. So, from the stripping-down and shedding of my physiognomy as a mask, it becomes a voyage through the world of the map of the mask. And this, too, is sustained and digested through the *commedia dell'arte*,[4] but maintaining all the while a certain distance from theatricality."

*I, for one, am convinced, and have always thought, that you're really a comedian from colder climes.*

"I'd like to be funny, but I'm also melancholic…"

*Trust me, it all depends on who's watching you, who's listening to you. I like that you have this sense of humour that weighs on you, like some black cloud hovering over you: every now and then you look up to see if it's raining, and you get angry. I like the fact that you basically know there's a certain degree of humidity that's good for you… but at the same time you like to present yourself all nice and dry. I think there's a degree of disguise, a cross-dressing in you that suspends things, also as a nod to Dada. You don't adhere to the character you're referring to because you create a pause, an interval – there's a disconnection, like a lazy eye between the mask and your body, a certain distance. What I like about you is this chronically adolescent side you have.*

"Late adolescent."

*Late gothic.*

"Now we're in total agreement."

*Let's get off the train, get down from the throne, and maybe I'll see all around us in the air a suspension that's a bit – how shall I put it? – threatening.*

"Those are what I used to call the *Tribù Tabù*, the "taboo tribes" I began to show in Volpaia, back in the days Luciano Pistoi[5] was there. It's a work-in-progress, insofar as they're the artists who've died *not* of natural causes, so they have this look that might even seem happy, but in truth…"

*You can never really get comfortable in this room. I've always said that, being a critic, I've never hung works of art at home, because I'm like a surgeon who, when he gets home, doesn't really want to see any blood on the walls. I've said so in other ateliers and studios, but in this case I really want to know whether these works keep you company, or if it's actually you who keep them company. Tell the truth!*

"It's the kind of 'keeping company' that makes the most of the pleasure of solitude, so it's a harmonious balance, maybe – who knows?"

*NarciJudas! No one has ever seen an Indian chief act as peacemaker between a critic and a white artist.*

"Oxymoron: bones, the black man, and gold = with a Coliseum of bones."[6]

*Ontani, off with the mask! It's high time we said so. What do you have to say in your own defence?*

"Weiwa is the androgynous warlock hired to teach, to educate little kids, and so he also teaches a love for art."

*Is this a highly educational work, or not? And is it also stereophonic?*

"These are some ceramics that were created in the Gatti workshop, the founder of which was one of the ceramicists who signed the Futurist Manifesto alongside Marinetti and Balla. This is Pinocchio Pannocchia, who rolls around and can change his face."

*Why?*

"Because that's his nourishment, that's his lie. So, let's go back to betrayal."

*Let's just say that art often chases after the myth of truth, while I, on the other hand, seek the myth of plausibility – and you?*

"I'm always all for a stylization of ideas, so for me truth is an unpredictable condition to be continuously contradicted."

*Alright, let's go back a step, let's go back and get behind our masks, see ya!*

"Long live art."

*Long live criticism. To paraphrase Goya, I could say that the sleep of reason creates masks. I salute you, NarciJudas, even in my sleep.*

"My name is *sbadiglio* [yawn] as in *sbaglio dell'io* [a mistake of the ego]. And the word *sbadiglio* also has the word *Bali* in it, so it's a homage to the island I love so much."

*But, if I'm not mistaken, we've met before.*

"Ours is an acquaintance that I hope is flexible, and changes over time, and contradicts itself."

*It changes over time and even changes space every once in a while, because earlier we were downstairs, in that "theatre of mortal remains", and now we've been promoted, and elevated to a higher floor, where you put the mask to sleep.*

"In fact, here you see Dracula, Endymion, the hermaphrodite, various mythologies and allegories that lead all back to the concept of sleep. My dream is to be able to sleep, so in my art there are always all these poses that facilitate a state of delirium; in this case, *lo sbadiglio*, the yawn, was born in Bali and carries with it a dancing desire of beauty."[7]

*I was just thinking of how uncomfortable you must be during Carnival.*

"No, on the contrary, I've always loved that painting by Brueghel that shows the battle between Carnival and Lent. This serious euphoria of mine is something else, insofar as the mask is a bearer of drama and even tragedy, the tragedy of entertainment."

*Just to clarify, I certainly don't think your work is an art carnival. Carnival is generally an explosion, a clockwork bomb, but in your case there's the time factor, because you follow through, there's a co-action, a repeated co-opting.*

"Yes, there's repetition, but there's also the conviction, or the illusion, that I'm not making a work, as I hate thinking that I'm working. So this playful game of mine, this repeated self-deluding conviction with respect to the interlocution of art, is an evasion, my way of avoiding the idea that there's some responsibility, some work to be done. A work is simply a desire to play with words, with the things that art exemplifies."

*Of course – and just now I was also thinking that we really shouldn't have a baby together, but I do find it cute that we're on a bed, putting all these thoughts, sentences, and words to rest: we're making language more comfortable.*

"It seems to me there's a whole slew of essays on how art is so celibate, texts talking about the lack of offspring, talking about procreation. But projections are something else altogether. Even in the precarious state of things, the art object is something that goes here and there; it's its destiny to be brought all around the world."

*But me, for example, as a critic, am I also authorized to do that, or not?*

"You're fully immersed within the rite, but I just don't think you have the air of that *sbadiglio*, that yawn about you."

*No, that isn't my realm, I'm cut out for something else.*

"But let's hope it's a pretty oversized cut, a size beyond all measure."

*I've spent so many hours with you, in your home, in this "theatre of mortal remains" or private dwelling, call it what you will, a studio or a place to rest, a place of fantasy and a place of horizontality, of deep rest in sleep. All the while I've kept in mind this idea, and I declare it with all my love, that the artist is my closest enemy. In your case, that's dangerous insofar as you have a lot of different masks, so I can never really catch you for who you are. There's always – how can I put it? – some escape route, some exit strategy on your part. What should I do, stalk you?*

"There's some hesitation, some indecision regarding the possibility and plausibility of a relationship that lives and even thrives on contradiction. My digressions are something that never avoids conflict and feelings, meaning."

*But do masks have to pay duty at customs?*

"I've even paid for a ticket the cops gave me at the airport in Rome because I had too many clothes, and when I asked just how many an Italian could have, they couldn't answer."

*But isn't excess established on the basis of some parameter? Didn't they have one?*

"No, there wasn't any, there was just clear evidence of a broad gamut of silken colours that, according to them, couldn't have all been only mine; but that's just a little anecdote…"

*No, au contraire, it gives you a good idea of how the everyday world – that quotidian stuff you're continuously trying to get rid of – just pops right up again through such lack of any sense of humour, the obtuseness of bureaucracy. But you're patient…*

"In fact, I was just about to say that this might also be the patience and seduction art exhibits when it runs up against such walls."

*One day I'll hide out, only to find you walking on water —
maybe on the sea at Ostia or Fregene, so not any real important sea.
But it seems to me that, by now, your lightness has taken on so much
weight that we're all taking a bit of it onto our own shoulders.*

"There is an illusion of at least walking on water through one's
gaze."

*Alright, fine, that's it for both of us.*
"Long live art, forevermore and *toujours*."
*And criticism.*

[1] This is a play on words: the original, rhyming phrase is "*critico d'urto più che critico d'arte*". As there is no rhyming equivalent in English, it has been translated literally as "shock critic more than art critic" (Translator's note).

[2] The phrase "*teatro delle spoglie*" which Bonito Oliva coined to address a recurring idea in art, has also been used by other writers and critics, and is translated here as the "theatre of mortal remains" (Translator's note).

[3] This was the nom de plume of late-nineteenth-century author and feminist Rina Faccio.

[4] This can also be read as a play on words, since *commedia dell'arte* is a well-known form of theatre that, translated literally, means "comedy of art" (Translator's note).

[5] Art critic, journalist, curator, and arts patron.

[6] This curious wordplay is untranslatable. The original reads "Ossimoro sono gli ossi, il moro e l'oro = col Colosseo d'ossi" (Translator's note).

[7] This is yet another play on words, "*il desiderio ballo del bello*" (Translator's note).

# Marina Abramović
Belgrade, 1946

New York
2006

*From the early 1970s your work focused on life and history. What importance does the presence of the body have in your work?*

"Since the early 1970s, my body has become the subject and object of my work. The theme has always been my life and history, from which I have taken personal elements that I have tried to transform into universal motifs."

*I remember that in the exhibition* Contemporanea *held in Rome in 1973 you gave a live performance involving your hands and knifes. In your work, is blood a colour?*

"The painter uses colour to paint blood. As a performer I do not use my blood as a colour but as blood. During the performance, I am inside reality: blood is blood, pain is pain, the body is the body."

*I recall, even before that, one of your performances with fire in Belgrade. Is this element purifying or destructive for you?*

"It's both. Only through destruction is purification possible. To be able to purify we often have to experience destruction."

*Your performances always defy existing boundaries and put the subject, yourself, to the test. What importance does the public have for you?*

"Martha Graham said that the place where the dancer dances is sacred. In my opinion, wherever there is a public, there is a sacred place. When there is no public, there is no performance because there is no dialogue."

*What difference is there between a social body and an individual body?*

"I'd prefer to make another distinction, the private body and the public body. When performers enter their mental and physical dimension, they leave their private body and transform it into a public body."

*Has your Balkan background, a culture situated on the border between different worlds, been a determining factor in your art of crossing boundaries?*

"Yes, Balkan culture represents the border between East and West. This is why I often define myself as 'a bridge'. I'm interested in the sense of time of the East and its extreme emotions, love, violence, hate, tenderness, which are necessary for heroism, legends and myths. In the Balkans, life is an extreme dimension where there is a need for strong will and determination to survive. All this is a part of my work where there is no frontier or boundary."

*At the end of the 1970s, you established an artistic association with Ulay. How did this change your work?*

"The biggest change concerned my ego. I accepted living with another ego, that of Ulay, and referred to this new presence as 'That Self'. This creation represented the fusion of female and male energy. In this way there were more possibilities but also more limitations; work became focused more on our relationship than on crossing boundaries."

*After your journey along the Great Wall of China, you re-embarked on your creative solitude. What were the differences?*

"The performance on the Great Wall was the first one without a public and, at the same time, it represented the end of the artistic collaboration and my relationship with Ulay. Immediately after the wall and before I began giving performances again, I produced a series of objects called *Transitory Objects*. The public, following my instructions, could use them and create a performance with them. Since then, my work has become more strongly linked to the participation of the audience, who became an integral part of the performance and not just spectators."

*Has access to the theatre modified the performative nature of your work? Has it developed greater inner reflection or greater spectacular tension?*

"In all my work I have only done one theatrical work which I consider a work in progress: *The Biography*. I began to perform this work in 1989 and every four or five years, in parallel with the changes in my life and work, I add a new part. Having such an open structure allows me the freedom to make an interpretation of my life."

*In the expression of oneself, biography plays a particularly important role. It is not a part of the present, nor a part of history, and never a simple unordered past. Even though there is a before and an after, biography is always an ordered past, organized into chap-*

*ters, with a specific objective; at the very least, it is an analysed sto-ry. What difference is there in your work between the subject and the object, between the body and your sculptures?*

"There is no difference between the body and the object. The Body is The Object. Therefore my *Transitory Objects* are not sculptures but veritable instruments that must be used by the 'body' of the public."

# Christian Boltanski
Paris, 1944



*In 1972 you began to bring clothing into art as a symbol of the human being's second skin. Does clothing represent past experience?*

"Clothing has always represented a second skin for me. It is at one and the same time an object and an object that refers to an absent subject. Used clothing still preserves the traces of the person who has worn it, even though the person who was inside it is no longer there. So it is a sort of hollow image."

*Very early on you developed an art that put identity at the centre of your reflection. Was this because of cultural anthropology, family background or the French tradition?*

"It is not so much identity as the membership of a group that is at the centre of my work. It is the identity of each person. In fact I think that everyone is unique and therefore different from all the others. If you want to look for a tradition it is undoubtedly the Judeo-Christian one of the uniqueness of souls."

*Identity implies looking and finding. Does art work through grief over some loss?*

"Creating art is not telling the truth but revealing a truth that is often linked to a lie, but that gives an account of a reality to the viewer. There is 'artifice' in the word art. It is not an exact science. It is something that can make people experience a complicated reality."

*The use of photography and objects in your work is often applied to the tragedy of the Holocaust. Is art only representation or is it reparation too?*

"I have never used images directly connected with the Shoah. If my work is linked to the events of the twentieth century, it is more in a symbolic way. It is not on the Shoah, but it is after the Shoah. In fact an understanding of human destiny can help to make it bearable.

One of the problems of our society is that we have lost touch with death, that we no longer see images of the old or dying people. If we could bring ourselves to accept this passage of time, old age would be easier."

*Does identity concern the subject, the destiny of a people or the psychology of the individual?*

"I have worked for a long time on what I called the little memory, which for me is what makes the difference between individuals. We exist because we have in each of our heads a quantity of information, of little stories, of different experiences. The tragedy of humanity is that history on a grand scale remains in the books and its memory is preserved, but that the fate and the little history which each of us possesses is going to vanish with us."

*Over the course of the years your work has opened up a great deal to the theatre. What does the stage mean for you? You now also make use of the installation. What function does real space have for you?*

"Theatre is an art of time and painting is an art of space. In a play there is a beginning and an end. Whereas when you go to an exhibition there is no scheduled time. So I became interested in linking these two kinds of art and introducing a vague notion of progression into my installations. Afterwards I conceived large installations with some friends in which actors, musicians and visual effects were mixed up in various places, such as opera houses, like the one in Reggio Emilia or the Théâtre du Châtelet in Paris, and factories. What interests me in this type of work is both the fact that it is not permanent and that it remains present in the memory of those who have seen it. In the earlier exhibitions or in the installations the viewer is not in front of something but is inside something. This makes him totally part of the work. He is not looking at a picture but is inside the picture."

*Can history be redeemed by art? And death?*

"Artists have always sought to struggle against death and to survive it with their art; at the same time we are well aware that we are bound to fail. Death always triumphs. But I believe strongly in the idea of transmission, that it is possible to pass on a feeling after one's death. Only artists have the possibility to move people they do not know."

*It seems to me that your work has taken on a philosophical breadth. Is your art is a question mark on the destiny of humanity?*

"I feel like a traditional artist and I raise the same questions that have been asked by other human beings before me. There are only a few decisive questions. The questioning before death, the importance of sex, the understanding of nature and the search for God. These issues are at once universal and timeless questions that each of us goes on asking ourselves. I wouldn't say that my art is philosophical but actually I do think that all art is close to philosophy."

# Pedro Cabrita Reis
Lisbon, 1956

Oporto
2006

*If art means "making space", what importance does architecture have in your work?*

"Being an artist, architecture is not, in itself, of pivotal importance in my thinking. Architecture, far from the eyes of art, is by vocation the political design of empty and open spaces and of the circulation within the city. In my work referential elements often emerge which seem to hark back to architecture *tout court*, but I think they reveal, first of all, my interest for the primordial act of 'construction'. 'Building' is a founding gesture that reveals what is human. It is the way we get to know the world, and the standpoint from which we perceive it. Making the 'house' is imagining the world. It is the place of the house that inevitably interests me. Built (and not created), it is in the long run the *mimesis* of the world that it helps us to discover. There is an obvious impossibility of a re-encounter with an unreachable and incommunicable nature that for us is irrefutably lost."

*What relationship does your work have with history?*

"History as an operative system doesn't seem to be of great use in art. I believe first of all that it is more productive to take on an infinite multiplication of individual and collective stories and times. It is impossible to make a drawing that reveals the place of a thought that can incorporate all that dramatic and magnificent cacophony. This may represent the impossibility of history, but inversely it is also the possibility of the work of art. In this profound noise as its territory, the work of the artist should be intended as the work of constructing memory. A memory that must not be intended as an inventory of what one remembers – one could indeed deem art to be the denial of nostalgia. I propose that memory be seen as a permanent state of a collection of symptoms of what is perceived 'now' of 'that' which will come 'after'. Something that is necessary to substantiate our necessity for a permanent continuation. A rejection of death. Perhaps it is nothing short of memory (projective and derivative, un-localizable), that can be seen as a refusal of history (narrative and ideological). The work of art therefore is like the place of what will 'happen' after. A mental projection (the universe of the author) that realizes itself as an act, in the moment of looking and through the eyes of what you can see *a posteriori*."

*What significance does the physical context in which you elaborate and formalize your ideas have in your creative process?*

"That context may, or may not, be important. My work has always been the result of the multiplication of diverse territories of thought, and this materialization continues to consume itself in diverse ways. Nothing is foreseen and nothing will have to be refused. At times, the location has that strange quality that brings to the revelation and the creation of the work. At other times, it can be configured and perfected, simply becoming rarefied into the spirit, until a particular moment whatsoever transforms it into something precise. At other times it is the perception of an instant in which, looking around, I perceive that something that I have been carrying with me for a long time, in a nebulous way, suddenly gains a luminosity – thus becoming a sculpture or a drawing. I am, in the end, always working and I refuse nothing. I am someone who collects things and keeps everything. Everything I see, hear, pick up from the street, even the ideas and the work of others. If the work can be, for some brief instants, the total beauty of the world, then it is the revelation of 'everything' that I have known, plus 'everything' I have imagined."

*Can external reality be moulded by the artist?*

"No. The artist's thoughts constitute his 'material'. Only the mediation offered by the eyes constitutes an intelligence of what lies outside, and thinking transforms that instant into the possibility of (re)presenting the World. The tree the eyes see is less complete than the tree drawn on paper. The drawing of the tree is the tree observed plus the thought that transforms it."

*The space that history offers is like a readymade or is it flexible and transformable?*

"The work is inherently the place where the eyes have been modified, 'transformed' by thought. Experiencing the work is knowing the world. It is sensing the multiplicity of the instances that converge within it, through the unificatory perception of the fragmentation of time, places and separate subjects. Constituting itself, for an instant, into the utopia of an impossible history."

*What counts more in your work, the object or the concept?*

"They are inseparable: a painting is a painting of an idea (it) of (its) painting."

*Does a morality exist in art?*

"No. Not even an immorality. Unfortunately, what seems to exist is an interminable procession of moralists, showing off pseudo-theories of doubtful philosophical interest and inundating us with loud and useless opinions of what is and what isn't important in art. They do nothing but create, cynically, a space where they are able to manoeuvre and fulfil their ambition of any fifteen minutes whatsoever of glory. Taking on for themselves the illuminated status of the guardians of artists and their works, they have the intention of attributing art with the mission of 'saving' the world, reducing it to the poverty of illustration and to an ideological desert. Such people have always existed, and will continue to exist."

*Your work resists the past and the present. True?*

"A work of art takes shape in an inevitable 'now'. If, on the one hand, its time is absolute and linked to the desire for eternity that it requires, on the other hand, it is only in the 'instant' that I 'see' it, that I am taken back to the emotion of the eyes, which probably constitutes the only form of total intelligence."

*Does art plan the future?*

"Art has history only in university courses and in the atelier of Time. It is indeed possible to say that a Caravaggio is still a future."

*Doesn't art bring into being an eternal present?*

"Yes, and this is why we can imagine Velázquez to be a contemporary of Barnett Newman, or that Ad Reinhardt discovers Giotto. An eternal present in which every art work summons, within itself and for itself, the dimension of an absolute time. Without history."

# Maurizio Cattelan
Padua, 1960

New York
2006

*Is the artist a biological mistake with respect to the work of art? In the sense that he dies and the work remains. Is art a yearning for immortality?*

"For every decision there is always a change of mind, every life always has its death. The idea of immortality makes me nervous. It makes me think that every little error and every bad deed of mine will stay there forever and will never be erased: we would all like to go back and change things, to have made different choices, to have said different things, to have created different works."

*Your work moves with extreme freedom, with playfulness and irony, between Dada and a Zen attitude. Are you an artist on the Silk Road between East and West?*

"I've always been fascinated by the East's flight from images and its terror of the representation of life and the human being. And, in the West, by its opposite: the obsessive and inescapable respect for the human figure, for our daily presence in the present and the projection of our life into the future. In any case, play is not included and irony is allowed only to those who look."

*Your art is certainly great publicity for art. It also works on the concept of icon, the recognizability of the subject tackled or of a public event. Does art have a political function?*

"Art has a mostly private function: it keeps me alive, it allows me to take on a new look over and over again and it has ennobled the fact of my being a champion of inadequacy. There are occasions in which art is capable of anticipating things and perhaps prefiguring scenarios and situations that are about to occur. In those cases it triggers a reaction in the public that undoubtedly makes it an agent of transformation or reflection, what would perhaps have been called politics in the 1970s. It is no coincidence that in today's world much of politics passes through the television: it is images that ask for a reaction from those who look at them, and no longer words."

*I still recall your participation in the 1993 Venice Biennale, at which you rented out your exhibition space at the Corderie. Was then concept the first matter of art?*

"That time at the Biennale I thought it would be more interesting to shuffle the cards and let someone else speak: certainly the message of that poster was far more interesting than anything I might have tried to say. It was a message addressed to everyone, that everyone could take away with them. In fact somebody ironically described me as a takeaway artist."

*From Pope John Paul II felled by a meteorite to the little Hitler rapt in prayer, your work always seems to be more a form of performative apparition. Are you an artist of epiphanies?*

"There are extraordinary images that come before everything else, long before thinking or going into action. The rabbit pulled out of the hat or the fat lady at a fair, for example: they are a perfect fusion of play and horror, between the explosive noise of a laugh and the embarrassed silence of a doubt. Perhaps the secret lies in the suspense: there are images that put the world on hold, as if they were pressing the button with two bars on the reader of the universe."

*After September 11, the collapse of the Twin Towers, the live CNN footage that documented the act of terrorism by Al Qaeda (which in its turn seems to have drawn on the aesthetics of Warhol's* Empire*), what surprising and performative value can art have? Personally, I prefer Andy Warhol, even in his detached, neutral, objective and impersonal perspective. I certainly don't prefer Osama bin Laden. Art is creative and creates life and understanding. Terrorism is a promoter of death and destruction. Behind Andy Warhol there is a culture that runs from Bratislava to New York, from Europe to America. There is even a futurist streak running through Warhol's cultural veins, when he says: "I'd like to be a machine." I think that Andy wanted to assert the principle of eternal eroticism of the machine that never stops, that is tireless. A bearer therefore of movement, and of thought too. The opposite of Osama bin Laden, who replaces movement with the fundamentalist obsession of religion; detachment with total adhesion to Islam, which does not allow for the separation of politics and religion. In any case, Osama and terrorism in general have introjected into their own destructive actions the trend of communication, fomented by television and whose indiscriminate use by Big Brother was prophesied by Warhol.*

"All the best works spring from death. New York was even more surprising than usual after September 11: in the space of a few months it proved capable not just of rebuilding itself, but also of taking a different direction, of transforming itself. With Warhol exactly the same happened: his best works came after he had gone."

*What difference is there between the social visibility of art and the spectacularization of a public event?*

"Spectacular events, from the fire-eater on the corner of the street to the launch of a cruise ship, have always attracted the public: when you are part of the crowd you feel protected, your voice sounds louder. Even though, at the same time, it vanishes. Social visibility is nothing in the mass spectacle, only the person who is at centre stage can have his say. But once he descends those few steps, even the protagonist disappears: each success is matched by a defeat, it can't be avoided."

*You rightly treat the history of art as a meta-reality in which the artist lives (this awareness has existed since Mannerism). Are your references to Pascali, Penone, De Dominicis and the showcase of pop art and hyperrealism without fulfilling the obligation of copyright a liberating attitude that has been transferred from advertising into art?*

"Any reference to real people and facts is purely coincidental. These words often appear when you watch a movie at the cinema or on television: on the box everything becomes timeless and sequences shot twenty years ago have the same power as those shot today. Advertising functions in the same way: it is timeless. If it works, it works and that's enough. For me copying and recycling has never been a strategic attitude, just a reaction to the constant buzz of images."

*From the sensational installation of the hanged children in the park in Milan to the miniaturization of two elevators on a baseboard at Phillips de Pury, is there a phenomenological perspective, that is to say one that suspends judgement and shifts all responsibility onto the viewer?*

"The viewer always has all the responsibility. I could never arrogate to myself the right to choose on the part of those who observe. It is not so much a question of suspending judgement as of accepting that the evaluations and comments of others control you. A French writer said: 'Don't wait for the Last Judgement. It happens every day'."

*Is it true that art is a question about the world and so the artist will never be able to come up with an answer? And if I ask you how much is 7 times 8?*

"Art gives no answers, it only asks questions. I can answer your question: 7 times 8 is 56. In 1956 Jackson Pollock died and the world shifted the focus of its interest from human feelings to the circulation of images."

# Braco Dimitrijević
Sarajevo, 1948

Zagreb
2006

*You're a classic international conceptualist with a strong European influence. Compared to the Anglo-Saxon and American conceptual art, that is centred on the objectification of the analytical statement, you transform its neutrality into a conflictive analysis that defines its language not only within itself, but also in connection to reality and context. You are a slalom Olympic champion, which means that you have the skill to avoid the obstacle and to keep going. The title of this conversation is* Art: forgetting by memory. *I believe that art is an oxymoron. Art is a conflictive ability to keep opposites inside and later synthesize them into a shape. Firstly I want to ask you if you approve this oxymoron: art means forgetting by memory historical reality, geography, intention, motivation, and creative drive or instead, as I believe, whether "forgetting by memory" means a disposal inside world's language, even though preserving a strong relationship with history?*

"I want to begin telling a story about Chagall: when he arrived in Paris he was asked why his paintings looked so much like Russia, his country. He answered by saying that he never cleaned the mud off his shoes: his native country's mud. I have never cleaned my country's mud off my shoes either; I never cleaned it off because I've never had it, but I've had a lot of dust: history's dust. Living in the urban context for generations I understood that it is History that shapes human behaviour. This is why I've always wanted to run away from history, trying to create a space that I called 'History's post space'. I've also published a book (*Tractatus post storicus*) in 1976 about this matter. It tells the story of two artists who have been living in the countryside, away from cities. They were neighbours. One day the king loses his dog whilst he is hunting, and he finds it in one of the two artists' garden, where he sees his work and invites him to the castle. The painter's name was Leonardo da Vinci, while the other artist has forever disappeared from human memory. This is obviously a fictional story but it is very indicative for general history, because it means that half of the story lacks of proof. It was very important for me to understand these mechanisms. I told myself that it is very interesting to be involved in visual art, since the world is full of blinds."

*In Italy we say "visually handicapped".*

"To be able to rise a potential doubt in each spectator I started this series of works involving strangers: I precisely used to walk down the street to meet random people and ask them if I could do a blow-up of their picture to display in public places. It was at the end of the 1960s that I displayed a picture for the first time."

*Framing the public is a very precocious work. The theme of a past Biennale edition was "spectator's dictatorship". You have not participated in this Biennale, you were "forgotten by memory". This work, that consisted in choosing a passer-by and in displaying his/her portrait in front of a museum, had the interesting aspect of turning upside down the monumental idea of history as the hero's portrait, a character who had a great role and performed a great action. You overturn this false merit system method and deal with the idea of mass society. The man-mass character ceases to be anonymous and is presented to History, post history and public's attention as a work of art. It is also interesting to observe that this anonymous figure is displayed outside, maintaining in this way its original context: this is Braco's double cross, born in Sarajevo but living in Zagreb.*

"With no boundaries, no limits."

*And no regrets. You take the anonymous, enlarge it, frame it, display it outside, following each one of the conceptual art steps. That said, what truly intrigues me about your conceptualism is its maintaining of the context relationship through the idea of post history, overtaking the lab neutrality trend of Anglo-Saxon and American conceptual art.*

"To better explain this chain reaction it is possible to say that every spectator looking at an image has the tendency to reach a conclusion."

*One of your first works has been shown in Zagreb, then Turin in 1970 and Naples in 1971.*

"This picture was installed at three in the morning in the same place that had been reserved for Tito's, Marx's and Engels' images. So people who saw the photograph going to work in the morning thought there had been a coup d'état. They got on trams or coaches without having the courage of asking to anyone whether this regime had really fallen. I found myself in a similar situation when Ilya Kabakov came to Paris in 1989 for the Centre Pompidou exhibition *Magiciens de la Terre*. He saw the biggest image I've ever done, 140 square meters, displayed on the Beaubourg façade. Kabakov said: 'I know this is your work but I'm not going to ask you anything…'."

*This is the typical fear of a society subject to dictatorship.*

"To end this chapter on anonymous passers-by I'm going to tell an anecdote: two days before I took the Beaubourg picture I went to Boulevard Beau Marché and stopped a person. I explained him the idea so that he might have accepted to be photographed, and he told me: 'You are quite stupid, this idea is not very original, Dimitrijević did it twenty years ago'. I was hit by the words of this guy who left me there with the photographer. I was speechless, because this person, a passer-by, my alter-ego, somebody who had a different conscience, a different way of thinking, made me understand that anonymous people are a metaphor to me."

*Could it not be possible that this person wanted to actually criticize you, telling you that after twenty years you were still doing the same thing?*

"I don't think so, because this is a method. All the geniuses, from Leonardo to Michelangelo, from Malevich to Duchamp, did at least one normal thing. In the same way I'm inspired by the stupidity that comes out of history: science-history. It will be absolutely normal to keep following this repetitive pattern until it will stop provoking this reaction, like the time in which Bruxelles Palais des Beaux-Arts went to Beijing in 1978 and one of them said looking at Mao's big image: 'This is one of Dimitrijević's passers-by'."

*The next step in your artistic career begins when you stop giving authority to anonymous people and start using images of intellectual people, of great writers, great musicians, great poets, philosophers, etc. You started to add objects to the images, like javelins hitting the target – obscure things that tend to wound the icon, represented by Kafka or others. I'd like you to talk about this transit, about this overturn, about the social analysis you conduct. Regarding this subject there are two particular works: one that we showed in Rome, at Casagrande's, and one that we showed at the São Paulo Biennale, where I invited you.*

"Yes, but before doing these works I did about five hundred installations with original pictures that I lent to museums."

*There is a sort of Darwin-evolutionary idea of passing time.*

"Even the world learns and makes progress from its own mistakes; when I was eighteen I wrote a quote that said: 'There aren't mistakes in history, history itself is a mistake'. The installations we presented at the São Paulo Biennale included very famous philosophers' and composers' images, even though their faces are completely anonymous. And just like javelins, I stuck cellos into the images. This work went by the title of *Against Historical Sense of Gravity*. Gravity is a physical term that cannot be applied in a sociological context, but what this title wanted to say was that maybe in art, in the social context, even physics laws can be deformed. Why did I call this work *Against Historical Sense of Gravity*? Because rules do not work with art. During an exhibition at the Tate Gallery twenty years ago, I displayed a Modigliani painting. This was followed by a huge argument and *Times* published an article that said: 'A three million pounds Modigliani has been put inside a wardrobe'."

*It is therefore important to say that the main aspect of this phase is represented by the capture and the physical quote, because you actually managed to have the original pictures to create the installations. You are able to obtain* Déjeuner sur l'herbe *or* Van Gogh's Self-portrait *and to place them in the pettiness and hell of a daily object that can be represented by a cart of oranges, completely disrupting in this way their position in the empyreal heaven of the history of art. You have therefore the ability of summarizing the sublime and material stupidity.*

"The title wanted to emphasize Modigliani's material value, considered that he almost never sold a painting. By using original works, for example a Turner or a Malevich, I didn't want to say that they were worth as much as a bicycle, but I wanted to emphasize the meaning statements that exist within every work of art. I was very irritated to notice that in certain museums some works were shown as meaningless *fetish* objects."

*You have to be reminded that when a bicycle is placed out of its context and moved into an art space it ceases to be a bicycle, while* Van Gogh's Self-portrait *remains the same.*

"Although in a post-historical context I want for the bicycle to remain what it is."

*Then you reverse it and move the bicycle to a pre-Duchamp situation.*

"Post-Duchamp. The installations involving a famous picture always present three elements. These elements aren't selected at random, and they act like a relation between three mirrors: each object has the tendency to emphasize the meanings of the other two. These triptychs go by the name of post-historical triptychs: a generic title with the idea of mentioning for example Van Gogh's *Self-portrait* (1888), or the *Bicycle* by Jean Paul Gautier…"

*Together with my critical complicity, you presented the last work of this series at the Musée d'Orsay at the end of 2005. You installed two of Van Gogh's* Self-portraits *linked to a sort of constellation made up of orange trees. Two questions: why a constellation? Why orange trees? Did you choose the colour orange because it is included in Van Gogh's pictures?*

"Yes, they were a little bit like the stars in Van Gogh's skies and they were also arranged in the same way as Halley's comet. The title for the installation was *Van Gogh, finally in heaven*. The shopping trolley was an obvious reference to the market and to movement, with two big wheels taking Van Gogh towards spirituality, and the comet's trace."

*With this series of works you seem to frame history of art again. There is also another series of which I would like to talk about now, and of which you presented one work in Rome. With this series you hit the triviality of collective taste, that kitsch taste that brought Strauss's last heir to be considered one of the greatest musicians in history. What you do is taking a series of overrated musicians or cultural characters, display them and "punish" them with an axe that somehow gets stuck into the icon. It is therefore a study on the icon; but what is the kind of judgement that this (negative) icon re-establishes?*

"A judgement that comes from the idea that there is only one little step between kitsch and blood and it depends on the social context."

*Please describe this work.*

"This work consisted of seven zigzagged photographs."

*Why zigzagged? Are you against tidiness? Subverting, subversive...*

"You tell me, I stuck a pickaxe in them."

*I unfortunately always see pickaxe as a negative tool. I look at it as a very Stalinist tool and it reminds me of Trotsky's murder. As you know, Trotsky's life has been under murder threat many times, but he always managed to escape. He wasn't although able to escape a paid killer from KGB, Siqueiros, who had already tried to kill him once but without succeeding. This confirms the idea that the artist is a biological mistake compared to the work of art. Siqueiros was potentially a murderer.*

"I believe that there is always a space reserved for a certain type of ideas, and that the space occupied by kitsch ideas does not allow other ideas to pass through. This is why I created this work called *Balkan-Waltz* that also presented a natural element, a red chilli, stuck by the pickaxe through the broken glass."

*Why the red chilli?*

"It is typically Balkan."

*Also Calabrian... So, let's move onto the last part of this interrogation, to understand how Braco's conceptualism is evidently a humus that moves the work of art outside the strict conceptual context. I believe Dimitrijević to be unfortunately a great artist. I said unfortunately because he is the producer of a work of art that I define classic, since it isn't a strict and scholastic expression of conceptual art. He uses conceptualism like an important element, because he grasped straight away that art is always conceptual. Leonardo said: "Painting is a mental thing". Dimitrijević proves us that photography is a mental thing as well, that art's iconography always presents an underground, under and inside the language, that allows it to have and to be a visual thinking: is art visual thinking?*

"Well, it's my choice. But I believe visual language to be much more important because it can communicate at the speed of light, faster than music and cinema."

*And what about the word?*

"It depends on how many letters it has."

*I don't know if in the Balkan Bible is different, but in the one I read it says that the verb came before the word.*

"There are others ideas before the Bible."

*For example?*

"For example that for human beings lights travels with a faster speed than that of sound."

*Going back to words, you wrote a few stories, it would be very interesting to understand their structure.*

"They are very short."

*As a final act, is there a work of art that you regret?*

"No. I wanted to do a retrospective, but I would need Leonardo and Piero della Francesca works and the insurance would be too expensive."

*Do you think you can use one of my pictures in your exhibition? As an icon.*

"Yes."

*So as a final act you should comment about my ABOrism, ABO, aborismo, aphorism: critics are born as such, artists are made, and as public you die.*

"Do you know what ABO means?"

*To me ABO means After Bonito Oliva, Art Before Obvious.*

"Double, or A.B.O.O., Bosnian Art all over."

*So?*

"It's nice."

*If you think so… I want to specify that "critics are born as such, artists are made" is a Roberto Longhi's quote and I only added "and as public you die" to it. Make a comment about it.*

"Aphorisms are the fastest way to say things through words. Images are so complex: like if you say that small books speak in the same way as big books. But it doesn't take long to read a small book."

*Small big man. What can we say to conclude?*

"Look, from the moon there is basically no distance between the Louvre and the zoo."

*Exactly, and we can say that iconography is inside Dimitrijević's work: image is a thinking spasm. I like concluding this way, thank you!*

# Jimmie Durham
## Arkansas, 1940

Berlin
2006

*In your work of destructuring linguistic codes, taboos, beliefs and commonplaces, does art have the function of reconstructing the anthropological unity of humanity?*

"This idea of an 'anthropological unity of man' is good; we have never had yet such a thing, have we? Even scientists, even scientists who are atheists, often speak as though humans were a 'created', that is, a completed project. Humanity is not a completed project. Certainly our knowledge is also far from complete. In Europe the dominant (but not the only) tradition of art has been that of monumentalism, of Belief as opposed to investigation. Should not art be an intellectual discipline? No matter if it is also often intuitive…"

*Your use of different materials, drawn from nature or from industrial production, is certainly at the service of a spiritual idea of art. Does that mean they have an apotropaic and magical function?*

"Well, the word 'spiritual' can be difficult; I must surely make more complications by stating that I love the world. (It might even, although I cannot see why, seem anti-intellectual to some.) I love materials – metals, plastics, wood, stone, and objects of every description. Spirit is everywhere, in everything. If one takes proper care, if one can be constantly attentive, juxtapositions can bring forth new voices, new thoughts."

*Your distinctly anti-colonialist vision also tends to make use of irony as a means of debunking social and cultural conventions. Does your Cherokee origin lead you to operate in dialectical terms with regard to Western civilization or in terms of complete opposition?*

"Cherokees have been colonized for four hundred years, which is to say that much of our 'cultural ways' have to do with resistance to a dominant power. I think that we have developed irony and humour dialectically, similar to the way European Jewish culture developed them. But more, before the invasions and enclosures natives of the Americas were completely 'in the world', not in a pre-defined part of the world. I feel that I can interact in

Europe not as a Cherokee, therefore, but as an artist in a multi-levelled contemporary society."

*In your work the object of everyday use is employed in accordance with the concept of bricolage devised by Claude Lévi-Strauss in his analysis of primitive cultures. Is this also the use that you make of materials in your creative process?*

"I like Lévi-Strauss's description of the phenomena which he calls 'bricolage'. When I first read it, it seemed a good description of some of my work. It is greatly pleasing when objects are willing to subvert themselves, their old limits. I feel that I am then really in the world, and that it is infinite."

*It is clear that nature is a central point of reference in your poetics as an artist. What is it for you, a symbolic place that condenses life and death, the transformation of things, the energy that moves the universe, the biological rhythm that governs the flows of humanity?*

"Nature is everything. I might add the word 'metathesis' to 'bricoloage'. For me, to 'observe nature' is simply to be alive. What, then, is our most natural response to life? It must be compassion."

*Stone is a material that you often use in your installations and your performances. Is it intended to emphasize an aggressive attitude towards the world (when you crush a car or a television set with a large boulder) or is it the material and symbolic form of an energy or a contact that you want to establish between different materials?*

"As I have written before, stone is unnaturally heavy in Europe, with the added weight of metaphor. According to his biographer Notker the Stammerer, Charlemagne once had a stone cathedral built in one day to impress a besieged city that he was there to stay. That is a very aggressive use of stone, but so is every cathedral and every Guggenheim Museum. If stone becomes the tool instead of the monument it brings us closer to the old nomadic concept of David as giant-slayer rather than giant."

*Your performance at Paliano and your month of lectures in Como (the former addressed to artists who have a particular feeling for birds and the latter to students at a Foundation) indicate a marked interest in the community of artists and in the social body in general. Is art communication, information, dialogue, confrontation, du-*

el, opposition to the world? What function does the word have in
your work? Does it have a Socratic function?*

"For me art is communication (and therefore dialogue), but
I have no message to communicate. I think art must be social, not
architectural, and not 'impressive'. I love it when interruptions occur. Words can interrupt art pieces at the same time that they interrupt an observer's intentions."

*In the film produced by Zerynthia (14 minutes, 35 mm) Anri
Sala plays the part of the successful artist and Mario Pieroni that of
the gallery owner who is getting on in years. Sala wanders through
the countryside around Valmontone, looking for and finding skele-
tons of animals, models and objects of everyday use, and then creates works in which he assembles different materials. The film lov-
ingly contemplates the Grand Canyon and California. Is it an autobiographical film?*

"No, it is not autobiographical but yes, it kind of is. I first came
to Europe in 1968 with the idea of never returning to the US (I
love Europe). But I came by a freight ship, on money saved at working stupid jobs and by selling my 1956 Chevy. If I could have come
by selling art, who knows if I would have been brave enough."

*Your works have always been anti-pop. They never celebrate
American consumer society. They establish relations between materials that are different and remote from one another in origin and
substance. In the end the coexistence of differences prevails in your
assemblages. Is this an invitation to harmony, to multiculturalism,
to environmental beauty, to complexity?*

"Yes, but always anti-pop. It seems too sad to me that capitalism can so easily and so constantly co-opt popular culture and
rent to us our own degradation. There is no energy there. I am
pleased that you say that 'coexistence of differences' prevails in
my work. Necessary complexity is our condition."

*I believe that in your work stone represents not just the weight
of matter, but also the energy that obliterates all hypocrisy. At the
same time an archaic and primitive feeling about the world that surrounds us predominates in your works. Does art seem to make the
invisible visible or the opposite?*

"I will begin an answer from a different direction, considering thoughts in previous answers. Cynicism is a kind of naivety:

it presupposes sufficient knowledge to justify itself when in reality we do not have sufficient knowledge to be cynical. There has always been much cynical art and it usually passes for 'sophisticated' art; it becomes commercially successful proving thus its sophistication. Declamatory art is ultimately heavy even if it is made only of neon. Investigative art can give energy. Like poetry it can make visible that which we were unaware of. It can change us. On the one hand, Nature is not cruel; it is much worse. On the other hand, Nature is not implacable, not indifferent, because we are not outside of it. We have invented the concept of compassion. That means that it is an intellectual, natural process. What stupid, crazy monkeys we are! But not always bad, and we still have not finished evolving even though we might blow ourselves up. In the 1960s we often spoke of 'liberation'. Shouldn't it be a constantly renewed theme?"

# Jan Fabre
Antwerp, 1958



*Maybe it's also because of your family history – your grandfather was an internationally renowned entomologist – that you have a strong sense of observation when it comes to nature. In your view does conceptual analysis or emotional synthesis prevail?*

"For me conceptual analysis and emotional synthesis have always been linked to sensory observation and the concept of experience which is based on the principle of traversing things starting with the exploration of one's self. This is why I find science so fascinating. My vision has an affinity with that of the scientist/entomologist who analyses the object of study in depth and detail and who at the same time observes the results based on the complexity of reality. Analysis and synthesis are two indispensable mental exercises with which to understand my field of research. My first laboratory in 1978 was in a tent in my parents' garden. It was a sort of wigwam shaped like two noses facing each other in which I was intent on creating new life like a modern-day Dr Frankenstein. I would catch flies and worms then I would pick the wings off the flies and using a scalpel I would attach them to the bodies of the worms. I was, you could say, creating new life. During these experiments I would draw illustrations and take notes, but smelling and creating new life through smell was for me the most essential process. This is why I built the tent in the shape of two noses. The development of smell for me is synonymous with delicacy and with animal instinct; and instinct, sense of smell and odour are a constant presence in all my work processes. More or less in that period through my family I came into an inheritance made up of books and manuscripts by the French entomologist Jean-Henri Fabre, as well as a collection of hundreds of boxes containing thousands of beetles. Over the years my interest in entomology has grown, becoming a font of inspiration both for my figurative art and my theatre. The knowledge I have acquired on territorial behaviour and the organization of space in insects is regularly used for the topography of my sets. And my actors and dancers often reproduce the behaviour and movements of insects such as, for example, ants and spiders. I have often used live animals on stage and I regularly insert animals, dead or alive, in my figurative art. I love the symbolical world that is evoked by certain animals. They place us in another world, put us in contact with another language and constantly make us face our human limitations."

*Beauty in creation exists. The diversity of nature shows us a diverse quantity of living beings. What relationship is there between art and nature?*

"My art has the task of expressing the divine, the deepest human interests, the lie of imagination, and it does this in a sensory way, thus showing a number of common traits with the manifestation of nature, of the senses, of perception. The beauty of nature is enclosed within itself while the beauty of art always poses a question to the spectator. Art should stimulate the body and mind. The sensory form of a work of art should always incarnate an idea or spiritual content. Nature for me also implicates the wonder and threat of the unknown. The presence of animals, the fable-esque elements, the dream-like sensation within my work constitute a veritable introduction to the comprehension of a forgotten language, a language we all have within us but which we repress as it incarnates the anarchy of nature. This is a language with a different logic to that of our civilized civilization, a language which is closer to the essence of things, with an empathy for life and other collusions regarding time and space. It is a language made of intensity, instinct and intuition. In wonder there is also the fear of 'power', which however must be present otherwise there would be no resistance. In many of my works power becomes even more powerful until it suppresses itself and impotence becomes the solution."

*In your work is the beetle a symbolic creature or just an empty frame which supports the form?*

"In my work the beetle symbolizes metamorphosis, the bridge between life and death, hope. Beetles have an incredible death drive and at the same time a vitality so strong as to be able to change appearance. At different points of their evolutional process their bodies at a certain stage cease to grow, only to be reborn, we can say, and start again under a new form: from larvae to the imago of a lightning bug. It is a sort of passage with the promise of a new and better life. This evolutional process, the behaviour and characteristics of the beetle inspire me in my research on the nature of future man.

We know that beetles have survived for thousands of years with their external shell or skeleton, while we humans only have an internal skeleton. We live in a sort of dualism with our bodies. It is a sort of paradox between the cult of the flesh and the cult of the skeleton. Our skeleton refers to the past but also to death. If we look at a skeleton we see our past but also our future. The skeleton is the cult of arrest, yet we live through our flesh. We move it both politically and socially and all that which moves and is in movement at the end withers, dies. It is in this dualism that we live. In my work this duplicity is evident, as is a strong sense of vulnerability which makes me reflect on what will really happen to humanity in order to survive in the future. Who is the future man? How can we improve him? How can a human being form an internal skeleton? How can we protect the flesh to make it live longer? This brings us back to the idea of living on borrowed time, of living in a state of post-mortem. Many of my sculptures meant to be a sort of research. They are bodies with a sort of external skeleton that works like a shield. They are bodies turned inside out which contain an internal void and an external skeleton."

*Is the modularity of the beetle that multiplies to fantastically become a robe a way to mould and formalize natural life?*

"Yes, the forms I wish to mould are sort of spiritual body. These are sculptures which refer to a future human image, or rather a human image that is recomposed with its own material turned inside out, an image which is not subject to the power of technology nor does it exalt mutation through technology. An example of a spiritual body as a sculpture is the series of angelic figures of beetles. I consider these sculptures as a sort of rite of passage, a transition from a certain situation to another. They are a type of intermediate beings in a state of transformation, just like the beetle is a metaphor for mutation and resurrection. The empty bodies are receptacles of memory, they contain the knowledge of the beetle. Spiritual bodies can always obtain a human form, which brings me to show the difference between the human and the divine. The human being is not asexual, static, exempt from sin… Angelical figures, like in *Mur de la montée des anges* (1993–94) have a seductive hyper-feminine form (inspired by three icons of Western culture: a bottle of cola, a Dior garment and an image of Mary), whereas the figures of monks, like in *Dÿe den nest weet Dÿe weeten. Dÿen roft Dÿe heeten* (1995), are masculine forms derived from an engraving by Brueghel in which sixteenth-century beekeepers, excerpted from a medieval universe, attain spirituality through their contact with the creatures.

Another example of the spiritual body comes from the sculptures that represent monks in the installation *Umbraculum, un lieu ombragé hors du monde pour réfléchir et travailler* (2001). They are sort of spiritual travellers of a future time, made from animal and human bones. They are bodies of nothing, without organs or blood. Bodies with a new skin, a skin that can no longer be wounded, free of stigmata, free of the Christian sense of guilt or the concept of sin. Bodies pervaded by gravity, acumen, elevation and glory that are not contemporary."

*What is the boundary between the beautiful and the horrible?*

"The boundary between the beautiful and the horrible, in my opinion, is found in the drinking fountain, which is the metaphor for the suture of the cranium. The premise is that the duality beautiful/horrible is inherent to human nature. This duality is intrinsically condensed in the way in which we come into the world as human beings. Vulnerable creatures as we are, from the symbiosis of the warm maternal womb we are abruptly pulled. In my creations I have investigated human birth in depth, the incredible intensity of the act itself. Bringing children to the world, for a woman, is the most beautiful experience accompanied however by the most atrocious pain. For this reason people can know the terror of beauty. The suture of the cranium, between beauty and horror, in Europe can be found, in my opinion, in Weimar-Bücherwald. While I was travelling in those parts I found that Goethe's villa, in which he wrote *Ifigenia*, was situated next to the Bücherwald concentration camp. The place that had propagated the ideal of classic romantic beauty was transformed in little over a hundred years into a place that would link the greatest beauty and the most horrible misdeeds. This thin line dividing the beautiful and the ugly explains why, as an artist, I propose to keep my distance from any form of ideology. Beauty succeeds moral, it is not linked to time or trend. Beauty liberates itself on different levels. It can be compared to a butterfly. If you hold it between your fingers you destroy it. Beauty is very expendable and very vulnerable. I often use the expression 'warrior of beauty' to define myself and my performers. Being a 'warrior of beauty' means being an artist. Fighting to believe in humanity, fighting for a good cause and believing in the vulnerability of human beings. The warrior of beauty tries to defend vulnerability, the indefinable, the irrational. The vulnerability of beauty must be defended because beauty or the human body are constantly in danger. Art can enclose beauty, but art is not always beautiful and beauty is not always art. In museums and galleries we often see works that are adapted to the perfection of those spaces, but which are in themselves very far from true beauty. Beauty is the colour of freedom. In my opinion beauty is based on a form of ethical values. However, much of my work can be considered beautiful; aesthetic for me is make-up. All my work must grow from ethical values, a sort of empathy towards someone, a defence of the vulnerability of life. I am a warrior of beauty. Perhaps I am out of time, out of place because I do believe in the power of beauty."

*Art can make any reality exemplary. The gaze of the owl becomes a sculpture blocked in its definitive form. What is the relation between the life of art and the death of life?*

"There is a strong link between that creative process and the relationship with death. Undoubtedly this has something to do with the fact that since I was young I have looked death in the eyes. At 18 and 20 years of age I was in a coma. Twice I found myself in that state of near death. The experience of passing from 'life' to 'death' to 'life' heavily influenced my way of life and my work. I have brought that up and ritualized it symbolically in my work. The celebration of death has become a recurring element in my theatre and in my figurative art. This is because of the fact that I have received a lot from life, so I am able to give a lot back. Moreover, in my life I have been able to convert a sort of aggressivity into vitality. There was a time when I was creating that I would be taken by a destructive impulse with no respect for death. As a young artist I had the feeling of being alone in the world. And if you have that kind of fear of life or death you become more aggressive. You begin to destroy. But the closeness to death has taught me accept and appreciate it. I still have the feeling that I'm fighting the external world, but now I appreciate death more. The celebration or the Carnivalesque aspect of death comes from a deep respect for it... The Glory of Death keeps us awake. Death is not outside of life. It accompanies life. For me death is part of life, death and life form a repeating cycle. The preparation for death and the process of passage from death to life, from the end to a new beginning are always present in my work. In the recent sculpture/installation *Boodschappers van de dood onthoofd* [Decapitated messengers of Death] there are seven owl masks on an altar, wrapped in Bruges lace. The numerology of the number seven mirrors the cyclical progression of days. The owl, the mythical night bird that sees and keeps watch in the darkness, symbolizes the guidance of the soul during the ritual of the passage. The seven decapitated owl masks are a personification of my multiple identities: the messenger, the sage, he who relativizes himself, the surveyor/guardian of spirituality, etc. At the same time, with the masks I want to give ritual functions and traditions back to civilized man. The masks incarnate both the delirious Carnivalesque body and the fasting disciplined body. They interpret in a subtle way all the functions of a body in a state of transformation or passage."

*Does the hermit presented in the Padula Charterhouse in the* Le Opere e i Giorni *exhibition, later taken to the Museum of Antwerp, metaphorically represent the identity of the artist on a journey of initiation and does that suffering bring sanity, or rather the spirituality of the form?*

"In *Sarcofagus Conditus (Self-portrait)* of 2003 I present my headstone with an effigy of myself. Is this a cavalier of desperation? The statue in the ancient sarcophagus is made with a typical Greek chalk (called 'sarco fagus', i.e. which eats the flesh), and I have substituted it with an empty covering of drawing pins. This forms a sort of spiritual body, a sort of new skin with antennae that work like a sort of immune system. This headstone is included in a series of works that express my process of preparation for death and death itself. It is a way of relating to death and the realm of the dead. The headstone with the statue works literally, you could say, as a sort of body in which the spirit can rest in peace and safety. In this way I am updating the original meaning of the sarcophagus as a final and safe place of rest."

*In the installation presented in the 2000 Valencia Biennale and in the one presented in Rome in 2006 an image of conflict between the artist and his double prevails. Is the creative process, therefore, always conflictive? Is it a battle in which there is no certainty of the result or of salvation?*

"The installation *Gravetomb (Skulls, crosses, swords)* of 2000, which I presented at the Valencia Biennale, is a sort of morgue. It is a space that works as a requiem for life and for art. It pays homage to three important elements in my universe: living animals held prisoner inside skulls honour mastery and love of materials; the sword is the indispensable weapon of the warrior fighting for beauty; and the cross of the tree of life is a spiritual reference to faith in the cycle of life. In this installation I have brought together, literally, the symbolism of the cross and that of the sword. The rigorously vertical form of the sword leads to a tail composed of animal material. I have turned the form upside down in order to turn the organic element into a rigid geometric form. In this way I try to return to the wild, the animal-esque in our civilized society. It is an attempt to re-establish harmony between culture and nature. Another meaning that emerges in this piece and in the film *Lancelot* is the conflict between the artist and his double. In *Lancelot* (2004) I am a knight of desperation in battle with an invisible adversary. Is it the enemy? Himself? A hidden force? Death? And even if the knight knows his battle is lost from the start – in the end death prevails over life – why does he continue to fight? The knight reminds us of Lancelot, an example of courage, whose search for the Holy Grail was in vane. The knight's incessant battle expresses the aspiration of the artist, who has become a model of human aspiration. At least the type of aspiration guided by values including hope, faith and love. And it is important that this aspiration continues each time it is expressed, because we can never give enough weight to Good, if only to contrast the power of Evil.

In *Gravetomb (Skulls, crosses, swords)* and *Lancelot* I also explicitly show that the conflict with myself is, foremost, a conflict with death. It is the fear of death that makes gods of us artists, that makes us heroes, stars, ourselves. I see the cemetery as the quintessential cultural institution, like a school of art and philosophy. Death plays a role that is not only destructive, but also strictly linked to life. Given that the cycle of the end and of birth is eternal, the cemetery can in the future become a lively and energetic museum. Worrying about the cult of the dead is a way to make the fear of death disappear. I would like to blur the boundary between life and death, because this, in my opinion, is the only way to lead a truly active, conscious life."

*You have also worked for many years in the theatre, using multimedia. Is it possible to speak about your work in terms of interaction with the public?*

"Interaction with the public does in fact characterize my work. For thirty years I have worked in figurative art and the theatre. Also, I have always written and been in performances. Yet I still don't feel like a multimedia or hybrid artist. On the contrary. I have always felt like a sort of *consilience* artist. There are always ideas and elements in my work that come together and pull away in time, stretching horizons, intersecting or needing to settle for a while before assuming a new form. This phenomenon of *consilience* has become clear to me thanks to a person who has always very much inspired me, Edward O. Wilson, entomologist, philosopher, biologist, who uses the term in his book *Consilience. The Unity of Knowledge*, meaning 'interconnection' of different disciplines. If one is able to move freely between various disciplines one may find *consilience*, with respect however to the peculiar laws of the medium.

My figurative art and my theatre are based on my individual performances of the early 1980s. My body – this strange body – is a sort of laboratory in which I awaken everyday. Therefore I felt the need of a confrontation between my body and the gaze of the spectator in order for dialogue to be born. I have continued to seek that dialogue between my body and the public without rest in my performances and my theatre. One important principle in theatre for me is the effect of catharsis in tragedy. The audience is placed in front of the darkest passages in the history of humanity, dragged through extreme pain and horror. Through this confrontation with deep suffering the soul is cleansed. In my plays I search for a similar effect. I launch an attack on the audience. I take the spectators on a journey with me. I show them human images they have forgotten or buried. I speak to their violence, to their dreams, their desires. In this way theatre has the effect of the plague, as described by Artaud.

In reality we are dealing with a reduction of tragedy to its essence. I want the audience and the actors to learn through suffering. My theatre is a ritual of purification with which I want to invoke a process of change. Not only the metamorphosis of the actor, but also that of the spectator. Perhaps I feel like a sort of Greek mystic. I know the functions of the ritual and the consequences of certain subtle blends. The Greek word 'pharmakon' indicates at the same time a medicine and a dangerous poison. This is the ambiguity of my way of operating and my representations. For those who act, dance or watch, my theatre has a poisonous aesthetic. But a poison that can perhaps heal."

*In your work, real objects are accompanied by those created by you. Nature, as seen in your work in Liguria, is a set that welcomes your intervention and establishes a critical testimony to the story. In which terms is your work social criticism, political intervention, conceptual reflection on the world?*

"The permanent installation *Il Rifugio (per la tomba del computer sconosciuto)*, 2005, that can be seen in La Marrana, was conceived as a sort of homage to the insect, the oldest computer in the world. At the same time with this piece I wanted to make a statement: that of digging a symbolical grave for unknown soldiers and unknown computers (insects) fallen in the area. In the magnificent Ligurian landscape I restructured an old barn transforming it into a crypt. I did this by placing a series of crucifixes with metaphorical names of insects, 'scarab, necrophorus, perforator…'. The Bic blue colour of the crosses remind us of the blue of the sky, as it appears in the blue hour, that magical time in which night slips into day. Through my position as an artist and my work I clearly assume an explicit point of view regarding society. I am an artist who lives and works *out of place, out of time*. In this sense I have never been a contemporary artist. I feel like an avant-garde artist because I believe in romanticism. Romanticism for me is living on borrowed time, having the courage to face things that are outside temporal imposition or tied to systems or structures. This is the sentiment that is enclosed in my work. I am an artist who believes in humanity, who believes in beauty. Nothing in my work has anything to do with cynicism, on the contrary, it is a constant refusal of cynicism. In figurative art nowadays there is a use of cynical language, a language of economy, a language of power. This is a language which does not belong to me because my language has a soul that is almost medieval, a believing soul, because I believe that thinking is an inheritance of the soul. All my works of art, my performances, my drawings, my sculptures hark to a faith in the vulnerable body and to the defence of it. They look at the human being and ask the question of how it can survive in the future."

# Alberto Garutti
Milan, 1948



*You come from a post-conceptual generation. More than the object you are interested in the concept. Does the dematerialization of the work have anything to do with an idea of spirituality in art?*

"What I like about conceptual art is its ideological matrix, its undetermined vocation, its great ethical drive, its mutations within reality. Moreover, the works of art have always been able to give form to a thought. For conceptual art the desire is strong to give an ethical sense to artistic actions and interventions. My work is moved by an ethical idea, by mutations of reality and – to use the term expressed in the question – it dematerializes in an attempt to become sublime in life.

Dilating the concept, it is as if art and life were to change roles. The work seems to hide and become invisible (the lights that signal the birth of a human being or glow-in-the-dark furniture, rather than the songs of the 1940s), but it's there. As if, adhering to the form of reality, it could be confused with reality itself, without losing its unhinging concreteness, in dialogue with immaterial systems and dynamics: economy, institutions, relationships between people… I do believe that there is, today more than ever, a latent need for spirituality, expressed in the most diverse ways. Supporting a football team, for example, is an expression of disinterested love; the large public participation that surprisingly we have been seeing at philosophy and literature these past years I think is a clear symptom of a need for spirituality. By now we are all conscious of creativity. Everyone knows more or less what it means, but abuse of the term has made it synonymous with something that is aesthetically pleasing. It seems that anything can go in the name of creativity. It's the passage from creative to artistic that interests me: as if creativity pushes towards art, which is a higher level. Art has something to do with existential spirituality. They live within the same meaning. If I want my work to be solid and have a form which adheres to reality it should offer itself poetically to the lives of people."

*Your work has moved from the production of singular objects presented in the traditional space of the gallery to projecting works that intercept society and a community of spectators that coincide with that of citizens. What is the relationship between art and politics?*

"This question has caught me off guard a bit because I'm of the idea that art is there, like a tree, its aim being the conservation of the species. It's as if I were considering the relationship between art and politics as analogous to the relationship between nature and politics. I think of art in fact as a cognitive experience that allows me to gather the sense of life. I think there is a sort of necessity in art that has to do with the necessity of nature. Doing public works of art I've clearly seen the dangers of the auto-referencing within the artistic system. I've understood that we have to 'move towards' a search for the work in question. And what is a work if not a meeting, an exchange of views, of imagination, of knowledge, in short of culture? 'Moving towards' is a gesture that contains a political idea. In this sense my work is political, precisely because it tends to instate relations and dialogue with the city as an organism of people, laws, ecological systems.

After participating in the Venice Biennale in 1990 many things changed in my work. The beginning of the Gulf War and the attention to the cultural change that would be provoked by the Internet soon after, made me look at life, at art and at my work in a different way. Moreover, it seemed to me that the gallery system was no longer sufficient to cope with the drive of an art that was becoming more involved in this evolution. It all began when, in 1991–92, I took on my first public commission for a piece in Peccioli, near Pisa. I was invited to pick a square or a street in which to do my work. For me, the priority was to do something that would not be refuted by the citizens. My aim was to touch the sensibility of the citizens, to do something that would have minimal environmental impact, something that could shift the linguistic level so as to avoid populist demagogy. All this meant, then as now, working in a political way, rather than creating a political work. Intervening in a public space not meant to host pieces of art, the artist must try even harder to move towards the 'spectator'. And in a city all the inhabitants are potential spectators. It is them that I address when I create a public artwork. This 'moving towards' is solidified in the captions that accompany my works. These are an integral part of the piece because they represent the most active part in the political sense. Think that for the Istanbul Biennale or in Kanazawa in Japan for the Century Museum of Contemporary Art the caption that I wrote was in fact a publicity campaign! I see the caption as a sort of utensil: a two-way device that activates different levels of reading for the piece, belonging as it does to the system of art and that of the city. In short, the captions which accompany my works are no more than an 'explicit declaration' of that moving towards those spectators who I feel are the recipients of the message. I think this is political."

*Does public art depend only on the context in which it is placed or the amount of people who make use of it?*

"In its nature art is only art when it is made public. In the case of so-called public art things are different. A work can be defined as public only when it is presented in a space that is not meant to accommodate art. The citizens of a city are not there to see artwork, as they would be if they had entered a gallery. In a museum the artist is responsible only for his work, whereas in the public space of a city he or she assumes a role that gives different responsibilities in terms of communication with people. As such, the manner in which one poses problems becomes determining. Therefore, I believe dialogue with the spectator, the basis of the existence of the work itself, should come to assume an even more important role now, in this moment when art wishes to live outside museums, strictly linked to the reality of life and, as such, to architecture, its context, the media and above all the public which is no longer that which is selected by a restricted artistic system. For this reason I feel the dimensions of the 'encounter' are important because art is, deep down, 'the art of the encounter': the artist must be able to come down from the pedestal of celebrity which the system has constructed resulting in the progressive and fatal marginalization from society.

My initial approach, with the collaboration of the institution, is to gain the citizens' trust through a series of meetings in order to understand how the work can speak 'about them' with a certain contemporary quality and sensibility, avoiding demagogic and populist forms. Each work is then integrated by a caption that explains in an elementary way the procedure at the basis of the piece.

In substance, my work consists of a strategy I like to define as 'Machiavellian' because it works on two levels – two sides of the same coin. The first is more popular, though in reality more contingent; the second is more specialized, critical and methodological. The caption is the point of entrance into these two interpretations. The one I did in the SMAK in Gent for *Over the Edges* reads: 'The streetlights of this square are hooked up to the maternity wards of the hospitals of Gent. Each time the lights slowly pulsate it means a baby has been born. This work is dedicated to all those born today in this city'. It's important for this to be comprehensible to everybody, less so for the work to be seen as 'art' to the passer-by. This is more for the insiders. Without these characteristics a public artwork risks not being public at all."

*Is there such a thing as a social function for art? Is its role dialectic, oppositional, or integrative with the reality that surrounds it?*

"Not exactly a social function. But art is the synthesis and coagulation of many things. It is more an oblique anticipatory view, as you wrote in *L'ideologia del traditore*. It directly and indirectly irradiates and modifies society. In the square of a suburb area of Bolzano, where I had a little room built as an annex of the Museion, I have found, meeting the citizens, the usual difficulties aggravated by their double culture – German and Italian. I felt rather uncomfortable, to the point of doubting if my interventions in the area were really necessary, finding this general disinterest for art. So precisely because of this indifference towards art that I had noticed, as is common in many cities, I came up with the idea of bringing a 'small museum' to the square, a sort of annex of the central museum. I commissioned the construction of that little room, camouflaged into its surroundings, in order to take the art right there, in that square. Now, when someone passes by, a sensor activates a light and a work of art is shown. As such, even those who are not interested in art find themselves visiting a museum for those three seconds. Every three months or so the work to be shown is swapped for another from the museum according to an established programme. It is now visited by many people, even students from all the schools of the area. This could perhaps be considered a social service. In planning this work I thought of government offices or churches. There was a time, for example, that a when a cathedral was built it was accompanied by many small chapels spread over the city or the surrounding countryside for those who wished to light a candle or place some flowers."

*Is art a social service? Your work in the Palazzo Doria Pamphilj in Valmontone, in the room of festivities, is accompanied by popular love songs chosen by the citizens. Did you want to produce collective creativity?*

"I believe that the artist should *also* have social responsibility. The vocation of the work of art is that of encountering the reality of the world even if the work is in fact elitist or specialist. Rather than collective creativity, I see it as collective 'artisticness', a more contemporary idea.

Nevertheless, one can't think that art doesn't consider places, contexts and what agitates them, nor that it is completely separated from the economic reality. I still think that this artistic system, that does work economically, is subject to change – changes that are already disclosed. Which direction it will take, I do not know, but I imagine it will be deep… In the case of Valmontone I used another logic that was not only that of choosing a room and showing my work along with other artists, doing a joint exhibition. Mario Pieroni, the curator, understood the idea perfectly. Starting with the premise of creating a work that could somehow meet the city and its inhabitants, I wanted to activate the critical mechanisms regarding the modalities of creating art in public places. I then went to find the people of the place who told me about the history of the building, the use people gave to it after the Second World War as a hospice for evacuees. The room that was given to me was used as a dance hall where people used to meet and chat about their days when they were younger. Together we dug out some records of the time and, using a hi-fi, some sensors and some speakers, the music would come on in the streets of the town every time someone walked into the room. The tunes reached everywhere, recalling those people who had once temporarily stayed in the building and had lived out their youth amidst the debris of a tragic war. It could be heard because of the echo, but the music was aimed 'outside', towards the city, like a gift. It is a work that has to do with memory and architectural emptiness. Sound was the most suitable material with which to achieve this. But the idea of intervening in public spaces without invading them, superimposing a project of mine on a collective memory was the main theme: I was interested in this critical position regarding the system."

*In other circumstances (such as the table and the chair for RAM in Rome, or the stand at A.B.O. at the Bologna art fair, 2006), with a sort of an artisan humility, you have chosen to make sculptures out of other people's objects. What is the difference between the artist and the artisan?*

"I wasn't thinking about the artisan or industrial origins of these objects. The idea came from imagining houses when their owners are out. The furniture remains still, silent, listening, as if it had a life of its own; from outside come sounds, the light of day, night time; the answering machine is on… places without their usual inhabitants are truly a great mystery. The title is: *What Happens in Rooms When People Go Away?*. What happens is that, when the room is closed and their owners turn off the lights, the furniture lights up because they are covered in phosphorescent paint. These objects – domestic and everyday – in the exhibition space are camouflaged to such a degree as to no longer be recognizable as art. The public will not see them as anything other than simple decorative objects. I wanted to modify the public perception of the work of art: we can only imagine, think, wait. It is within this immaterial tension that the work is unveiled. The work is only fully carried out when it encounters its spectator. To the latter we ask for patient effort in looking for it.

If in the public space I want the artist to move towards the spectator, here in the specialized space of the museum I ask the spectator, who for me is always the true protagonist, to assume the responsibility of being the one to move towards the artwork, of looking for it, giving things an auratic character. Art is everywhere, everything we see around us is already a potential exhibition. He who decides to turn it into such is the spectator. It's the development of a sort of an opposite process to that of Duchamp: I think that today the object, the work of art has a great desire to move out of the museum, but the moment in which the work returns to reality it loses its own aura. Therefore it is the spectator, the artist being the first spectator, who can give it back its aura. Without considering that our society is ever more ubiquitous…"

*For the* Arte all'Arte *exhibition you restored a space for the local band, in Sardinia you built fountains with variable water jets (for the Tiscali office), in Bolzano you constructed a welcoming house for art, in Rome you built the Fountain of the Wolf in the courtyard of a gallery. Is art the vaporization of a social idea, aesthetic intention, individual ethic or just the fruit of a laboratory for the search of new forms?*

"Just like in Peccioli in 1994, for *Arte all'Arte 2000* at Colle Val d'Elsa, I set up a budget, well, an economic system, to show that I define 'critical, ethical and amorous' an idea of a method. The same thing in Cagliari, where water is hardly abundant: for the Tiscali office I did something which could answer ethically to the request for fountains by making some irrigators instead. In Villa Manin I set up an enclosure inaccessible to people allowing nature to freely run its course, just like in Bolzano I created a 'service' for a marginalized area in the outskirts by building the annex to the Museion we were talking about earlier. In Rome, in the exhibition at the Magazzino d'Arte Moderna, all the experience I got from these public works was used in a private context: the restoration of a condominium – let's say public – fountain regenerated those works in a private space…

I consider my works of art as mechanisms working on the city on different scales, finite and infinite, visible and invisible; devices able to silently modify contexts and relationships. The spectator becomes the client, the artist is 'at his service' and the work can even not be recognized as such. I repeat: the work constitutes systems and procedures of relations between the institutions, ecology, economy, people."

*In my Padula Charterhouse exhibition* Le Opere e i Giorni *you confirmed the secret of the Carthusian cell and the monumental silence which surrounds it by hiding under a wall a gold leaf. Is art also the fruit of an alchemical process? The application of the oxymoron of "unveiling by concealing"?*

"I think that the work of art, in the past as in the present, in order to be beautiful must also be good. There must always be this double value, declared or unknowing. Art is always a positive project; the vehicle of problems, of questions; carrier of life, of evolution and of a cognitive process. The work has no truth, what matters is the mystery of the visual event, its inexpressible undecodability; its undefinable, unteachable essence. It is as elusive as an enigma, and as such it possesses a power of attraction that not even the passing of time can erode. Viewing the work of art requires a special act of faith, precisely because nothing is completely revealed. Everything is hidden and secret. Then there is the theme of emptiness, of imagination as narration, of emptiness as an infinite possibility of images and thoughts…"

*After 9/11, which punctured the collective imagination not only of Americans but of the entire world, performance art entered a crisis, that self-referential art which, imitating fashion, was aimed entirely at communication. But under the dress there was nothing! Do you think that your work, which comes from very far away and from a noble creative experience, participates in the new trend of a type of creativity which positively addresses an active ethic and a reflective and spiritual aesthetic?*

"Certainly it was after the Twin Towers came down that everybody realized they were all in the same boat, inside a complex problem that spares no one. It was after the Twin Towers that public art gained its officialism, the knowingness that art must 'relate to', as well as the beginning of a trend as you say. But I can't bear trends and in fact my public art dates back to the early 1990s. For me the Gulf War and the arrival of the Internet were precursors to 9/11. Fashion has turned public art into a neighbourhood party, instead it is form that is important. It is necessary to be able to dialogue with the recipients of the work, the citizens, but it is essential to pick out a modality that is the expression of a thought. The artwork in turn produces a theory, the theory produces a second work and this second work produces yet another theory.

Having said that, I think that there has been an interest in moving away from a modern ego to a contemporary ego, impregnated by a sense of the collectivity. The contemporary ego moves within a logic of shared sensibility, of collective intelligence, and all this is easy to confront. Even those who have nothing to do with culture participate in this newly diffused sensibility. An example is the mad cow episode. Whoever sits down to eat, though perhaps not getting into philosophical disquisitions, is fully aware that if he or she eats a steak it isn't the same as the steaks of fifty years ago as the animal has been raised on food which is full of chemicals. In other words, everything implicates everything and the responsibilities are ever greater. Encountering a city is also an extraordinary opportunity to give back value and form to the artistic operation."

*Does art leap over the past and ride into the future? Does the artist, in accepting public commissions, maintain the present or plan the shaping of collective taste in the future?*

"Nowadays everything is accelerated by the media; the present means accepting the past and the future, and in the present the work of art is concretized by adhering to reality. But art has always done this. For example, when Mantegna was called to Mantua by the Gonzaga to paint the fresco in the bridal chamber he had to face a series of problems caused by that space: the lighting, the architecture, the narrative, the demands of his client. In short, the work adheres to that reality. Great artists, by accepting this challenge, have developed new strategies and a new language. This apparently limiting 'constriction' has for centuries produced an artistic quality of the highest level. Nowadays everything has changed even though I like to believe that there are new clients for the work who I see as the recipients – us, that is. Marketing experts know this problem all too well."

# William Kentridge
## Johannesburg, South Africa, 1955



*You have a huge experience of working in films and theatre, animation and photography, which represent a fundamental multimedia background to your work. Is time a structuring aspect of what you do?*

"I do not think it is time in itself so much, as transformation, which of course implies time. If you have a static image, you have a frozen fact. If you invoke the world of animation, film, or theatre, you have process and transformation at its heart – transformation from image to image, transformation in subjectivity and history – and time is the medium in which this happens. The animation itself is a way of trying to make visible this invisible passage of time."

*Is your cinematographic work, which is based on a gradual process of cancellation, the result of intense figurative realism?*

"At the Johannesburg Art Foundation where I trained as a teenager and student, there was a big emphasis on figure drawing (although the Foundation in general produced abstract painters), and working within the field of animation and working monochromatically my reference points were black and white photography and cinema, both of which are essentially, although not exclusively, figurative."

*What is the conceptual value of your work?*

"I have no idea of the conceptual value of my work. I suppose it has within it a resistance to the disappearance of the artist behind technology – the idea that there is a difference between a handmade drawing based on a photograph, and the photo itself. I also think that the hours of work embodied in the drawing can have a power in themselves and at best give a feeling of agency. I'm not sure if this is a conceptual value."

*Is your interest in film and theatre also partly the result of an idea of art as total work?*

"The idea of a total artwork is perhaps a generous way of describing the interest involved. Rather through a series of fortunate accidents and failures, I was unable to embrace one medium on its own wholeheartedly, nor abandon others which still had an interest for me. So that, without there being anything so clear as a plan, I found myself working in the theatre as well as in the studio, and making work that encompassed performance, music, stage and projection."

*What importance does photography have in your work?*

"I think photography manifests in the work in different ways, sometimes simply as a reference, a store of information, to be used alongside or in place of a sketch book – this is the shape of that tree, this is the different shape of a hand as it moves from extended palm to fist. Second, there is something in the greyscale of a silver nitrate photograph, which whilst not the same as that of charcoal, certainly has an affinity with it. So that sometimes you think of the drawings as handmade photographs, although charcoal is laid down rather than silver nitrate washed away. The third level is in controlling the image, the way a photograph can be cropped, printed, the lighting changed within it – which has suggested strategies for working with images. Fundamentally there is the question endlessly posed by photographs, abut those surfaces on which our gaze meets the world. How much of the photo is the world and how much is our projection onto it? This seems to me the heart of what it is to look at a photograph or drawing."

*Is your work partly the result of a critical vision of reality?*

"I think some key lectures and books I read at university, particularly Alexandre Kojève on Hegel, made me realize that the world could be understood as process rather than fact, and showed the centrality of contradiction as part of the world."

*Does art have a social function? And in what way can it play a part in progress in the world?*

"I think art has a personal social function. So much of who we are is constructed through the films we have seen, books we have read, particular chapters in books, specific sentences within chapters. These are moments of different art forms that confirm and expand who we are. I have a deep belief in art's role in the creation of subjectivity. I don't think I would go much further than this. I think this is a most optimistic view of art's social role. On a broader social level, I think artists have a less than glorious past."

*For Mozart's opera* The Magic Flute, *you adopted the role of total author. Like a great Baroque artist, such as Bernini, you have become a director of all the arts, moving between music, literature, set design and direction. Does art imply contamination and over-stepping boundaries?*

"I used to believe that to work in several fields would of necessity mean that one was a dilettante in each one. Temperamentally I was unable to restrict myself just to one form, though for many years I did try this. Secondly, I discovered that the strategies, demands and ways of thinking about one art form were productive of working in another. So there were images and ideas for drawing that came out of theatre productions, and ideas for staging and theatre strategy that came out of a drawing. There is often a combination of different art forms in one piece, for example in *The Magic Flute*, and then a fragmentation afterwards, where ideas from the work find expression in other forms – a set of sculptures for example, a suite of etchings, a particular animation. Some of the drawings that I have done that have seemed the most interesting to me, were essentially applied drawings, drawings done in the service of a film or a piece of theatre – images I would never have come to if simply thinking about drawings."

*Does art have a liberating function? In your case, have your South African origins had an even greater effect on creating a need for socially responsible art?*

"I think the particularities and political pressure in South Africa in the 1980s, when I was starting as an artist, were such that it made one confront directly how engaged, disengaged, socially responsible or agitprop one's work is. I had started making work directly in the service of others – a Leninist approach to what images were needed. But in the end there was too much of a dichotomy between the false certainty of these images and the sense of uncertainty and ambiguity I felt about the world. When I allowed myself to be irresponsible, it became possible to start feeling in touch with the work."

*Is there a Wagnerian matrix in your work, given your preference for music and the multimedia staging of many of your shows?*

"For me Wagner always conjures up an idea of certainty about the world, of being able to plan a huge programme of work in advance, seeing oneself as a national representative, involved with the forging of a *volk*. So I do really hope that my work is not Wagnerian."

## Fabio Mauri
Rome, 1926–2009



*Mostly because of generational coincidences, your work seems to move around the zeroing of the image and reflection of the space of painting. I am asking you therefore: in the vast interdisciplinary area of your personal culture, was there any space for phenomenology?*

"I started painting when I was very young, almost a baby. My family was often talking about my great grandfather, a member of seven European Academies and winner of the Kassel Price. I therefore wanted to be a painter. And because of my other paternal grandfather Achille, a theatre manager of *caffè-concerto* and the theatres Argentina and Apollo of Rome (now Eliseo), Trianon of Milan; and because of various authors like d'Annunzio, Pirandello and Petrolini, I thought I would certainly want to be in the theatre. Later, I shared this passion with my young friend Pasolini. Pier Paolo eventually chose literature and not only poetry, instead of painting. He used to tell me that cinema was more immediately alive. From the very beginning I got involved in the idea and practice of avant-garde; I was trying to find out the way in which every means of expression could pour itself into another, and could freely be used as a unique expressive tool. I was sharing this feeling with avant-gardes that seemed dead. They were, by all means, not! The zeroing you are talking about goes with this attempt: to free oneself from a culture oppressed by styles and prejudices, to recompose a reality after verification of its true significance. The phenomenology of my work is reintroduced in two ways. The first way lays in titles: to title inadequately raw materials laid out as a line of samples. This is to signify that sense and significance is a reality with many layers, it does not wear out with its identification or comparing differences. The second way consists on an acquisition of objects already made (bicycle, tobacco, record) as solid bodies of historic phenomenology: their historic deletion is immediate."

*Your work starts measuring itself with history. Urban images appear together with questions about the past regime of our country. From phenomenology to ideology?*

"In 1971 at a public exhibition, I have re-examined my past youth. Fascism and war emerged with their intimate links. I retraced the origin of European thought, ineffective and useless in comparison with the immediate effectiveness of American thought, as well as political Russian thought. I realized that fascism and war were not obligatory events for remembrance as one would be inclined to think, but they were violent crossings, terrifying, false and deadly, deprived of any thought. Stupidity engenders death. I saw this with my own eyes. I have seen pure idiocy killing idiots and non idiots – I have revisited mentally the time of a precocious adolescence among a beloved family; the milieu, the circle was intellectual and generous, only fascism was awkward although trying to look familiar. It was invading schools, streets, public life, newspapers and radio, it sounded as a geographic phenomenon, not political and almost natural, in which we were by pure chance or for incredible luck. Its military spirit infiltrated everywhere, even during a parade of wet nurses; it was incredibly clashing and all was ending on an exclamatory tautology.

Life can offer to a young boy slightly talented better advantages than the hitches of the capricious events of an ideology. Till the day, I remember so well, of the war declaration. That day and the following years, reality overturned. Aggressive words turned into reality, till every most horrid detail. It was like a song which had only been dull and then had suddenly turned in a real extermination of people, of desperates full of blood, mutilated, compelled with a necessity of hate. The world had no inner evidence and was like a menacing obligatory helmet to be warned, due to menacing predication cried out by obscure lips deprived of any sense. Fascism counts on foolish people and through obedience makes them exactly what they are."

What is Fascism: *a pedagogic informative performance. In what way is it connected with your past experience?*

"*What is Fascism* is a performance in memory of a past personal experience with Pasolini and other friends from Bologna. We were taken to Florence in the occasion of Hitler visiting Italy in 1938. 'Young intellectuals' were supposed to debate over 'the mysticism of Fascism', about their political ideas; there were sports meetings like boxe for instance and artistic meetings like dance and singing. Since the early morning in our camp, we could hear the voice of Edoardo Spadaro: *È primavera…* – it is spring, wake up you little girls. These 'little girls' were the *piccole italiane*, equivalents of us young *Balillas*, heavily militarized. We had no terms of comparison except in our families to what one could think about the world – libraries did not sell but permitted books. In all social places and in the institutions and schools, every conversation used to happen without trueness. Reality, the sun, the rain, our youth were 'fascism', a sort of idea of nature that was pretending to be so simple to the point of resembling a most healthy ideology.

In 1971 I very badly wanted to exhibit the microphone of Mussolini. I had found it, but there was no way to buy or to borrow it. I therefore changed this exhibition into a performance at the Accademia Silvio d'Amico in Rome. Giorgio Pressburger had invited me together with Kounellis, Pistoletto, Germano Celant and you. It was within a class on modern art. So I did *What is Fascism*, which is the expositive introduction of ideology as an historical constant of contemporary experimentation.

Completely taken out of memory and technically formalized, this performance has a value in itself as a sort of ceremonial mass. Even without a proper public. In this performance, the existence of memory is brought back according to a judgement on the experience and even if through channels of irony, beauty, music and aesthetical symmetries, one feels a clear condemnation. *What is Fascism* is a poisoned apple."

*Your research strips off itself to the point of isolating only one figure on the scene. What is the relation between the subject and the social body, or between the body of the actor and the spectator?*

"My work tends to isolate a person from the scene. For instance during *Ideology and Nature*, a young girl undresses and redresses herself with her black and white military strict uniform, to the point of tearing to pieces the ideological form of her outfit. If I have understood the question, in my opinion there is no difference between the subject and the social context.

*Ebrea* is a composite exhibition that contains a performance. A young girl on her growing adolescence, undressed of her clothes, is cutting her hair and she sticks them on a small camping mirror. She is portraying her own identity, the star of David. There can be diversity between the body of the actor and the spectator, as the critical distance, the obligation of the point of view is different. I am using the public as an involuntary participant, but active in a composition of clean conscience. During *What is Fascism* the public is seated in the corporative platforms and helps giving a truthfulness which relies precisely on true facts of political experience. Present unawareness and past unawareness share the same aspect. The public has no problem in resembling something that it is fatally not, but for one or another reason is compelled to interpret (including the amusement of a show). The performance is a vase without cover, as time has proved. Art, if we think better, does not come and go, does not hit and afterwards withdraw its hand. To make art, attempting a composition of poetry or dramaturgy, goes only in one direction, it proceeds with the identification of the world and art itself. In more intense moments of culture, actuality retraces contemporary links with other moments of thought and language, and modernity finds itself in company with one or another classicism. This is how we call the well-established fruit of a time that has decoded and built patterns and repeatable specimens."

*Your work investigates the theme of the body of the artist to the point of projecting on Pasolini's body film pieces. What is time in this type of work?*

"At the base of the projection on Pasolini is his *Gospel of Saint Matthew* and the film *The Desperates of Sandors* by Miklós Jancsó. It is the idea that the relation mind/world is a projective one: a projection containing memory, imagination and culture and producing (mostly autonomously) further language, that is to say a brand new meaning. We can see the world because we are aware of its plot. An artist, as any other thing or any other being, acts as a screen – actually, he *is* a screen. Projecting the film on Pier Paolo's body is a symbolic attempt to make the author responsible – responsible of everything, and particularly of his own story. This is my way to point out that making art is a phenomenology of discernment. I would not know what the idea of 'time' could be exactly in this work on Pasolini. Maybe there is no time. I suspect that time itself does not exist and that the times of the earth are exaggeratedly scattered. I think their enumeration is not exact nor useful. It seems to lead us to a non-objective relativism, something of a fantasy. This tendency of mine may sound as a contradiction, but actually it is only a specification. I personally mistrust fantasy, I had to resist it for a lifetime."

*From the white screen of the 1950s to the screen full of history of the 1960s and 1980s. Art can be ideologic?*

"Yes, art is ideological because man, from whom it starts and to whom it is directed, is by nature ideological – it is a condition of the human mind and behaviour. Ideology, in my opinion, is a personal 'under-theory' of the world and of life, it is a scientifically uncertain building of personal experience. When a number of different ideological experiences find affinity between themselves, great ideologies about the world are created, the more pitiless and horrible. Radical solutions are essentially blind and deft. With the fall of the Berlin Wall, stupidly, 'the end of ideologies' was shouted and even art lost its breath with this cry. I must confess I was scared. Ideology seemed to disappear, but reality would have sank in the roots of the 'ideological man' and would have restarted from there to carry on its battle – a chiefly ideological battle. And so it was. For reasons of ideology nations, regions, and continents fight. They fight for high and old ideologies as well as for just born ideologies. Every ideologist thinks that his palate or his belly is the epicentre of a unique conception of the world, for which to fight till death. The dimension of the absurd is extra strong. One has to reflect on it because it is simply real like the flatting of the wheel of a bicycle. And it is equally and simply an unreality, unbearably unreal. The capacity of error of man is an extended biological damage. It surprises me all the time. Ants don't have it. Or they are not subjected to it.

On this subject I made my show at the Venice Biennale of 1978. It was called *The Evil Numbers* and it was about reflecting on the error of calculation and judgement in man; to start with the evaluation of 'quality' in political, social and artistic thought. Modern time commits suicide in order to save one instant of clearly ideological existence. They pretend that in the achievement of a common ideology one could find individual security, or personal happiness. Of course this is not true."

*In what way the autobiography can interfere with history?*

"Autobiography interferes with history inside the destiny of the world as the wings clapping of a butterfly. But naturally this depends on whose is the autobiography: the one of Julius Caesar happened later, for instance, when his biography had already taken place and had already been influent. Autobiography is often only a chronicle and not a story with a significant meaning. One should define 'what history is' at that point. It is possible to think that history is the gathering of events that puts together the largest number of men around a shared matter of fact. It is an elementary definition and certainly only sufficient for time being. History is also a war, an earthquake, a geographical discovery, a political power or a drawing by Leonardo da Vinci. History is a remarkable event or meaning that cannot be eliminated, shared by everybody. It is not necessarily positive, it is quite expositive. It explains how things go, how they have gone and how they might go in the future."

*Your last installations in Rome have a clear tendency towards a form of total art. From literature to architecture. Which is the space for man?*

"These installations follow my usual tendency through years. I am happy to give this impression of following total art. Futurism and Expressionism were going after that. These cultures have formed my mind. I use the world as a language, the container as what it contains, the world as it seems to me, the world in which happily or painfully I live. Language indicates directions, what matters and what dos not matter (for me), what has mattered and what could matter (for others). Judgement finds its own field of experience and rules any part of the composition. Hybridization between ideas and language is continuous. So many things in life have a resemblance with the fusion of bodies. It is an extended reality, not a pure metaphor. In the work of art, man is always present even if the author is talking about insects. Word is already man, sign is already man. Man is the consciousness of the existence of the world, that is to say, of the world even without him. The cry of man is already man as the bark of the dog is already the dog. I am saying this to give value to the man as well as to the dog. And probably to the world."

*The* horror vacui *of the white screen has been exorcized through a working process that has lasted fifty years. Can you fight death with the death of language?*

"I do not think one can defeat death with the death of language. It is quite the contrary – that would be giving death a short cut. I don't believe that art has this power. Its aim remains an artifice, one controlled and measured. Art forces any madness and intellectual strength into the syntactic logic of language. Art is a minor product of desperation, from the point of view of the concept and experience of reality. But maybe I am wrong and ungrateful."

*Can still life, which represents the identity of language, its definitive exemplarity, redeem the biological error of the precarious life of the artist?*

"Yes, I do believe that still life could redeem in its exemplarity the biological error of the precarious life of the artist. As the drawing of the beloved woman or other things of the sort. Man does not stay on earth for a long time. He only lives the day before his death I mean, but he leaves traces of thoughts and deeds and scatters objects around. Thought and art are objects and real traces. One takes care of these traces of others who are no more there. Meanwhile one leaves other traces, the present ones, maybe our traces also, for others who are not here or are not yet here. If they will be here, they will ask themselves what we had intended to do. Art often knows it. Art can say it."

# Dennis Oppenheim
Electric City, Washington, 1938

New York
2006

*In your outdoor works did land art signify a love of nature?*

"For me, land art had nothing to do with the love of nature. I can't speak for the others, but most of the artists doing it lived in New York. Land art for me came from a hard look and intense involvement in minimalism and other art theories centred around phenomenology."

*In these operations of yours, what was the value represented by the physical scale of the work?*

"Undoubtedly, one of the major influences coming from land art was its effect on the scale of sculpture. I used the term 'activation of land', thus implying both a kind of physical alteration of the site and the conceptual presence of the artist. It was not at all uncommon for a work to span several miles, either physically or conceptually."

*In my first book,* Il territorio magico, *I published a work in which you are photographed in an open space in which the natural context encounters the presence of a book placed on your body. What relationship is there between nature and culture?*

"Again, nature was not an influence on land art until ecology was brought in. Then, ideas involving seasonal change, temperature, elevation and other characteristics of the site were brought into the work. The term site-specific was coined then to describe a work's relationship with where it was placed. If the work was a hole in the ground near a boundary line, one could say it had a strong relationship to the site."

*In your work land art certainly does not spring from the anthropology of the cowboy, from the myth of unspoiled nature and the romantic yearning for space. What relationship do you have with European culture?*

"In my mind American land art was not inspired by the American landscape but by the dematerialization of the art object. It was for me an extension of minimalism, to include depressions and negative spaces in the earth. This catalyst then moved quickly to include large land areas, ecology and site specificity. The Euro-

343

pean landscape, although different from that of the US, would have been able to act as a format for these ideas."

*Subsequently your work has acquired a strong sense of irony. What importance does the piece in which a metal puppet repeatedly bangs its head against a bell have in your long creative adventure? What does it represent?*

"I've always jumped around a lot. Occasionally one work will stand out from the others done at a particular time. This in itself is not unusual. *Attempt to Raise Hell* (1974) seems to always present the audience with a high wattage experience that is also meaningful. Coming from the core of body art, this violent action of lunging forward and smashing one's head against a large iron bell results in a ringing, a long drawn out sound emanating from metal hitting metal, right at eye level."

*Going further, your work has naturally opened up to architecture. Does your art have a social function?*

"In the 1970s one wanted to stay away from functionality, it was a bad word meaning your art had to be controlled, or applied to fit a need. But later work appeared involving a functional characteristic. This is simply a form of fusion, one art form moving into another. Presently, architecture and sculpture seem to be sleeping in the same bed."

*I remember that in Venice you even turned a real work of architecture upside down, presenting it physically in terms of a large sculpture. Does turning something upside down imply subversion, revolution or just playfulness?*

"*Device to Root Out Evil* did invert a typical country church, allowing the pitched roof to penetrate the ground. My interest is not blasphemous but formal. The object, when turned upside down, cantilevers its major portion precariously out in space. It leans and tilts, the roof spearing into the ground like an arrow. This is a church actively in pursuit of evil."

*In your latest works the installation has become a route through which the public moves with its emotions. The work has gone beyond the categories of painting and sculpture, of video and photography. What does multimedia mean to you?*

"All of the boundaries once separating the arts have fused so you can compound them, one on top of the other, into a generalized thrust. The inclusion of more than one art form in this way is so common, one is inclined not even to bring up the fact that it is multimedia."

*In the uncertainty of the new century is it possible to speak again of utopia or of little utopias of art?*

" Some artists are more affected than others by what is going on around them, they often bring it into their work. Others are dealing with concepts, unmoved by anything else."

*Is art only concerned with aesthetics or does it spill over into politics?*

"Art is not necessarily political. But artists are."

# Marc Quinn
London, 1964



*Your work starts from the idea that mankind is a biological error.
How can art rescue it?*

"It's the opposite. Mankind is the only possibility that could exist. If you look at the theory of evolution according to which the environment creates what inhabits the environment, then therefore there can be no biological error. Every biological reality is a product of the environment. What's interesting is that art can help you see your environment and see how you inhabit it."

*Sometimes technology has been part of your work. Is art the only way to humanize it?*

"I don't think it's about humanizing technology. Sculptures like the frozen heads, for instance, are about the way we depend on technology. In order to remain as a sculpture, the frozen-blood head has to be kept frozen all the time and kept plugged and electricity has to be continuously present. In a way, it's about dependence. It could be dependence on drugs, dependence on anything like that, but also the way that we are all dependent on the environment and electricity and all that. It's interesting that since I first made this sculpture, the first blood-head ten years ago, people are now much more aware of the whole idea of dependence on the environment. That side of the sculpture for me becomes more and more interesting. Technology can also be interesting to understand old things in a new way, such as with the DNA portraits. The mapping of the human genome is an amazing revolution for humankind. It's the first time that we can see the instructions to make ourselves. It's equivalent to realizing that the earth goes around the sun, not the other way round. It's one of those great revolutions in human thought. Technology has different meanings in different works. Take for instance the frozen-flower sculptures: what I love about those is that when the flower freezes it becomes its image. Yes, when the flower freezes it does become its image, so you see the transformation of an object into an image happening in front of your eyes. I mean the biological flower dies, but its image perpetuates. The whole connection between image and object is one of the main things I'm thinking about all the time."

*Your work seems to involve alchemical processes. Can art transform the world?*

"I believe art is always about transformation. What alchemy is about is the will to transformation, it is not necessarily actually changing materials. But if you make an artwork it has to transform, and when it transforms that makes it interesting. For instance, take the frozen-flower sculptures I was just talking about. When you get real flowers and you dip them into frozen silicon, they transform. They stop being real flowers and they start to become an image of a flower that's exactly the same shape as a real flower. The Kate Moss sculptures for me are all about that same separation between image and object. Someone like Kate Moss, whose image has a life of its own completely separate from her own biological life, is functioning the same way as the flower. When you look at the marble sculptures I did of people who had lost limbs, which to me is also the other side of the Kate Moss sculptures, it's about what can be beautiful. It's taking the idea of the fragmented, classical statue and then transforming that into being a sculpture about wholeness. Always transformations, flipping from inside to outside, reflections: this is what gives art its ability to make us look at life in a new way."

*Nature goes from birth through death in all its transformations. How can art stop life's dissolution?*

"Art can't stop life's dissolution. In a sense, you could say that the frozen flowers are about stopping life's dissolution, but in fact they tell you the truth, which is that a perfect image can only be achieved through biological death. In other words, for the flower to remain beautiful forever, it must die. If you have a movie star who dies young, their image stays perfect forever like Marilyn Monroe. But if they live on to be old and maybe embarrass themselves, then people just kind of get bored of them. Their image doesn't live on. It's much more important to choose life than image."

*The language of art seems to paralyze time. Does your art search for an eternal present?*

"What's really interesting to me is the way that you can tell the difference between an artwork and an artifact, in that an artwork is always in the present moment. I'm looking across my studio now and there's a Roman sculpture there of a boy, but it seems like it was made yesterday, because it has a continuous present moment. There's a kind of time travel. I'm looking at this ancient sculpture and I'm communicating with the person who made it 2,000 years ago. Whereas, if it's just a pot, it just becomes an object from that period. I think this really is the difference between an artwork and everything else. An artwork is something that in a sense travels through time, carrying its present moment with it forever. You could say that the frozen sculptures are in a way articulating that in a literal way. The frozen sculpture has to be perpetually frozen, it has to be perpetually in the present moment. A work of art is always in the present moment, and the sense that the present moment exists only when someone looks at it is not within the work. It's someone bringing their attention to it that creates that moment."

*Even the artist is a biological error with respect to his art. Do you think the artist can be rescued by searching for immortality through his work?*

"It would seem to any reasonable person that biological immortality is impossible, and not something to be worth looking for. When you freeze yourself in vat of liquid nitrogen like Walt Disney, you're doing the same thing that ancient Egyptians did. You'll end up in a museum, you won't end up coming to life again. What I think is interesting is that your thoughts, your ideas and your emotions can be immortal in the sense that if you make artworks that last then you communicate with generations of people who have not yet been born. I think that's very exciting. As I said, I'm looking at this Roman sculpture, and there's an emotional communication with someone who died 2,000 years ago. So, in a sense, even though I don't know who the artist is, he is immortal and the ideas feeding his emotions are immortal. That's why art sort of transcends the barriers of time and I think that's one of the exciting things about it."

*Does art have a symbolic role, or does it make new models of real behaviour?*

"Do people make images that reflect themselves, or do they mould themselves to images? I think the answer is both, but it's interesting the idea of moulding yourself to images and that's why I was interested in the idea of the Kate Moss sculptures in a way, because it's about the image that our desire is moulding by making her the most popular model in the world, but also an image people are moulding themselves to. It all begins in childhood. When a child sees another child doing something it copies it. We all live by images and we all live by inhabiting images, and I think that, depending on what images we inhabit, we can create or destroy our lives. That is one of the deepest questions of art and life."

*How do art and science pursue each other?*

"Art and science are two very different things because science is trying to find out facts about the world, and art is trying to create, I would say, matrices where meaning can occur, or thoughts can occur. On the other hand there are times when some revolution in science, like the sequencing of DNA, can bring about the possibility to make artworks that deal with profound issues about our existence in the world. In that case, when I'm making the DNA sculptures using real DNA, I'm using the techniques of science, but I'm using them for the purposes of art. The way that I use it by taking the DNA, putting it in a frame and then putting it in a gallery is not how the scientist uses the same techniques."

*What's the relationship between your art and religion?*

"To me art is a sort of concrete philosophy. It's a way of creating objects or images that make us think about what it is to be a person in the world. These questions are the same questions that religion has tried to answer for people. The fact that these questions exist is the reason that religions have occurred – because people want answers to these unanswerable questions. It's normal that the same areas can be dealt with by religion and art, but I don't think that religion gives someone an answer, whereas I think art poses a question and knows no answer."

*You observed that the public admired the fragments of classical sculptures displayed in the British Museum even though they were mutilated, and you introduced the dignity of a new kind of beauty. You gave classical shape to subjects that were authentically mutilated by diseases or accidents. Is art a form of restoration for mankind? Is art able to restore harmony, proportion and symmetry to our everyday lives of insecurity and fear of terrorism?*

"What art can do is make you think about things you know in a new way, and sometimes that can make you question things, or might bring you serenity or hope. Making these marble sculptures of disabled people was a quite interesting process. It all began with the conceptual idea of seeing the people looking at the fragmented classical statues in the British Museum and thinking: 'If someone looked the same in real life, these tourists would react in the opposite way'. When I actually made the sculptures of people whose bodies were a similar shape, but obviously they were whole and not fragmented, then it became about something else. It became about celebrating diversity of bodies and diversity of what could be beautiful, and somehow break away from the narrow band that only Kate Moss is beautiful. The only reason that some things are unacceptable is that we decide that, and there's nothing intrinsic within them that makes them unacceptable. It's just how we decide to think about them."

# Ettore Spalletti
Cappelle sul Tavo, Pescara, Italy, 1940

Cappelle sul Tavo<br>2006

*The theme of the invitation that I gave to the artists is "Art: to forget 'from memory'". What I want to know from you Spalletti, is, when you're developing the form, the design and the colour of a work, you seem very wisely to forget 'from memory'. I mean the street you took and whether you went by foot, by car, or by bike to reach your studio, and whether it was raining, snowing or a sunny day. Do you in actual fact believe that forgetting "from memory" is the miracle or the oxymoron of the creative process? I have singled out this co-existence of oppositions, because on observing your work there is no trace of everyday life. There is on the other hand work that isolates itself, becomes objective, or rather, being abstract it does not represent you, nor is it in favour of you.*

"I'm very happy to hear these words you have just pronounced."

*Tell me if you agree and why.*

"I do agree with you. I'll talk to you about colour, and in this way I hope to answer your question. My colours are never just layers of colour. My colours are always atmospheric colours. Why do I always use the colour blue? Because blue never appears in its true essence on a surface but it is all around us continually, we are immersed in it. The same with pink; I use pink because it is the colour of complexion, it is a colour that can always be transformed according to our emotions. These are the main reasons why blue and pink characterize my work. I use grey because it is a neutral colour, but it is also a colour that consents the use of all other colours. So what does a colour exactly mean to us? I believe it means where that colour is capable of taking our imagination to. Sometimes, the colour yellow takes me so far and so inside light that I have difficulty in remembering I'm a figurative artist. I like to think that colour can always take me somewhere different, to a place that unfolds internally within me but with different motives and different rules. Does that answer your question?"

*Yes, I liked that very much. I believe, we could say that Spalletti's painting, if that's how we choose to call it, is done by a figu-*

*rative painter. The design, the colour, the vaporization of the colour, and also colour as powder, represent an idea of time and an idea of space. This is the linguistic dimension you utilize to describe reality.*

"In fact, sometimes I use figurative titles too, but it is more important for me to speak about something else."

*What?*

"My works are untouchable, but at the same time they communicate an important value: tactility. Everyone wants to touch them."

*And leave their fingerprints.*

"I ban my works from being touched but at the same time I am scolded for making works that motivate such strong desire. I believe this has to do with the meaning of life right now. These days we are able to get into contact with everything, but there is no reason why the things we like necessarily have to be touched."

*Just now you have touched on the quintessence of art: complexity, ambivalence, ambiguity, amorality and morality. Art is complex, and it is interesting to see that Spalletti's art is crying out to be touched but at the same time he is banning that. Spalletti's paintings are very expensive, so we deduce that the wealthy have permission to touch them. I'm just making a demagogic joke, as we are close to election time. What I really mean to say is that it's interesting to see how your work encourages temptation. I would like to talk about the theme of the "Temptation of Saint Ettore". How do you experience the creative process? Is it a moment in your life when you feel maximum involvement?*

"I never know where to look, or when that moment will come about. I like to spend a lot of time in my studio, not only working, but just strolling around and feeling colour all around me. This process could go on for quite a few weeks, sometimes even longer, and after having observed colours in different lights, the moment comes when I start painting. This is probably the best moment. Lately, I no longer wish to accompany my paintings to exhibitions."

*Your paintings are thirty years old – I mean, they are old enough to go on their own…*

"I had an exhibition in England, and I was very pleased to see that my paintings were hung very well without my intervening. My paintings are much more competent than I am."

*So is it true that you are a biological mistake with respect to your paintings?*

"If you say so…"

*No, I'm asking you, if you don't mind answering.*

"I don't know."

*Let's go back to talking about colour. Do you think reality is black and white or in colour?*

"Black and white are the only colours that have no dark or light."

*Don't you think that white embodies everything? I myself believe white is hybrid, it certainly couldn't be defined as the artist's First Communion.*

"White is often indicated as the sum of all colours. But for me it is also a colour that has no dark and no light. What it does have is a fine preciseness in which you can find the taste and the quality of knowledge. You can always find white in all my colours. When it is laid on a canvas a thin powder returns to the surface and gets on your fingers. What can I tell you about my paint? Paint on a canvas or on a palette instead of pouring it into a glass, are two completely different moments: in the former, paint becomes a painted layer on the surface of a picture, whereas in the latter, a glass full of paint gives us the sensation of being completely submerged in colour. This is the extraordinary experience of painting and painting in fresco as well."

*I believe you are an archi-painter, precisely because of your strong and energetic use of colour. However, your paintings lack in depth and yet they are not even two-dimensional since the spectator becomes lost inside them in a sort of pulverization of colour that spreads everywhere. You're a chromatic polluter! Justify yourself!*

"I'm very happy to be here with you."

*There's something else I want to ask you seriously though, not provokingly. It should be useful for understanding your work. I hope the public will not be scandalized when I define Spalletti as an existentialist. He is a painter who creates a biography, using the Freudian notion of negation that is a form of confirmation. Freud said that to negate doesn't mean to deny, but to confirm, by way of a type of (psychological) procedure. Spalletti is an archi-painter who works in depth but his painting appears two-dimensional. He assails real-*

*ity with an architectural idea of colour, and it's not a coincidence that his anthropological, cultural and linguistic matrix is the fresco. This is the last theme I will be dealing with you, Spalletti: the importance and the lesson of painting in fresco in your work.*

"A fresco is paint penetrating into wet plaster and giving a particularly wonderful depth to the colour. On the other hand oil painting is completely different. It is perceived as a layer of paint on the surface of the canvas that seems to put the palette and the canvas in direct relation with each other: we could almost say the picture becomes the palette of colour. My experience is unusual and not easy to describe or understand. The idea of colour has always been of profound and utmost importance to me: especially the idea of being immersed in it and what it is able to return to me in terms of expression of my desires."

*But getting back to the fresco, I get the feeling that there is some detail in the fresco that you particularly like, something that is cancelled and has lost its narrative imprint but has conserved its skin. This is the idea of memory.*

"That is a beautiful thing."

*Paradoxically enough, you transform the process of the fresco – where paint is supposed to be applied quickly and dry quickly – into a sort of slow motion. What importance does a 'slowing down' process have in your work, if you do agree this dimension really belongs to you?*

"The narration is lacking, don't you see? Many works we observe recount philosophical thought, tell a story, and this is important. The Renaissance and the preceding period tell the story of art patrons, the most important of which was the Church. All the artists, from the less talented to the great geniuses of the time, painted the story of the Annunciation or the Deposition. However, when I look at a Raphael's painting of religious subject, I feel a strong presence of another story underlying what is painted on the surface. The same thing happens to me when I observe paintings of artists I admire, and whose story and place in history I completely ignore. In artwork in general, historic thought has a weight that is significant and, in my opinion, gives the direction somehow. And then you meet an artist like Caspar David Friedrich, for example, and you find it so difficult to understand that incredible 'lengthening' of nature, perhaps it's part of his own make-up, his personality."

*For instance, in Friedrich's well-known picture of the man in ecstasy in front of nature, where do you place yourself, facing nature or turning your back?*

"Achille, your questions are so difficult."

*You spoke about Friedrich because you express desire, you're tempted by the sublime.*

"I am in front of, and with my back to, contemporaneously. There are certain moments when I feel and appreciate transparency, that's when I feel light going right through me."

*Do you enjoy being in an ambivalent position?*

"I don't know what you mean."

*You said yourself you are in front of, and with your back to, contemporaneously. Like Duchamp's door that closes a room only to open onto another at Rue Larrey in Paris.*

"There was a time when I found Duchamp's works extraordinary and he secured all my attention; but now I'm not sure. At home I like to have a painting, and I like the painting, and therefore I paint pictures, and even a sculpture becomes colour, it flattens out, it returns an image to me. I like my story. I also like Duchamp's door, but it's not my story."

*Are you more fond of Duchamp or Mondrian? Though I believe neither of them are congenial to you, they are too secular and too rationalist.*

"I love the Dutch painter."

*Who? Vermeer?*

"Yes, but I don't know why he is so important."

*He works on light.*

"You know, after the picture has been decided, I set out to work. There is a lot of repetition in my work, for ten days I have to lay the colour on at the same time every day, otherwise it would dry unevenly and the chromaticity would alter."

*So you are the wet nurse of your paintings at the beginning!*

"It's a very long process. I only start at the last minute when I make an abrasion and the pigments that create the colour are released, so the colour is ready to be applied. When I first started working, I was always making mistakes and a thick coating used to build up from trying to get the colour right. With time I have improved and I get things to work now."

*What do you think about the powder in Baschenis's paintings? He is a seventeenth-century artist who painted musical instruments in the trompe l'œil style and also painted powder. I am saying this because I would like to understand the difference in your case between the powder and the paint and between design and painting. Is there a difference?*

"The powder is paint for me, and therefore also painting."

*So what does powder and paint mean? Time?*

"Yes. But you have no idea of what is happening to you. There's this thing that gradually starts leaving you, that starts existing on its own, without a trace of intelligence or memory. It's a bit like what I wrote about this black surface here. There's no story, moon, or nature, it's like freeing everything and letting it be born internally."

*So, Spalletti is the author of families of paintings that are not related to each other. And he reassures us: his paintings are emancipated after twenty years, each one is free to go on its own way.*

# Franz West
Vienna, 1947



*You received your formation in the cultural climate of the Viennese Actionism, but since the beginning your work has focused on analysing the established convention between the work of art and its fruition. Is art an act of transgression that involves both artist and public or is it a communication of the principles that inspire it?*

"Both. I believe that if you try to limit art to certain modalities you bar all access to the things that are perhaps not defined with precision or defined in an incorrect way."

*Does your work have greater conceptual or behavioural value?*

"Behavioural value…"

*It seems to me that there exists a great attention to the fruition of your pieces on the part of the public. Is art interactive by nature? Does it require participation or simply contemplation?*

"Both. On the one hand the function of the sculptures in papier-mâché is a merely contemplative consideration, while on the other works like *Passstuecke* and *Mobili* clearly require the participation of the public. In my experience it's not possible to have both things at the same time, therefore you might even say this is stupid. (If, in the drunkenness of contemplation, this were converted into gestures you would probably get expressive forms similar to the cult of the body and expressionist dance, as for example Rudolf Steiner in the first half of the twentieth century.) This is obsolete, ridiculous. It means that faced with raw reality, we are exposed to ridicule, we find ourselves unarmed. This does not mean that the quality we find in contemplation is insignificant; on the contrary. For me, tending as I am towards slight depression, it provokes such a sense of abandon that the bitterness and the less appetizing side of life have the effect of a censorious device from which we must escape."

*The languages, materials and techniques used by you are multiple, all of them aimed at creating a fusion between art and life. But is there a threshold between the banality of the everyday and the creative act and its exemplarity?*

"For the artist the everyday is exemplary. It acts as a model, it is the threshold between art and life; we do not aim to remove the quotidian but rather to give it an artistic vision."

*I remember your installation in the MoMA in New York where the chairs you projected became confused with those in common use in the museum. I also remember that in your exhibition at the Whitechapel in London you presented a sort of large phosphoric seat with which you offered to the public a lucid fruition of your work. Does a spirit of Fluxus exist in your work?*

"Of course! In fact I see my seats as graphics that can be used. This is precisely the imaginative leap from the everyday. Art disappears, you can sit on it, you can't see it anymore but it remains in your conscience."

*In the piece named* Invention *you propose once more a free fruition of the work. Is art an anarchic discipline, transformation of the world, or simple analysis of the principles that regulate the artistic system?*

"I could see the transformation of the world in the terms of Wittgenstein, who in his *Traktatus* claims: 'I am my world'. In this way I can also understand the rest. I don't think of it in a solipsistic way, but perhaps monadically."

*In the Padula Charterhouse you presented an installation which interacted with a piece by Tamuna Sirbiladze in which you portrayed the everyday and the arid banality of daily life. Do you wish to normalize art or resuscitate everyday life?*

"Both. But not in a missionary sense. I try to give life to eventual dispositions in an interactive way!"

*Contrary to Duchamp who created the metaphysics of the everyday through the ready-made, your innovation is subtle, silent and conceptual. Do you wish to promote the hierarchic succession between art and life, between poetry and prose, and bring about the democracy of a concentrated community that lives free from all conventions of relations with events? Where does the role of the artist-creator end and that of the creative public begin?*

"There was once a Chevrolet Malibu parked on the side of the street in Peekskill, New York. On 9 October 1992 a meteorite weighing 12.6 kilograms pierced it and created a crater under the car."

*You always accompany your work with performances that verge on music or theatre. Does multimedia aid creation?*

"The elements of multimedia are literally tied giving life to a creative act which however is not detached but maintains its relationship with the nature of my process of formal invention."

*Some times you have projected tables and chairs, as you did for RAM, and you have occupied an artistic space with the banality of everyday objects. Is art only analysis of its system, transgression, deconstruction, transformation, or is it liberation from the conventionality of thought and market? Do you consider yourself an undisciplined interdisciplinary?*

"Of course! The table which was sent to RAM is now called *Ramme* (sledgehammer) and I would like to do a video in which 4–6 people break down, or rather smash, a door. This is the disciplinary interaction that constitutes the theme of our conversation. It is the dissolution of the bark that is an integral part of our substantial fabric."

# Sisley Xhafa
## Pec, Kosovo, 1970

New York
2006

*Here we are with Sislej Xhafa, a Balkan artist from Kosovo, an Albanian who lives a cosmopolitan life between New York and now a little in Italy too. Xhafa is an artist with whom I have for years enjoyed an exchange of views, collaborations and invitations to exhibitions I have organized. He is an artist who works absolutely and paradoxically within a Duchampian realm, having eliminated any sign of indifference and neutrality from Duchamp's synergy, always introducing, on the other hand, a quality of estrangement which he expresses through the materials and the object itself, raising questions and developing a discussion on identity. I would like to start from his latest work, realized for an exhibition whose scientific project I directed, curated by Giusy Caroppo, in the castle par excellence, Castel del Monte, Frederick II's castle where Sislej created and presented a tormenting work. It consists of a painting, filtered through a photographic technique, in which a non-European figure embraces a heater. I found connections between this work and Leonardo da Vinci's* Mona Lisa, *where the figure of the non-European expresses a complicity but also a perplexity, a vagueness, a warm happiness. We can say that we have an object that, in some way, offers protection, and from which we can infer, if possible, the idea of the exodus, of nomadism, of being caught unprepared, of uprooting. I found this work to be very intense and particularly happy. This meeting can allow us to anticipate the round table of* Which Europe? *by asking Sislej Xhafa, a border artist in the most geographic and personal of the terms, if is it true that art has its own peculiarities or can it no longer help being boundless?*

"Identity. It's a very complex question and I believe that we have a European identity here too. The question of identity is something which quite rightly measures itself with the very old phenomenon of geographical relations. A question of presence and, above all, a new metabolism of reality itself which allows us through art, however, to address certain nationalized stereotypes taking on a creativity which must not however become a tool for art, because the artistic language must go beyond stereotypes and

"

nationalisms. In respect to the latter, I come from a certain country but today I feel Bolognese, tomorrow perhaps I will be Romanian. In my work *The Sun* there is a ray, not only intellectual; the presence of new identities, which are being formed and are following an interesting and healthy evolution in this country, is truly important."

*Have you finished? Laconic, as well as Balkan. I would now like to aim at something bigger and understand if we can say that your work has an ideological value. Apart from introducing an ethos of resistance, because I do believe that it contains an ethos of resistance and even a subjective and existential sense, besides an ethical sense, is it possible to talk about an ideology of art today in your work and in your research?*

"I personally believe that the role of the artist must simply be to do a good job, that's all. Then, quite rightly, critics and the others codify us."

*Don't be like Cucchi… I asked you a question, answer me otherwise I will torture you: is there an ideological importance to your work? From your point of view, not from mine, what do you think?*

"I don't think there is an ideology, because I don't care about leaning towards a position of refusal or one that goes in the opposite direction. I am more in favour of a collaboration. When I talk about collaboration I think that in the 1960s and 1970s we accumulated an extraordinary experience with the artists that worked on ideologies, on political relations. I think that today we don't need to be codified; personally I believe that there must be a type of collaboration. For example, I did something in a waiting room of the police station of Gand, I furnished it, transforming it completely."

*In what way?*

"It was an operational police headquarters and I fitted it out in a luxurious way, with big philosophy and human history books. I put whisky, champagne, a mirror from the eighteenth century."

*A brothel, practically…*

"Quite rightly the police invited people in. I am talking about this because I believe that I can find my brother, my father and my sister in the police force."

*You have a family of police officers?*

"No, I am speaking in general. They do questionable work for us, but instead of having a rigid position I believe it is possible through art to create a dialogue, create new spaces, ours, yours, create more welcoming spaces. The policemen of the police station were very happy about the installation because it didn't disturb their work. They continued working for a month and a half and then they asked me to transform three buildings, three floors into a real sculpture."

*You brought them whisky every day, I bet the police were happy.*
"Yes, bravo."

*Did you also bring them women? Don't the policemen of Gand chase women?*

"If the police go after women? I think so. Going back to the problem of ideology: we must not talk about left, or right. In this sense ideology doesn't exist anymore; there is indifference and this is topical. It's the result of an economic development and we must ask ourselves many questions without being ideological and try to collaborate. It's pointless saying: McDonald is no good. To do a work, to go about creating a reality, you must collaborate and, in my opinion, the collaboration today is surely more useful if we face the truth. Because it's true that the economy has no limits and thanks to this we are here. It is important not to protest but to collaborate and through this collaboration something worth reflecting on together could emerge."

*If art is the result of a purely ideological force it is schematic and one-way; art is, as I have always said, an oxymoron; it is complex, ambiguous and cross-eyed – therefore, in some way it goes beyond. So the artist can well be a conservative and produce a revolutionary work of art. I will give you some examples: Balzac is a conservative writer, Marx and Engels said that Balzac was one of the most revolutionary writers in that he had written* Eugénie Grandet. *All his novels are an important fresco of the society of the nineteenth century, developing a profound knowledge of the world. Céline, who was a wretched person at a human level, an anti-Semite, brought the French language to life through an absolutely impressive literature, so, as you can see, ideology escapes us and in the end it has a rich ambivalence and it allows us to drag it on our side, like a blanket, and there is no need for the artist to declare himself ideologically on the left or the right. I would like to say, without making political propaganda, that art is in the centre, in that it is nourishment, a matrix, a root which spreads, branches out, and opens itself to a thousand influences.*

"Personally, then, I believe that for each of us artists, doing a work does not take on a qualitative aspect, each of us does something in which he believes in. The rest belongs to the time of the critics, to those who will speak. I believe in a fresh attitude that takes you inside a space, whatever it be, a gallery, or a specific site in the city. The role of the artist is surely to trust himself, without this becoming something exhibitionist and a priority. Trusting oneself means also understanding one's capacities. The final product is then judged on the basis of the quality, in any case the role of the artist is to bring a fresh attitude. Art, the art work, is not even in the centre, it lies always underneath."

*Underneath what?*

"Underneath your trousers, underneath your jacket, underneath the table, always underneath."

*It's on top and underneath, not only underneath… I don't agree, because I want to remind you of the definition of the concept of the feast. In anthropological terms the feast overturns the everyday. The everyday is inhabited by a hierarchy, the feast is the space in which high and low, left and right, get confused continually. Art in this sense is the space of the feast in which under and over can get mixed up, where it is not even necessary to have the rhetoric of the underground, of the underneath at all costs.*

"No, I didn't mean that, I meant to say something else. When you are underneath, it becomes a process. When you are on top it becomes, however, a final work. Each one of us has energies, some stimuli that live inside, that's what I meant by underneath."

*And in your case, what work do you do? Which elaboration, which breathing exercises do you do?*

"With all respect to those artists who are painters, as far as I am concerned I don't even need a studio for example. My studio is everywhere."

*A fruit shop…*

"Bravo."

*Here we have a victim of Xhafa's work, a person who has bought a work called* Self-portrait *for his collection. What is this self-portrait like?*

"If I knew I wouldn't have done it. Personally, however, I ask questions with Art, as you know. However, I worked for three years thinking about how a self-portrait could be defined today. Then, in the end, after a lot of work, I finally understood that personally I am a watermelon, an organic watermelon that weighs nine kilos. And after two months, quite rightly, you throw it away because either you eat it or it rots… And then you go to the market and buy a new watermelon of nine kilos. I think this is the organic aspect of us living creatures. I am a man of the earth, I come from the earth. The other aspect is that we are made up for 90 percent of water, we are red and we are anyhow surrounded by a standardized world. The watermelon has these characteristics, then you judge for yourself…"

*So, tell me please what value does the research of a form have in your work.*

"Certainly the form is important, but it cannot be more important than the operation itself which must have the freshness in the novelty of the work itself."

*I believe that your work is not ideological because you do not have the presumption of ascertaining that art is an answer. Art is a question about the world, don't you agree? In this sense, you are a problematic Balkan artist. There is also an ironic power to your work. A great German writer called Goethe used to say: "irony is the passion that frees itself in detachment".*

"For one thing, irony is fundamental for me, above all for one reason, above all because it is an operation that leaves people room to think, that's not to say that I want to make a declaration. I respect all the declarations made by artists who apply them to their research with a precise aim. I personally don't apply them because I believe that declarations don't leave others room to think. For me, irony is an approach in which you give space to people where the spectator can define how to relate to the work, he can say: it makes me sick or everything is fine. That's it, you leave room, you create an approach that isn't manipulative. Irony is fundamental."

*How much participation and how much detachment is there in your work?*

"Active participation."

*When we did the last edition of the San Gimignano L'arte all'arte, founded by Mario Cristiani, you presented a little truck that used the Duchampian process, the famous work by Duchamp where sugar cubes become marble. But more important is the writing that accompanied the work close to the tree. I would like you to tell us how this work was born, what this writing says and if you can confirm what it says.*

"I must say, first of all, that this work was born as a site specific work. The artistic interventions completed in the city, in my opinion, are extremely difficult because they are works in which you must be very careful not to offend anyone, you must really share your work with people, that is with common people, the people that are not ready for art and that live in a society that sees art as something strange. Each of us has a particular sensibility. With these works I took into consideration the richness of the territory, the thing I feel is of fundamental importance in Montalcino: wine."

*It is also an aesthetic richness as well as a material one, of Tuscany and of Montalcino.*

"Then I even took marble into account, one of Carrara's products of a natural quality. I think that wine not only has positive effects but negative ones as well. I highlighted this fact with an operation in which an Ape 50 car weighing 6 tons, made of marble, capsizes."

*Yes, just like when a small truck skids off the road. And what does the writing near the tree say?*

"Wine is the richness of the territory and the Ape is a sign of the technical revolution."

*The Ape naturally is the name of a vehicle, but at the same time here is the ambiguity, one thinks of the beehive, thinks of the earth, of the farmer's society. Going on, another work that allowed the meeting in Teano between ABO and Xhafa was the Biennale of 1997. I walk inside the Biennale, go through the gardens and I see a young man coming towards me, dressed like a soccer player, with a ball under his arm, wearing a t-shirt. You continue the story...*

"We meet, I kick the ball, then we say hello. The operation that I wanted to carry out with this work, I repeat, was very important: I didn't want to use art as a nationalist instrument, as a stereotype. But in this case, given that the Biennale of Venice, I believe you can confirm this, represents firstly a political approach above the artistic approach, I made a simple observation: the Albanian pavilion didn't exist. I wanted to do something with this in mind that would question identities. I asked myself : how come Luxemburg with a population of only 300,000 had a pavilion but India with a population of 1 billion didn't? Did that mean that India didn't have artists? I wanted to do something, make a mobile pavilion, a pavilion that walked, a pavilion that didn't have a physical structure, architectural, something in itself. Walking and dribbling transformed itself into a soccer game. I would kick a ball and then someone would kick it back, and we would end up playing, trying to play as fairly as possible. Anyway, it was an event that was called *Clandestine Albanian Pavilion* in that I had entered the Biennale illegally: here we have it, this was the first challenge for me. I wanted to challenge myself and, above all, question something that goes beyond borders. It's correct to raise the problem, because my country is not only a developing country, it doesn't just engage in folkloristic activities, there are other things going on. There are people that come from developing countries where you find not only economic wealth but also cultural richness, like Italy which is in constant transformation. There is an identity crisis in Europe. I just wanted to highlight this fact: it's important not to manifest a colonial attitude, no offence to France, Holland and Great Britain. I didn't want an Orientalist attitude with statements that justify the capacities of the newly arrived, I didn't want geographical relations."

*You need to keep in mind that the Venice Biennale was born in 1893, thanks to the Mayor Selvatico of Venezia, who organized this project along the model of the Paris Universal Expo, where in the nineteenth century each country had its own exhibiting area to promote its national products. The Biennale of Venice has its Gardens with its pavilions that still today host the country and on which the nation has cultural sovereignty, while the territory belongs to the Municipality of Venice. When I was the director of the Venice Biennale in 1993 I faced this problem; I created a Biennale which*

*I called trans-national. Why? Because before 1993 there was still the model of the Universal Expo in place and it came back into being after 1993. What is the Universal Expo? It is the contraposition of differences. In 1993, however, I realized the coexistence of differences, getting Nam June Paik invited to the German pavilion, giving the Hungarian pavilion to Kosuth, hosting a number of artists from different countries in the so-called national pavilions, as is typical of a good Neopolitan, sneaking in artists who shared an affinity, to then reach Aperto 93, which has always been an exhibition of research par excellence and which I first curated in 1980 with 120 artists. After 1993, the pavilions closed up again. This idea was no longer to be because there was no longer a director who had the problem of overcoming the antiquated issue of identities of the Biennale like the Universal Expo, at heart. An old autarchic and national Biennale where each country always presented itself, came back into force. I even influenced the choices, it was me who pushed America into inviting Louise Bourgeois who was of French origin; I was interested in all this. Sislej basically defends the idea of a hybrid art, the coexistence of differences and the play of interpersonal relationships and contacts.*

"I believe in the individual creativity of the artist, leaving aside the nation. I say it openly and simply, I am from Kosovo. They ask you what your country is doing for you and what you are doing for your country. A simple question that starts from you. I lived in Italy for twelve years and so I love Italy, it's really a beautiful country. It has, however, many contradictions, negative things and aspects. I had bureaucratic problems when I lived in Italy, I sweated hard to get a residency permit. In the United States, where I have lived for the last five years, I got my permit just after one year, the green card, and within three years I will become an American citizen. Why doesn't Europe adopt the same system as the one used in America? Because the Americans are different, they are a new nation and we can't do things as they do but we can say that you must not look just at the economic aspect, we can improve things by basing them on a multicultural reality. We must confront ourselves with an identity that is always growing and is always different in every moment. I believe that art can do this. Art can question things."

*Last question and then we will finish off. I always offer one of my sayings for commentary. In your case, being a border artist in the system of art, I would like to ask you what do you think of this: "Some go down in history and others in geography"?*

"Some go down in history and others in geography… men make history, and then destroy it."

*And women make geography.*

"Yes, the women. But I believe that geography is our mental obsession. We think that we are living within a border but in the end it's always a question of sovereignty. I believe only in confronting oneself with others, but mine is not a defence, it is not insecurity that produces fear. We must try to understand others without judging them."

# Pier Paolo Calzolari
Bologna, 1943



*I want to begin this interview in 1967, the year in which I arrived in Bologna to direct a small avant-garde publishing house, Editrice San Pietro. It was during that year that I happily came across your work. When I walked into your studio I saw an installation that almost seemed like an apparition. It was an artificial lawn with a dove. What really stroke me was that it seemed that you already had inside an Eastern ability both of intervention and dissolution. At the time Bologna was bursting with ideologies, but your work didn't seem to be tied down or blocked by an art-politics correspondence. This is not because your work is lyric, it is in fact a mistake to consider Calzolari as a lyric artist, but because you are an artist that sends a philosophical observation through image. How did this first work come to life? The time in which this work was created is also very impressive: you did it in 1966 and it was supposed to be realized in 1967.*

"First of all I want to thank you for two things: one by mentioning that my work cannot only be referred to as lyric but that it contains an expansion attempt, and two by realizing – although this is part of your understanding qualities – that my work didn't mean to be an attempt to escape from Italian and Bologna's reigning ideologies of the time. That work didn't live in a particular idea or ideology. The imaginary theme, my curiosity, was a link with the Eastern world, and more precisely with Byzantium. It was in fact constituted by three classic Byzantium chromatic elements: green, red and white. There was the idea of the strength lines that, because of my affiliation with Venice, were probably virtual lines, those dove's lines that crossed the space. There was also the fact that people used to quickly march wearing red socks, almost moving in a compulsory way along the green lawn. Someone who truly understood what I was trying to say was Carlo Scarpa, the architect. He read it as a simple desire to aspire to Byzantium, to those key elements: three colours and some strong points represented by the red socks worn by people and by the flight flow of the doves. In this sense it is all anti-ideological."

*It has to be said that there was an element of participation because the public was invited to wear the red socks, to step in, to stop and to move. Which means that there was an active time element, which was also a generational trend. Walking out of the image, stepping off the frame, life's drive, blending life and art, paying respect to the public, giving it a main role, although it was a relative one since it was all about entering history of art. Do you agree that someway your work contributed to the idea of rendering life aesthetic?*

"I don't know whether you remember the title of the work, because you just hit the point. This work went by the name of *Progetto per un lavoro pubblico benvenuto all'angelo* [Project for a public work welcome to the angel]. The idea was to diversify the ideology of public relationship with the political relationship with the public, and therefore to lead it towards aesthetic. Regarding aesthetic, I've been formed or formed myself as an instrument; sometimes I wonder who made me instrument and who made me play, but in truth I formed within myself as an instrument that lives inside aesthetic. I consider aesthetic as an ethical/aesthetical relationship, as a blending. My work has certainly a strong complicity with all of those things that become aesthetical and that therefore become a reality that aesthetically and, consequently, ethically live in the world. With all the possible limits, since it's clear that I only move inside that discipline, in that measurement of things, I just wouldn't be able to do otherwise."

*I want to tell you that this is probably the reason why we never met so often, even though respecting each other. I want to publicly give you credit for having the courage to be a solitary artist. You took part in many personal and international collective exhibitions, to fellow artists' gatherings, but I truly believe that your solitude has been very constructive for your work, as well as being a destiny, a constraint, a suffering. Everything is ambivalent and bivalent. It wasn't a case that you prematurely introduced active temporality in your work. I remember that already by the end of the 1960s, you started to use primary elements such as water, ice, fire, temperature. This is why I've always seen your work moving from figurative to abstract and to entropy.*

"This process is very important."

*How did it start?*

"It's difficult to say; I can definitely say that my formation in Venice has had an important role, but then there would be so many things that I could say."

*Do Bologna's existential elements, for example its eroticism and vitality enter in your work?*

"Bologna formed me a lot, although sometimes in a negative way. Like when you talk about solitude: solitude is not an action, it's a heroic choice. Sometimes it is forced, but one is beneficial for the other."

*What do you mean?*

"To be forced is not just negative but it is also part of the construction of your reality. Something definitely very interesting that you said is that few critics and few readers sensed that my work starts from 'figurative' and moves towards abstraction. I believe, in a very simple and humble way, that this is how it started. I don't believe in abstraction as a deliberated leap from void to void. It in fact seems to be a daily and organically consumed distillation that makes things 'others', so much that they become abstract, although the starting point has to be strongly physical, otherwise it would all seem too uncertain and wouldn't touch my soul."

*What did the active representation of time in your work mean in such an existential atmosphere?*

"It's very strange, but it starts from a very simple and basic thing. I had my very first doubt about the relationship between time and tearing of things over time and about the primary and physical structure of the work, when I tried to paint the white that was reflected by the lagoon onto the marble at Riva degli Schiavoni. Using all of my skills, I tried six times to stop this sublime questioning moment of light over white. But the more I stopped the moments, the more it became a dead and rigid thing. I understood in a humble and indirect way that there was something that had to change. There was a relationship between light and reflection, both of marble and water, of indirect light that would consume and fall into matter. The first ice works were born from this: this is what ice's white is, not a technological matter. It is an idea that comes from my youth, a doubt, inability, powerlessness to witness this strange constant osmosis that existed within paint's classic terms. I can observe things differently today while before

I was forced to use different media especially because of the general art's context of the time, since before 1966 painting was dead, apart from some exceptional cases."

*There was American pop art on one side and the great Anglo-Saxon experience on the other.*

"It was becoming impossible to use painting for emotions and vitality, so I had to try to use other instruments even through Arte Povera."

*To revitalize painting through the use of extra materials, like Anselmo or Kounellis. I know, and I understood straight away your instinctive conscience and knowledge of the history of art. It is therefore clear that introducing time to devitalize painting's space was not a punishment. Can this time, this vibration that activates and modifies the image in every instant, also be anthropologically linked to your Jewish culture background?*

"Although in a very vague, faded and indirect way the Jewish link exists."

*For example?*

"From my mother and my stepmother. And also through the idea of condemnation and acceptance of each other, of a strong structure, of Christian-Catholic Western culture, which is very penalizing, and is based on bearing the other side that, on a theological level, has never refused the sentence and has accepted to carry it instead and to relate it in different contexts. This is the lesson that certainly comes from the cells, probably because of the DNA."

*And this is probably why we should also say that your work is un-iconic.*

"It even becomes un-iconic when I face the idea of still life, like I'm doing lately. I think I manage to remain un-iconic. There is an impossibility to codify an image, because an image has, in my formation and education, such a richness, such a resounding and returning echo, that can never set in iconography."

*In 1971 I invited you to the Paris Biennale and you won. We were all so proud that you won the Great Prize at the Young Artists Biennale in Paris, because it was the most important international prize at the time. We were all really happy, I also remember the great gallerist Sonnabend's joy. I remember that your work managed to capture the attention of the jury, of which I wasn't part of, not on-*

*ly through the scream of the work, but through its extraordinary shape, through your concentration that gets transformed into shape. It was as if you sucked the jury's attention towards the silence of your work, instead of making it scream ad attack. This is, in my opinion, another aspect of your work: to be able to carry the public on the verge of a silence that can communicate, understand, and contemplate your work. This is your works' Eastern aspect. Right?*

"It is absolutely so, and now please allow me a brief shift, digression – or maybe regression, I'm not sure. The idea of my work is very simple, it refers to a visit to a temple, and for temple I mean a synagogue as much as a Catholic church, or a mosque, there is no difference. What I want to say is that the physical space, the gathering place of attentive people, resounds with passage footprints, on symbols on marble, on carpet, on things. It simultaneously lives on things, on divulged ideas and on the idea of the thinnest and most hermetic moment. In brief, I've always seen the sculpting aspect of my work inside the temple in which resides the work of those who pay attention to the temple: the smells, the symbols on marble, on floors, on woods and rugs, to the whispers that were there, to the voice of desire that lives inside us, to echo's trace. There's also another part of my work that looks at sculpting in a physical way, considering the objectification, that always springs from a general context. As if the borders of a rug on which a person is concentrating on touch and close him in a space, an object dimension. I've always seen my work as something that moves within this objectification, that moves around the rug, the smell, the sign, and the entirety of the empty space, filled with voices and desires of the past. So there is a kind of fluctuation between objectification and an unsaid but induced totality. I don't know why I'm saying this, maybe because it's a less linear way to answer your question."

*We could say that you revitalized painting through sculpture.*

"I think we could say that, and it is quite singular. I think that by not giving one up I tried to ride the other, to touch it, to see how one could vibrate into the other. I don't think that they are such different fields. They belong to your and others' desire. It's a crossing point that lives inside everyone's desire. In any case I've never seen such a fracture between them, so I tried to live them both."

*What is the relationship between your work and the real space in which you arrange it? Is it just a further expansion of a frame?*

"It is a very difficult question, because it's not always possible to choose the perfect space. Celebrating the union between your work and space is not always possible. It should be the temple's recreation, where the work is able to bang and vibrate. Where the temple becomes prayer with a wrapping humour. I confess that it is not always this way, it is very difficult to happen, but this would be the ideal situation."

*Your work always seems to appear like an epiphany. This epiphany needs to have a friction with the space that is going to hold it. This is going to be a laic space: a gallery, a museum, a collector's home, an alternative space. In any case we know that it is not going to be a temple. And I think that this friction, this de-placement can add further fascination to the work.*

"It's a charming question, but I believe that there certainly is a clash between a laic space and what we define as other, but this fight, this right desire, is the artist's right to make a laic space vibrate and to recreate the epiphany for a moment, for an instant, by chance. In short, I claim the artist's right to constantly look for an epiphany. It is something very objectionable, very questionable, but it definitely is an artist's and a dreamer's right. Betting and surprise happen when a dreamer manages to slightly make his epiphany vibrate, to give a sound of desire to a laic space and to harmonize the two even just for a second, overpowering in this way the codification and rigidity of laic history."

*Yours is definitely a dynamic epiphany which with the ice introduction seems (following the great Venetian school) to be a memory, an attempt to capture light. So what do the fire, the flame and the candle flame mean in your work?*

"I often tried to find some answers to these very questions. I don't think it is neither an archaic nor a primitive matter. I actually think that they represent a memory, a prayer, the daily action of repeating, of summoning. The first emotional action that, although repeated, still remains *the emotional act*. It is the moment in which you do something for someone, or for yourself of for anything close. Fire or small flame are a gateway moment from the daily poverty of your being. It is quite related to the idea of prayer,

374

even though not church prayers. We can say that it is the moment of suspension from the desire of linearity."

*Does the use of these primary elements find its origin in Jung or Freud?*

"If I had to choose I would probably say Jung, but considering how his theories have been used I find it difficult to take a side. Let's say that it is a way to peacefully accept the habits that have been left behind, not always with consciousness, but not randomly abandoned. It's like a dance moment, where people try to communicate with God and can't find the right language, where an adaptor has the ability to be a corporal and sign translator for people's confused requests addressed to an entity that is another. This is the primary elements' use."

*At some point during the 1960s you decided to freeze the light and introduced neon. It was as if this vibration would solidify. What did this shifting in your work mean?*

"Sometimes it is just like a mixed idea of light. That is like the use of natural, candle and neon light or two light spheres that unite and blend without any contradiction like two fireflies, not lights. Otherwise I used neon to make writings. It was a relationship, a whisper: I always saw poetry as something exceptional, something endemic, something that you don't want to have, but if you have it you don't want anyone to touch it. You can even go down a tube station and be surrounded by tired and pale people when suddenly a bell rings and it's poetry again, embracing you and absorbing you and assaulting you – actually, successively assaulting you. I find the written letter – and I appreciate the element of poetry – to be something to decode and analyse. I find the attempts to formalize flashes in neon, small segments of poetry, from Chlebnikov to Pound or, in an infinitesimal way, of small writing attempts that try somehow to be and to get close to poetry very awkward; but in another case the use of these artists, of these poets certainly speaks of a voice, of a bell that follows you and assaults you when you are very far from it. You go to a factory, to an office, to a war and I don't know why but this inner voice embraces you. I believe that it is something that creates a sculptural space, something that physically occupies a space. Therefore whatever I used that wasn't in relationship with light, which is the way, I almost always used it in this sense. An attempt to take this writing and send it back to the space that concerns poetry, the plastic space, in the same way that masses have a voice and sound, if we just want to listen to them. It is very simple and naïve but this is how it is."

*Don't you think it has also something to do with Bible's statement "In the beginning was the Word"?*

"I simply think: word was. I can't even think of saying "in the beginning" because without it I don't have any knowledge, I don't even have light."

*What does the introduction of word through your writing mean in your work?*

"The hope for it to become sculpture somehow, to be a relaxed and flexible voice that organizing itself in a plastic way can create a central point between who's looking, who is perceiving and me. That it may acquire visual axes, strength lines, strengths that are certainly not Tintoretto's ones. They are sharing signals. It is a writing that, if possible, tries to find its voice through plastic lines. It isn't a very well organized sentence but this is exactly what I mean."

*You employ materials such as lead or tobacco, where the first represents endurance and plasticity and the second reminds of smoke and consumption. Is there a dialectics beginning in your work?*

"I don't want to say this, I want to declare it, but I would also like to use your flow of ideas to talk about Arte Povera. I believe that some basic points that Western culture doesn't put into use certainly represent the Franciscan dimension, that teaches to democratize and Orientalize things. As Saint Francis used to say, this means that it is necessary to listen and to give voice to the spiritual and camouflage abilities to become able to understand, to be similar to the voice of things, to matter, to people, to creatures and to beings. A creatural sense that can be interpreted in its most material aspect. Following these ideologies we can say that one of the many Franciscan senses is to pay respect to things. It is similar to horizontality, to water's murmuring and it establishes a relationship based on mutual dignity and listening. It makes matter a rich humoural voice, a very strong creatural voice."

*Saint Francis spoke to human beings and creatures. Do you speak to materials?*

"I don't see a big difference, after all sound and wind change depending on things and materials. Matter has a voice: lead is tearful, very sad, vast, grotesque, baroque and violent, humbly repeating and copying what it covers. What I want to say is that I don't believe animals to have a different life from things."

*Do you agree if I say that, on a critical level, there was a dogmatic use of the Arte Povera word during the 1960s and 1970s?*

"I totally confirm it. During the late 1960s and early 1970s I wrote a text that went by the name of *Casa ideale* [Ideal Home] that was later used in different situations and that was addressed as Arte Povera's house, which wasn't its sense. For me it was the house in which I looked for horizontality. In my opinion it was used totally contradicting those strong ideological paradigms that opted to justify the Arte Povera."

*This is because ideology usually excludes, whereas you tend to include. You celebrate cohabitation, you celebrate coexistence. Is this Franciscan?*

"It could be, but I think this is based on another level: in this context Arte Povera is certainly the only twentieth-century non avant-garde movement. By this I mean that it is not a very Western movement, since avant-garde has always been a Western, Oedipic pyramidal direction."

*This is what I call linguistic terminism. Can you explain me why you do not consider Arte Povera as an avant-garde movement?*

"Because I think that many artists tried to have an horizontal relationship rather than a vertical or pyramidal one. We can say that a vertical relationship would be the idea of avant-garde as a negation. This is a careful cohabitation attempt, a moment that gets formed and legitimized from indicative and edifying attitudes, in abnormal situations that have their starting point in the year zero, in Gutai."

*I believe and also wrote that Arte Povera is more linked with Fluxus and Gutai rather than simply being inspired by the vitality of Futurism. For example I wrote that Zorio is linked to Fluxus, while I think that you could be connected to Gutai and Mono-Ha. Is this possible?*

"Not only it is possible, but I actually wish it to be this way. I think that in this way Arte Povera can be read as a more elastic, rich and vast idea rather than the one of merely being a *post-futuristic movement.*"

*There is a strong ethic of coexistence in your work that, as it later happened, led you to have your own style of painting. You also used an instrument that has a very important history in Western art, also from the point of view of a linguistic evolution.*

"During 1972 I was profoundly thinking about the horizontal questioning of the matter, and it was an attempt to revitalize painting, the mother of things, by re-codifying it – although I felt that it couldn't be a leap in the dark. This is why I started by doing a few corporal monochromatic paintings, using object and sound structures in a painting context. I'm not going to tell you about the results because there was also a suspension and condemn moment. Probably because I wasn't happy with this passage I took three or four *télescopage* years, studying painting in its totality. Three conscious sabbatical years where painting would spring in the precise point that I wanted, where the highly tactical greys of seventeenth-century painting could re-emerge. I interrogated myself till I had no more requests to satisfy, and then I went back on my path. Even in this case painting managed to give me matter, richness and confrontations. I find that what I've done in 1972 has been very positive and I'm still able to use that experience today. I obviously don't see any fracture from my point of view."

*The use of colour in your work has a very high quality. Compared to the general cultural atmosphere it wasn't afraid but it had a ring to it and its own eroticism. It had a sort of joy to live that was in contrast with the sense of guilt that politics was trying to introduce in the artistic world during those years to decrease cyclostyle artists and guardian angels, almost pushing them to resign from their solitary, aristocratic, subjective and creative status. Is that so?*

"It is for me. I don't know if my vision about art and painting can be considered aristocratic, but it's certainly high."

*You have always maintained a strong subjectivity when talking about art or used extra-pictorial materials. You've always kept your ego, your subject and subjectivity; is painting an almost hedonistic confirmation of this presence?*

"I probably have some hedonistic aspects, merits or sins, but I certainly never nurtured them. I always portray myself in the same way, repeating the same sentences. The first one is my big problem, that is tearing me apart since I was a boy and it refers to what I said before: who made me an instrument, and who plays me. I say this stating that I'm a laic and not a religious person. Despite this is a clear problem followed by consequences, one can imagine from these topics who makes you instrument and plays you. And the second important thing to mention is the one that I declare through my work: what happens to the dream when the dreamer dies? This is a question that expropriates the egocentric and ideological position of the artist, shifting it towards a slightly vaster context."

*So art is not an answer, otherwise it would become a sort of dogma, and I agree with this. Art is a question. Is art a question?*

"Yes, I totally agree with it. Art is in fact a constant question, first of all for the artist. It is a question in itself, a desire in itself, a defined longing, but it can never be the possibility for an answer or a definition."

*At some point you introduced sound in your work, music, with a sort of Wagnerian spirit to it, an idea of a total art. Is it possible to look at it in this way?*

"Although I respect Wagner very much and I have a big sympathy for his music, I think that the Occitan or Northern Spanish cloisters, where the faithful sing hymns to the saint to whom the church or cathedral is dedicated, are a more humble and less pompous answer. I see art as an attempt to assemble totality. It was a sixteenth-century's idea that said that art's highest point was a great Leonardesque painter, or a princely fishing's great preparation, where everything was used, from falling water sound effect to science. I believe that art's reference point is an ensemble of emotional and instrumental relationships."

*I've always observed that you tend to "sit" your works. There is always a non-rhetoric and non-monumental aspect to it. There is always a soft material. Is the mattress the space where the artist dreams? Is the meeting with the public in a dimension of drowsiness possible?*

"It has to be. I believe that the artists' desire for a dimension of drowsiness is necessary for their cohabitation with art and with the intelligence of dreams. In any case, I definitely consider it an inertial and essential passage for a moment of participation to art."

*Moving forward from the 1990s to today, in the early years of 2000 your work began to consider the issue of entropy. Is art anti-entropic or the perfect place for entropy?*

"These are questions that you ask people like you, people who work on art's existential problems. I'm an artist so I'm not able to answer this question. But I believe that maybe art isn't and shouldn't be entropic, although it is true that sometimes the answers to the world that surrounds us or the use of analytical abilities towards the world are entropic. I think that when an artist is living or perceiving this moment has to avoid public and listeners."

*I think that by introducing real time through the elements, like water and fire, you produce entropy, but with an anti-entropic aim and hope. What does hope represent for you as an artist?*

"Difficult question asked to a man that is an artist. Hope is the filling of what you don't have. It is the ambition of what you can sense but it's not the sense of filling a void, it's a fierce project, a way of being, that tends to plan things daily, to decipher things in a too explicit way."

*Your creative adventure works, in a very existential and philosophical way, within the reality of your starting always from a humble understanding. According to you, is a constant state of imperfection necessary to make art?*

"I would say so because I agree with those basic elements dictated by people such as Guénon. I follow art's idea of perfection, mainly in its aesthetic function but especially in its primary one, which is for example the function of who makes a table or an object that encloses or has to enclose something. To make a table means to think on who is going to use it, who will sit on it or at it. To make a table that is completely stable and suitable for who is going to lean on it is a work of art in itself. I try to rescue simplicity from the marshes of ideology."

*Through your work you've tried to broaden materials' demography as well as your sensitive state and to hook it to the contemplation of the social body. This is its original starting point, but*

*I think that your work has an ascending dimension. This is the last question. I say that your work could be described with this sentence: "fight with the angel". I remember a ladder in one of your works, what is that ladder?*

"The ladder is a symbolic element, and it certainly has an ascension will to it. The problem with it is that we don't know how many steps or passages it has. There is also a strong complicity between the ladder and who climbs it, a participation. It is clear that the ladder has an ascending-symbolic function, but it all depends on how it is formed. It can have more or less steps, it can be more or less steep, but it cannot be decisive on its own. A ladder can only live depending on who climbs it, step by step, as if praying, accepting the multiple passage. It represents an ascending action, but it is also very cruel because your time is ending while you climb and it precisely settles your prayer, will and desire's potential. So in that precise moment my will is ascending, but is a very cruel, qualitative and selective ascension."

*What is the demon in your work?*

"Non-continuity. The gap between a moment of work and another. It's the doubt of dementia, of losing the thread, or to find the thread again but in a wrong way that leads me to wrong observations and to false frenzies and desires. Demon means to lose desire. This is the only demon that I truly feel in my work. I could also say complacence and self-appreciation – that is another big demon."

*I think, and you confirmed it, that in your relationship with words, drawing and writing there's a will of sealing the work with your handwriting. Would you say you owe something to the great German Romanticism?*

"It is true that I wrote about the sublime and that this automatically takes you back to German Romanticism, but in reality I link my work to the Italian cultural whirl of complexities. I connect it to the sixteenth-century idea of the sublime, where sublime didn't coincide with beauty, and beauty didn't coincide with good will. Beauty was becoming cruel. And when it was cruel, when the saint's masturbation became a moment of total corruption, in that moment Pan's veil ripped, and what was blessed wasn't blessed anymore but it became a slurry, rich and emotional blending instead. I see the sublime as it was seen in Italy during the sixteenth century. So I don't think I owe anything to German Romanticism that, considered individually, I don't even like."

*Does your distance from German Romanticism rise from the fact that it is nocturnal? An hymn to the night? Is yours an hymn to the light?*

"Yes it is, because this hymn to the night is the attempt of an alibi, an attempt to hide that this can be done in broad daylight and that it isn't a gateway but a daily pragmatism. I believe that for German Romanticism the night often becomes a pretentious alibi, a moment to move away from life-line and from straight-life. And I think the right way is not nocturnal but in the daylight, where conflicts and pitiful things become sublime, striking, clear, not lunar but solar. I believe that the idea of daytime and the sun is important because it creates a clear fracture between two moments: the idea that the cruel, the sunny, the daytime, the sublime, the pietas, the tragedy, the abnormal and the maniac are the magma of daily pathos and the idea that it is instead a confusion allowed by the nocturnal."

*Does your statement of being an Italian and Mediterranean artist take you to confirm the existence of a genius loci in your work?*

"I can definitely say it exists: there is no doubt about it. There are many genius loci in Italy; there is such a high concentration and cohabitation of different genius loci that makes Italy a very spoiled and lucky country because it has the chance to live in this mosaic of hundreds of influences. What is very interesting is the different culture between *genius loci* that come from different areas. Still, they cohabit with each other. The richness of the Italian artists is that they have always been able to cohabit, to be a plurality, and this goes from Squarcione to Roman art."

*Yet you lived with a generation of artists who worked in a Duchampian way on the idea of internationality, neutrality and objectivity of language. Is there a difference between you and some of your colleagues of the time?*

"Of course there are. Arte Povera's group of artists was a constellation of different methods that sometimes would collide or slightly touch but there was a bifurcation, there were differences. I'm not condemning anything, I just want to publicly admit that I have a big difficulty in absorbing Picasso when only three years earlier Monet was working on his *Water Lilies*, and then move on to Pollock. I have problems thinking about Bonnard's lights, or about Duchamp's mean and extreme intelligence. Duchamp was in my opinion a man who, in a very bourgeois way, especially hated art although loving it at the same time. To be able to absorb art, he used to first destroy it in a Cartesian way. I am on the other less winning side, and I can't do otherwise but to define myself as Italian and Mediterranean artist."

*So wouldn't you say that in your work and in art in general exists a typical avant-garde value of language discovery?*

"I would say so, but in the way in which a window gets divided in five, three and two parts, in a double and triple lancet window. In the same way that Japanese art manages to suddenly find language and sound within a total loss. Of course language discovery exists, it is possible for at least five languages, different cultures and dialects to cohabit, but not as a new language: I basically don't believe in Esperanto."

*Language discovery typifies Western art, but you have your own system and cohabitation ethic; you are also open to an Eastern spirituality and this attitude of coexisting differences constitutes the deterrent of your whole creative painting.*

"My answer is yes. Undoubtedly rondo is the *Leitmotiv*, but what really stimulates me to make art is constituted by these elements, by the coexistence that constantly jumps from an image to an idea and then back slightly changed. I wouldn't have any interest or curiosity otherwise."

*Good.*

# Dan Graham
Urbana, Illinois, 1942

New York
2007

*I think that you are the conceptual artist who has shown by far the greatest capacity to take conceptual art out of its tautology and who has had the greatest effect on behaviour with your analyses.*

"Before that I was doing magazine pages, I was doing conceptual things earlier, pages of magazines. In fact, Joseph Kosuth had a stupid idea of tautology. My work was more like Roy Lichtenstein's, it was sarcastic humor, and maybe it was closer to Stanley Brown."

*The question is this: your openness. For example, let us take* Lax, Relax, *a work from 1969…*

"It was about Dean Martin. Dean Martin had a television programme. Everybody thought he was drunk and lazy, because he was Italian and in America everybody was trying to relax, but America was very puritan and to relax was a bad thing, to be lazy was a bad thing. People thought that Dean Martin was a lazy Italian and they thought he was immoral because everything was lax. He had sexual affairs with everyone, he was drunk supposedly, but my piece is a little bit like a therapy, it's like yoga, it's like 'breathing in' and 'breathing out', and so the audience was also breathing in and breathing out.

The idea is that women had to relax, breathe in and breathe out, relax, and the men also had to relax, breathe in and breathe out. So you hear the breathing and of course men come closer to women… The rhythm becomes closer, it's like a good sexual relation and the audience hears and sees each other breathing, so they become more and more relaxed and start breathing again."

*Your work also establishes a relationship with anthropology. I'd like to know whether you agree and in what sense.*

"I agree."

*Why?*

"You are correct. When I was thirteen years old I read the books of Margaret Mead because her books were involved with sex. Margaret Mead was an anthropologist interested in feminism. I also read Lévi-Strauss… It was about the family from an anthropological point of view, against sociology. It's not critical, it's political, but making jokes. My work was very much influenced by Oldenburg."

*Oldenburg and…?*

"And Roy Lichtenstein. Especially Lichtenstein and also Flavin."

*At the end of the 1960s, conceptual art concluded with a reflection on itself. You are the only artist who instead uses your analysis to tackle reality, social, political, anthropological…*

"Well, I think what relates me to conceptual artists like Laurence Weiner is poetry. For instance in my first work, *Homes for America*, I was very much influenced by the *French New Novel*, that was related to Flaubert. *Homes for America* was a kind of poetry. Also I was really very much related to Jean-Luc Godard. And I was related to rock 'n' roll, the Beatles, Nowhere Men… It was all about the suburbs. That was a bad cliché. My work was a kind of poetry, like Lawrence Weiner's. I think that his early work was amazing although he didn't do conceptual art until 1968. Lawrence and Kosuth didn't even work before 1968. Kosuth did not invent anything at all, but I shouldn't say this, because he is like the pope, he is a very important person in Rome and I should not say nothing bad about the pope."

*What importance do psychoanalysis and Freud have in your work?*

"I think my work comes from a more popular psychology. In the 1980s, it was all about social psychology, social therapy. In the 1960s everybody had his own psychological idea. I was more interested in Marcuse."

*The Frankfurt School?*

"No, Wilhelm Reich."

*Do you remember* The Sexual Revolution*?*

"Yes, but do you know Félix Guattari? He was a psychoanalyst of the Russian school. And Marcuse took a lot from Wilhelm Reich. I remember that I had a Russian therapist in the early 1970s."

*You know that in America, when John Kennedy was president of the United States, Wilhelm Reich's books were burned because they were considered immoral?*

385

"No! That was the Eisenhower period. Because of the worry about communism."

*I think that they were burned because Reich tried to create a connection between Karl Marx and Sigmund Freud. It was the presence of Marxism that upset people.*

"Reich was a Marxist."

*Wilhelm Reich had created a machine that liberated people, which was called "orgone box". But on the plane of analysis he was important.*

"That was late in his life, he was completely crazy. You understand that his most important theory was that cancer is caused by the fact that people feel guilty and hold everything in their body. Reich said that cancer was psychosomatic, and I think he was right."

*Reich's most important idea was the analysis that he made of the failure of the Russian revolution, drawing on the concept of submissiveness to authority. He said that the revolution had failed because the political class that had carried it out was shaped by tsarism. It had had an education characterized by a deep mental block and this had led to the development of a hierarchized society, a society of the submissive-authoritarian type.*

"No, I think it's the Russian character."

*What function does art have for you?*

"The country that opened his arms to Wilhelm Reich was Yugoslavia. There was this very famous 1971 film titled *WR: Mysteries of the Organism* by Dušan Makavejev."

*Does art have a liberating function for you?*

"I agree with Marcuse that art should be a bad play. Reich wanted to go towards our origin. He spoke about the sexuality of children. Also in my work I go back to the early impressions of my childhood."

*So is that why you sometimes develop an interactivity in your work? Because interactivity avoids a static, authoritarian contemplation? Because interactivity makes the public a protagonist?*

"When I was fourteen years old I read Jean-Paul Sartre's *Being and Nothingness*. He talks about the child becoming a person when the child sees himself seen by other persons. I was very much influenced by what I read when I was fourteen."

*Then in the 1970s your work progressively opened up to architecture. What is the relationship between art and architecture in your work?*

"In the early 1970s I was reading Michel Butor's book *La Modification*, and Aldo Rossi read the same book, and I was very involved in city planning. My first work concerning architecture was a suburban city plan. I thought then that the idea of the white cube of the gallery was a stupid idea, I was more interested in relating my work to the urbanistic plan. But my biggest influence was science fiction and especially a film by Elio Petri: *La decima vittima* (1965)."

*I remember. You use transparence in the construction of your structures. What is transparence in you opinion? A motif of continuity with the world, with society? Or is it a way of avoiding the isolation of art?*

"I do not absolutely want to create isolation. My work is part of the landscape. When I use curved material in a park, through the reflection boys see themselves very big like supermen. On the opposite and convex side women see themselves very thin and beautiful. I think that the most interesting fact in the 1990s is the phenomenon of narcissism, people had one child, they bought things for the child and things for themselves as children. I deconstruct that idea."

*I remember that at Documenta you showed this work in which there was a glass wall and behind it the action of a performance. What was the glass wall in that case? Did it allow the public to see, but separate it from the action? What was it then? Was it a form of isolation of art? Of separation?*

"What? Which one do you mean?"

*Perhaps it was Jan Hoet's?*

"Jan Hoet didn't want me in his Documenta. He was really against me. I was the very last one in his Documenta because he didn't want me to be included in the show. There was no space for me."

*There was this thing, there was this wall of glass.*

"I did an environment in 1981."

*1976, Venice Biennale (it was the work* Public Space/Two Audiences *for* Arte-Ambiente).

"That was the best show Germano ever did. It was a very important piece for me."

*Why?*

"The Venice Biennale was like a world sphere and every country had its own pavilion. And what I did was a showcase window situation. And the people became the objects. I was interested in the perception process. So they saw each other seeing each other through the glass and wanted to communicate. What I was trying to show was the sociological relationship. I think it was a very important piece but I made a mistake because I used a white wall. But the show was so incredibly good. The team was good."

*A good exhibition.*

"Very good."

*What importance does light have in your environments?*

"It's very important. For me light is very important, it's absolutely crucial. My work is not so different from Mies van der Rohe's. I deal a lot with landscape. My real mentor in art was Dan Flavin. Of course Flavin learned a lot from the Parson school. He was going to become a priest.

*A Protestant priest?*

"He was Catholic."

*Who? Flavin?*

"He was Irish and German. But now I am referring to him in terms of light."

*I think that in his work there is also a kind of romantic sensibility.*

"It's not conscious, but I think it's probable, because Flavin is very cold. But he's romantic. In 1991, in the Carnegie, I put a piece at the entrance. I'm not as cold as Flavin."

*Yes. But light in Flavin is neutral, it's statistical, it's eternally the same. In your works light has a rhythm in time, because there is transparence.*

"But actually Flavin's things should be seen outside. His outside pieces are amazing. I think Flavin is more expressionist than I am."

*What function does time have in your work?*

"It's very important. First I smoked marijuana. I was very

much influenced and involved by the music of Steve Reich and
La Monte Young and finally I was really influenced by science
fiction. Science fiction in the 1960s was all about time paradoxes.
I also studied physics. We all were really interested in Eisenberg
in that period."

*Planck?*

"Well, I don't know Planck but I know Eisenberg."

*The idea of elimination. And music?*

"Well, I was introduced to Boulez and also to Luciano Be-
rio. He had a cetain influence on Michel Butor. But I prefer rock-
'n'roll, especially psychedelic rock'n'roll from Los Angeles. And
The Kinks from England. For me music is spiritual, almost a religion."

*And Richard Wagner?*

"No, I don't know Wagner. But I have the same birthday
as Bach. In fact, I do prefer rock'n'roll. I prefer Chuck Berry to
Wagner."

*I like Chuck Berry too. But I asked this question because you
lean towards an idea of total art. This idea has its origin in Richard
Wagner.*

"In fact I just change what I do often. The most total art
I've done is my rock'n'roll publisher. I like Jean-Luc Godard."

*À bout de soufflé / Breathless?*

"Not so much. I like the architecture."

*Do you know Libera?*

"I've never seen Libera. I have such an enormous love for
Terragni, specially his *Casa Rustica*."

*You know what we call this architecture? Rational-fascist.*

"We call it Rationalism."

*They were fascist architects who took their inspiration from
Rationalism.*

"But you have to understand that for Mussolini social housing was important. Actually the *Casa Rustica* in Milan is amazing social housing."

*The Casa del Fascio in Como. What relationship is there be-
tween Terragni and your pavilion (Portal, 1994)?*

"Terragni was an idealist."

*Why?*

"Because he believed in social housing, he believed in religion. He was a Catholic. He also was in love with Dante. He was an innocent person."

*And you? You are not innocent? You are American, so you are guilty.*

"No I'm an Aries. Terragni is an Aries… he also loved Futurism."

*For me your work is very important because you go beyond minimalism, beyond conceptual art, beyond rationalism. You complete this idea of an art that is born from a project. That's why I said total art, with psycho-sensorial elements and an interactivity with the public. So in this sense it is a social art.*

"Well, I have to say that minimalism is no such thing. Carl Andre loves Constantin Brancusi, and Dan Flavin loved Barnett Newman. I am sure that people think that minimal art wasn't psychological. But it was psychological in fact. I believe that Donald Judd was a very frightened person. Things are really complex. But there is a kind of misunderstanding. One thing about Sol LeWitt you have to understand: his work is full of humor. He told me that his structures are like playgrounds for his cats. Also Roy Lichtenstein was very emotional. He was a Scorpio and his first wife was schizophrenic. So the woman who cries is his wife. Of course I had to break with minimal art and I took another direction."

*The last question. Nature: what weight does it have in your work?*

"I think the sky is very important. But actually I'm influenced by Michael Snow."

*Me too. I like him. He is a Canadian artist.*

"Yes. You know Michael Snow's best friend was Steve Reich? And I was a friend of Steve Reich too. For me, the baroque is really important. In the 1980s and 1990s you find a new fashion, the postmodern buildings of corporations, they became kind of baroque. But of course I absolutely prefer the nineteenth century. Georges Seurat for example, and maybe for my interest in light. That's why the sky is so important."

*And Magritte?*

"I don't think I know so much about Magritte."

*To end: why are you still an artist in 2007?*

"Being an artist I can meet brilliant students, and I'm also very influenced by the ideas of the students. And because as an artist I can get air tickets to travel. I don't get business class but I get the travel."

*That's a Flavin-style answer!*

# Maurizio Nannucci
Florence, 1939

Florence
2007

*We both know that your creative path started from a deep experience with concrete poetry. In what way did the composing method of such experience subsequently influence your work?*

"In my experience concrete poetry meant opening my artistic practice to a linguistic observation and to experiment a synthesis between image and word, meaning and context. It meant creating works in which spontaneous intuition, rules, rational structure but also unforeseen and random situations would merge. The radical use of the text as medium favoured the abandon of any traditional support. During those years it was necessary to overtake the historical-geographical limits of an environment and to look for a vaster international reference territory in which to operate and confront each other. By then I was already trying to travel as much as possible, taking distance from the place where I lived. My interlocutors where from all over the world: Germany, Brazil, United States or Japan. This meant expanding one's horizon, being able to look beyond, to send signals and receive answers. We were in the middle of the 1960s, and I was then participating in the first real international artists network, which was set up as a 'new territory for perceptibility', where painters, musicians, poets and philosophers coming from different disciplines, cultures and ideologies would commit to begin an observation on the artist's role and the ways of interpreting a work of art through language. My *mind machine*, my creative medium, was at the time a small Olivetti typewriter… white and coloured papers… my studio was a desk, wherever I was! At the same time as I was working on the hundreds of pages that would compose the *Dattilogrammi*, created between 1964 and 1966, I was interested in sign and notation systems related to sounds. I worked at the Musical Phonology Studio of the Florence Academy of Music for more than five years, realizing sound effects, electronic music and computer music. I used to get very stimulated when working in a group because individual identity would disappear, merging into an open project that would result in a collective work. This was very distant from the artist's individualism I was accustomed to, and it was something that from then on became a constant practice for me. Apart from the semantic potential that made possible an image elaboration based on the signifier/signified, sign/image, I was attracted by the white's page potential, because it represented the symbol of a new space. It wasn't just about filling that space – I preferred emptiness to abundance. Environment to page. Urban space to painting. Concrete poetry looked into linguistic and typographic systems and structures such as tautology, which would later become a fundamental aspect of conceptual art. During those years experimenting was pushing beyond, taking for granted a series of results. Going over the page's borders I could sense that the problem was space, intended as a medium. So I moved my attention onto problems dealing with communication and linguistic visibility inside the urban environment."

*As if to say that you moved from eye measurement to cognitive body knowledge.*

"I gained a better knowledge of the context in which I was operating when, in 1967, some of my *Dattilogrammi* appeared in Emmett Williams' *Anthology of Concrete Poetry,* a book that gathered authors and artists coming from apparently different backgrounds like Fluxus or minimal and conceptual ones. Concrete poetry had truly been a multidisciplinary fusion and a key platform for the linguistic turn of all those new artistic experiments that were moving away from painting. During that same year I created works such as *M/40*, a sort of typewriters' keyboard mapping, a sign for each page, a series of infinite combinations and textures; *Faber Polychromos*, a catalogue or list of the chromatic scale of a box of crayons, where each of them was consumed on a sheet of paper; or *Alfabetofonetico*, my first neon writing. As you well know since we met during that time, concrete poetry and electronic music have been fundamental for my experience: an open door through which I could penetrate the links between light and space, continuum and discreet, provisional and definitive, a nucleus of concepts that would have a central role in all of my work."

*In what way did the analytical singularity of the poetic experience impress a conceptual mark to your work?*

"My constant challenge is to stimulate an analytical approach to reality. I've always favoured the cognitive processes of artistic actions: the analysis of codes, entropy and reduction against formalism, eye satisfaction and the *Gegenwelt* of illusion. It has to be said that by analysing communication systems I want to emphasize the potential freedom of imagination that comes out of these choices and that often has not the possibility to emerge. Since then my practice has remained positively suspended between the medium's reality and the experience of the subject."

*During the 1960s and the 1970s there was a constant ideological and political pressure that also broke into the world of art. Do you think that the works you did during those years have to be still looked at in the same way?*

"The dynamics of the new avant-garde practices and the elaboration of alternative systems of diffusion were the references I carried on together with my research, always bearing in mind their ideological and political potential. The Situationist utopia of *détournement* suggested appropriation practice as a medium to create a permanent transformation of the world. This is how a series of political actions of mine were born: numerous publishing enterprises, the organization of exhibitions and events, the creation and collective management of no-profit areas such as Zona – founded during the 1970s – and Base art projects, active since 1998. All of these 'artist's actions', whether carried out alone or in a group, gave me the chance to acquire knowledge and to reflect; they have been moments of great creative freedom that gave birth to a series of events (some of them inedited) such as the Piccola Stampa exhibitions, artists' books, artists' audio works sound archives and Zonaradio, a real radio station dealing with this type of experience. And finally there's the Zona Archives project that gathers materials and documents concerning any artistic marginal practice from the 1960s up to our days, thousands of documents that can be consulted and used as part of a great collective and personal diary. This project is an essential aspect of my artistic work. It lives together with the big neon installations, with the thousand photographs featuring botanical gardens, with artist's books and with my 'multiples'. It is an open attempt, still in progress, to help us reflect on our own cultural, social and political identity."

*Are words in your work a medium or a vaporization of sense?*

"I'm interested in fluid, flexible, and easy to shape and transform materials, where the non-material meaning gets close to the zero point of representation, to be able to intervene, moulding writing, composing and decomposing. Besides, the physical virtues and the meaningful physicalness of language can be expressed with colours. Words are raw material, media to be elaborated, but also simple meanings. Colour and light are in my work the impenetrable elements that give that status of immanence to language, which doesn't have to expire within the image nor to get isolated within the meaningful in respect to the environment. Texts' positive and communicative dimension implodes, when they are visible and occupy a space, to find a new sense of reality that does not completely expire within the sign of a statement. Word opens the door to image and vice versa. It means to make material, senses, text and colour cohabit to transform matter into meaning: in this way, both perceiving and seeing become clearer."

*Does your neon writing have a link with the work of Bruce Nauman and Joseph Kosuth?*

"Neon writing had a really big impact on our everyday perception during that period. At least, on some of us. Neon light wasn't only an opportunity for a new, non-material and persuasive artistic method to create a more impacting communication, but it was also the chance to look beyond the traditional space of the use of a work of art and to open to the urban context working with those very media that defined it. Neon was a new, high-quality material that lent itself well for this purpose. This is why I believe that many of us who were working on language, were fascinated by the environmental potential of the luminous neon sign."

*Do colour and light also have a metaphorical meaning to you?*

"Neon light's nature is very similar to the one of a phonetic or musical soundtrack. My choice to use neon has to be related to the experiences with sound and concrete poetry we were talking about earlier. I'm referring in particular to the *Dattilogrammi*, that were born in the organization of black and white on the surface of the page, in the matt and shine monochrome alternation – of red on red or blue on blue, like a surface switching on and off. I'm also referring to my sound and radio works, to the installations and the 'auditions' of electronic music that I brought around Europe with me, which often became an integral part of my exhibitions. After all, the sound that spreads through the magnetic tape's track and the neon writing's luminous track have the same irradiating potential in space and the same rarefied and volatile basic condition."

*With respect to the North American experiences, it seems to me that your identity as a European artist finds its originality within the search of a beauty that breaks through the equilibrium between form and function. Is that so?*

"I believe that the relationship between beauty, form and function is is to be searched in the innovative strength and formal rigour expressed by the artists belonging to the historical avant-garde of the past century: Kazimir Malevich, László Moholy-Nagy, Josef Albers... As in a semiotic game, I often set myself to abandon colour and canvas and follow a pattern beyond their spaces, although I find it hard to relate my work to art's tradition, even the avant-garde. This is the role of art historians and critics... Many artists tend to refer to tradition and lineage. I experience my work more like a constant flow of energy, sort of space where I can walk in and out, rather than a linear consequentiality in time."

*Where do you find your inspiring cosmos within time's flow?*

"Each one of my relationships and bonds is part of contemporaneity. I like to study what is contemporary, to live inside its pragmatism and uncertainties, to get to know and appreciate other artists' work, to foster and keep a lot of contacts, to travel, see exhibitions, visit studios, libraries and museums. It's always been this way for me. Weiner, LeWitt, Matta Clark, Higgins, Filliou, Cage, Finlay, Byars, Toroni, Kosuth, General Idea, Raetz, Coleman: some of them are friends of mine, some are colleagues I met along the way, others are artists who have passed by Zona. What's important is that their work has been and still is a reason for observation and comparison. As for Italy, I mostly think of Lucio Fontana, the first one to open up to an international context. I belong to the same generation as Colombo, Agnetti, Anselmo, Paolini, Mochetti, Boetti: each of us, each through his own work, abandoned painting and sculpture's traditional practice to pursue a de-structuring of form. I also do believe that political practice made a clear shift between European artists and American conceptualists and minimalists. If we analyse the origins of the American and European radical ideologies of those years, we discover that political practice was a common, daily reality in Europe – especially in Italy. They were two very different worlds, as was different the role of artists within society and their potential for political change. Different theories and practices that gave very different results in time."

*Does the use of colour follow a desire to emphasize the aesthetics of the daily environment in which your work is placed?*

"As I was saying before, I've never been interested in emphasizing reality's aesthetics but rather in raising the level of perception of reality. This level has not only to do with the quantity of information, but also with the quality of the medium employed. I soon gave up representation to follow an absolute form of abstraction. This way of facing the issue of what a work of art is does not want to be an escape from reality. I aim to beauty as a distraction: a work of art doesn't have to be just a project, an image or an iconic representation of the project. I tried to reach this goal acting directly onto reality and not by separating elements from reality and transforming them into art. From this choice many works were born, realized in the urban context. I'm referring to my latest public works that aim to create a very precise spatial direction, like the one I did at the Lenbachhaus in Munich, or Villa Arson in Nice, the façade of Altes Museum in Berlin or Plaza Redonda for the Valencia Biennale. But I'm also referring to my earlier works, where the sense of disorientation and dizziness was more immediate."

*Your work is based on dizziness and meant for effect…*

"In some of my early works I still let the surfaces interact, although works such as *Corner* and *Redline* made me understand that the perfect location for what I do is the neutrality of a wall, environmnental space and urban landscape. A good example of this use of the surface is the installation featured at the Montepulciano exhibition *Amore mio*. It was an investigation on the relationship between colour & surface and colour & light in four monochromatic squared panels, one for each wall, where the neon writings

'Blu Klein' (Klein Blue), 'Rosa Fontana' (Fontana Pink), 'Bianco Malevich' (Malevich White) and 'Giallo Albers' (Albers Yellow) were meant as tributes to these artists and were totally immersed in luminous reflections and in the reverb of the recorded sound of my heartbeat. I'm still very close to two works I've done in the 1970s: one was a small airplane that dragged the blue writing 'Image du ciel' while flying across the Venetian sky during the 1978 Biennale; the other changed the colour of urban lighting on two street in Volterra in 1973. These were two bold actions that opened to the future and that suddenly altered the familiar aspect of two cities, meeting people's habits and giving life to new spatial references."

*Your multimedia and interdisciplinary approach establishes a strong relationship with architecture. Is this something that only comes from Futurism or has something to do with Constructivism as well?*

"Multiple disciplines and media were, during the 1960s, practices that allowed processes of better cultural knowledge, and they were very distant from today artists' neo-conceptual media quoting, where they have the tendency to easily read and embezzle many symbols of the works created during those years. Your question reminds me of a project by Sant'Elia, where the sign 'Propaganda luminosa' [Bright propaganda] was placed in one of his utopian architectural projects. It was a great intuition, but I'm very far away from this historical approach even in respect to architecture. In my opinion architecture means facing with a complex and fascinating reality, with a vast diversity of spatial coordinates that have to be organized in a functional, rational and creative way, bearing in mind the goal to improve the quality of both life and individual conceptual experience. From my artist point of view intervening in architecture means enlarging the perception of space, stimulating multiple possibilities of interpretation, a sign that would make colour simultaneous, light penetration and language strength tangible. It also means to step in the democratic dimension of the *polis*, in the urban context, adding text to space. In some of my works can be observed a clear gestalt ancestry, a module, a constant structure, and the variations, the open and fluid game of interpretations and of different languages. This is the case of *Transit – A light journey* presented in 2000 at the Architecture Biennale in Venice – a work where history and contemporaneity are side by side, where a series of neon writings in different Mediterranean languages were installed onto ferries landing-stage – or like *Polifonia*, showed at the Rome Auditorium and planned by Renzo Piano – where a double neon writing path crosses the entire foyer creating a polychromatic and luminous horizon that wants to stimulate thoughts, images and observation about art, architecture and music. In this case it is the context of the meeting point between space and subject that I put into practice. I can only arrange a situation, but I don't mean to completely control it. This is why I want to provoke a conceptual observation in the public. I'm positively interested by that suspension I was talking about earlier."

*Does the use of your personal handwriting in neon draft represent the subjectivity that you want to impart to the surrounding scenery?*

"Tension between concept and image, between mind-set and form, directed my research towards a particular care of form that, as my work states, must be abstract, it must change, it must give pleasure, it has to be original, to have the proper dimensions for the chosen space that is going to hold it, but not necessarily integrated, depending on a pure aesthetic that is to be regarded in its highest intellectual, idealistic and ethical meanings. I prefer openness and fluidity to limits and closure. In this same way calligraphy and the geometric structures in which I write letters and words have to be interpreted. They are both my mark and a meditative exercise to complete a thought and to give a definitive and original shape to the writing. My texts are never quotations, they are all born by me after a long and careful consideration of the space, on the relations between art, language and image, and on the sensual potential of communication. *Anthology*, the book that gathers all of my writings since 1967, has a strong relation with all the times and places that I've been through. To write and to read means measuring and measuring oneself with space and time."

*Your work establishes relationships with literature and philosophy. Does your art want to found new knowledge processes of things or does it simply want to confirm its contemplative value?*

"They are multiple sides of the same coin. The historical contradiction of which I was talking earlier, rule and exception, planning and the unexpected. Word, language and text are both medium and objects that come from experience, and this is why experiences are regulated by language. I like to study reading and representation: printed, written and oral language built within different contexts and materials. During the years scales, measures, places and spaces haven't been the only ones to change, but this happened to medium's role and strength as well. We live in a world where images are omnipresent. Image power has grown so much that image waves attack us everyday. Inside this tide text, which has always been the base of our culture, is everyday more substituted by the pictorial. Although it is only text, the written word, that can save our collective memory and its secret of persisting."

*From concrete poetry to conceptual art. From a careful visual geometry of literature to a formal order rather than expression… In what way does your neon writing become sculpture and colour become paint, and how does industrial material come in contact with architecture?*

"My works are born from a careful reading of the architectonic space and of its details. I look at this relationship as to a mutual exchange. Architecture gives me a system of volumes, lines, angles, and a geometry that inspire me in a different way every time, depending on place and circumstance. At the same time, the presence of one of my works pays back with the value of a new connotation of the space in which I worked, creating a context of multiple temporal perception where colour, light and meaning interact with each other. It is in such an exchange dynamic that *The Shadow of Light* and *Blauer Ring* were born. The first installation was presented at the Fridericianum in Kassel and it was a big bright circle hanging from the ceiling, a polychromatic cosmogony made of hundreds of neon signs and words, while the second, installed in the German Parliament's Library in Berlin, was a 90 meters long blue light loop with a text stating freedom and equality's values. Being able to give back the right inspiration to see, think and live the space in a new and unusual manner to the architect and the public, is a way to contribute in building a democratically free and cultured subject. I'd like to conclude this interview with the two statements that you,

Sergio Risaliti and I installed at Forte Belvedere in Florence for the *Orizzonti* exhibition. The political strength of that particular work was in line with an almost maieutic art function."

ART IS NOT INTENDED TO BE PERFECTLY TRANSPARENT IN MEANING / IT IS A DISCONTINUOUS INTERACTION BETWEEN MAN AND THE ENVIRONMENT / A GAME BETWEEN A ORDER AND DISORDER / OPPOSITION BETWEEN LIMITS AND TRANSGRESSION / AN EXCHANGE BETWEEN CENTER AND PERIPHERY / WHERE IMAGES ARE REPLACED BY NEW FORMS OF LANGUAGE.

EVERY PLACE HOLDS THE POSSIBILITY OF A NEW GEOGRAPHY / SHIFTS IN PERSPECTIVE MOVE IDEAS TO FUTURE WORLDS / BY DEFINING ART AS A FIELD OF EVENTS THE ARTIST INVENTS SPACE THAT UNFOLD THE NEED AND THE DESIRE FOR TRANSITION / FROM PAST TO PRESENT TO FUTURE / WHERE THE FLOW OF TIME OPENS NEW ZONES OF IMAGINATION

# Gianni Piacentino
Cozze, Turin, 1945

Turin
2007

*Since its early years your artistic activity and research has never been influenced by the myths of energy and nature that used to be theorized during the second half of the 1960s. Were you fascinated by speed instead?*

"My early works revolved around the energy of fundamental geometric elements that became tangible and concrete in a dimension and in a colour. The aspect of nature in art always seemed to me like a nineteenth-century element. I was certainly more fascinated by speed devices than by speed in itself. My passion for motorbikes was born long before riding them fast."

*Car myth and eulogy of techniques seem to derive from Futurism. Does your love for motorbikes and cars come from there?*

"I never liked Futurism: it had excessive theory and over-decorated paintings. The eulogy of techniques has to be done by good technicians and not by unrealistic artists. In any case I don't like myths. What has really been important for me is the role that constructors, engineers and panel beaters had from the 1920s to the 1950s: an extremely creative time for vehicle and airplane mechanics."

*You always preferred the material aspect of a work to that of the process, following clean shapes that almost challenge Design. What kind of relationship exists between art and industry in your opinion?*

"I've always believed that a work should be 'well done' and 'properly finished' in order to be called a piece of art. I don't know what type of relationship exists between art and industry… I guess there exists a lot of cross-breeding. In my case I can say that industrial products certainly help increasing art's creative possibilities and making them last longer in time. Industries have also been improving the quality of their products, which means that art's idea of quality undergoes changes."

*Your work has without a doubt anticipated 1990s objectistics but it is its project value that seems to prevail. Does this value constitute the ethic of making art?*

"I think that the ethic of making art has more to do with the constant and disciplined control of its technical realization, and with a critical ability for changes and improvements during any phase rather than with the project aspect. A sort of technical and emotional engineering."

*Unique pieces have always defined art's production. Is it essential for you?*

"Yes it is. Even though it generally happens to work better and to have a stronger impact if it is a group *unicum*: in this way, especially during the enthusiasm of the beginning, it is possible to observe various movements, personal singularities that can blend in each other. It is a fact that the knowledge of very similar and repetitive things is easier to comprehend."

*Starting from Duchamp and along a particular contemporary art line, the object constitutes the strategic element; but in your work there is no trace of an* objet trouvé *or of a design elaboration. Is the artistic value to be found in the anti-functionality of the produced shape?*

"I like to construct missing pieces that do not exist both in reality and in the history of art, objects that feature the aesthetic elements of mechanics and aerodynamics – topics that are of a big interest for me. The combinations appear more often tense than harmonic, and the lack of function leads to a different perception than the one reserved to the 'real' and functional objects."

*Your work presents an "objectification" of the subject. The shapes are inscrutable, neutral and impersonal. Is your art deliberately and simply urban?*

"It is the piece of art that counts, not its maker. The shapes are impersonal because they belong to the actual pieces and not to their maker. It is definitely not naturalistic art but artificial – the result of a human artifice. It is related to our environment, but to its technical aspect rather than its natural one. Nowadays vehicles seem to outnumber trees in a city."

*Your works have the ability to fit in any space, crawling even down the walls. They never act as antagonists or in a conflicting way with the daily objects that surround us, or with the artificial city landscape in which we live. Would it be possible to say that you realize a sort of silent and rigorous infiltration in the context of our lives?*

"From 1966 to 1968 my abstract geometric shapes (the X, the triangle, the pole…) have abandoned the sacredness and symbolism of art and become more 'concrete': tables, windows, doors, precisely in order to be less incisive in our daily environment. I believe that a work of art has to have the ability to go unnoticed, without compelling a constant attention. It has to be something to get to know and observe but also easy to live with."

*You seem aware of Nietzsche's prophecy about the "crystallization of the world". Does the elegance of your works respond to this philosophy?*

"The shapes of my works are elegant only because they want to reflect an idea of beauty, similar to that of Classic art. I think that Nietzsche's prophecy has more to do with a front cover world and TV, something far removed from the history of my work."

*It seems that your entire investigation wants to give a logo to speed, a nobility to cars, and a modernity to sculpture, to weld the unique aspect of the artistic product with the modular standard of the industrial product. Yet your work seems to possess a sort of metaphysics to it, an alienation that transforms the object that you've created into something rare and lonesome. Is this an attempt for a new creative way of thinking of a work of art that is destined for a "modular" public?*

"'Signing' speed and aerodynamics with static symbols is my biggest conceit (a juvenile dream?). Cars that are important (because of their beauty or efficiency) are noble per se. My search can be considered as a metaphor for remarks and admiration. Industrial standard means (not always) high quality of materials in concrete objects, something that art often neglects. I don't want to create a new thinking model, but it can perhaps be said that a properly done and less 'artistic' piece may expedite the approach of a 'modular' public."

# Ghada Amer
Cairo, 1963



*Your work is the outcome of a long cultural journey, the crossing of two different cultures, of the East and the West. Right from the outset you operated in a context where you had to affirm your identity as a female artist. Was art for you at the beginning an act of moral and political resistance?*

"For me art is still a moral and a political resistance as a female artist and as a hybrid. Of course, not to forget the visual level that is as important. The whole point is to try to combine all three facets. It is like writing poetry, making sense with beautiful and powerful words. It is important for me to touch people and make them react on a personal and emotional level."

*A distinguishing trait of your art is always its great attention to the human body, which has been veiled if not altogether denied by Islamic culture. Was that the reason why your first output emblematically dealt with the burqa?*

"I wanted to make my own burqa, in case I was forced to wear it. It was in 1995 and conservatism in Egypt was more and more resplendishing, so I got very scared and I decided to make my own burqa – it is the only way I found to defend myself."

*Eroticism is a recurrent feature in your artistic quest. Is it a form of reversal of its repression in certain types of civilizations?*

"In all types of civilization! According to my experience and how my work gets shown and censored I can tell you with facts that sexuality is repressed in many many cultures…"

*How did your passage and long stay in Paris affect your work?*

"I stayed in Nice, not in Paris. And I did not 'stay', I grew up there so it is my second home. It made me aware of my hybridism, it made me hate it… I had a lot of problems concerning my origins while I was growing up. Being an Arab in southern France was not a walk in the park, neither was being a female. Growing up in a Muslim household in a Western country in the midst of a growing conservatism back home was very confusing. I am doing the work I do because of my growing up in France and being confronted with all of those questions since a very young age."

405

*In your art eroticism has gradually taken up the explicit figurative forms of sex and sexual positions that echo the Kamasutra. Does art have a liberating function for you?*

"Yes of course, I am doing this art to liberate myself, not to liberate the others! I have always talked about sexuality and I do not think that my work now is more explicit. It is just people can read it easily because now they know what I am embroidering. I deal with other subjects too but only sexuality is the one that people talks the most about!"

*Can the subjectivity of women – which is denied in different ways both in the East and the West – be communicated through art in such a way as to impact the collective conscience of society?*

"I do not understand this question – what do you mean by subjectivity of women?"

*Manual dexterity is always present in your work – a historical sign of the female condition but also an active statement of the body. In time, your embroidery has lost its explicit references to sex and achieved, it its loose threading, an abstract vibrancy. Is it an influence of abstractionism that is so close to American culture, considering also that you have now moved to New York?*

"I do not agree at all, I am not sure that I get influenced by the cultures I live in, when I move to America I become American when I move to Europe I become European – it does not work like this. At least for me. Once you know that you don't belong or that you are a hybrid, then you really *are* a hybrid, you take whatever you want and leave whatever you want anytime. Besides, I have always loved American painters *before* moving to the US – I knew them and travelled to see them. Culture now is global and you do not have to live in a specific culture to be influenced by it. I chose to live in New York because it is good for art business. I know that in France, for example, they cannot talk about business in art as if art was a 'pure' object not polluted by money! I wanted to paint with my thread. I have always loved abstract expressionism – so I have been working hard to re-invent a new form of painting that would be equal to abstract expressionism but totally taking it by reverse. First because I am a woman, second because I wanted to make a work that would take for ever to finish and not just the expression of somebody's anger in five minutes, and finally I wanted to oppose low art (needle work, manual art, folkloric art, etc.) to high art (painting in oil or acrylic).

*At the same time you have acquired a manual skill that is pictorial and goes beyond embroidery strictly speaking. A painting where the human body is represented frontally, which is typical of urban civilization. Is this a sign of a maturing multicultural approach?*

"Do not understand this question as well... At least it is not a question that you ask for an artist. I did not know that urban civilization represents the human body frontally – which is very interesting. In this case I am very urban even without this kind of representation. I am not comfortable in the jungle. I went once and stayed half an hour and it was the worst thing I have ever experienced!"

*Your art embodies a value – which is being highlighted by the ongoing clash between civilizations – as well as the coexistence of differences. Is art a collision with the world or is it a pacification that overcomes all ideological formulas?*

"I would say it is a pacification that overcomes all ideological formulas. Art speaks in general about the "human being", does not matter where he comes from or where he will go at the end. It speaks about his joy, his pain and we all share this at the end – joy and pain. When I hear a poem from China, it is beautiful and I understand it, it talks to me. When a Westerner reads Jalal al-Din Rumi, I am sure that he understands."

*In your art, nature, in terms of technique, themes and materials, has had a big role. Is your penchant for organic forms, for the curving line, for oscillating lines – such as in your composition for the gardens at the Padula Charterhouse – also a statement on the sensitiveness of doubt, fragility and delicacy?*

"It might be, but it is difficult for an artist to say why he or she is drawn to any forms. It is not a decision, it is very intuitive (at least for me). It may be because I may come as well from my Arabic culture that is used to curves and decorative art."

*From my point of view, art has no sex. Can we affirm that sex is androgynous?*

"Art has a sex of course, it has *both* sexes – masculine and feminine. But sex remains sex."

Katharina Sieverding
Prague, 1944

Düsseldorf
2008

*How did Joseph Beuys's artworks, social behaviour and teaching in the Academy influence your work?*

"As I studied medicine first, then art, Beuys's position of Social Sculpture was the missing link between Science, Art and Politics. I was interested in analysis and diagnostic processes of organisms, systems and structures and decided to use the instruments of expanded optical media and their critical and theoretical shift towards modernist attitudes."

*Do you think that art in the 1970s, politically open-minded, was partly a critic operation on the social context or even a re-establishment of the human anthropological unity?*

"Art in the 1970s meant to me questioning and criticizing any hierarchy of institutional spaces, presentation, artistic authorship, genius authority and aesthetic canons. And of course the gender revolution in terms of representation and participation."

*Has art got a liberating role for the subject or even for the collectivities that benefit from it?*

"Neither liberation for the subject nor the collectivity – in its best sense, it was a liberation of the arts from the apolitical autonomy and institutional neutrality of art."

*Does art develop new processes of knowledge of the world, or does it just assert the artist/creator's identity?*

"For sure, but only if it doesn't assert the role of creation but investigates the cultural, scientific, economic and social knowledge and the hegemony of globalization."

*Your work has always had an easy level of communication to people. Is this a democratic element of art?*

"This results from my interest in the people and in the materialism of the media, and in its investigation of the relation between information and politic communication."

*Your work has also been a research of your identity as a female artist. Is art a kind of fight too?*

"No – but strategy, resistance and resiliency."

*I guess that in your artistic investigation there is something of the great German Romanticism. Is there any breaking from this tradition?*

"I don't see my research in that particular context or tradition."

*Even though lots of artists of the 1970s and 1980s kept on combining an impersonal, neutral and objective language, close to the leading position of English research, you focused on the subjective representation. Is there any autobiographical line in your work?*

"For sure, but in a controversial sense: photography allows autobiographical strategies as a non-linear narration, but as an unexpected surprising interface of past and future. For example, in the production series called *Die Sonne um Mitternacht Schauen* of 1990 I discovered the meaning of the golden portrait – a series of 1973 – nearly 27 years later. In no other media you can use, recycle and actualize the same materials into a future context."

*Do the photographic persistence of your figure, the enlargement of your face, the monumental representation of your body bring to the image a conflict between the I and the world? Or are they just a narcissistic statement of the artist?*

"No, they are not. This pictorial strategy is meant to be an integrational, general, large surface within other large-size statements in the cultural context of representational image-politics. It has to be large because it mixes up the strategies of large-format advertisements, movie close-ups, political public imagery, etc. with established representational large-size formats in painting, art-history and film. The convention of 'narcissistic' interpretation for me is sexist and anti-feminist. The personal appearance in public images was a participatory political strategy especially in the 1960s and 1970s."

*Art, your art, is a formulation of mourning, the loss of human unity, the fall into the partial result of everyday life. So, do you think it may be considered as an affirmative gesture to a better future?*

"I do not think so. It is not a formulation of mourning but a statement, or better a formulation of resistance. The artistic decision is an exemplary representation of the power of the media."

*Is art a declaration of war against linguistic conventions, or better the affirmation of new social behaviours?*

"Neither, nor. For me art has the power to formulate and practise criticism. Art could cooperate as an intervention within theoretical debates – for example of Giorgio Agamben's *State of Emergency* and *Homo Sacer*, Derrida's *Scoundrels*, *Multitude* and *Empire* by Antonio Negri and Michael Hardt, Slavoj Zizek's *Iraq. The Borrowed Kettle* or Susan Sontag's *Regarding the Pain of Others*."

*Does art – with the dictatorship of style – fix and force the imagery of the artist-creator or does it develop a strategy of peace, the affirmation of value, the coexistence of differences?*

"We are living extreme cultural, social and political transformations. We should reflect and visualize the global conflicts to deconstruct power structures in their effectiveness, especially those of the new war regimes after 9/11."

# David Tremlett
St Austell, Great Britain, 1945

London<br>2008

*Your work lives in every possible space, both public and private. In any case it doesn't need to be confined inside the frame. When this border crossing started?*

"As a sculpture student I always dealt with space and volume, and working outside in the land, travelling, writing and drawing on walls and ceilings were no different. I made work on paper as a natural part of this procedure and this continues as an integral part of the process."

*The wall drawings are done in houses, in the underground stations, in the churches and in many other places. Does the context modify your work?*

"Of course. Every work is site specific; it only works for that space. There is a relationship with the architecture, with the purpose of the project and the location. Whether locations have a strong public use or a very private meaning, my intentions for the outcome are purely aesthetic."

*Your work is based on an idea of variable geometry, which is that of straight line and curved line. Does this form of eclecticism develop more vitality in the work?*

"Variable geometry has regularly played a role in the work, but the experience is first a primary motivation, then a personal form of geometry. It all comes from life: in some ways lines, geometry, colours, etc. are just part of what I see."

*Colour is always present in your work and it is arranged in different ways. The chromatic tone is almost always very strong. Does it represent for you the eroticism of the work? Does it represent your desire for communication with the external world?*

"Colour is our daily occurrence (unless colour-blind); it's there for us to savour everything – from human flesh to a brick wall; colour gives us tangibility. I believe that whether it is blacks and greys or primary colours or strange mixtures they are the bricks, the clay, the steel and the marble of my constructions."

*Your work is different from the American minimalism. It always implies a complexity that is not reducible to a simple project.*

411

*Does the realization of the work represent an added value?*

"My work, I think, starts from a simple beginning and gets more complex as it develops – but formally remains straightforward. The end result is the experience over time. I feel there is a difference between a desire to reduce and the need to cut away the unnecessary; in my case it was always the latter, so that what is left is the purest possible."

*Your references run from Rothko, Kandinsky, Klee, Malevich up to the concrete painting of the 1940s. On the background of these historical references, does the passage from the painting to the wall imply an amplification of the artist's secret work? Does it mean an attempt to involve a greater number of viewers?*

"I was never influenced directly by painting – although I never ceased to love many paintings. My background was sculpture, I studied sculpture and stayed within the tradition: all I have made was always concerned with the notion of space. Once a space has been created and used in a particular way, then numbers of viewers are inevitably involved. The influences have been a crossing of architecture, the Constructivist period in Russia, Dada, late-nineteenth- and early-twentieth-century photography, modernist furniture and architecture and wall and ceiling painting, from Italy to the Middle East."

*You have been a forerunner of public art. You worked under the commissions of both public and private institutions, in open and closed spaces, and in spaces that are not commonly used for exhibitions. Does public art involve a political behaviour? Or is it the artist's wish to affect the collective feeling?*

"My intention is not to make work of a political nature, unless of my own choosing; as for my art or any other artist's work, the effect should always be the change of a human's vision or perception. The honest answer to the idea of art and politics is that all art is political, because it exists in a political domain; the decoration of a hut in a part of Africa has the same political ramifications as the Catholic church with a ceiling of saints – just their reasons for being are different. There is a difference between the intention to make political art and the awareness that the art you make exists within a political framework."

*The realization of your work always involves the presence of a large number of collaborators. Do you think that the author is only you who made the project or we can talk of a "collective" artist?*

"I think that there is a difference between those who technically help and those who creatively help. In my case I was always a 'hands on' artist, delegation of work was only a method of completion and natural assistance. As for collective art, this would be a group making decisions and therefore the result would be collective – something I have not done yet."

*It is very clear that you try to bring art near to life, the work project to the daily experience. What you think should be the function of art in the modern society?*

"I probably go against the trend in that I prefer art to be a challenge and a force for change, not a confirmation of known values. In this way it can become more exclusive, but also of greater social importance in a modern society. I am not so interested in what we know – more in what we don't."

*Your work, arranged in many parts of the world, has a big circulation and, at the same time, talks to every architecture that receives it. How is it that your work becomes the protagonist as to the context? In which way your shapes do not constitute a mere decoration?*

"I have always worked and lived with the one idea, that life and work are difficult, a challenge; and that they remain interesting only if they stay that way. So, working as I do in many different types and styles of architecture allows me to express that concept. To decorate the inside of buildings is the work of an interior designer or decorator; but my approach is never about compliance or attraction. In my experience, the more difficult the space, the simpler is the outcome of the art; the more simple the space, the more complex the art."

*The historical avant-garde has got us used to the big utopias, to the generous desire of transforming the world with the experimental forms of new languages. After the collapse of the ideologies, is the role of art purely ecological, in the sense that it can only improve the quality of our life?*

"Not true; the challenge is to create a new ideology, or anarchy. Ecological ideas are all fine within the context of changing a contaminated world, but the contaminated intellectual and philosophic world should be changed by folk like artists, writers, musicians, etc. If we are unable to clean up the intellectual crap that is all around us as artists, then we should accept the role as painters and decorators."

*If we can't speak any more of big utopias, you're surely one of the artist who have always fostered the little utopias of the work. After so long time, at the end of the first decade of the twenty-first century, which is for you the resistance level of art towards the world?*

"As I just said, just keep on pushing the awkward and the complex, don't allow too many to understand what's going on and leave a big mystery wherever you go – this can be where ideas start. And, above all, never think that you know what you are doing!"